IBM® Personal Computer

Troubleshooting & Repair

For the IBM PC®, PC/XT™, and PC AT®

Robert C. Brenner

SAMS

A Division of Prentice Hall Computer Publishing

11711 North College, Carmel, Indiana 46032 USA

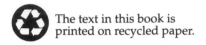 The text in this book is
printed on recycled paper.

International Standard Book Number: 0-672-22662-6
Library of Congress Catalog Number: 89-61435

95 94 93   9 8 7

Interpretation of the printing code: the rightmost double-digit
number is the year of the book's printing; the rightmost single-
digit number, the number of the book's printing. For example, a
printing code of 92-6 shows that the sixth printing of the book
occured in 1992.

Acquisitions Editor: *James Rounds*
Developmental Editor: *C. Herbert Feltner*
Illustrators: *Don Clemons and Bill Hartman*
Indexer: *Don Herrington*
Compositor: *Cromer Graphics*
Cover Graphic by: *Ned Shaw*

Printed in the United States of America

This book is dedicated to my parents, Florence and Chuck Brenner, for giving me the opportunity and inspiration to become all that I can become.

Through encouragement and always expecting me to do my best, they made me eager to learn and unafraid of hard work. Their zeal to make the world a better place through actions, belief, and midwestern determination has resulted in a family of achievers. I'm proud of them, and through them, of myself.

To the Reader

WARNING: Dangerous voltages and currents are present in the IBM switching power supply. Only trained technicians should troubleshoot and/or make repairs in or around the power supply.

WARNING: Dangerous voltages and currents are present in the circuits of the display monitors used with the IBM PC, PC/XT, PC AT computers. Only trained technicians should troubleshoot and/or make repairs to the video display terminals.

CAUTION: Modifying or removing components from a board or adapter card may void the manufacturer's warranty on the product.

Overview

Contents

Preface

The personal computer has become an integral part of our society, and the PCs produced five and six years ago continue to play a useful role in our lives. Contrary to what proponents of "the newest, the fastest, the biggest" schools preach, the IBM PC family of computers are still viable for business, home, and educational use.

Managers are becoming more computer-wise and are evaluating their options carefully. Less easily swayed by bright, loud, and demanding marketing hype, today's managers are slower to push aside the old trusty PC for a shiny, new ultra-personal computer, just because it has all the latest bells and whistles. The PC is still more than adequate for most jobs, and productivity is greatly enhanced by having one.

With the continued use of machines that are up to eight years old, the number one priority is making sure that the PCs remain healthy and on-line. Some of the older machines develop power problems, disk-drive problems, and heat-generated problems. In addition, many of the so-called PC problems are misdiagnosed. This makes the knowledge of troubleshooting and repair techniques critical to the continued use of personal computers.

Whether a user opts for on-site repair, carry-in repair, mail-in repair, or do-it-yourself repair, the final decision depends on the nature of the machine's usage and on the budget of the user. If a day of downtime would seriously affect your productivity, then on-site maintenance may be appropriate. If replacement or repair is not critical, or if spare equipment is available, carry-in or mail-in service may be adequate. But, if you want to greatly reduce your repair expenses, everything you can do to find and correct the problem yourself will have a direct impact on your bottom-line productivity and profit.

There's no question that computer repair is big business, and it's growing greatly as more large companies enter the repair field. Either you try to make the repairs yourself or you pay dearly to have them done. Contrary to what the repair industry may insist, if you can operate a PC, you can probably fix it when it fails. And, the troubleshooting and repair experience of "doing-it-yourself" will probably not be the ordeal you imagined. This book will show you how.

Not only is this book suitable for home and business use, it is also suitable for education. Schools and universities that teach microcomputer repair need a text that can guide the student through troubleshooting and repair procedures for a well-known and widely accepted machine—the IBM PC. This book was developed to meet all these needs.

Drawing on Howard W. Sams & Company's COMPUTERFACT® series of manuals and on the manufacturer's service data, *IBM Personal Computer Troubleshooting & Repair* provides a descriptive text and an easy-to-understand explanation of the troubleshooting and repair procedures necessary for repairing the IBM PC family of microcomputers. It was written to fill the documentation requirements of the using public, and also to support those service centers and small shops that repair IBM personal computers.

Although this book can serve as a text for a course in microcomputer troubleshooting and repair, its intent is to make better repair technicians out of us all and extend the operational life of our personal computers. A good repair manual should not just help locate and correct computer malfunctions, it should also provide guidance in preventing further failures. This book does just that.

With these guidelines, you should be able to isolate and correct most IBM PC, XT, and AT equipment failures. This book has brought me much success in my own troubleshooting, and I trust it will do the same for you.

Robert C. Brenner

Acknowledgments

This book could not have been produced in the time and with the accuracy required without the support and direct involvement of many people. Certain individuals gave more than expected, and to them I wish to extend special thanks.

To my wife, Carol, who kept the house a home during months of fourteen-hour days. To my son, Dan, whose technical experience shined even more brightly during his efforts to support me during development of the detailed troubleshooting chapters in this book. To Paul and Gail Hunt, owner-managers of Personal Computer Rentals of San Diego, for offering their facility and equipment during this project. To Personal Computer Rental employees Dan Ledesma, Ben Villalobos, Rich Fletcher, and John Zarling for their technical support. And to Jerry Mosley for his fine close-up photography.

Trademarks

All terms mentioned in this book that are known to be trademarks or service marks are listed below. In addition, terms suspected of being trademarks or service marks have been appropriately capitalized. Howard W. Sams & Company cannot attest to the accuracy of this information. Use of a term in this book should not be regarded as affecting the validity of any trademark or service mark.

COMPUTERFACTS is a registered trademark of Howard W. Sams & Company.
IBM PC/XT is a trademark of International Business Machines Corporation.
IBM, IBM PC, IBM PC AT, and PC-DOS are registered trademarks of
    International Business Machines Corporation.
MS-DOS is a registered trademark of Microsoft Corporation.

Mylar is a registered trademark of E. I. duPont de Nemours and Co., Inc.

PageMaker is a registered trademark of Aldus Corporation.

TRI-STATE is a registered trademark of National Semiconductor Corporation.

Word is a trademark of Microsoft Corporation.

WordStar is a registered trademark of MicroPro International Corporation.

Description of the PC, XT, and AT Computer Systems

The first step in the successful troubleshooting and repair of the IBM PC, XT, or AT computer is to learn all you can about the computer and how it works. You don't need so much technical knowledge that you could almost redesign the computer. However, you do need a good understanding of what the particular IBM computer looks like, how it's connected to other devices, and how it operates. This knowledge is necessary before you can recognize and localize problem symptoms to a particular part of the computer and expect results in your attempts to find and correct a failure.

This chapter is the beginning of your journey into the interesting world of microcomputer repair. It provides a descriptive overview of the IBM PC, XT, and AT computers. Although you are not expected to know a lot about computers, a basic understanding of electronics will be helpful.

This book was written to guide both the novice and the experienced user through the operation, troubleshooting, and repair of the IBM PC, XT, and AT computers. The text will describe the system configuration for each of these IBM personal computers and how each computer system works. Then you will be introduced to problem analysis and eventually corrective repair. In this chapter, a high-level systems view is presented for the IBM PC, XT, and AT to acquaint you with a particular machine and the types of devices (such as printer, display monitors, and disk drives) that you can connect to it. In this book we will use the term PC when referring to the original IBM PC, XT when referring to the IBM PC/XT, and AT when referring to the IBM PC AT.

All computers are manufactured using a wide variety of component parts. These components are referred to collectively as *hardware*. Hardware includes the box or case containing the electronics, the disk drives, the boards, and even the individual components on the boards. When viewed as an operational system, this collection of hardware can be functionally partitioned into specific units. Every computer system, whether a mainframe, minicomputer, or a micro-computer can be partitioned into the same five basic units shown in Fig. 1-1:

▶ An arithmetic logic unit.

▶ A control unit.

▶ A memory unit.

▶ An input unit.

▶ An output unit.

The *arithmetic logic unit* (ALU) performs the adding, subtracting, multiplying, dividing, comparing, and logic operations. The *control unit*, shown just above the ALU in Fig. 1-1, regulates the operation of the computer and enables it to communicate with the operator and other devices in the system. The control unit fetches and interprets instructions and causes certain parts of the computer circuitry to respond to those instructions. The ALU and the control unit can be considered the nerve elements of the computer's brain. Adequate power and a good system clock are vital to the operation of the computer. The system clock will be discussed in Chapters 2, 3, and 4.

The *memory unit* shown at the bottom of Fig. 1-1 is the remembering part of the machine. It stores programs, data, calculations, and results. Two types of memory are included in most computers: temporary storage called RAM (random-access memory) and permanent storage called ROM (read-only memory). The ROM memory chips are permanently programmed with specific computer instructions and special data. This permanent information is called the computer's operating system. You will see the expression *Basic Input/Output System* or BIOS used to describe the operating system in ROM. There is also an

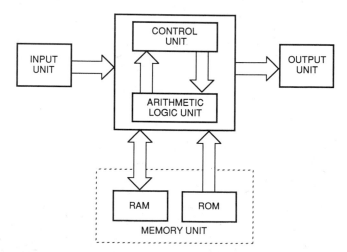

Fig. 1-1. The five basic parts of a computer.

operating system called DOS (Disk Operating System) that is loaded from a disk when you boot up your machine. Whether stored permanently or temporarily in memory, any sequence of computer instructions is called a *program*. Programs are called *software*. At least one of the ROMs in each IBM computer has an operating system program permanently stored in it; a hardware component containing software is called *firmware*.

The RAM memory in the IBM computer is sometimes called *system memory* or *main memory*. Information stored in RAM exists only as long as power is applied to the computer. When power is removed, the programs and data stored in the RAM are lost unless first transferred (copied) to external permanent memory. The external memory used with the IBM PC, XT, or AT computers is normally a floppy disk drive or a hard disk drive. Most PC computers have two internally mounted floppy disk drives. The XT and AT usually have one floppy disk drive and one hard disk drive. Additional disk drives can be connected externally to the IBM computers. However, this is rarely done since the external drives require separate power supplies.

Communication with the computer occurs through the input and output units. These interface devices are called *peripherals*. A peripheral can be just about any type of device connected to the computer. Most peripherals are connected to interface adapter boards plugged into expansion sockets inside the computer.

One peripheral, the keyboard, connects directly to the system board. The IBM PC includes a direct cassette connector on the system board.

An input device allows commands, programs, and data to be entered into the computer. It enables the operator to "talk" to the computer. The keyboard, a mouse, joysticks, game paddles, graphics tablets, light pens, microphones, and analog-to-digital converters (ADCs) are all examples of input devices.

The computer communicates with the environment and the operator though an output device. Output devices include monochrome and color display monitors, printers, plotters, speakers, and digital-to-analog converters (DACs). The computer acknowledges input commands by sending information or control signals to these output devices. Thus, the character for the key pressed on the keyboard (input device) is displayed on the monitor screen or printed on the printer (output device).

Some devices are used for both input and output. These bidirectional peripherals include the mass storage devices (floppy disk drives, hard disk drives, and archival storage tape systems) and MOdulator-DEModulators (Modems) which enable computer-to-computer communications over long distances.

The arithmetic logic unit and the control unit can be combined into a single integrated circuit called a *central processing unit* (CPU) as shown in Fig. 1-2. Microprocessors are also called CPUs because they can be designed to perform

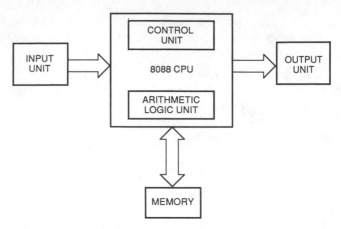

Fig. 1-2. The control unit and the arithmetic logic unit can be combined to form the central processing unit (CPU).

the same functions as the central processing unit in a large computer. In the PC and XT, an Intel 8088 integrated circuit (IC) is the systems central processing unit. In the AT, the central processing unit is an Intel 80286 IC. The CPU accesses memory (fetches an instruction), interprets what the instruction means, performs the action required by the instruction, stores the results or routes the results to an I/O device, and then fetches the next instruction in the program and repeats the sequence. This sequential process was described by mathematician John von Neumann in the late 1940s. Today, every desktop or laptop computer operates as a sequential "von Neumann" machine. In the future, microcomputer systems will include multiple processors and operate on many instructions at the same time in a parallel "non-von Neumann" architecture.

The Basic IBM PC and XT Computer Systems

The IBM PC and its successor, the IBM PC/XT, are architecturally the same although the XT has three more expansion slots than the PC. Programs written for the PC will also run on the XT, and any interface board originally designed for the PC will also work in the XT. Table 1-1 compares the characteristics of the IBM PC, XT, and AT computers.

Several hundred peripheral interface devices and accessories have been designed for the IBM PC family of personal computers. With the wide variety of peripheral devices available, an IBM PC or XT system could be configured from a selection of peripherals as shown in Fig. 1-3.

A typical IBM PC or XT system is comprised of the system unit with keyboard, a monochrome or color display monitor, two disk drives, and a printer. The following pages will describe the system unit and the keyboard. Display monitors and disk drives are described separately in this chapter.

Table 1-1. Comparison of the IBM PC, XT, and AT Computers

System	PC	XT	AT
Processor	8088	8088	80286
Speed	4.77 MHz	4.77 MHz	6–8 MHz
ROM	40K	40K	64K
RAM	16/64K	64/256K	512K
	64/256K	640K*	
Floppy drive	360K	360K	1.2 Mbyte
Hard drive	—	10 Mbyte	20–30 Mbyte
Expansion slots	5	8	8

*An XT with 640K RAM on the system board was introduced by IBM in 1986.

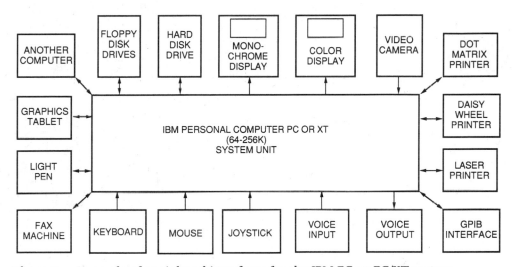

Fig. 1-3. Example of peripheral interfaces for the IBM PC or PC/XT system.

System Unit

The system units for the PC and XT are shown in Figs. 1-4 and 1-5. The system unit is the main component of the computer. Inside the system unit is the system board or motherboard. The system board includes expansion slots for peripheral adapter cards and expansion boards. The PC has five expansion slots and the XT has eight. The system board also includes several memory and control ICs. The system boards for the PC and XT will be described in detail in Chapters 2 and 3. Also inside the system unit is a switching power supply, and two standard-height, double-density, 5.25-inch floppy disk drives. The XT usually has a single floppy disk drive and a hard drive. On the right side, near the back of the system unit, is the ON/OFF power switch.

Fig. 1-4.   System unit and keyboard for the IBM PC.

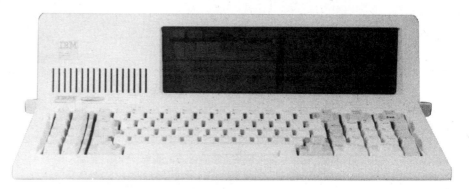

Fig. 1-5.   System unit and keyboard for the IBM PC/XT.

Keyboard

The detachable keyboard (Fig. 1-6) has 83 keys that can generate all 128 ASCII (American Standard Code for Information Interchange) characters. It can also generate special symbols and graphic shapes. In all, the keyboard can cause the machine to generate and display (or print) 256 characters, shapes, or symbols.

Viewed from left to right, the keyboard includes a set of function keys, the main keyboard array, and a numeric keypad. Some of the keys on the numeric keypad are also used as cursor control keys. The ten programmable function keys on the left side of the keyboard are used to execute specific programs or to initiate special software routines. The functions of the individual keys can be programmed by the software designer. Some applications programs allow the user to define the purpose of each function key.

Also provided on the IBM keyboard are special keys such as Shift, Up-Down-Left-Right arrow keys, Caps Lock, Num Lock, Scroll Lock, Back Space, Enter, Home, Pg Dn, Pg Up, End, Del, Ins, PrtScr, Tab, Ctrl, and Alt. The functions of each of these keys and key combinations are described in the IBM *Guide to Operations* manual.

All 83 keys have automatic repeat and a 10-character type-ahead buffer to let you type at rapid speed without getting ahead of the computer processing of each keystroke. Each of the 83 keys have a tactile feel with an audible click to provide positive feedback that key action has been completed. Electronic circuits inside the keyboard enhance key operation and permit keys to be redefined for increased programing flexibility. Some keys can be used in combination to cause special actions such as system reset.

There are two plastic feet on the bottom side of the keyboard housing that allow the keyboard to be tilted in one of two positions for optimum typing comfort. A plastic ridge above the top row of keys can be used to hold a book or report between the keyboard and the display screen. It can also be used to hold templates for special application software. A 6-foot coiled cord connects the keyboard to the system unit.

Fig. 1-6.   Detachable keyboard for the IBM PC and PC/XT.

The Basic IBM PC AT Computer System

The IBM PC AT computer is designed around the Intel 80286 microprocessor and utilizes a 6-MHz or 8-MHz clock rate. (Later versions of the IBM AT utilize a 12-MHz clock.) The Intel 80286 CPU in the AT is an advanced high-performance microprocessor that is upward compatible with the Intel 8088 in the PC and XT computers. The AT is powered by a 192-watt power supply and is equipped with a clock/calendar circuit that is backed up by a special long-life battery. There are five models of the AT as described in Table 1-2.

Table 1-2. The IBM PC AT Model Product Line

Model	Features
Model 68	256K RAM, 6-MHz clock, single high-density 1.2-Mbyte floppy disk drive.
Model 99	512K RAM, 6-MHz clock, one 1.2-Mbyte floppy disk drive, and a 20-Mbyte hard drive.
Model 239	512K RAM, 6-MHz clock, one 1.2-Mbyte floppy disk drive, and 30-Mbyte hard drive.
Model 319	512K RAM, 8-MHz clock, standard keyboard, one 1.2-Mbyte floppy disk drive, and a 30-Mbyte hard drive.
Model 339	512K RAM, 8-MHz clock, enhanced keyboard, one 1.2-Mbyte floppy disk drive, and a 30-Mbyte hard drive.

The AT shown in Fig. 1-7 is designed similar to its predecessors, the PC and XT. It has the same number of expansion slots (eight) as the XT, and programs written for the PC and XT will also run on the AT. Many of the interface boards designed for the PC and XT will also run in the AT, but here the similarities end. The AT is more powerful and faster than either the PC or XT.

The AT is a popular personal computer, and hundreds of peripheral interface devices and accessories can be operated with this machine. Some of the 8-bit interface adapter boards designed for the PC and XT, such as the display adapters, will also work in the AT. The typical IBM AT computer system is comprised of the system unit with keyboard, a monochrome or color display monitor, a floppy disk drive, a 20- or 30-Mbyte hard disk drive, and a printer.

System Unit

The AT system unit is larger than its PC or XT predecessors. The large, boxy-looking system unit shown in Fig. 1-8 is the main chassis of the AT computer. It contains the primary components of the computer. The major component is the large printed-circuit board laying flat in the bottom of the system unit cabinet. This board is called the system board or motherboard. Like the XT, the AT system board has eight expansion slots for connecting interface adapter cards and other accessories. However, not all of these expansion slots are the same as on the XT. The AT system board will be discussed in detail in Chapter 4.

The AT system unit also contains a 192-watt power supply, a half-height, 1.2-Mbyte 5.25-inch floppy disk drive, and a 20-Mbyte or 30-Mbyte hard disk drive. The ON/OFF power switch is located on the right side near the rear of the system unit.

The indicator panel on the left side of the system unit front panel includes a security keylock to lock the system unit cover and disable the keyboard. The

Fig. 1-7. IBM PC AT computer system.

keyboard remains disabled until a special key is inserted into the lock and rotated to the System On position. This special round key is similar to security keys used for alarm systems and vending machines. The keylock provides protection for the system by preventing unauthorized use of the computer. When the system is locked, anyone who turns on the power will get a display message requesting that the F1 key be depressed. However, since the keyboard is locked and no key entry will work, access is denied.

Keyboard

Two types of keyboards were developed for the IBM AT as shown in Fig. 1-9. Both keyboards are a little larger than the keyboard used for the IBM PC and XT. Neither of the AT keyboards can function with the PC and XT machines. One of the AT keyboards has a low profile with 84 keys including 10 function keys; the other keyboard is an enhanced keyboard with 101 keys including 12 function keys. Both keyboards were designed with important improvements over the

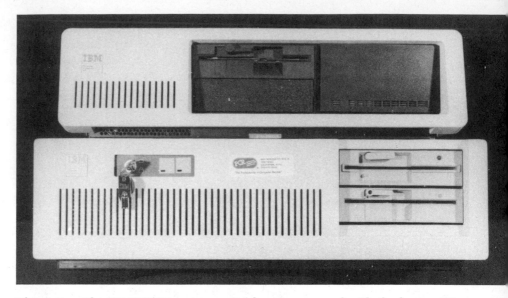

Fig. 1-8. The IBM PC/XT system unit (above) compared with the larger AT system unit.

Fig. 1-9. The two keyboards developed for the IBM AT.

earlier IBM keyboards. The Backslash key was relocated, the Shift keys are larger, and indicator lights were added to display the state of the Caps Lock, Num Lock, and Scroll Lock keys. The larger keys have flat tops like most users have always wanted.

The layout of the IBM AT keyboard is delightful, but for some reason IBM chose to relocate the Esc key from a perceived standard location to the other side of the keyboard. Some users have speculated that the move was made to position this control key to a location convenient to the cursor control keys. In its new location, the Esc key gives the AT operator single hand control over viewing text, menu item selection, and quick program exit. The PrtScr (print screen) key was also relocated. Many touch typists wish IBM had designed a CTRL key into the right side of the keyboard to speed program usefulness.

Six keyboard layouts are available including U.S., U.K., French, German, Italian, and Spanish. The detachable keyboard connects to the rear of the system unit through an extra long 10-foot coiled cable. The keyboard can generate all 128 ASCII characters as well as special symbols and graphic shapes. Using the Ctrl and Alt keys, along with the other keys, the computer can produce and display (or print) 256 characters, shapes, or symbols.

Viewed from left to right is a set of function keys, the main keyboard array, and a numeric keypad. Some keys on the numeric keypad double as cursor control keys. The ten programmable function keys on the left side of the original AT keyboard are used to execute specific programs or to initiate special software routines. The functions of the individual keys can be programmed by the software designer. The 12 function keys of the IBM AT enhanced keyboard are located across the top of the keyboard. The key caps on the enhanced keyboard can be removed and replaced for customized key layouts.

Also provided on the keyboard are special keys such as Shift, Up-Down-Left-Right arrow keys, Caps Lock, Num Lock, Scroll Lock, Back Space, Enter, Home, Pg Dn, Pg Up, End, Del, Ins, PrtScr, Tab, Ctrl, Sys Req, and Alt. The functions of each of these keys and key combinations are described in the IBM AT *Guide to Operations* manual.

All 84 keys (101 on the enhanced keyboard) have automatic repeat and a 16-character type-ahead buffer to let you type at a rapid speed without getting ahead of the computer processing of each keystroke. The keys are typematic in that holding a key down will repeat a steady stream of the selected character on the screen. A 0.25- to 1.25-second delay can be programmed into the AT to define how long a key must be held down before it is recognized. When the system is powered up, the keyboard is initialized to a 0.5-second delay and a 10-characters-per-second typematic rate.

The keys each have a tactile feel with an audible click that provides positive feedback that key action has been completed. Electronic circuits inside the keyboard enhance key operation and permit keys to be redefined for increased programming flexibility. Some keys can be used in combination to cause special action such as system reset.

Output Devices

There are many output devices that can be connected to the IBM PC, XT, and AT computer systems. These devices include display monitors, printers, modems, plotters, and the speaker, which is built into the system unit. Display monitors and printers, which are common to almost every PC, XT, or AT system, are described in this chapter.

The Display Monitor

The most common way for the PC to communicate with the operator is by means of the display monitor. The type of display monitor used depends on the information you want to see on the screen. When the IBM PC was first introduced, two types of display monitors were available: a monochrome (single color) monitor for displaying text or a color/graphics monitor for displaying images, shapes, and brilliant colors. The display required for graphics could be a black-and-white monitor, a composite color monitor, an RGB color monitor, or even an ordinary television receiver. While a television receiver is adequate for graphics and color, it is not acceptable for 80-column text. Television receivers are barely acceptable for 40-column text although they were used extensively with early personal computers.

The IBM PC, XT, and AT computers can support many different display monitors, both color and monochrome. The display monitor connects to a video adapter board plugged into an expansion slot on the system board of the computer. The video connector is accessible through a slot in the rear of the system unit. Initially, only two video adapter cards were available for the IBM PC—a high-resolution text-only Monochrome Display Adapter (MDA) and a good graphics, poor-text Color/Graphics Adapter (CGA).

The MDA enables the computer to generate and display 25 rows of 80 characters each in white on black (green on black) with the IBM monochrome monitor, black on white (or black on green), blinking, highlighted, or underlined. This adapter board also has a connection for a parallel printer.

The color/graphics adapter (CGA) board supports both text and graphics. The CGA interface provides options for two types of text (25 rows of 40 characters or 25 rows of 80 characters) and two types of graphics (medium resolution and high-resolution). The monochrome display adapter produces crisp, readable characters and is fine for word processing and spread sheet applications. But it cannot produce circles, curved lines, or other graphic shapes. The color/graphics adapter provides a mixed bag of capabilities. It can produce medium-resolution graphics in 4 of 16 colors or high-resolution graphics in monochrome. However, the character resolution is poor in the text mode and it has been criticized for causing eyestrain after extended use. The IBM Color Graphics Adapter board is shown in Fig. 1-10.

To upgrade its standard color/graphics interface and utilize new IC technology, IBM introduced two new display adapters in 1984: the enhanced graphics adapter (EGA) and the professional graphics adapter (PGA). At the same time IBM also introduced two new display monitors to be used with these improved graphics adapters.

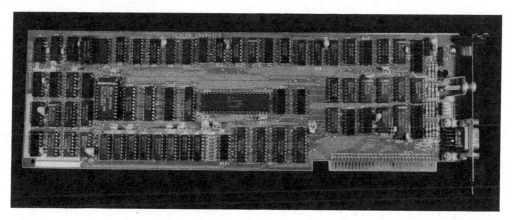

Fig. 1-10.   IBM Color/Graphics Adapter board.

In a single integrated adapter, the EGA board combines monochrome text, monochrome graphics, or color/graphics capabilities. The EGA board supports more colors, more displays, more memory, and more modes than either the MDA or CGA display adapters. It supports three different types of display monitors: IBM Monochrome, IBM Color, and IBM Enhanced Color. EGA has become the most common standard for IBM graphics display. The IBM Enhanced Graphics Adapter board is shown in Fig. 1-11.

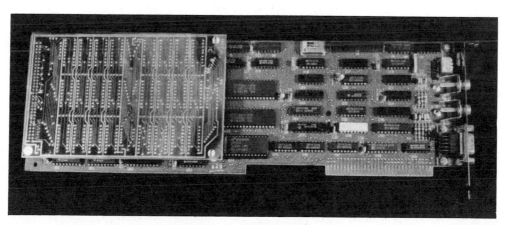

Fig. 1-11.   IBM Enhanced Graphics Adapter board.

Until the advent of the Professional Graphics Adapter (PGA), IBM display monitors received digital signals from the video adapter board. Although this digital interface proved sufficient for most applications, analog circuitry has a capability for infinite primary color combinations and can produce subtle differences in color shading that exceed the capabilities of most color/graphics cards. Therefore, more RGB display systems are being introduced with analog signal interfaces. The PGA is IBM'S first analog video standard.

The four display standards for the IBM PC, XT, and AT computers are compared in Table 1-3. The MDA, CGA, and EGA display adapters are described in detail in Chapter 5.

Table 1-3. Comparison of the MDA, CGA, EGA, and PGA Display Standards

Display	Type	Resolution	Colors
MDA	Monochrome	720 X 350	None
CGA	Color	320 X 200	4 of 16
EGA	Color	640 X 350	16 of 64
PGA	Color	640 X 480	256 of 4,096

Printers

Many types of printers can be used with the IBM PC, XT, and AT computers. Standard 9-pin dot-matrix printers, 24-pin near-letter-quality dot-matrix printers, and full character daisy-wheel printers are commonly used with these computers. The recent introduction of low-cost laser printers and thermal ink jet printers have given PC users the ability to generate high-quality hard copy output.

In all cases, the printer is interfaced to the microcomputer using a parallel or serial adapter board plugged into one of the expansion slots. Some users have more than one printer connected at the same time—a dot-matrix printer for drafts or working copies and a letter-quality printer for final documents.

Mass Storage Devices

There are three primary types of bidirectional data storage devices that are used with the IBM PC, XT, and AT computers. These three types of storage devices are floppy disk drives, hard (fixed) disk drives, and tape backup drives.

Most original IBM PC systems included two floppy disk drives. Many PC owners have added fixed drives to their machines. This upgrade usually requires replacing the original 62.5-watt power supply with a higher-rated power supply capable of handling the increased load of the hard drive.

The first XT computers were equipped with a full-height floppy disk drive and a 10-Mbyte fixed drive. Later, 20-Mbyte fixed drives became standard for the

XT. The full-height floppy disk drive in many XTs have been replaced by two half-height floppy drives.

The standard drive configuration for the AT was a half-height 1.2-Mbyte high-capacity floppy disk drive and a 20-Mbyte or 30-Mbyte fixed drive.

Floppy Disk Drives

The PC and XT floppy disk drive controller board can accommodate up four floppy disk drives (two internal and two external). However, more than two floppy drives are rarely used with these machines.

The early IBM PCs with the DOS 1.10 disk operating system formatted floppy disks to eight sectors per track on each 40-track disk. With DOS 2.0 and higher, the PC and XT could format floppy disks to nine sectors per track. Each 40-track 5.25-inch double-density floppy disk can be single-sided or double-sided, depending on the drive used. The first IBM PCs were equipped with single-sided floppy disk drives using DOS 1.0. The disks are magnetically partitioned during formatting into 40 tracks of 512-byte sectors. This format provides 163,840 bytes of storage for single-sided, double-density disks (184,320 bytes with PC DOS 2.0 and higher) or 327,680 bytes of storage for double-sided, double-density disk drive system (368,640 bytes for DOS 2.0 and higher).

The AT computer is configured with one high-capacity floppy disk drive and a hard drive. The half-height 5.25-inch dual-sided drive provides 1.2-Mbyte storage capacity. It can read both 160/180K single-sided disks and 320/360K double-sided disks. Because the high-capacity drive formats floppy disks at 92 tracks per inch, it cannot write standard 48-tpi PC format disks. The track space on the AT drive squeezes 80 tracks into the area normally reserved for 40 tracks on the PC and XT drives. An optional 360K disk drive is available for the AT that enables the same disks to be written onto and read from any PC, XT, or AT. A 720K double-sided 3.5-inch minifloppy disk drive is also available.

Up to two high-capacity 1.2-Mbyte disk drives can be connected to an AT system. Both a 1.2-Mbyte high-capacity, half-height drive and an optional standard 360K half-height floppy drive can be installed in the same AT. The IBM standard 360K drive is marked with an asterisk on the front panel to distinguish it from the high-capacity drive. An external 3.5-inch microfloppy disk drive can also be connected to the AT.

Hard Disk Drives

The primary difference between the PC and the XT is that one of the floppy disk drives was replaced with a 10-Mbyte hard (fixed) disk drive. Up to two hard disk drives can be connected to the XT through the fixed disk controller card that plugs into one of the expansion slots on the system board.

The typical hard disk drive installed in the XT has two disk platters providing four read/write surfaces inside a sealed unit. Each surface is partitioned into 306 tracks and each track is further divided into 17 sectors of 512 bytes each. This partitioning yields 10,653,696 bytes or 10 Mbyte of data storage capacity for the hard disk. The hard disk drives used in later XTs partitioned the disk platters into 612 tracks, which resulted in 20 Mbyte of storage capacity. In Chapter 3 you will learn how the hard disk drive works with the controller card in the XT system to store and retrieve information.

There are many differences between the XT and the AT. The increased performance standard of the hard disk drive used in the AT is a significant improvement to most users. The 10-Mbyte hard drives in the early XTs had a 85–100 millisecond access time while the 20-Mbyte drives in the early ATs had an access time of 40 milliseconds. A year after the AT was introduced, IBM brought out a 30-Mbyte hard drive option for the AT.

The 20-Mbyte hard drives used in the very early AT machines were designed and built by Computer Memories, Inc. (CMI). The CMI drive did not have an automatic "park-and-lock" feature, so the drive was very susceptible to damage caused by head crashes. An inadvertent jar of the drive unit or unexpected loss of power could cause the head to land on the disk surface (crash) and destroy information or the disk media. Often the damage didn't show up until weeks or months later when the operator attempted to access the damaged area of the disk. This problem was corrected when improved hard drives were installed in later ATs.

Although IBM offered the AT with 20-Mbyte or 30-Mbyte hard drives, many disk drive manufacturers worked hard to increase the amount of data that the AT fixed drive could hold. These manufacturers soon offered 40-Mbyte, 60-Mbyte, and 80-Mbyte hard drives for the AT. Today, hard drives with capacities of up to 300 Mbyte have been designed to work with the AT personal computer.

One or two fixed disk drives can be connected to the AT system. The typical 20-Mbyte hard disk drive has four disk platters providing four read/write surfaces inside a sealed unit. Each surface is partitioned into 615 tracks (plus a landing zone). Each track is further divided into 17 sectors of 512 bytes each. This partitioning yields 21,411,840 bytes or 20 Mbyte of data storage capability. The 20-Mbyte AT drive can transfer data at 70K bytes per second. This is approximately 60 percent faster than the 44K-byte-per-second transfer rate of the XT hard drive. Chapter 4 describes how the hard disk drive works with the controller board in the AT system to store and retrieve digital information.

Backup Storage

Four major types of devices are used for backing up data in a PC, XT, or AT computer system. These storage devices include: floppy disk drives, removable hard disk cartridge drives, tape cassette drives, and tape cartridge drives.

While cassette tape storage is slow and often frustrating, magnetic tapes do provide an excellent way to provide archival storage for large amounts of data. Many more files or pages of information can be stored on a good audio tape cassette than can be stored on a 5.25-inch floppy disk. The IBM PC includes a connector for cassette interface. Some archival storage systems use a video tape to hold long-term computer data. Tapes with 20-Mbyte to 40-Mbyte storage capacity are common. A 20-Mbyte tape can hold over 21 million characters of information, or about 10,000 pages of text. Both of these methods are becoming outdated due to the rapidly increasing popularity of tape cartridge units.

Backing up a 20-Mbyte hard disk onto 360K floppy disks is extremely slow and awkward. The 1.2-Mbyte high-capacity floppy disk used in the AT is faster but still awkward. A 10-Mbyte hard disk cartridge is fast and convenient for backup, but is relatively expensive. Tape backup is popular and cassettes, cartridges, and tape reels are common. Tape cartridges store more data than cassettes and are becoming the standard backup device for the PC, XT, and AT systems. The prices of tape cartridge units have dropped considerably due to their increased popularity.

Tape backup comes in three operating modes: streaming, file-by-file, and disk emulation. Streaming drives copy data off the hard disk in a continuous stream, accepting the data as one long file. This type of transfer is fast and simple, but it doesn't give you the ability to save and retrieve individual files. Start-stop file-by-file drives copy data in blocks providing break points between files. The disk emulation mode lets the tape respond to DOS commands as a hard disk would. Disk emulation is slow and data is stored sequential, but the drive does let the user access specific files.

Connections

The monitor, keyboard, and various peripheral devices are connected to the computer through specific connectors located on the back of the unit. Most of these connectors are on the adaptor boards that plug into the expansion slots on the system board.

IBM PC

The connections at the rear of the IBM PC are shown in Fig. 1-12. On the lower left are two power connectors—one female and the other male. The female connector on the far left provides ac power for the display monitor. The male connector just to the right is for the ac power cord. The round opening with vents to the right of the power connector is the air intake for the internal power supply fan. To the right of the air intake port is a 5-pin circular connector for the keyboard cable. Next to the keyboard connector is a 5-pin circular connector for cassette data input/output. This connection is not available on the XT or AT. Since the cassette connector is not used on the XT or AT, a tape backup system must be connected through an interface board plugged into one of the expansion slots on the motherboard.

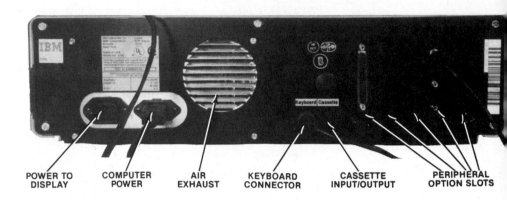

| POWER TO DISPLAY | COMPUTER POWER | AIR EXHAUST | KEYBOARD CONNECTOR | CASSETTE INPUT/OUTPUT | PERIPHERAL OPTION SLOTS |

Fig. 1-12.   The connections at the rear of the PC system unit.

The system expansion slots on the motherboard are for connecting peripheral devices to the system. The IBM PC motherboard has five expansion slots. The rear panel of the system unit has five slotted openings that provide access to the connectors on the back of the interface boards plugged into the expansion slots. This allows cables from display monitors, printers, plotters, and other external peripheral devices to be connected to the interface boards.

IBM PC/XT

The connections at the rear of the IBM XT are shown in Fig. 1-13. The connectors on the XT are essentially the same as the connectors on the PC except that the cassette interface connector has been removed and there are eight expansion slots rather than five.

IBM PC/AT

The connections at the rear of the IBM AT are shown in Fig. 1-14. The female connector that provides ac power for the display monitor is shown on the far left. The male connector next to the display power connector is the input connector for the ac power cord. The single 5-pin circular jack to the lower right

Fig. 1-13.   The connections at the rear of the IBM PC/XT system unit.

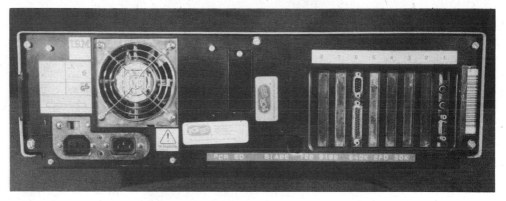

Fig. 1-14.   The connections at the rear of the IBM PC AT system unit.

of center is the keyboard connector. The long rectangular opening on the right provides access to the connectors on the rear of the interface cards plugged into the expansion slots on the system board. These connectors allow the cables from external peripheral devices to be connected to the interface cards. Like the XT, the AT has eight expansion slots.

IBM PC Internal Components

Disconnect all cables and power cords from the rear of the system unit and move all external equipment and devices away to provide a clear work area. Note the five screws on the rear panel that hold the cover housing to the system unit chassis. Using a nutdriver or a flat-blade screwdriver, remove these five screws and put them in a container so they won't get lost. Turn the system unit around so the front faces you and slide the cover towards you until it clears the chassis. You may have to tilt the cover up slightly as you pull it forward. After the cover has been removed, look into the system unit. Except for the boards plugged into the expansion slots, the inside view of the PC system unit should look like that shown in Fig. 1-15.

On the left is the system board or motherboard. At the top of the system board are the five expansion slots used to connect peripheral devices. On the lower left of the system board are four banks of memory chips. Up to 256K of RAM integrated circuits (ICs) can be installed on the system board. Also, in the lower left corner is the speaker that provides beeps and other sounds during operation.

The switching power supply is located in the top right of Fig. 1-15. It provides the electrical energy needed to operate the computer, the display unit, and the disk drives. Space is provided in the lower two thirds of Fig. 1-15 to house two floppy disk drives (only one floppy disk drive is shown). These drives connect to the system board through an adapter card plugged into one of the expansion slots.

The densely packed 8-1/2 inch by 12 inch system board is mounted at the bottom of the system unit. The multilayer board contains the primary electronic components of the IBM PC. Fig. 1-16 is a photograph of a typical 64K-256K PC system board. (Older PCs may have the 16K-64K system board installed, which is similar to the 64K-256K board.)

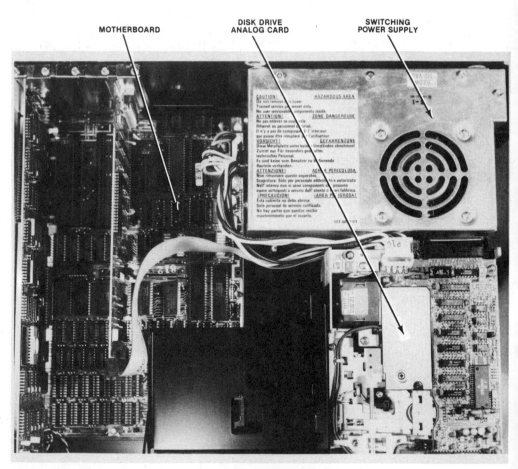

Fig. 1-15. Inside view of the IBM PC system unit.

Fig. 1-16.   Photograph of the 64K–256K IBM PC system board.

As you can see, most of the ICs on the system board are mounted in a common direction with pin 1 of each chip in the same position. This is important when repairing the PC because it helps prevent installing an IC backwards. ICs are marked with the package positioned so that pin 1 is at the lower left corner of the chip. If you inadvertently install a replacement IC with pin 1 facing the wrong way, you can quickly tell by the upside down lettering and numbering that it is mounted incorrectly.

Each IC also has a corresponding code (U23, U36, etc.) that relates to its identification on the circuit diagram or schematic. The code is stamped on the system board near the chip. In addition, the IC locations are marked in increasing order from left to right and from top to bottom. This is helpful in quickly locating a particular IC.

The major chips on the PC system board will be discussed in detail in Chapter 2. In all, 99 chips are mounted on the PC system board. These chips comprise the CPU, the memory, the timer, controllers, and input/output circuits.

IBM PC/XT Internal Components

Disconnect all cables and power cords from the rear of the XT system unit. Using a nutdriver or a flat-head screwdriver, remove the five screws on the rear panel that hold the cover housing to the system unit chassis. Turn the XT system unit around so that the front faces you and slide the cover towards you until it clears the chassis. You may have to tilt the cover up slightly as you pull it forward. With the cover removed, observe the layout of the XT internal components. Fig. 1-17 is an inside view of the XT system unit.

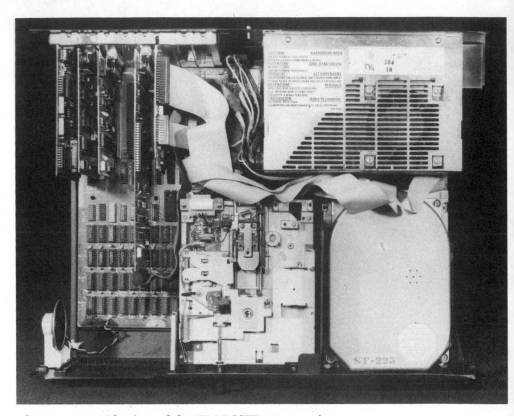

Fig. 1-17. Inside view of the IBM PC/XT system unit.

As you look into the XT system unit from the front, the system board is on the left. At the top of the system board are the eight slots used to connect peripheral devices. The distance between slots is less than that on the IBM PC, so component height on some non-IBM boards may be a problem. On the lower left of the system board are four banks of memory chips. Up to 256K of RAM can be installed on the system board. An XT with 640K of RAM on the memory board was introduced by IBM in 1986. The speaker is in the lower left corner of the system unit.

The switching power supply is located in the right rear area of the system unit when viewed from the front. The 130-watt power supply provides more than twice the energy as the power supply used in the IBM PC. The two disk drives are mounted in front of the power supply. The floppy drive is mounted on the left and the hard drive is mounted on the right. Two of the eight expansion slots are behind the floppy disk drive and can only accommodate short expansion boards.

The XT system board is mounted at the bottom of the system unit. This multilayer circuit board contains the primary electronic components of the XT. Most of these components are integrated circuits (ICs), which are often referred to as *chips*. A typical XT system board is shown in Fig. 1-18.

Fig. 1-18. Photograph of the PC/XT system board.

Most of the ICs on the XT system board are mounted in a common direction with pin 1 of each chip in the same position. This is important when repairing the system board because it helps prevent installing an IC backwards. If you inadvertently install a replacement IC with pin 1 facing the wrong way, the lettering and numbering will appear upside down when compared to the other ICs on the board.

Each IC has a corresponding code (U23, U36, etc.) that relates to its identification on the circuit diagram or schematic. The code is stamped on the XT system board near the chip. The chip identification labels on the board are marked in increasing order from left to right and from top to bottom. This is helpful in quickly locating ICs.

The most important of the 99 ICs mounted on the XT system board will be discussed in detail in Chapter 3. These chips include the CPU, the memory, timer, controllers, and input/output circuits.

IBM PC AT Internal Components

Although larger than the PC and XT, the AT is housed in a similar slide-on case which is held together by five screws on the rear panel. Turn the power switch off and remove all cables and power cords from the rear of the system unit. Turn the key switch to the UNLOCKED position and remove the key. Removing the back panel from the system unit (attached with plastic fastener strips) will expose the five screws that hold the cover housing to the system unit chassis. Use a nutdriver or flat-blade screwdriver to remove the five screws. Turn the system unit so that the front panel faces you and slide the front cover towards you until it clears the chassis. You may have to tilt the cover up slightly as you pull it forward. Except for the boards plugged into the expansion slots, the inside of the system unit should look like that shown in Fig. 1-19.

On the left side is the large system board with eight expansion slots near the top. The expansion slots are used to connect peripheral devices to the AT system unit. Six of the expansion slots have two sockets. One is a 62-pin socket like that on the PC and XT, and the other is a 36-pin socket for the expanded capability of the AT. On the lower left of the system board are two rows of RAM memory chips. These chips comprise two banks of 16-bit RAM memory. Each IC is a 256K by 1-bit dynamic RAM. Up to 256K of memory can be installed on the system board of the original ATs using 64K by 1-bit or 125K by 1-bit DRAMs. The first AT system boards used strange-looking piggyback memory chips to get 512K of RAM. The newer AT system boards (Fig. 1-19) are socketed for 512K in two banks of 256K each. The speaker is in the lower left corner of the system unit facing the front panel.

The switching power supply is in the right rear corner of the system unit. Just to the left of the power supply is a small battery backup pack as shown in Fig. 1-20. The battery backup pack is attached to the rear panel with a plastic fastener strip and plugged into a socket on the system board. (Earlier ATs used two screws to fasten the battery backup pack to the rear panel.) The 6-volt battery backup pack maintains the system configuration information and an internal real-time clock when the primary power is turned off.

The one or two half-height high-capacity floppy disk drives are mounted on the right side of the system unit in front of the power supply. The fixed drive is mounted in the center of the system unit next to the floppy drive(s). Recall that

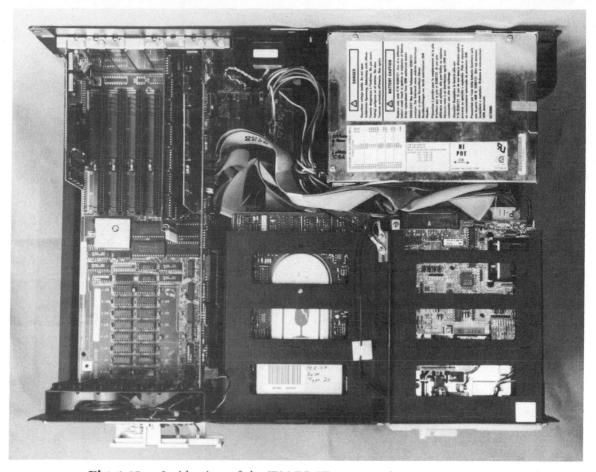

Fig. 1-19. Inside view of the IBM PC AT system unit.

three mass storage devices can be installed in the AT (two floppy drives and a fixed drive, or one floppy drive and two fixed drives).

The densely packed 12-inch by 13-inch AT system board is mounted in the bottom of the AT system unit. This multilayer board contains the primary electronic components of the IBM AT. The technology advancement of the PC AT over the earlier PC and PC/XT can be seen in the very large scale integration (VLSI) IC components mounted on the system board. One such VSLI component is the 68-pin Intel 80286 Microprocessor (U74) mounted in the center of the system board. A typical AT system board is shown in Fig. 1-21.

Most of the chips on the AT system board are mounted in a common direction with pin 1 of each chip facing towards the lower left corner of the board. This is important during repair because it helps prevent replacing ICs backwards. IC chips are typically marked with the packages positioned in the same direction. If you inadvertently install a replacement IC with pin 1 facing the

Fig. 1-20. The IBM PC AT battery backup pack.

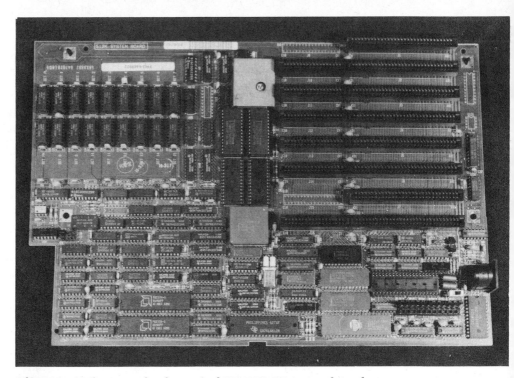

Fig.1-21. Photograph of a typical IBM PC AT system board.

wrong way, it should be readily apparent because the lettering and numbering will be upside down compared to the other ICs on the board.

Each IC also has a corresponding code (U23, U36, etc.) that relates to its identification on the circuit diagram or schematic. This code is stamped on the circuit board near the chip. The chip identification labels are marked on the board in increasing order from left to right and from top to bottom. This is helpful in locating a particular IC.

The important AT system board ICs will be discussed in detail in Chapter 4. In all, 128 ICs are mounted on the system board including the 80286 CPU, 64K of ROM memory (expandable to 128K), either 256K or 512K of RAM memory, special RAM memory to maintain system configuration, a real-time clock, controllers, and input/output circuits.

Questions for Review and Discussion

1. Describe the five basic parts of the IBM personal computer.
2. Give three examples of input devices.
3. Give three examples of output devices.
4. Name two devices that are both input and output devices.
5. What are the primary differences between the PC and the XT?
6. How many keys are on the standard IBM PC and XT keyboards?
7. Describe the major technological advancement of the AT computer over the PC and XT computers.
8. What is the primary difference between the floppy disk drive used in the AT and the floppy disk drives used in the PC and XT?
9. What is the advantage of tape cartridge backup over other storage backup systems?
10. How are most peripheral devices connected to the IBM PC family of computers?

Detailed System Operation of the IBM PC

In Chapter 1 you were introduced to the IBM PC family—the PC, the XT, and the AT personal computers. Chapter 2 describes the operation of the IBM PC computer. Chapter 3 will describe the XT and Chapter 4 will describe the AT. Circuit schematics and block diagrams are used to ease your understanding of signal and data flow.

The schematic symbols used in this book conform to the Howard W. Sams & Company COMPUTERFACTS standard symbols. A number enclosed in a box is used to represent a common voltage source. An active low signal is normally represented by a signal label with a bar over the top. Because printing the "not" bar over signal labels is awkward in a text such as this, the active low representation of a signal will be indicated by the symbol * following the label. Thus, the active low signal for reset will be represented as RESET*. Other symbols should be self-explanatory.

This chapter begins where everything in your computer starts—at the power plug. As shown in Fig. 2-1, power is furnished to the computer power supply through the ac power cord. The switching power supply produces the required voltage sources for the system board, the adapter boards in the expansion slots, and the floppy disk drives.

Power Supply

Inside the PC system unit chassis is a rectangular metal box containing a switching power supply. The back of the supply is exposed through holes cut into the rear of the system unit chassis. A fan is mounted inside the power supply to remove hot air generated by the supply and internal computer components.

Fig. 2-2 is a block diagram of the switching power supply. When rocker switch S1 is ON, line voltage is applied through slow-blow fuse F1 to the switching

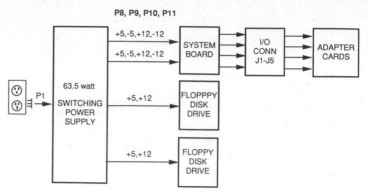

Fig. 2-1. System power requirements for the IBM PC.

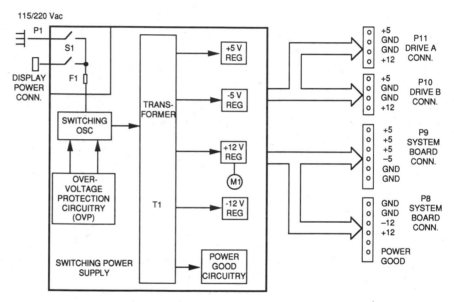

Fig. 2-2. Switching power-supply block diagram.

power-supply circuits. Switch S1 also provides 0.75 amps of filtered 120-V ac power to a display monitor receptacle at the rear of the power-supply housing.

As current begins to flow into the supply through fuse F1, a switching oscillator begins to provide ac input power to transformer T1 and the regulator circuitry connected to the output of T1. The regulators convert the ac input power into usable direct current (dc) voltage levels for the system components. One output drives cooling fan motor M1 and provides +12 volts to power the system's dynamic memory and the internal 5.25-inch disk drive motors. Another output provides a +5-V dc source to power the ICs used throughout the computer system. The −12-V dc source is used for driver circuitry on a communications adapter. A −5-V dc source is used for the dynamic memory chips on the system and expansion boards.

The +5-V dc source is also used as a power supply reference to produce a POWER GOOD signal for the system board about 100 ms after the source voltages have reached their desired level. The POWER GOOD signal is applied to the 8284 clock generator on the system board. If the source voltage drops too low, the POWER GOOD signal will disable the clock generator and shut down the system.

The power supply output voltages are monitored by internal circuitry to prevent catastrophic damage to the system or adapter boards should an over-voltage or overcurrent condition occur. A power-supply shutdown occurs if either the +5-V or +12-V dc outputs exceed 200 percent of maximum rated voltage. The supply also shuts down if current to any output exceeds 130 percent of nominal level.

Because high voltage is present in the PC power supply, we will not cover troubleshooting and repair of the power supply in this text. Power supply problems should be referred to experienced technicians. In most cases, it is more practical to replace a defective power supply.

IBM PC System Board

Fig. 2-3 shows the component layout for the IBM PC system board. This drawing will help you identify components as they are discussed. It will be also helpful during troubleshooting. An alphanumeric identification code is printed on the system board near each component. This code identifies the components in block diagrams and schematics. The integrated circuits (ICs) are often called "chips." Chips are identified in this text and on schematics with a "U" prefix designator followed by a number. The quad D flip/flop in chip location U26 is a "74LS175." The 74175 label identifies the IC as a quad-D flip/flop. The "LS" indicates that this chip is a low-powered Schottky type of IC. Other chips may have no center designator, or a different designator, such as a single "S" for Schottky, or "ALS" for advanced low-power Schottky.

Whenever replacing a component, it is important to use the same type of device as the original. Component characteristics including speed of operation are identified by the markings printed on the device. Using a 74S175 as a replacement when a 74LS175 is intended can cause unpredictable operation after the computer as been repaired. Remember to verify the center designator whenever you replace a component. A list of the chips with their center designators can be found in Appendix B.

8088 Central Processing Unit

The IBM PC was designed around the Intel 8088 Central Processing Unit (CPU)—an 8-bit version of Intel's 16-bit 8086 CPU. The bit size is determined by the number of binary bits in a data word. The 8086 works with 16-bit data words.

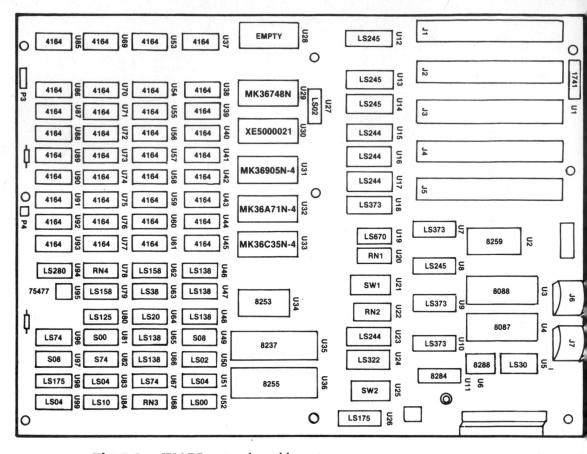

Fig. 2-3. IBM PC system board layout.

Although the 8088 can work with 16-bit data, only an 8-bit data bus path is available to enter or exit the chip. In the IBM PC, the 8088 is designed to work with 8-bit data.

With 20 address lines (AD0–AD7 and BA8–BA19), the 8088 CPU in Fig. 2-4 can directly access one million bytes of memory (two raised to the 20th power is 1,048,576). These address lines enable a physical memory address range between 00000H and FFFFFH (the "H" means "hexadecimal"). Sixteen of the address lines also access up to 64K of input/output (I/O) memory. The IBM PC I/O is memory mapped (looks like an address to the CPU) for easy access by CPU U3 and by application software.

The 8088 instruction/function format is identical to that of the 8086 micro-processor, so U3 also supports 16-bit operations, including multiply and divide. U3 is driven by the +5-V dc power source. The 8088 CPU and related circuitry is shown in Fig. 2-5.

Pin limitations caused Intel to design the 8088 to time-share part of its 20-pin address bus with the data bus. The lower eight address lines also serve as bidirectional data lines. During the first half of a microprocessor instruction

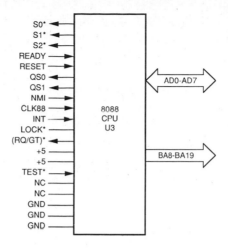

Fig. 2-4. The 8088 Central Processing Unit (U3).

cycle, bits AD0 through AD7 contain address information and are part of the 20-bit address bus. During the last half of the cycle, these eight bits contain data. Time-multiplexing the bidirectional address and data signal paths enables the microprocessor to access a large memory space while keeping the CPU package size small. The 8088 CPU is also designed to support an 8087 math coprocessor with its own local instruction set extension.

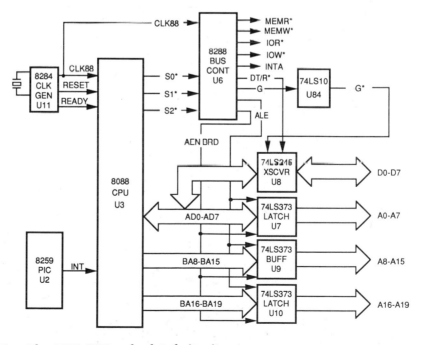

Fig. 2-5. The 8088 CPU and related circuitry.

When 8088 operation begins, the CPU places an address on its address bus, accesses a memory location, fetches a byte of instruction data, interprets and executes the instruction, placing the results in a location determined by the instruction, and then fetches another instruction to repeat the sequence. The 8088 can collect up to four instructions in a queue; so while it's busy internally executing a current instruction, another part of U3 can be loading other instructions enabling maximum program execution speed.

The CLK88, READY, and RESET signals from the 8284 clock generator U11 enable 8088 operation. During operation, CPU U3 sends special status signals to 8288 bus controller U6. The bus controller uses these signals to generate sophisticated bus control and command functions.

The 8088 status signals S0*, S1*, and S2* are decoded by 8288 bus controller U6 to generate timed command and control signals. Access to system or I/O memory is achieved using memory read (MEMR*), memory write (MEMW*), I/O read (IOR*), or I/O write (IOW*). The active low memory read command (MEMR*) causes the system memory to drive its stored information onto the data bus. Its companion command, active low memory write (MEMW*), causes the memory to record the information presently on the data bus. Peripheral devices are controlled using low IOR* and IOW* commands. These commands instruct I/O devices to drive data onto or read data from the PC data bus. If an I/O command is to be executed, only the lower 16-bits of the address bus are used. This gives the 8088 CPU 65,536 (64K) directly addressable I/O locations. An addressing scheme that represents I/O devices as addresses is called "memory-mapped I/O."

Bus controller U6 also generates an interrupt acknowledge signal (INTA) that informs a programmable interrupt controller on the system board that an interrupt has been recognized by CPU U3. Interrupts are described later. Several other control signals (DT/R*, G, and ALE) control the address buffers and latches, and the data transceiver connected to CPU U3.

8087 Math Coprocessor

The 8087 numeric processor extension (NPX) math coprocessor was designed for complex operations requiring powerful arithmetic instructions and data types including fractional values, sine, cosine, logarithms, and square roots. The 8087 can perform number-crunching applications at rapid speed and with extreme accuracies. The 8087 coprocessor (U4) handles numeric data over a wide range of values including integer and noninteger numbers. It can produce precise results with a large number of significant digits and can handle calculations involving real and imaginary numbers. Integers up to 18 digits long and floating point numbers from 16 to 80 bits wide can be used. The NPX has built-in math instructions for add, subtract, multiply, divide, absolute value, arctangent, tangent, square root, log base two and log base e. Both the hardware and the software interfaces to the 8087 are compatible with the 8088.

A prewired 40-pin socket (U4), located next to the 8088 CPU (U3) on the system board, was designed to hold the optional 8087 math coprocessor. As shown in Fig. 2-6, the system board is configured so U3 and U4 share the same multiplexed address/data bus, the clock, reset, and other system board signals.

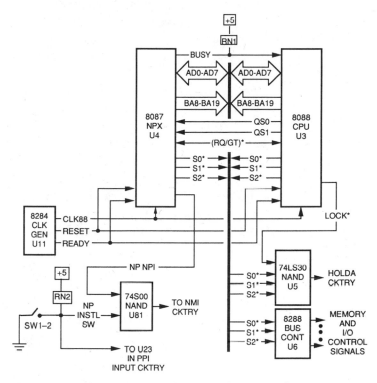

Fig. 2-6. The 8087 math coprocessor (U4) interface circuitry.

Both the CPU and the math coprocessor monitor and decode the same instructions and bytes of an instruction stream. This allows the 8087 to monitor and decode instructions synchronously with the 8088 CPU without introducing any CPU overhead. Thus, coprocessor U4 knows at all times what instruction was just fetched. The coprocessor and CPU instructions can be mixed in a program, and the 8087 can process instructions in parallel with and independent of the 8088 CPU.

An instruction that requires 8087 action appears as an escape (ESC) command followed by a special code. When an ESC instruction occurs, U4 looks at the byte following the ESC instruction to see if the coprocessor should respond. If the ESC instruction and following byte are for coprocessor execution, the 8087 takes control over the system busses.

A BUSY signal from U4 tells the CPU when the coprocessor is executing a numeric instruction. If the CPU samples BUSY and finds it low, CPU execution continues; otherwise the 8088 goes into an idle state and the 8087 continues using the system board circuitry.

To assist U4 in monitoring CPU operations, status lines QS0 and QS1 are connected between the 8087 coprocessor and the 8088 CPU. The CPU sends these signals to U4 to cause the coprocessor to read and decode instructions synchronously with U3.

Coprocessor U4 can interrupt the 8088 CPU whenever U4 detects an error or exception. If an incorrect instruction is sent to U4, such as a command to divide a number by zero, U4 will generate a numeric processor interrupt (NPI) that results in a nonmaskable interrupt (NMI) to the CPU.

System board switch SW1 position 2 is open (OFF position) when an 8087 coprocessor is installed. Some IBM PCs with the standard 67.5-watt power supply have experienced intermittent problems when an 8087 coprocessor was installed. The 8087 draws 0.457 milliamps of current and dissipates up to three watts. If the PC system also contains several power-hungry expansion boards, the switching power supply can become overworked causing excessive heating of the power-supply circuitry. This can cause intermittent CPU lockup, power-on self-test failure, suspicious RAM memory malfunction, unreliable disk drive write operation, and even power supply failure. Installing a larger power supply usually prevents system failures caused by an 8087 coprocessor.

System Support Chips

The 8088 CPU on the IBM PC system board is configured to work with special system support chips. These chips include the 8284 clock generator (U11), the 8253 programmable interval timer (U34), the 8255 programmable peripheral interface (U36), the 8259 programmable interrupt controller (U36), and the 8237 programmable DMA controller (U35). Each of these chips and their associated circuitry are discussed in the following paragraphs.

8284 Clock Generator (U11)

The 8284 clock generator (U11) produces several clock signals that help the CPU process millions of bits of information each second. As shown in Fig. 2-7, a 14.318-MHz crystal (Y1) is connected across the 8284 and causes U11 to produce three clock signals—CLK88, OSC, and PCLK.

The 4.77-MHz clock signal, CLK88, is the system operating frequency for the 8088 CPU (U3), the 8087 math coprocessor (if installed), and the 8288 bus controller (U6). The 14.318-MHz OSC signal is used by the color/graphics adapter board to develop synchronization and horizontal scan signals. The 2.386-MHz peripheral clock signal, PCLK, is divided down to 1.193 MHz and used to step the counters in the 8253 programmable interval timer (U34).

The clock generator also receives external status inputs and produces two important handshaking signals. The POWER GOOD signal from the switching

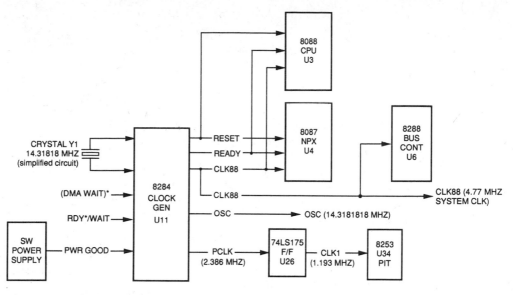

Fig. 2-7. Block diagram of clock circuitry in the IBM PC.

power supply causes U11 to generate a reset signal (RESET) that initializes the entire system to a known start-up condition. RESET causes the 8088 CPU to start operating at address FFFF0H. System start-up will be discussed later. The clock generator also produces a ready signal (READY) that tells CPU U3 and math coprocessor U4 if a slower component or device has completed its process. The active processor can then continue with its own processing and no longer wait for the slower device.

8253 Programmable Interval Timer (U34)

Fig. 2-8 shows the circuitry associated with the 8253 programmable interval timer (U34). This IC performs three important functions: it generates a time-of-day clock tick, it refreshes the dynamic RAM memory, and it helps produce sound from the PC's internal speaker.

Inside U34 are three individually programmable 16-bit down-counters. The 2.386-MHz PCLK signal from clock generator U11 is divided by 74LS175 quad D flip-flop U26 to produce a 1.193-MHz clock input that goes to each counter inside U34. Each counter can be preset when the PC is started. Depending on the setting of each counter, three timed outputs are generated: OUT0 (IRQ0) to U2, OUT1 to U67, and OUT2 (TIMER/CNTR2) to U63. Each output occurs at a frequency determined by the input clock and the software programmable U34 internal counters. This feature lets U34 generate accurate time delays while minimizing program overhead.

Once programmed, the counters operate automatically. Upon count start, the 8253 causes each counter to clock down from its preset delay value until the

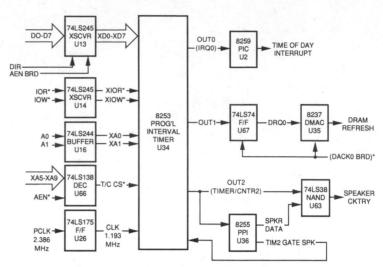

Fig. 2-8. 8253 programmable interval timer and related circuitry.

count reaches zero. At this point, the counter sends out a count-complete signa[l] (OUT0, OUT1, or OUT2) and rolls over backwards to its preprogrammed prese[t] value so the countdown can begin once more.

OUT0 becomes IRQ0, the time-of-day interrupt that occurs approximatel[y] 18.2 times each second. OUT1 occurs 66,287 times a second and causes the 823[7] direct memory access (DMA) controller U35 to access the dynamic RAM every 1[5] microseconds. This periodic access is called "refresh."

OUT2 is labeled TIMER/CNTR2 and helps produce speaker activation sig nals. TIMER/CNTR2 can be varied by presetting the OUT2 counter with differen[t] values, each producing a unique output frequency.

8255 Programmable Peripheral Interface (U36)

The 8255 programmable peripheral interface (PPI) electronically connect[s] peripheral equipment to the 8088 CPU. As shown in Fig. 2-9, U36 connects [a] bidirectional data bus (XD0 through XD7) with three programmable PPI I/O port[s] (Port A, Port B, Port C) under control of specialized read/write control logic.

During system start-up U36 is electronically configured so Ports A and [C] function as inputs and Port B becomes an output. This basic input/outpu[t] configuration requires no handshaking for information transfer. No clock pulse[s] are required to step data through U36. Whatever is present at a port can b[e] accessed simply by addressing that particular port. Data to and from the dat[a] bus, XD0 through XD7, and the PPI is under CPU control. Control words an[d] status information are also passed back and forth between U36 and the CPU ove[r] the data bus.

Port A connects to 74LS322 keyboard input register U24 and to configura tion switch SW1 via 74LS244 buffer U23. Depending on the status of output Por[t]

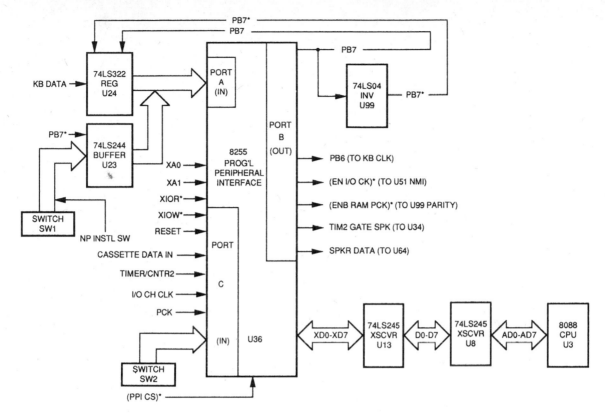

Fig. 2-9. The 8255 programmable peripheral interface U36 circuitry in the IBM PC.

B bit 7 (PB7), Port A reads either the keyboard (PB7 high) or system board switch SW1 (PB7 low). SW1 defines the number of disk drives installed, the type of display connected, the amount of system board memory installed, and if a math coprocessor is on the system board.

Port C receives information from the cassette data input circuitry, the 8253 programmable interval timer (U34) counter 2 output (TIMER/CNTR2), I/O chan nel status circuitry, a RAM parity checking circuit, and memory configuration switch SW2. SW2 defines the number of RAM banks in the I/O channel. Its configuration causes the PC to recognize up to eight 64-Kbyte I/O memory banks. Table 2-1 describes the assignments for SW1 and SW2 system board switches.

The settings of both manual switches are read by the 8088 CPU through the 8255 PPI (U36). A software program examines the inputs to Ports A and C and interprets the data to determine the system configuration.

Port B sends information to the speaker, to timer U34, to the cassette motor, and to the parity test circuitry. Port B also sends programmed data waveforms (SPKR DATA) to the speaker. Active low signals (EN I/O CK)* and (ENB RAM PCK)* enable RAM parity checking and monitoring of the I/O channel status lines that are read by Port C (I/O CH CLK). Bit 6 of Port B (PB6) is used to drive the keyboard clock line low (when PB6 = 0), and PB7 is used to cause Port A to read SW1 (when PB7 = 1) or the eight bits of keyboard data (when PB7 = 0).

Table 2-1. System Board Switch Assignments

Switch	Function
Switch Block 1:	
1	Number of installed 5-1/4 inch diskette drives
2	Math coprocessor installed
3	System board memory
4	System board memory
5	Type of display connected
6	Type of display connected
7	Number of installed 5-1/4 inch diskette drives
8	Number of installed 5-1/4 inch diskette drives
Switch Block 2:	
1	Amount of installed memory
2	Amount of installed memory
3	Amount of installed memory
4	Amount of installed memory
5	Amount of installed Memory
6	Always off
7	Always off
8	Always off

8259 Programmable Interrupt Controller (U2)

The IBM PC is designed to function in an environment of interrupts. Interaction with the 8088 CPU occurs using interrupt signals. Interrupts can be caused by the operator (e.g., pressing a key on the keyboard), peripheral hardware such as disk drives and video displays, and software programs that need to interact with other programs or hardware.

When the 8088 recognizes an interrupt, it transfers control to the location of an interrupt handling subroutine that services the interrupt. Then control is returned to the CPU or the software program that was running when the interrupt occurred.

Software interrupts are part of the program code that is executed by the CPU. These interrupts occur as designed during program execution. Problems in the memory hardware can cause a special nonmaskable interrupt (NMI) to the 8088 CPU. All other hardware interrupts begin as external interrupt request signals to an 8259 programmable interrupt controller (U2) that is preset to accept interrupt requests in a priority order. As shown in Fig. 2-10, the output of U2 is a CPU interrupt signal (INT) that connects directly to the 8088 CPU (U3).

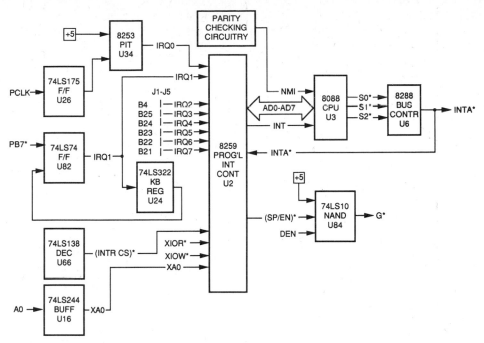

Fig. 2-10. 8259 programmable interrupt controller (PIC) U2 and related circuitry.

The 8259 programmable interrupt controller handles up to eight priority interrupt requests and requires no clock input. It responds to any interrupt request input once it is properly configured during system start-up. Its ability to handle multilevel priority interrupts minimizes software and real-time system overhead.

Priority setting during start-up lets U2 respond correctly when several devices attempt to interrupt CPU operation at the same time. The device with the highest priority is serviced first. Higher priority inputs can be masked (effectively ignored) without affecting the interrupt request lines of lower priority inputs.

IRQ0 is the highest priority interrupt. It causes a time of day clock tick. The second highest priority interrupt (IRQ1) is used during keyboard entry. Table 2-2 lists the assignments for all eight interrupt request inputs to programmable interrupt controller U2. If two request lines become active at the same time, the request whose number is closest to IRQ0 is serviced first.

When a hardware interrupt request occurs, U2 sends an INT signal to CPU U3 causing the 8088 to pull status outputs S0*, S1*, and S2* active low. This status code is interpreted by the 8288 bus controller (U6) causing two interrupt acknowledge (INTA*) signals to be passed back to U2.

The first INTA* signal communicates to the 8259 that the request has been recognized and that an interrupt acknowledge cycle is in progress. The CPU locks out other devices from gaining access to the bus and then causes bus controller U6 to generate another INTA* signal. When U2 senses this second interrupt acknowledge signal, it places a byte of data on the address/data bus

Table 2-2.　8259 Hardware Interrupt Request Listing

Interrupt Request	Type of Interrupt	Function
IRQ0	Type 8	Timer
IRQ1	Type 9	Keyboard
IRQ2	Type A	Reserved
IRQ3	Type B	Asynchronous communications (secondary), Synchronous Data Link Control (SDLC) communication, Binary Synchronous Communications (BSC)
IRQ4	Type C	Asynchronous communication (primary), SDLC communication, BSC (primary)
IRQ5	Type D	Fixed disk (if installed)
IRQ6	Type E	Floppy diskette adapter card
IRQ7	Type F	Printer/display adapter

(AD0 through AD7). This data represents the interrupt type (Type 0 through 255) associated with the device requesting the interrupt. The CPU uses this byte to develop an address pointer to an interrupt vector table containing a jump instruction to a service routine elsewhere in memory.

For example, pressing a key on the keyboard produces IRQ1 causing U2 to generate INT. CPU U3 responds by sending an all-zero S0*-S2* code to 8288 bus controller U6 causing it to return an INTA* signal back to U2 starting the response sequence. When the second INTA* is received by the interrupt controller (U2), it places the appropriate interrupt vector (09H for IRQ1*) on the data bus. CPU U3 uses this vector to produce the address in memory where a jump instruction to the actual service routine is located. The final physical address for the keyboard service routine is 0E987H. A program at this location reads the keyboard data and resets the system for the next key entry. Hardware interrupts are serviced in priority sequence. Once the highest priority interrupt has been serviced, the next highest priority interrupt request to the 8259 programmable interrupt controller receives CPU attention.

Hardware interrupts that originate with an interrupt request to the 8259 interrupt controller can be masked (ignored) by command from the CPU. However, there is one hardware interrupt that can never be masked. Instead it must be immediately recognized and serviced by U3. This interrupt is called a nonmaskable interrupt (NMI). Whenever a "catastrophic" event such as a parity error occurs, a NMI is generated causing CPU U3 system operation to stop. A NMI interrupt can also be caused by an 8087 math coprocessor malfunction or a failure in the I/O channel circuitry.

8237 Programmable DMA Controller (DMAC)

An 8237 programmable DMA controller (U35) is used to improve system performance in the IBM PC by allowing external devices to directly transfer information in large blocks (up to 64K bytes). When activated, U35 causes the 8088 CPU to suspend normal operation and pass control of the system buses to the DMAC. Programmable DMA controller U35 can conduct data transfers at rates up to 1.5 megabytes per second. Innovative circuit design ensures that U35 takes bus control only at the correct moment. When the DMA is active, U35 causes the CPU's address, control, and data buffers to appear disconnected (go tristate) from the system board circuitry. U35 then causes the 8284 clock generator to pull READY low, forcing U3 to wait while U35 conducts the DMA transfer.

As shown in Fig. 2-11, DMAC U35 contains four independent request (DRQ0 through DRQ3) and four independent acknowledge channels (DACK0 through DACK3) which can automatically reinitialize to a preprogrammed condition following each DMA process. Each channel has a 64K address and word count capability.

Special logic circuitry inside U35 resolves priority contention when more than one DMA channel requests service at the same time. The four DMA request channels (DRQ0 through DRQ3) are independent but in a fixed priority with DRQ0 holding the highest priority (DRQ3 lowest). Each DMA request signal must be held until a corresponding acknowledge signal (DACK0 BRD, DACK1, DACK2, or DACK3) is generated.

When a DMA request line becomes active, U35 produces a Hold Request DMA (HRQ DMA) signal. HRQ DMA results in the generation of a DMA WAIT signal that pulls the 8284 clock generator READY output low. The low READY output causes the 8088 CPU to be electronically disconnected from the system and gives DMA controller U35 direction over the address, data, and control buses.

Every 72 clock cycles (15 microseconds), programmable interval timer U34 generates OUT1 sending an active high DRQ0 to U35 producing (DACK0 BRD)* and causing a memory access that refreshes the charges in the dynamic RAM (DRAM) ICs on the system board. Acknowledge signal (DACK0 BRD)* is also buffered through 74LS244 U15, relabeled DACK0*, and passed to pin B19 of expansion slots J1 through J5 for refreshing DRAM memory installed on system expansion adapter boards.

The other three DMA request channels (DRQ1 through DRQ3) come from pins B18, B6, and B16 respectively on connectors J1 through J5. For example, DRQ2 comes from the floppy disk drive adapter card. These request signals result in active low DMA acknowledge signals DACK1*, DACK2*, and DACK3 * that tell an individual peripheral that a DMA cycle has been granted. The DMA request signals are often used to generate chip select signals on I/O boards.

DACK2* and DACK3* are also passed to 74LS670 4 × 4 DMA page register file (U19). Because the DMA controller can only handle one 64K memory page at a time, U19 is used to increase the DMA capability from 64K to a full one megabyte of 64K pages. U19 can transfer up to 1 MB of data in 64K page increments. Each time 64K of data has been transferred, an internal counter fills and generates a terminal count pulse (T/C)* that signals the completion of a DMA operation. This signal is used by the system board and adapter cards to keep track of DMA cycles.

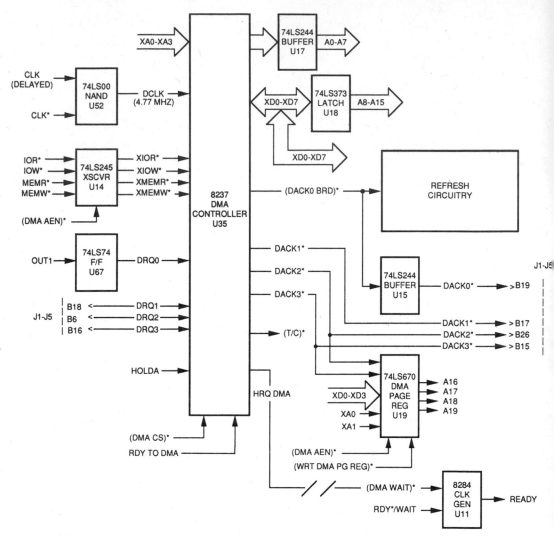

Fig. 2-11. 8237 programmable DMA controller U35 circuitry.

Memory Configuration

The PC system board can contain up to 256K of installed random-access memory, but the CPU can physically address up to one million memory locations (addresses 00000H to FFFFFH, where H means hexadecimal). This section describes the circuitry and signals associated with the onboard and I/O memory.

Memory Addressing Scheme

The system memory of the PC includes read and write random-access memory (RAM) and read-only memory (ROM) residing within one megabyte of address locations. The CPU can also access up to 64K of I/O devices. Each device appears as a unique memory location. Some devices, such as the floppy disk controller on the disk drive adapter card, can have several addresses assigned to certain registers in the controller. Memory-mapping the I/O within a 64K byte dedicated I/O memory space enables easy access by the CPU. As shown in Table 2-3, the one megabyte system memory of the 8088 CPU in the IBM PC is partitioned into a number of dedicated and reserved areas.

Table 2-3. Memory Allocation for the IBM PC

Hexadecimal Address	16K/64K System	64K/256K System	
00000	64K RAM on system board		←
0FFFF		256K RAM on system board	
10000			
3FFFF			640K
40000	576K RAM on expansion cards		
		384K RAM on expansion cards	
9FFFF			←
A0000	reserved		←
AFFFF			
B0000	Monochrome video RAM		
B3FFF			
B4000	reserved		128K
B7FFF			
B8000	Color/graphics video RAM		
BBFFF			
BC000	reserved		
BFFFF			
C0000			←
	256K ROM		256K
FFFFF			1024K

The allocation of the first 64K of system memory is described in Table 2-4. The lower part of system memory is reserved for interrupt vectors and the

BASIC I/O system (BIOS), BASIC high-level language, and BASIC and Disk Operating System (DOS) data areas. From location 00600H to 0FFFFH is 63.5K of user defined RAM memory space.

Above address 0FFFFFH is 576KB of RAM. Some of the RAM is mounted on the PC system board and the remaining RAM can be mounted on expansion cards. Note that the total available memory resides in the first 640K of memory space. As shown in Table 2-3, the 128K above address 9FFFFH is reserved for video and attribute display data and the 256K above this is dedicated to ROM.

ROM is designed to reside in the address space bounded by C0000H and FFFFFH. The allocation of these 262,144 locations (256K) in both the 16K/64K and 64K/256K PC systems is described in Table 2-5.

The top 16 bytes of ROM memory (locations FFFF0H through FFFFFH) are reserved for specific 8088 CPU operations including a jump to the initial program loading routine. When a reset occurs, the CPU always begins executions at location FFFF0H where a jump instruction is stored to shift program execution to a special routine elsewhere in memory.

The I/O space in the IBM PC is logically separated from the system memory space using special control signals defined by a code from the CPU to the bus controller. The I/O memory space covers addresses 0000H to FFFFH (64K bytes). Special commands enable data transfers between I/O devices. The allocation of I/O memory is described in Table 2-6.

Table 2-4. Allocation of Lower 64K of Memory (16K/64K and 64K/256K Systems)

Hexadecimal Address	Memory Content
00000 0001F	BIOS interrupt vectors 00-1F
00020 0007F	
00080 000FF	DOS interrupt vectors 20-3F
00100 001FF	User interrupt vectors 40-7F
00200 003FF	BASIC interrupt vectors 80-FF
00400 004FF	BIOS data area
00500 005FF	BASIC and DOS data area
00600 0FFFF	63.5K user area

Table 2-5. ROM Memory Space Allocation

IC Label	Hexadecimal Address	16K/64K System	64K/256K System		
	C0000		System expansion and control		
	C7FFF				
	C8000	16K Hard disk control		192K	
	CBFFF				
	CC000	144K			
	EFFFF				
	F0000	16K		16K	
	F3FFF				
U28	F4000	8K Open socket		8K	
	F5FFF				
U29	F6000	8K ROM Cassette BASIC			
	F7FFF				
U30	F8000	8K ROM Cassette BASIC		32K	
	F9FFF				
U31	FA000	8K ROM Cassette BASIC			
	FBFFF				
U32	FC000	8K ROM Cassette BASIC			
	FDFFF				
U33	FE000	8K ROM BIOS & POST		8K	
	FFFFF				

256K ROM

Some system board ICs are directly accessible using I/O write or read commands. Other locations in I/O memory space are reserved by IBM or a chip manufacturer. For example, IBM designed locations 060H through 063H to access the 8255 PPI while Intel reserves addresses 0F8H through 0FFH (8 bytes) for its own future hardware and software products. The system BIOS software ignores these eight bytes.

Fig. 2-5 shows how the four memory command signals: system memory read (MEMR*), system memory write (MEMW*), I/O read (IOR*), and I/O write (IOW*) are generated. These signals are passed through a transceiver to produce buffered signals XMEMR*, XMEMW*, XIOR*, or XIOW*. Each signal is also passed to a dedicated pin (B11 through B13) on expansion connectors J1 through J5 for use on peripheral boards. These signals are typically connected as enable inputs to gates used in memory or I/O operations.

Table 2-6.   IBM PC I/O Address Map

Hexdecimal Address	Access Function
000–00F	8237 DMA controller (U35)
020–021	8259 programmable interrupt controller (U2)
040–043	8253 programmable interval timer (U34)
060–063	8255 programmable peripheral interface (U36)
080–083	DMA page registers
0A	NMI mask register enable/disable
0C	Reversed
0E	Reserved
0F8–0FF	Reserved for 8088 upgrades
100–1FF	Not usable
200–20F	Game control
210–217	Expansion unit
220–24F	Reserved
278–27F	Reserved
2F0–2F7	Reserved
2F8–2FF	Asynchronous communications (secondary)
300–31F	Prototype card
320–32F	Hard disk
378–37F	Printer
380–38C	Synchronous data link control (SDLC) communications
380–389	Binary synchronous communications (secondary)
3A0–3A9	Binary synchronous communications (primary)
3B0–3BF	IBM monochrome display/printer card
3C0–3CF	Reserved
3D0–3DF	Color/graphics
3E0–3F7	Reserved
3F0–3F7	Diskette
3F8–3FF	Asynchronous communications (primary)

Read-Only Memory (ROM)

The IBM PC system board is designed to hold six 8K-by-8-bit read-only memory (ROM) chips, although only five are installed (U29 through U33). Thirteen buffered address lines (XA0 through XA12) connect to each chip as shown in Fig. 2-12. A special chip select signal (CS3* through CS7*) enables a particular ROM to place eight bits of data on its output.

Of the 262,144 bytes of assigned ROM memory space (C0000H to FFFFFH), locations C0000H to F3FFFH are reserved for future ROM code and the adapter cards connected to the system. If a hard disk is installed, it is allocated address space C8000H to CBFFFH. Addresses F4000H to F5FFFH were reserved for part of the original Cassette BASIC code but BASIC required less actual memory space so these addresses are allocated to an empty socket (U28) which is not shown.

The next four ROM chips (U29 through U32) are assigned address space F6000H through FDFFFH and contain the 32K Cassette BASIC object code. The

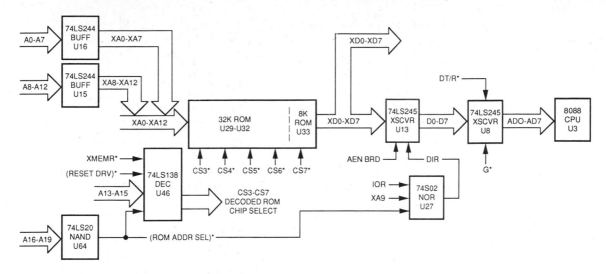

Fig. 2-12. IBM PC ROM circuitry.

remaining 8K ROM (U33) is allocated address space FE000H to FFFFFH and contains the basic input/output system (BIOS) routines for the IBM PC.

Permanently stored in U33 are short programs called "I/O drivers" that enable communication with external devices such as printers and mass storage. U33 also contains dot patterns for 128 special characters for graphics display operations and the codes to control the time-of-day clock, cassette operations, a power-up self-test (POST) sequence, and disk bootstrap loading of DOS. All address locations below C0000H are dedicated to random-access memory (RAM).

The computer's power-up self-test program occupies 2K of the 8K BIOS ROM U33 and includes a series of tests that occur each time power is applied. These tests check the 8088 CPU (U3), the keyboard, the video display adapter card, the cassette recorder, the floppy disk interface, and the ROM and RAM. The RAM test contains five different write/read operations that check the entire installed RAM memory. Each memory test writes and then reads and checks a different bit pattern in memory. Testing systems fully populated with RAM can take up to 1.5 minutes. If the computer is restarted with power already on, part of the power-up self tests including the RAM tests are bypassed, reducing the initialization time by almost 40 percent.

Fig. 2-12 also shows the ROM chip select circuitry. Addresses A13 through A19 cause a valid chip select signal (CS3* through CS7*) only when certain enable signals are present and address lines A16 through A19 are high and A13 through A15 are between binary 011 and 111. This produces a chip select signal for one of the ROM chips only when an address of F6000H or higher is placed on the address bus. F6000H correlates with CS3* and the first BASIC ROM U29. CS7* enables ROM U33 when an address FE000H or higher is applied.

Data from ROM is buffered through 74LS245 transceiver U13 onto the data bus (D0 through D7) and into the 8088 CPU (U3). Direction (DIR) and enable (AEN

BRD) signals cause U13 to pass data from the buffered data side (XD0 through XD7) to the data bus side (D0 through D7) and into 74LS245 transceiver U8. Active low data transmit/receive (DT/R*) and G* signals cause U8 pass data from the D0 through D7 side to the address/data bus side (AD0 through AD7) for action by the 8088 CPU (U3).

Random-Access Memory (RAM)

The first IBM PC contained a system board designed to hold up to 64K of type 4116 16K-by-1-bit random-access memory (RAM) chips. These system boards were later replaced with an updated design containing up to 256K of type 4164 64K-by-1-bit dynamic RAMs (the 4564 version was used in some systems). Using expansion slots, a user can install an additional 384K of external RAM giving a total of 640K of available RAM per system. Most PCs have the 64K-by-1-bit RAM boards, so this book focuses on the newer system boards. Older board designs function much like the system boards described in this book, so the user should have no difficulty following this text and relating the information to either system board.

Four rows, or banks, of nine RAM chips each are mounted on the system board. The ninth chip (shown at the top left in layout diagram Fig. 2-3) stores a parity bit associated with each 8-bit word in a particular row of RAM. RAM is parity checked during readout. This operation will be discussed later.

Fig. 2-13 shows the circuitry associated with reading or writing a typical bank of 4164 (MK4564) 64K-by-1-bit RAM chips. Bank 0 is shown alone for simplicity.

Eight address lines (MA0 through MA7) and a single data in line (MDn) and a single data out line connect to each RAM chip. This is why Fig. 2-13 shows two data paths at the top of RAM.

Sixteen of the 20 system address bus lines (A0 through A15) are multiplexed into eight RAM chip address lines to access each of the 65,536 dynamic memory cells in each chip in each bank of memory. Each memory access affects an 8-bit word plus its parity bit. These sixteen address bits are multiplexed simultaneously into all nine chips in a selected RAM bank. Using row (RAS0) and column (CAS0) strobe signals, a row address is latched into the RAM chips first, followed by a column address. With a special write enable signal (WE*) that defines a read or write operation, these three signals enable access to RAM Bank 0 as shown in Figure 2-13. A similar process accesses the remaining banks of memory. Reading or writing is simultaneously accomplished on all nine chips in the data word (data plus parity).

Refresh

Each dynamic RAM is comprised of 65,536 tiny memory cells. In each memory cell, a logic 1 is represented by a tiny stored electric charge. Since this charge can leak away, each storage location must be periodically accessed to restore the

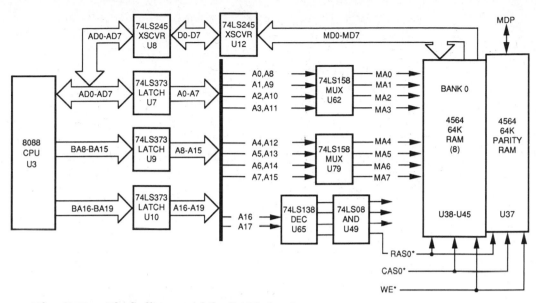

Fig. 2-13. Block diagram of the RAM circuitry.

charge in cells that are in the logic high condition. This periodic memory access to restore charge is called "refresh." Depending on the manufacturer, dynamic RAM (DRAM) chips must be refreshed every two to four milliseconds.

Each time a DRAM location is read, the same memory cell is accessed in all nine chips associated with a selected bank of memory chips. All the memory cells in that bank are refreshed together, and memory cells that held a logic high are recharged to the full logic 1 charge condition. Refresh is accomplished by performing a memory read cycle within each two to four millisecond interval. Any cycle in which a row address strobe signal becomes active will refresh an entire row of memory cell locations. Each dynamic RAM is designed so its output buffer is electronically disconnected from the memory data bus until the column address strobe signal is applied. Thus, refresh can occur without ever activating the column address strobe. This row-strobe-only refresh prevents data output during refresh and conserves power during the memory cycle.

Refresh begins when the OUT1 signal from the 8253 programmable interval timer (U34) sends a DMA request signal (DRQ0) to DMA controller U35. Since OUT1 occurs every 15 microseconds, the memory accesses caused by OUT1 are well within the two to four millisecond (2,000 to 4,000 microsecond) refresh requirement. Refresh affects the dynamic RAM on the system board and on any I/O expansion boards.

Parity

A ninth chip in each bank of RAM stores a bit corresponding to the parity of the 8 bits in each word of data. During memory write operations, each data word is evaluated to determine the number of binary 1s contained in it. If the count of 1s results in an odd number, a 0 parity bit is stored in a special memory chip (parity memory). If the number of 1s is even, a 1s parity bit is stored in the corresponding location in the parity memory chip causing the total (data word plus parity) to have an odd number of 1s.

During memory read, the parity of the 8-bit word read out of memory is checked by the 74S280 9-bit odd/even parity generator/checker (U94) shown in Fig. 2-14 and compared with the memory data parity bit (MDP) read from the corresponding location in the parity RAM. A new parity value is calculated on the 8-bit data word and then compared with the stored parity value. If the two parity values (computed and stored) are equal, the data word is accepted by the CPU or processor and system operation continues. However, if the two values differ, a nonmaskable interrupt (NMI) occurs, causing the machine to halt with "PARITY CHECK" displayed on the screen.

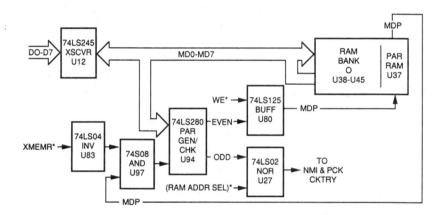

Fig. 2-14. Block diagram of parity generator/checker circuitry.

Parity generator/checker U94 detects (but not corrects) errors in RAM data retrieval. Both the even and odd parity outputs from U94 are used although the system is designed to establish odd parity. To do this, a complete 8-bit data word (MD0 through MD7) is passed to U94 at the same time it is applied to RAM. If the number of high bits in the data word is even, the EVEN parity output goes high. If the number of high data bits is odd, the ODD parity output goes high and the EVEN parity output goes low.

During a write operation, the EVEN parity output is passed into 74LS125 quad 3-state buffer U80. When enabled by WE*, U80 causes the even parity bit to become the memory data parity bit (MDP) input to parity RAM U37 (Bank 0 selected in this example). This is the bit that is compared with a new calculated parity bit during memory read. Also during a memory write operation, the output from 74S08 quad 2-input AND gate U97 is held low disabling the parity check circuitry of U94 until a read occurs.

Keyboard

IBM provided two types of keyboards for the PC. The older IBM Type 1 keyboard has a 23-row by 4-column momentary contact pushbutton array. The newer Type 2 keyboard has a 12-row by 8-column capacitive key matrix. Both designs function alike and differ only in the keyboard matrix configuration and in the way an on-board single-chip microcomputer is connected to the I/O cable. The Type 2 keyboard is more common, so it will be described in this text.

Inside the Type 2 keyboard are a handful of components including four ICs, a capacitive key matrix, and a few discrete components (capacitors, resistors, and an inductor). The 83 keys on the board connect to the switch matrix. Each time you press a key, a switch is closed at a crossover point on the X-row by Y-column capacitive matrix. This matrix is scanned by an internal dedicated processor (M1) that senses the open or closed contact condition of each crossover in the matrix. When a switch is closed, the processor generates a bit stream code (scan code) that is passed through the keyboard cable onto the system board and into the 8255 PPI (U36) which in turn provides the data to the 8088 CPU (U3) for interpretation and action.

The keys are typematic in that pressing a key generates a scan code indicating a closed (make) condition. Releasing the key produces an open (break) scan code. Therefore, a code is generated for both switch closing and opening (make and break) conditions. The keyboard is controlled by a 40-pin Intel 8048 microcomputer (M1) inside the keyboard and an interface controller on the system board. M1 is a completely self-contained 8-bit microcomputer with an internal 1K-word by 8-bit preprogrammed ROM and a 64-word by 8-bit RAM. The keyboard circuitry is shown in Fig. 2-15.

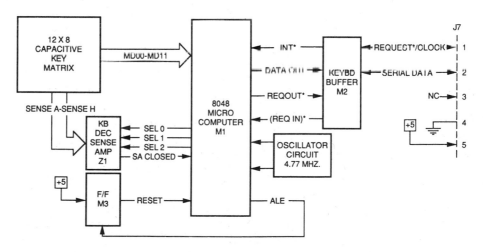

Fig. 2-15. The PC keyboard circuitry.

The 8048 microcomputer (M1) continuously scans the key matrix detecting key actions and generating serial scan codes that are sent to the PC system board as SERIAL DATA information. M1 also contains a power-on self-test that checks its internal memory and then checks for stuck keys. It maintains a bidirectional serial communications flow with the system board and executes the handshake protocol required for each scan-code transfer.

An external oscillator circuit connected to M1 generates approximately 4.77 MHz as a reference frequency for chip and keyboard circuitry operation. M1 divides the oscillator pulses by three to create a request out signal (REQOUT*) that is passed through keyboard buffer M2 onto the system board as a keyboard clock pulse (CLOCK). The serial scan data is sent out of 8048 M1 through keyboard buffer M2 and the keyboard cable onto the system board. An address latch enable signal (ALE) from M1 clocks flip-flop M3, periodically resetting M1 so it can rescan the keyboard matrix.

Every three to five milliseconds, M1 scans the 12-row by 8-column keyboard capacitive matrix. Twelve of the M1 I/O pins are connected to the keyboard matrix. Three pins form binary weighted inputs to keyboard decoder/sense amplifier Z1. Select inputs (SEL 0, SEL 1, and SEL 2) are decoded to activate a particular keyboard matrix sense output (SENSE A through SENSE H). The condition of a selected and decoded sense line is returned to M1 by Z1 as the SA CLOSED signal.

Key action is recognized by M1 scanning the sense lines (SENSE A through SENSE H) and reading the input lines (MD00 through MD11) to determine which intersection point is active. When a key closure is detected, a timer program in M1 waits a few milliseconds to let the key bounce settle out and the key condition to stabilize before reading the MD00 through MD11 inputs. Then 8048 M1 stores an 8-bit scan code in its internal RAM memory indicating that a key closure has occurred. If a key is held down longer than a half second, M1 causes the same scan code to be generated at a rate of ten times each second. Internal RAM enables M1 to buffer up to 16 key scan codes, permitting type-ahead operation.

The release of a key closure is also detected by M1 causing the eighth bit (bit 7) of the scan code to be set high. This effectively produces a break code that is decimal 128 higher. In addition, M1 also searches the keyboard array for phantom switch closures (several interconnections simultaneously made and falsely encoded). If two keys are pressed, causing closed switches in the same column, and one of the two rows containing a closed switch has another switch closed, a phantom switch condition has occurred. M1 usually ignores these conditions, accepting only legitimate double and triple key closure operations (such as Ctrl-Alt-Del). Although a fast typist can press keys every 20 to 30 milliseconds, a keyboard scan is performed in 3 to 5 milliseconds. This allows the matrix to be scanned several times for each keystroke, effectively eliminating incorrect data encoding.

M1 generates a unique scan code for each key action as shown in Table 2-7. A specific scan code is generated when a key is pressed and another scan code (128 higher) is generated when the key is released. Pressing the ENTER key causes M1 to generate the hex code 1CH (00011100 in binary). When your finger is removed from this key, the 8048 (M1) generates the code 9CH (10011100 in binary). Only the high bit has changed. This is the same as adding 128 to the original scan code value. Once this code has been generated and passed to the system board, the scan code signal drops to 0 (00H). Uppercase characters and special functions can be generated by pressing the Shift/Ctrl/Alt keys and one or more character keys.

Table 2-7. Scan Codes Generated by Pressing the Keys on the IBM PC Keyboard

Key Number	Key Label	Scan Code		Key Number	Key Label	Scan Code
1	Escape	01		43	\	2B
2	1	02		44	z	2C
3	2	03		45	x	2D
4	3	04		46	c	2E
5	4	05		47	v	2F
6	5	06		48	b	30
7	6	07		49	n	31
8	7	08		50	m	32
9	8	09		51	,	33
10	9	0A		52	.	34
11	0	0B		53	/	35
12	-	0C		54	Shift	36
13	=	0D		55	*	37
14	Backspace	0E		56	Alt	38
15	Tab	0F		57	Space	39
16	q	10		58	Caps Lock	3A
17	w	11		59	F1	3B
18	e	12		60	F2	3C
19	r	13		61	F3	3D
20	t	14		62	F4	3E
21	y	15		63	F5	3F
22	u	16		64	F6	40
23	i	17		65	F7	41
24	'	18		66	F8	42
25	p	19		67	F9	43
26	[	1A		68	F10	44
27	]	1B		69	Num Lock	45
28	Enter	1C		70	Scroll Lock	46
29	Ctrl	1D		71	7	47
30	a	1E		72	8	48
31	s	1F		73	9	49
32	d	20		74	-	4A
33	f	21		75	4	4B
34	g	22		76	5	4C
35	h	23		77	6	4D
36	j	24		78	+	4E
37	k	25		79	1	4F
38	l	26		80	2	50
39	;	27		81	3	51
40	'	28		82	0	52
41	`	29		83	Del	53
42	Shift	2A				

Pressing a key (or set of keys) causes M1 to generate a signal telling the system board circuitry that SERIAL DATA is coming. Then M1 clocks an 8-bit serial scan code through M2 out the keyboard and onto the system board. This code is sent least-significant bit first. The keyboard interface circuitry on the system board is shown in Fig. 2-16.

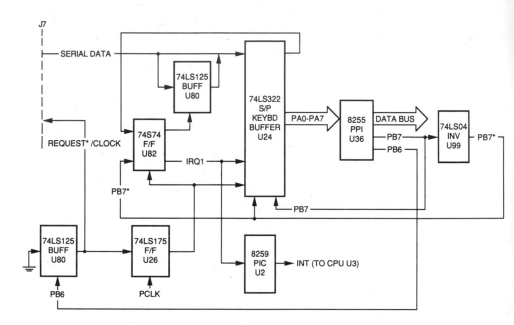

Fig. 2-16. System board keyboard interface circuitry.

Scan code data (SERIAL DATA) passes through the keyboard cable into 74LS322 serial/parallel keyboard buffer U24. Flip-flop U26 clocks the scan code data into U24. Keyboard buffer U24 is wired to function as a serial-in/parallel-out buffer. Thus the scan code data is serially entered into U24 and converted into a parallel signal for the 8255 PPI (U36) port A (PA0 through PA7) input.

As the last of the 8-bit scan code is shifted serially into U24, an interrupt request (IRQ1) is generated causing the the keyboard buffer (U24) to pass the parallel scan code data to port A (PA0 through PA7) of the U36. IRQ1 also results in a CPU interrupt that causes the keyboard scan code to be read from U36 port A (PA0 through PA7) into the 8088 CPU (U3). The scan code is converted by U3 and the BIOS ROM into an ASCII code representing the character selected. (An ASCII conversion chart can be found in Appendix B.) The 8-bit scan code and the 8-bit ASCII character code are stored in 32 consecutive locations of a 16-character circular buffer in the system board RAM. This interrupt also clears the system so it can respond to another keyboard interrupt request.

By capturing and translating keystrokes, BIOS can determine if the key-stroke action included any special keys such as Ctrl, Alt, or Shift. When BIOS converts the scan code to ASCII, it enables the calling program to interpret the code as a software code character string or data input. BIOS then recognizes the character as a special password or passes it to an active output device such as the display adapter board or a printer adapter board.

Video Display

Except for the keyboard and a tape cassette recorder, all I/O peripheral devices connect to the PC through dedicated adapter cards plugged into one of the expansion slots on the PC system board. Several video display adapter cards are available for the PC. A monochrome display adapter was introduced with the first PC. Since then, color/graphics adapters, enhanced graphics adapters, professional graphics adapters, and other display standards have been introduced.

Since these display standards are adaptable to the IBM PC, XT, and AT computers, a separate chapter has been devoted to displays. To understand how the display is produced by your computer, refer to Chapter 5.

Floppy Disk Drive

The IBM was designed to interface with various mass storage devices including 5.25-inch minifloppy disk drives, 3.5-inch microfloppy disk drives, hard (fixed) disk drives, and several types of tape backup storage. Because the basic PC comes with two floppy disk drives installed, this is the configuration that will be described here. Chapters 3 and 4 cover the hard disk interfaces to the XT and AT machines. Descriptions of these hard disk drives should help you understand the construction and function of the fixed disk drive you may have connected to your PC.

The original IBM PC floppy disk drives could store up to 160K bytes of data on single-sided disk media. The BIOS was later upgraded to use drives that could format disks for double-sided, double-density 360K-byte operation.

In writing digital data to a floppy or fixed disk, the data is sent from the system board through a disk drive adapter board into the disk drive unit itself. Digital data representing logic 1s and 0s are applied to the read/write head inside the drive causing a magnetic field to transfer the information onto the magnetic disk media. During a read operation, the read/write head senses the information stored on the disk and interprets this information as digital data.

Disk Drive

The first floppy disks were single-sided in that only one side was used for recording and readback. With computer users demanding more and more mass storage capability, disk drive manufacturers soon introduced drives that could use both sides of the disk. These double-sided disks increased the memory capability from 160K bytes to 320K bytes (for 8-sector disks) and to 360K bytes (for 9-sector disks).

Microfloppy disks increased the disks density to 720K bytes. Thin, high-capacity, 5.25-inch drives can format the minifloppy disk media into 80 tracks, 15 sectors-per-track, and 512 bytes per sector for a total of 1.2 Mbytes of available storage (600K bytes per side).

Each disk drive has circuitry that translates digital command signals from an adapter board into electromechanical actions (for example, drive selection, motor on/off, and head movement) and that senses disk media or disk drive status (for example, Track 0, write protect, ready to read/write, and write fault). The disk drive also contains an analog circuit board that senses, amplifies, and shapes data pulses read from, or written to the disk by the magnetic head.

Floppy Disk Controller

The 5.25-inch IBM disk drive adapter has connections for two internal and two external double-density disk drives. As shown in Fig. 2-17, DMA transfer is used to move data to and from the disk media in the drives. DMA transfers can occur in blocks of up to 32K bytes. Interrupt IRQ6 and DMA request DRQ2 are the primary handshaking and control signal interfaces with the PC system board. The disk adapter (and hence each disk drive) appears to the system board as I/O locations 3F2H, 3F4H, and 3F5H. Recall from Table 2-6 that I/O addresses 3F0H through 3F7H are allocated to the PC floppy disk drive electronics.

The heart of the disk drive electronics is an NEC μPD765 (or equivalent) floppy disk controller (FDC). The FDC directs the operation of up to four double-density disk drives. It simplifies the architecture of the disk drive adapter write (precompensation) and read (data recovery) circuitry. FDC U6 contains a data bus interface buffer, DMA read/write control logic, a status register and data register, serial interface control signals for the floppy disk drives, and drive interface control for drive head movement and the reading and writing of data. Six functions are performed by the FDC:

1. Manage the writing of data to up to four disk drives.
2. Control track and head selection.
3. Monitor the magnetic head for track sector placement.
4. Control the disk drive magnetic head.
5. Receive data read from the disk.
6. Conduct error checks.

Up to 15 disk commands can be executed by FDC U6, including: disk formatting, seeking, writing data, writing a deleted track, reading data, reading the identification marking for tracks and sectors, reading a track of data, reading

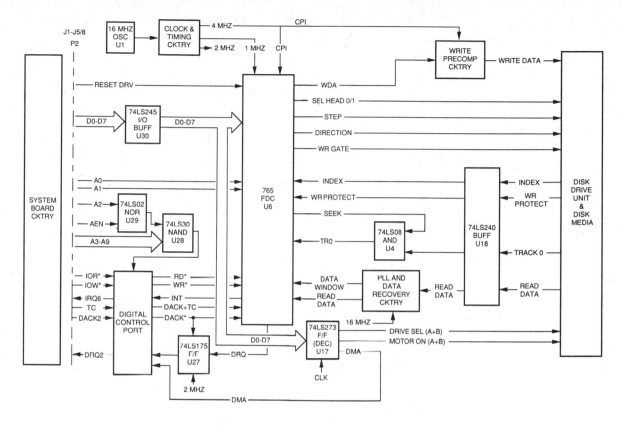

Fig 2-17. Floppy disk drive adapter block diagram.

deleted data, and sensing interrupt and drive status. Multiple 8-bit bytes from the 8088 CPU on the system board specify which operation is to be performed.

A MOTOR ON signal causes the spindle motor in the selected drive to rotate at 300 rpm or 360 rpm depending on the drive. A STEP signal causes the read/write head of the selected drive to move one cylinder track in or out for each pulse depending on the logic level of the direction signal. A logic high causes the head to move one track cylinder toward the spindle for each step pulse. It moves one track away from the spindle if DIRECTION is low.

The SEL HEAD 0/1 signal energizes the upper head (Head 1) when low, and the lower head (Head 0) when high. The WRITE DATA signal causes a magnetic flux change to be recorded on the disk surface for each low-to-high transition. The WR GATE signal disables or enables write current in the read/write head.

The INDEX signal indicates drive detection of the disk media index hole during its current disk revolution. READ DATA pulses occur each time a flux change is sensed by the magnetic read/write head of the selected drive. The TRACK 0 signal goes high when the read/write head of the selected drive is positioned over Track 0. The WR PROTECT signal becomes active if a write-protected disk is detected in the selected drive.

The write circuitry on the disk drive adapter board generates a composite clock/data bit stream, WRITE DATA, that is sent to the disk drive unit. This circuitry also sends a direction signal, a SEL HEAD 0/1 signal, and a STEP pulse to the disk drive.

Data Transfer

A DRQ2 DMA request from the adapter board to the 8237 DMA controller (U35) on the system board causes the 8088 CPU (U3) to relinquish control of the address and data buses so the DMA controller can communicate with the drive adapter board and cause data transfer. DMA acknowledge signal (DACK2*) is passed back to the disk drive adapter board and used to set the board for data transfer to or from a data buffer in the FDC (U6).

Prior to data transfer, the starting address and number of bytes to move are passed to the DMA controller on the system board. Once data transfer has started, DMA continues until the specified number of bytes have been transferred. When transfer is complete, system control is returned to the CPU.

During DMA transfers, I/O read and write signals (IOR* and IOW*) are generated by the 8237 DMA controller. When a transfer has been completed, the DMA controller sends a terminal count signal (TC) to the adapter board. This causes the FDC to generate an interrupt (INT) that becomes IRQ6 out of connector P2. IRQ6 indicates that the execution phase has ended and that the results of an operation can be read. IRQ6 is passed to the system board causing the interrupt controller to interrupt the 8088 CPU. An interrupt handling routine examines the transfer result for errors and then resets the interrupt request. Using DMA channel 2, data is transferred at 31.25K bytes per second (32 microseconds per byte).

Since the information read from the floppy disk is a composite of clock and data, separation must occur to extract the useful information out of the signal. Every 16 microseconds the serial data is assembled into 8-bit bytes and transferred to memory. After synchronizing with the data stream, special separation logic provides a data window to the FDC that differentiates data from clock information. FDC U6 uses this window to reconstruct the data that was previously recorded on the disk.

As information is written, an error detection value is computed and stored on the disk with the data. This value is called a "cyclical redundancy check" (CRC). When the data is later retrieved from the disk, a new CRC value is computed on the data read out and compared with the original stored CRC value. If a match occurs, all is well. A mismatch results in a CRC error and a second read attempt by the system software. If there is another mismatch, an "unable to read" disk error occurs.

During a read operation, composite read/clock data, write-protect status, index information, and Track 0 information are passed from the selected disk drive into the disk-drive adapter card. Two disk-drive connectors are on the adapter card—one for each drive pair (A&B) and (C&D). The composite clock/data bit stream, READ DATA, from any one of the four drives is passed through data recovery circuitry that strips the data off the composite information and reshapes it to ensure clean logic levels before passing it to the floppy disk controller. After isolating the data from the READ DATA bit stream, FDC U6 reassembles the data bits into 8-bit bytes for transfer to the 8088 CPU or system board memory.

Cassette Interface

On the rear of the system unit chassis is a 5-pin circular connector for interfacing a cassette recorder/player to the PC. While this is one of the least used of the PC interfaces, you may want to use a standard audio cassette as a medium for archive or backup storage. Between 500K bytes and 2M bytes of information can be stored on a good audio cassette tape. The popularity of the cassette/computer interface declined with the meteoric rise in the use of floppy and hard disk drives, but recently the need for data backup and archive storage caused the design and introduction of over thirty tape-drive backup systems for the PC family. Some disk file backup systems use video tape.

Your IBM PC comes with a built-in tape backup interface. The cassette interface port can be controlled by software stored in Cassette BASIC ROM. With this software, you can write and read data through Cassette Port J6, shown in Fig. 2-18.

Data are sent to the port using the 8253 programmable interval timer (U34) OUT2 line. After passing through the 74LS38 quad 2-input NAND gate (U63), the data are stepped down by a resistor voltage divider and passed through microphone connector P4 to Cassette Port J6 as a series of 0 or 0.075 volt (75 millivolts) signals. By connecting the DATA OUT line to the MIC input on a cassette recorder, digital data can be stored on a standard audio tape. If the AUX connection on the system board is used, the J6 DATA OUT signal is 0 or 0.68 volt (680 millivolts), suitable for the AUX input on a cassette recorder.

Data retrieved from a cassette player enters J6 as DATA IN and is passed through relay K1 into an MC1741 operational amplifier where its signal level is converted to a digital logic level (0 or +5 volts) and passed into the PC4 input to Port C of 8255 PPI U36 as CASSETTE DATA IN. Between 100 and 200 characters per second (0.6M to 1.2M bytes per minute) can be read into the PC through this path. This is extremely slow compared to the fast tape backup systems that connect to the PC through adapter cards, but it does represent an economical backup solution.

The cassette motor is turned on and off by the MOTOR signal from the 8255 PPI. PB3 of Output Port B is buffered through 74LS38 quad 2-input NAND U63 and 75477 relay buffer U95 into relay K1. When the output of U95 goes high, the contacts of relay K1 close and energize the cassette motor. Likewise, removing the voltage from K1 opens the contact and turns the cassette drive motor off.

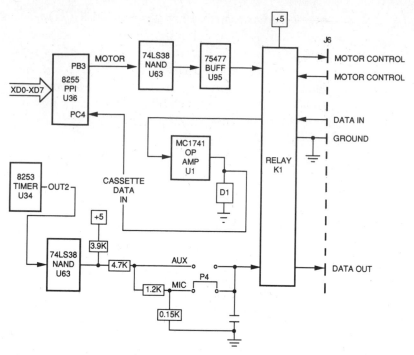

Fig. 2-18. Cassette input/output port circuitry.

Other Input/Output Devices

A wide variety of devices can connect to a basic IBM PC system through specialized adapter cards. These include expanded and extended memory, a hard disk drive, hard disk card, modem, facsimile machine, printer, specialized display, mouse, joystick, trackball, light pen, plotter, graphics tablet, and other computers in a small area, local area, or wide area networks.

The open architecture of the PC provides ample opportunity to expand a system with the requirements of the user. Just keep in mind that the PC switching power supply can only drive a limited number of components. Consider installing a larger power supply if you intend to stuff your machine to its expansion slot limit.

System Start-Up

There are two ways to "start" your system. You can start the computer by switching the power on or, if the computer is already turned on, you can simultaneously press the Ctrl, Alt, and Del keys, resetting the system. The former method is called a "cold boot." Its begins with a cold system—nothing operating. The latter method is called a "warm boot." Power is already present and the initial start-up tests have been successfully performed. All you want to do is reset the system so you can start from a known condition and run an application program.

When power is first applied during a cold boot, a series of specific actions occur. These actions begin when electrical power is applied to the motherboard, causing the system clock to begin pulsing through the circuitry. The 8088 CPU accesses BIOS ROM U33 and begins running a bootstrap program that loads and then pulls itself up to full readiness (the word bootstrap or "boot" refers to the computer pulling itself up by its own bootstrap). During this process, major system components are tested and the hardware is initialized to a known condition, ready to accept and respond to the operator keyboard commands. The basic I/O operating system (BIOS) lets the hardware and software communicate. It also controls how the I/O will work and how the system board and CPU will interact with the outside world (display, keyboard, and disk drives). The first part of the 8K BIOS ROM includes a 2K power-on self test (POST) that checks the system and then sets the system up for operation. Once the boot-up has occurred, the control of the system is passed to the operator for command.

Software Structure

The physical hardware is an important part of any computer system, but it's of little use if it can't do functional work. A system is not complete without software. It takes software to make a computer generate a letter, print a spreadsheet, or draw an image on the screen.

Three types of software programs are provided with your PC—a low-level hardware operating system called "BIOS," a disk operating system called "DOS," and a high-level language called "BASIC." The hardware operating system (often called a system monitor) resides permanently in ROM. It's the software that gets the computer running the moment power is applied. In the IBM PC, the monitor is stored in a part of 8K ROM U33. As the lowest and most basic level of code, BIOS (for Basic Input/Output System) has been aptly named. Software such as BIOS that is permanently written into hardware is called "firmware." Part of BIOS is loaded into RAM from the system disk during start-up, so BIOS is both a firmware program and a software program. BIOS loads and runs other programs. It causes the PC to start up in a known condition, it tests the primary system components, and it lets you communicate with the computer. The BIOS contains short routines that load the boot program from the disk and begin the bootstrap process. It is what causes your keystrokes to be recognized and your commands to be accepted and acted upon.

The next higher level of software is the disk operating system (DOS). DOS is an extension of BIOS. It is larger than BIOS (20K versus less than 8K) and handles many I/O data transfers. Both BIOS and DOS are designed to optimize the interface between the 8088 CPU and user programs. The BIOS and disk operating system keep everything straight and responsive. They direct the flow of information between keyboard, screen, memory, and mass storage.

But DOS goes beyond BIOS by providing file management tools for interfacing with the floppy and hard disk drives installed in your system. DOS lets you format disks, copy, erase, and rename files, generate a directory, and perform a myriad other functions related to the mass storage interface.

The third type of software is a high-level language called BASIC for Beginner's All-purpose Symbolic Instruction Code. Rather than generating custom programs using hex code and assembly language, BASIC lets you write code using English language statements such as READ, PRINT, GET, and LET. Each BASIC instruction is interpreted by the 8088 CPU using a ROM look-up table. An interpreter program in BASIC ROM converts each source instruction into an object code instruction that can be readily recognized and implemented by the CPU. When this code is executed, the next instruction in the program is then fetched, interpreted and executed. This sequential process is time-consuming, but writing code in BASIC is easy to learn and simple to understand.

Other high-level languages, such as FORTRAN, C, and Pascal, use compilers that load and interpret a complete program in one step, converting the source code into executable object code. The object code program can be run at much faster speed than running an interpreted program code. Many companies sell commercial software packages that were written using these high-level languages. These software packages include: Word from Microsoft Corporation, PageMaker from Aldus Corporation, WordStar from MicroPro, and many others. Collectively, these programs are called "application software."

When you think of a computer system, you should view it as a combination of hardware, software, and firmware. It takes all three parts to function as a system.

Summary

This chapter provided a detailed study of the operation of the IBM PC system. The information presented enables you to partition the PC system into simple building blocks for failure analysis and troubleshooting. As you recognized by studying this chapter, each building block can be analyzed and then connected to the others to form the complete IBM PC system. By understanding how the computer and software interact and function, you are able to quickly recognize and isolate trouble symptoms in one of these building block circuits.

Questions for Review and Discussion

1. Why has the 8088 been described as the "heart" of the IBM personal computer?

2. Which has higher priority, INT or NMI?

3. What happens on the system board when an IRQ6 signal is received?

4. How would you reconfigure the PC system to recognize an installed 8087 coprocessor?

5. What causes the clock signal to begin pulsing on the input to the 8088 CPU, U3?

6. Describe the RAM refresh process.

7. How does the computer determine what size RAM is installed?

8. How does the system board know if an address on the address bus is intended for system memory or an I/O device?

9. If you switched your PC on and nothing happened, where would you look first in analyzing the problem?

10. What function does the READY signal perform?

Detailed System Operation of the IBM PC/XT

The last chapter described the operation of the IBM PC personal computer system. Chapter 3 describes how the XT works. Because the IBM PC and XT are almost identical (primary difference is in the hard disk drive), much of the material in this chapter will be similar to Chapter 2. In describing the operation of the XT, circuit schematics and block diagrams have been included to enhance understanding.

As mentioned in the last chapter, the schematic symbols used in this book conform to the Howard W. Sams COMPUTERFACTS standard symbols. A box enclosing a number represents a common voltage source or test point. Because printing a logical "not" source bar over an active low signal label is awkward, the symbol * will be used to represent a signal that is active when low (zero volts). Thus, an active low RESET signal will be represented as RESET*. Other symbols should be self-explanatory.

Power is furnished to the XT power supply by an ac power cord plugged into an electrical socket. As shown in Fig. 3-1, a switching power supply provides energy to the system board, the adapter boards plugged into the expansion slots, and the floppy and hard disk drives.

The Power Supply

The IBM XT operates on either 120 or 230 volts. Most personal computers in the U.S. work on 120 volts. The XT can operate on both 50 and 60 Hertz alternating current (ac). Unlike its weak cousin in the PC, the XT power supply furnishes 130 watts to the computer system. This is twice the power furnished by the PC power supply.

Fig. 3-2 is a block diagram of the switching power supply. Rocker switch S1 applies 120-V ac to the power supply through a 5-amp, slow-blow fuse (F1). A receptacle at the rear of the power supply provides 0.75 amps of filtered 120-V ac to a display monitor.

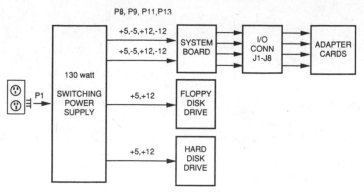

Fig. 3-1. System power requirements for the IBM XT.

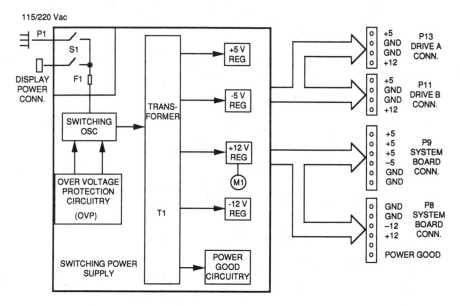

Fig. 3-2. Switching power supply block diagram.

A switching oscillator drives transformer T1 and regulator circuitry converting the ac input power into usable direct-current (dc) voltage for the system components. One output provides a regulated +12-V dc source to connectors P8, P11, and P13. These connectors provide power to the internal 5.25-inch floppy diskette and 10-Mbyte hard disk drive motors. Another output provides a +5-V dc source to connectors P9, P11, and P13 for the system board and the adapter cards. The +5-V dc source is also used as a power supply reference to produce a POWER GOOD signal that is passed through connector P8 onto the system board. This signal is the start flag for system operation. One output drives an internal cooling fan M1 and provides +12-V dc to connector P8 for the XT expansion slots. Both the +12-V dc and −12-V dc voltage sources can drive a communications adapter plugged into an expansion slot.

The power supply output voltages are monitored by internal circuitry to prevent damage to the system or adapter boards should an overload or overcurrent condition occur. A protection circuit shuts down the power supply if either the +5-V or +12-V dc outputs exceed 200% of maximum rated voltage. The supply also shuts down if current to any output exceeds 130% of nominal level.

High voltages are present in the XT power supply and power supply problems should be handled only by experienced technicians. Troubleshooting and repair of power supply problems is beyond the scope of this book. In most cases, replacing the defective power supply is the most practical action.

IBM PC/XT System Board

Fig. 3-3 shows the layout of the primary components on the XT system board. This drawing will be helpful in identifying the components to be discussed. It will also be helpful during troubleshooting. An alphanumeric identification code is printed on the system board near each component. This code identifies the components in block diagrams and schematics. Integrated circuits (ICs) are also called chips. Chips are identified in this text and on schematics with a "U" prefix designator followed by a number. The IC in chip location U21 is labeled "74LS175." The 74175 identifies the IC as a quad-D flip/flop. The "LS" indicates that this is a low-powered Schottky type of IC. Other chips may have no center designator, or another designator, such as a single "S" for Schottky, or "ALS" for advanced low-powered Schottky.

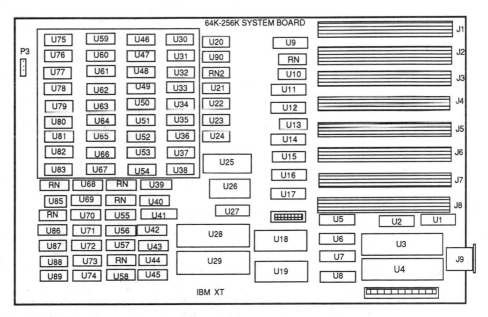

Fig. 3-3.   IBM PC/XT system board layout.

When replacing a component, it is important to use the same type of device as the original. Component characteristics including speed of operation are identified by the markings printed on the device. Using a 74S175 as a replacement when a 74LS175 is intended can cause unpredictable operation after the repair has been completed. Remember to verify the center designator whenever you replace a component. A list of the chips with their center designators can be found in Appendix B.

8088 Central Processing Unit

The XT is designed around the same 8088 Central Processing Unit (CPU) used in the IBM PC. The Intel 8088 is a third-generation microprocessor and an 8-bit version of Intel's 16-bit 8086 microprocessor. The bit size is determined by the number of binary bits in a data word. The 8086 works with 16-bit data words inside or outside the chip. The 8088 works with 8-bit or 16-bit data internally but only with 8-bit data external to the chip. To read or write 16-bit data requires two separate operations (one for each byte).

Since the instruction/function format of the 8088 is identical to the 8086 microprocessor, U3 also supports 16-bit operations including multiply and divide. U3 is driven by a single + 5-volt power source. In the IBM XT, U3 is configured to support an 8087 coprocessor. An 8288 bus controller (U8) provides bus control and command for the system.

With 20 address lines, U3 has a physical memory range between 00000H and FFFFFH (the H means hexadecimal) and can directly access over a million memory locations (two raised to the twentieth power is 1,048,576). Sixteen of the address lines also access up to 64K of input/output (I/O) memory. The I/O of the XT is memory-mapped for easy access by CPU U3 and by application software. This means that I/O devices appear as memory locations to the CPU.

Because of pin limitations, U3 uses a time-multiplexed address and data bus that permits some of its pins to serve dual functions as shown in Fig. 3-4. During the first half of a microprocessor instruction cycle, the lower eight bits (AD0 through AD7) are part of the 20-bit address bus (A0 through A19) over which U3 communicates with the rest of the XT system. During the last half of a micro-processor instruction cycle, these same eight lines are bidirectional and contain data (D0 through D7). Time-multiplexing the address and data lines enables access to a large addressable memory space using fewer IC pins.

During each cycle of system operation, the 8088 CPU places an address on the system board address bus, fetches an instruction from the memory location addressed, interprets and executes the instruction, and places the results in a location determined by the instruction. The CPU then fetches another instruc-tion and the sequence repeats. The 8088 can collect up to four instructions in a queue. While it's busy executing a current instruction, another part of U3 can be loading other instructions, thus enabling faster program execution speeds.

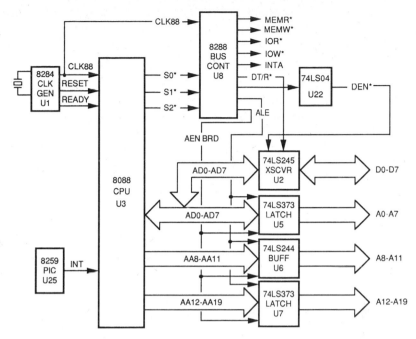

Fig. 3-4. The 8088 CPU and related circuitry in the XT system.

The status of CPU U3 is passed to an 8288 bus controller (U8) as a status code comprised of signals S0*, S1*, and S2*. These signals are decoded by U8 to generate timed command and control signals. Four of these signals enable access to system or I/O memory. The memory read command (MEMR*) causes the system memory to drive its stored information onto the data bus. Its companion signal memory write (MEMW*) causes the memory to record the information presently on the data bus. Peripheral devices use I/O read (IOR*) and I/O write (IOW*). These command signals instruct I/O devices to drive data onto or read data from the data bus. If an I/O command is to be executed, only the lower 16 bits of the address bus are used. This provides 65,536 (64K) of directly address-able (memory-mapped) I/O.

An interrupt acknowledge signal (INTA) from U8 indicates CPU recognition and intended action for a received interrupt request. Interrupts are described later. Several other control signals enable address buffers, latches, and trans-ceivers in the CPU circuitry.

8087 Math Coprocessor

The 8087 numeric processor extension (NPX) math coprocessor (U4) was designed for long, repetitive operations requiring powerful arithmetic instruc-tions that can handle fractional values, sine, cosine, logarithms, and square roots. The results of these mathematically complex operations involve extreme accuracies and rapid calculations. The 8087 can support these operations while using the same circuitry as the 8088 CPU. Both the hardware and the software interfaces for the 8087 coprocessor are compatible with the 8088.

Handling real and imaginary integer and noninteger numbers over a wide range of values, coprocessor U4 can produce precise results with a large number of significant digits. Integers up to 18 digits long and floating point numbers from 16 to 80 bits wide can be used. The 8087 has built-in math instructions for add, subtract, multiply, divide, absolute value, arctangent, tangent, square root, log base two, and log base e.

The system board contains a prewired 40-pin socket next to the 8088 CPU U3 for the optional 8087 math coprocessor. As shown in Fig. 3-5, the XT is configured so U3 and U4 share the multiplexed address/data bus, clock, reset and other system board signals.

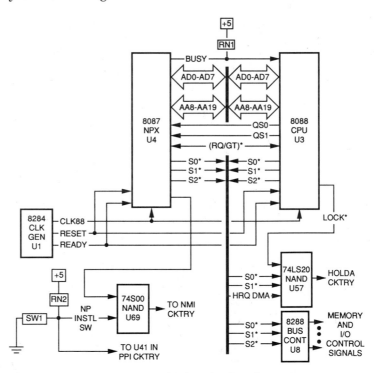

Fig. 3-5. The 8087 NPX coprocessor (U4) and related circuitry.

Both the 8088 CPU and 8087 math coprocessor monitor and decode the same instructions and bytes of an instruction stream. This lets the 8087 and 8088 monitor and decode instructions simultaneously without introducing CPU overhead. Thus, U4 knows at all times what instruction was just fetched. Instructions for CPU or coprocessor execution can be mixed in a program, and the 8087 can process instructions in parallel with and independent of the 8088 CPU.

A numeric instruction that requires 8087 action appears as an escape (ESC) command followed by an instruction code. As soon as an ESC instruction occurs both the 8087 and the 8088 decode and execute it. The coprocessor looks at the byte following the ESC instruction to see if the 8087 should respond. If coprocessor action is intended, the 8087 takes control over the system bus and acts on this coded command.

A BUSY signal from U4 informs the CPU of the coprocessor's internal status. BUSY is high while the coprocessor is executing a numeric instruction. It causes the CPU to wait for the 8087 to finish its processing and return BUSY low before using the system buses. As long as BUSY is high, the 8088 waits in an idle state allowing the 8087 to control signal and data flow in the system. Normally, the 8087 coprocessor sits idle, monitoring the 8088 CPU instruction code as it comes out of memory. The 8087 will respond and request the system buses only when it senses a coprocessor instruction.

While the 8088 CPU has control of the bus, its status line signals are passed to the 8288 bus controller (U8). During coprocessor operation, the 8087 generates five of the eight combinations of S0* through S2* signals for encoding by U8. These status signals cause U8 to generate memory and I/O access commands.

Status lines QS0 and QS1 connect between the 8087 coprocessor and the 8088 CPU to help the coprocessor monitor CPU operations. The 8087 can interrupt the 8088 CPU whenever the coprocessor detects an error or exception. If an incorrect instruction is sent to U4, such as a command to divide a number by zero, U4 can interrupt the CPU for error condition servicing.

System Support Chips

The 8088 CPU on the XT system board is configured to work with special system support chips. These chips include the 8284 clock generator (U1), the 8253 programmable interval timer (U26), the 8255 programmable peripheral interface (U29), the 8259 programmable interrupt controller (U25), and the 8237 programmable DMA controller (U28). Each of these chips and their associated circuitry are discussed in the following paragraphs.

8284 Clock Generator (U1)

The operation of the XT computer begins with and is maintained using clock pulses and several important control signals that are generated by the 8284 Clock Generator (U1). A 14.318-MHz crystal is connected across two pins of U1. The crystal causes U1 to generate clock, command, and control signals for the XT and its expansion cards. As shown in Fig. 3-6, U1 produces a 4.77-MHz CPU clock signal (CLK88) for the 8088 CPU (U3), the 8087 math coprocessor (U4), and the 8288 bus controller (U8). It also produces a 14.318-MHz clock signal (OSC) for the color/graphics adapter board that is used to develop synchronization and horizontal scan signals, and a 2.386-MHz peripheral clock signal (PCLK) that is

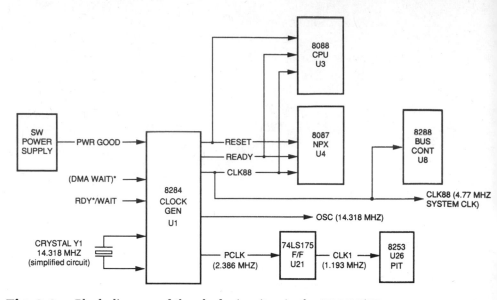

Fig. 3-6. Block diagram of the clock circuitry in the IBM PC/XT.

divided down to 1.193-MHz and used to step the counters in an 8253 programmable interval timer (U26).

The POWER GOOD signal from the switching power supply causes U1 to generate a system RESET signal that initializes components on the system board and adapter cards. When RESET is applied, it causes the 8088 CPU to generate FFFF0H, the first address for program start-up. Using external status inputs (DMA WAIT)* and RDY*/WAIT, U1 generates a READY signal that tells the 8088 (U3) when a slower device has completed its process. U3 can then stop waiting and continue with its own processing.

8253 Programmable Interval Timer (U26)

Fig. 3-7 shows the circuitry associated with the 8253 programmable interval timer (U26). U26 generates a time-of-day clock tick, requests the DMA controller to periodically refresh the dynamic RAM in the system, and helps produce sound from the internal speaker.

Inside U26 are three independent 16-bit downcounters. The 2.386-MHz PCLK from U1 is divided by 74LS175 quad-D flip-flop U21 to produce a 1.193-MHz CLK1 signal. CLK1 steps each of the three preset counters in U26, producing timed output signals OUT0 (IRQ0), OUT1, and OUT2 (T/C2 OUT). Each output occurs at a frequency determined by CLK1 and the U26 software programmable internal 16-bit counters. This lets U26 generate accurate time delays while minimizing program overhead.

Once programmed, the counting operation of all three timers is automatic. Upon count start, the 8253 causes each counter to clock down until its preset

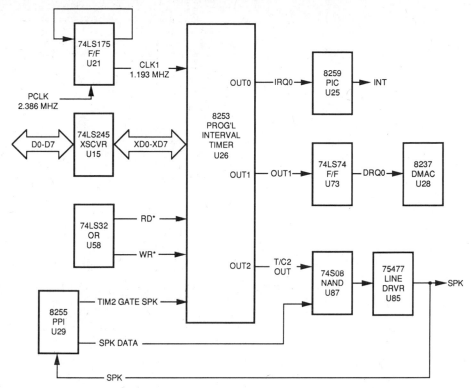

Fig. 3-7. 8253 programmable interval timer circuitry.

delay value reaches zero. At this point, the counter generates a count-complete output signal (OUT0, OUT1, or OUT2) and rolls over to its preset value so the countdown operation can begin once more.

Timer 0 output (OUT0) becomes IRQ0, the time-of-day interrupt that occurs approximately 18.2 times each second. IRQ0 is passed to a programmable interrupt controller as a time-of-day interrupt request. A second counter produces a 66.287-KHz (15 microsecond) OUT1 signal that becomes a direct memory access request (DRQ0) to the 8237 DMA controller (U28). DRQ0 causes a dynamic RAM memory access operation at least every 15 microseconds. This programmed access is called "refresh." The refresh operation will be covered in detail later.

A third counter produces an 896-Hz square wave OUT2 signal (T/C2 OUT) that helps activate the internal speaker. Unique speaker sounds can be generated by changing the preset value in the OUT2 timer.

8255 Programmable Peripheral Interface (U29)

The 8255 programmable peripheral interface (PPI) electronically connects peripheral equipment to the 8088 system bus. As shown in Fig. 3-8, U29 interfaces a bidirectional data bus (XD0 through XD7) with three programmable I/O buffer ports under control of specialized read/write control logic.

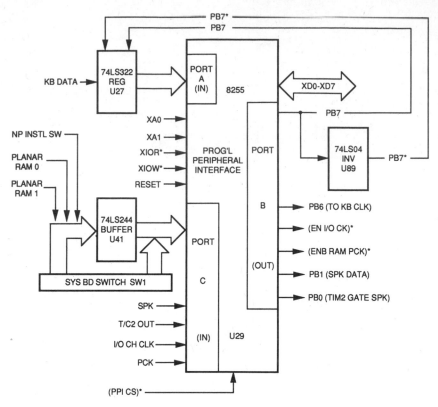

Fig. 3-8. 8255 programmable peripheral interface circuitry.

During system start-up, U29 is configured so its A and C ports function as inputs, and its B port functions as an output. Then data and PPI control signals are passed to and from the bidirectional buffered data bus (XD0 through XD7) under CPU control. No clock or special handshaking signals are required for information transfer. Once configured, whatever is present at a port can be accessed simply by addressing that port.

Port A is connected to 74LS322 serial-to-parallel keyboard register U27. Under control of output Port B bit 7 (PB7), Port A becomes the pathway to the 8088 for keyboard data.

Port C receives T/C2 OUT from interval timer U26, the status of the I/O channel (I/O CH CLK), the status of RAM parity checking (PCK), and the system configuration as determined by the position of system board switch SW1. This eight-switch DIP package defines the amount of RAM installed in the system, the type of display monitor being used, the number of 5.25-inch diskette drives attached, and whether an 8087 math coprocessor is installed. Table 3-1 describes the function associated with each of the eight switches in SW1.

The settings of switch SW1 are read by the 8088 CPU through port C of 8255 PPI U29. A software program examines the input to port C to determine the system board configuration. Use of system components and memory utilization

Table 3-1. System Board Switch Assignments

SW1–x Position	Function
1	Normal OFF, ON for loop POST test
2	OFF if 8087 installed
3–4	Amount of system board memory
	3 OFF / 4 ON 128K
	3 ON / 4 OFF 192K
	3 OFF / 4 OFF 256K
5–6	Type of monitor being used
7–8	Number floppy disk drives attached

depends on the SW1 configuration settings. An improper memory setting results in part of the memory not being read or used during operation.

Port B outputs information to the speaker, to interval timer U26, to enable the I/O channel check (EN I/O CK)*, to the parity test circuitry (ENB RAM PCK)*, and to the keyboard. PB6 is the keyboard clock (KB CLK) and PB7 is the keyboard data input register enable.

When PB0 is at logic high, its TIM2 GATE SPK output enables a counter in interval timer U26, generating a square wave for the speaker. PB1 sends programmed data waveforms (SPK DATA) to the speaker.

8259 Programmable Interrupt Controller (U25)

The IBM PC/XT, like the IBM PC, is an interrupt-driven machine. A normal 8088 CPU operational sequence can be temporarily suspended while another device or function is being serviced. Interrupt signals are used to control these functions.

During operation, external devices inform the CPU of a need for attention using dedicated interrupt signals. CPU operation can also be altered by system failure or software programmed interrupt signals. Software interrupts occur as part of a program and are interpreted internally by the 8088. Problems with an installed 8087 math coprocessor or in the memory hardware cause a nonmaskable interrupt (NMI) that is sent to a dedicated 8088 pin. A NMI interrupt causes system operation to stop. Other hardware interrupts cause an INT signal on another dedicated 8088 pin. This interrupt causes the CPU to perform preprogrammed functions.

When the 8088 recognizes an interrupt, it stores the condition of the program it's currently executing and then begins executing software code stored at a new program location. There are 1024 memory locations (00H through 3FFH) dedicated to storing up to 256 four-byte interrupt vectors which point to service routines stored elsewhere in memory. When the 8088 completes servicing an interrupt, it returns to the software program it was executing before the interrupt occurred. Internal 8088 program-related interrupts are serviced before external hardware interrupts.

Except for the NMI interrupt, all other hardware interrupts are recognized and handled by 8259 programmable interrupt controller (PIC) U25, which is preset to accept selected interrupt requests in a priority order. These external interrupt request signals are connected as shown in Fig. 3-9.

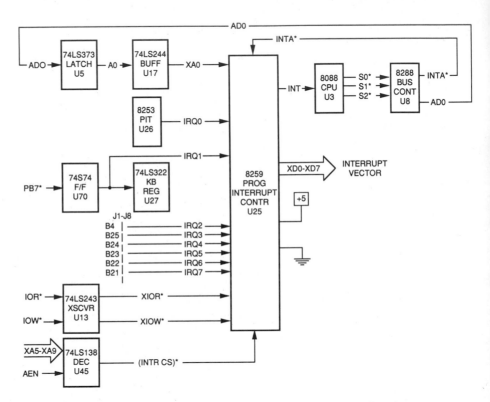

Fig. 3-9. 8259 programmable interrupt controller U25 and related circuitry.

The 8259 interrupt controller (U25) handles up to eight priority interrupt requests and generates a logic-high interrupt signal (INT) to the CPU. It requires no clock input and responds to any interrupt request once the control lines are properly configured. Its ability to handle multilevel priority interrupts minimizes software and real-time system overhead.

During start-up, the 8259 PIC is tested and then preset to respond to interrupt requests by priority. This lets it respond correctly when several devices attempt to interrupt the CPU at the same time. The device with the lowest interrupt number has the highest priority and is serviced first. Higher priority inputs can be masked without affecting the interrupt request lines of lower priority inputs.

The highest priority interrupt is IRQ0. It causes a time-of-day clock tick. The second highest priority interrupt (IRQ1) is used during keyboard entry. Both the IBM PC and IBM XT are designed to handle interrupts in the same manner. Table 2-2 in Chapter 2 lists the assignments for all eight interrupt request inputs to the 8259 programmable interrupt controller. If two request lines become active at the same time, the request whose number is lowest (closest to IRQ0) is serviced first.

When an interrupt request is sensed, U25 produces a corresponding INT signal that is passed to CPU U3 causing the 8088 to pull status outputs S0*, S1*, and S2* active low. These status bits are decoded by 8288 bus controller (U8) causing it to generate a sequence of two active-low interrupt acknowledge (INTA*) signals.

The first INTA* signal communicates to the 8259 PIC that the request has been recognized and that an interrupt acknowledge cycle is in progress. CPU U3 locks out other devices from gaining access to the bus and then causes U8 to send a second INTA* signal to U25. When U25 senses this second interrupt acknowledge, it places a byte of data on the address/data bus (XD0 through XD7) representing the interrupt type (Type 0 through 255) associated with the requesting device. The 8088 CPU uses this byte to develop an address pointer to an interrupt vector table containing a jump instruction to a service routine elsewhere in memory.

8237 Programmable DMA Controller (DMAC)

The 8237 direct memory access controller U28 is designed to improve system performance by allowing external devices to directly transfer information in blocks of up to 64K bytes. DMA is used to perform data transfers with the floppy and hard disk drives. DMA is also used to refresh the dynamic RAM memory in the XT system. Fig. 3-10 is a block diagram of the 8237 circuitry.

The DMA controller (U28) causes the 8088 CPU to suspend normal operation so U28 can take over the system address, control, and data buses. The DMA controller can conduct data transfers at rates up to 1.5 Mbytes per second. Innovative circuit design ensures that U28 takes bus control only at the correct moment. When the DMA is active, the CPU address, control, and data buffers appear disconnected from the system board circuitry. The I/O and memory control signals are then generated by U28. If more time is required during an active DMA cycle (accessing a slow memory or I/O device), a ready signal (RDY TO DMA) is placed at the input to U28 causing the DMA controller to insert wait states in the DMA cycle. U28 also causes the 8284 clock generator (U1) to pull READY low, forcing the CPU to wait while U28 is conducting the DMA transfer.

DMAC U28 contains four independent request/acknowledge channels which automatically reinitialize to a preset condition following each DMA process. Each channel has a 64K address and word count capability so blocks of data as large as 64K can be transferred with a single command. Typical disk drive transfers are in 32K byte blocks. Logic in U28 resolves priority contention

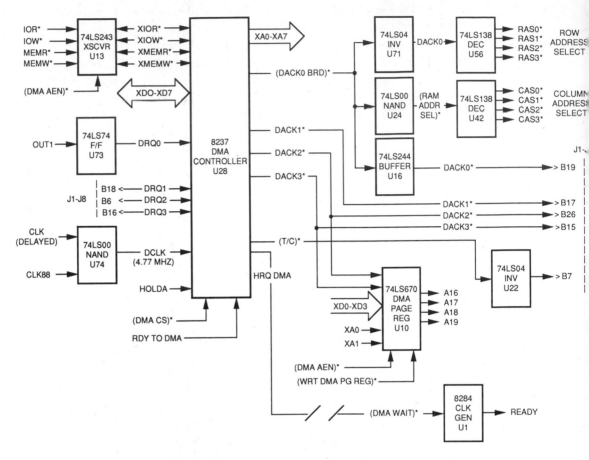

Fig. 3-10. 8237 programmable DMA controller U35 and related circuitry.

between several DMA channels requesting simultaneous service. Internal timing
is achieved using the 4.77-MHz DCLK input.

In an idle state, U28 samples the four DMA request lines (DRQ0, DRQ1,
DRQ2, and DRQ3) with each DCLK input pulse to determine if any channel is
requesting a DMA transfer. These DMA request lines connect U28 to individua
input channels from peripheral circuitry. DMA requests are not timed or preset
but occur under control of the requesting device. They are, however, in a fixed
priority with DRQ0 holding the highest priority and DRQ3 the lowest. DRQ0
produces a memory refresh cycle every 15 microseconds. DRQ1, DRQ2, and
DRQ3 come from the expansion slots and initiate I/O data transfers with periph
erals. For example, DRQ2 initiates floppy disk transfers. Each DMA request
signal must be held steady until U28 responds with a corresponding DMA
acknowledge (DACK0 BRD*, DACK1*, DACK2*, or DACK3*).

When a DMA request line goes high, U28 produces a hold request (HRC
DMA) that results in the generation of a DMA WAIT signal pulling the 8284 clock

generator READY line low. The low READY output causes the 8088 CPU to be electronically disconnected and gives DMA controller U28 control over the address, data, and control buses.

The first DMA request (DRQ0) is developed using OUT1 from the 8253 programmable interval timer. Every 72 clock cycles (15 microseconds) OUT1 occurs, producing an active high DRQ0 input to U28. Thus, every 15 microseconds, DMA channel 0 is activated and DMAC U28 produces DACK0 BRD* resulting in a memory access that refreshes the charges in the dynamic RAM (DRAM) ICs. Refresh will be covered in the section on random-access memory. DACK0 BRD* is also converted to DACK0* and made available for external memory refresh over pin B19 of expansion slots J1 through J8.

The other three DMA request channels (DRQ1 through DRQ3) are generated on external adapter cards and passed to U28 via pins B18, B6, and B16 on connectors J1 through J8. These external DMA requests result in DACK1*, DACK2*, and DACK3* acknowledge signals that tell individual peripherals that their request for a DMA cycle has been granted. The acknowledge signals are typically used for chip select in the I/O circuitry. DMA requests also cause U28 to generate a memory address and to signal the destination to read the address bus.

DACK2* and DACK3* are connected to 74LS670 DMA page register file U10. Because the DMA controller can only handle one 64K memory page at a time, U10 is used to increase the DMA capability from 64K to a full one megabyte while retaining the 64K page boundary. The 64K data boundary is stored inside U10 and made available whenever DMA address enable (DMA AEN)* goes low. The condition of DACK2* and DACK3* cause U10 to generate a unique page address data word on address lines A16 through A19. When (DMA AEN)* returns high, the address outputs from U10 electronically disconnect from the address bus. This permits the DMA controller to use the same address bus circuitry as the CPU.

Each time 64K of data has been transferred, an internal word counter fills (reaches FFFFH) causing U28 to generate a terminal count signal, (T/C)*, that signals the completion of a DMA operation. This signal is used by the system board and adapter cards to keep track of DMA cycles.

Memory Configuration

Although the XT comes configured with up to 256K of random-access memory (expandable to 640K with an expansion card), the 8088 can address up to one million bytes of storage. This memory space ranges from addresses 00000H to FFFFFH. The XT operating system determines how much memory is installed by reading the position of the system board switch SW1 connected to the 8255 PPI. When memory is added, SW1 switch settings are changed so the software can recognize the memory configuration being used. This section describes the circuitry and signals associated with the onboard and I/O memory in the XT.

Memory Addressing Scheme

The XT system memory includes random-access memory (RAM) and read-only memory (ROM) allocated to specific areas within the one megabyte of address space. The XT I/O memory is memory-mapped I/O in that peripheral devices are perceived by the 8088 CPU as specific physical addresses within a 64K I/O memory space. Special system memory or I/O memory control signals define the type of memory (system or I/O) being accessed.

As shown in Table 3-2, the one megabyte XT system memory is divided into a number of dedicated and reserved areas. All memory locations are expressed in hexadecimal. For convenience, a hexadecimal-to-decimal conversion table is included in Appendix B.

The 8088 CPU accesses memory in 8-bit bytes. Thus, 16-bit word operands are accessed in two bus cycles. Also, 16-bit instructions are fetched one byte at a time (two cycles).

The four 64K memory banks on the system board let users expand the system RAM to 256K before adding expansion cards. Up to 384K of expansion card memory can be added. Just before production of the XT was stopped, IBM was producing the machine with a full 640K of RAM on the system board.

The IBM PC and XT both allocate memory the same way. About 2K of lower memory (addresses 00000H through 005FFH) is reserved by design as described in Table 2-4 of Chapter 2. The rest of the first 64K of memory (Bank 0) is available for user program and data storage. Interrupt vector memory allocation is the same as that for the PC. Each of the 256 possible interrupt types in an 8088 based system has a service routine indicated by a 4-byte pointer in this memory space. The pointer elements are stored in reserved memory prior to the occurrence of interrupts. Intel reserves addresses 00000H through 0007FH (128 bytes) for 32 specific interrupts (Int 0 through Int 1F).

Read-only memory (ROM) is allocated to the address space bounded by C0000H and FFFFFH. The allocation of these 262,144 locations (256K) in the 128K/256K XT system is described in Table 3-3.

The 16 bytes at the top of addressable memory (locations FFFF0H through FFFFFH in ROM U18) are reserved for specific 8088 CPU operations including a jump to the initial program loading routine. When a RESET occurs, the CPU begins operation by generating address FFFF0H where a jump instruction is stored, shifting program execution to a special routine. In both the PC and XT, this jump redirects operation into the BIOS program.

The XT I/O space is separate from the memory space, although I/O devices can also be configured to be addressable within the memory space (memory mapped I/O). The I/O memory space covers addresses 0000H to FFFFH (64K bytes). The allocation of I/O memory is the same as that shown in Table 2-6 in Chapter 2.

Some system board and adapter board ICs are directly accessible using I/O write or read commands. Other I/O addresses are reserved by IBM or a chip

Table 3-2. Memory Allocation for the IBM XT

Hexadecimal Address	128K/256K System		
00000	128K RAM on system board		
		256K RAM on system board	
1FFFF			
20000			640K
3FFFF			
40000	412K RAM on expansion cards		
		384K RAM on expansion cards	
9FFFF			
A0000	Reserved		
AFFFF			
B0000	Monochrome video RAM		
B3FFF			
B4000	Reserved		128K
B7FFF			
B8000	Color/graphics video RAM		
BBFFF			
BC000	Reserved		
BFFFF			
C0000			
C7FFF			
C8000	Fixed disk control	256K ROM	
CBFFF			256K
CC000			
FFFFF			1024K

manufacturer. For example, Intel has reserved addresses 000F8H through 000FFH (8 bytes) for future hardware and software products.

Fig. 3-4 shows how the 8088 status outputs cause the 8288 bus controller to generate memory read (MEMR*), memory write (MEMW*), I/O read (IOR*), and I/O write (IOW*) memory control signals. These signals are used throughout the system board and are typically connected as enable inputs to ICs used in

Table 3-3.   ROM Memory Space Allocation

IC Label	Hexadecimal Address	128K/256K System		
	C0000	32K		
	C7FFF			
	C8000	16K Hard disk control	System expansion and control	192K
	CBFFF			
	CC000			
		144K		
	EFFFF			
	F0000			
U19		32K ROM cassette BASIC		32K
	F7FFF			
	F8000			
	FDFFF			32K
	FE000	8K ROM BIOS & POST		
U18	FFFFF			
				256K ROM

memory or I/O operations. They are also made available to adapter card cir
cuitry via pins B11 through B14 on expansion connectors J1 through J8.

Read-Only Memory (ROM)

As in the PC, the top 256K of addressable memory (C0000H to FFFFFH) is
allocated to ROM. The XT system board is designed to hold up to 64K of ROM
but only 40K of ROM is installed—one 32K ROM chip and one 8K ROM chip
These two memory chips are designed to occupy addresses F0000H through
FFFFFH.

A 32K ROM Cassette BASIC high-level language is stored in U19. Perma
nently stored in 8K ROM chip U18 are short BIOS programs called "I/O drivers
that enable interface operations. U19 also contains dot patterns for 128 charac
ters and graphic shapes, and code to control the time-of-day clock, the power-up
self test, and disk bootstrap loading.

The power-up self test occupies 2K of the 8K BIOS ROM U18 and includes a
series of tests that occur each time power is applied. These tests check the 8088

CPU (U3), the keyboard, the video display adapter card, the floppy and fixed disk interface adapters, and the ROM and RAM. The RAM test contains five different write/read operations that are conducted on each location in the entire RAM memory. Each memory test writes and then reads and checks a selected set of bit patterns in the same memory location. The RAM tests can take up to 1.5 minutes if your system board is fully populated. The power-up self tests are bypassed if the computer is restarted with power already on. This warm start reduces the initialization time by almost 40 percent.

Fig. 3-11 shows the XT ROM circuitry. Fifteen address lines connect to each ROM chip. A special chip select signal (CS6* or CS7*) enables U18 or U19, placing eight bits on buffered data bus XD0 through XD7.

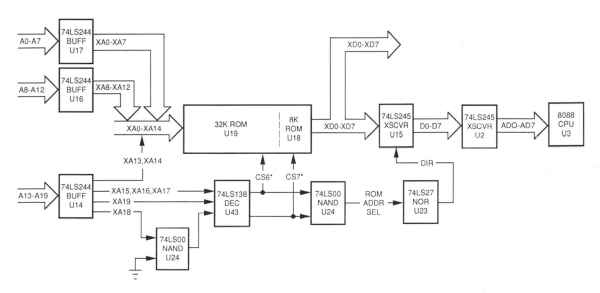

Fig. 3-11.   IBM XT ROM circuitry.

Of the 262,144 (256K) memory space addresses allocated to ROM (C0000H to FFFFFH), 192K locations (C0000H to EFFFFH) are reserved for system expansion and control. These addresses are accessible from adapter cards. For example, the hard disk is allocated address space C8000H to CBFFFH. The top 64K of ROM is designed to be accessible on the system board.

System board ROM chips U18 and U19 are allocated to the 64K address space F0000H through FFFFFH. Locations F0000H to F7FFFH are used by the 32K BASIC object code ROM U19. The socket containing BIOS ROM U18 has an allocated address space of F8000H to FFFFFH, but only an 8K ROM is installed. Chip select signals CS6* and CS7* from decoded addresses XA15 through XA19 determine which ROM will be accessed. CS6* enables the 32K BASIC ROM (U19) whenever MEMR* occurs and the address bus contains a value between F0000H and F7FFFH. CS7* enables the 8K BIOS ROM (U18) when the address is between FE000H and FFFFFH.

When a ROM location is addressed and its chip select is pulled low, eight bits of data become valid on the buffered data bus lines XD0 through XD7. The 8-bit data word is determined by the combination of the lower fifteen address bits (XA0 through XA14). The buffered ROM data passes through 74LS245 transceiver U15 onto the data bus (D0 through D7) and through another 74LS245 transceiver U2 into the 8088 CPU (U3).

Random-Access Memory (RAM)

The IBM XT system board is designed for up to 256K of 4164-type 64K-by-1-bit RAMs. An additional 384K bytes of expanded memory can be installed using a memory expansion card. This allows up to 640K bytes of available RAM memory in a system. Most XT systems are fully populated by the user with 640K of RAM.

The RAM system board chips are mounted in four rows, or banks, of nine chips each. The ninth chip is used to store a parity bit associated with each 8-bit word in a RAM bank. Parity is used to detect an error in a memory data word. All of the RAM is parity checked during readout. Parity will be described shortly. Table 3-4 relates system board RAM memory banks and addresses to physical components.

Table 3-4. 64K RAM Memory Address to Chip Identification

Address Range	D7	D6	D5	D4	D3	D2	D1	D0	PAR
00000–0FFFF BANK 0	U38	U37	U36	U35	U34	U33	U32	U31	U30
10000–1FFFF BANK 1	U54	U53	U52	U51	U50	U49	U48	U47	U46
20000–2FFFF BANK 2	U67	U66	U65	U64	U63	U62	U61	U60	U59
30000-3FFFF BANK 3	U83	U82	U81	U80	U79	U78	U77	U76	U75

Fig. 3-12 shows the circuitry associated with a RAM read or write operation. For simplicity, only Bank 0 is shown. Note that each bank of RAM chips has nine address lines (MA0 through MA8) connected to it, with separate data input and output lines for each chip. Only eight of the address lines are required to access a type 4164 RAM because the memory array is comprised of 65,536 dynamic memory cells in a square matrix and is accessed by row and by column, suggesting that the XT board was designed for later upgrade to 256K-by-1-bit RAM chips. The 256K RAM chip requires nine address bit inputs. This is

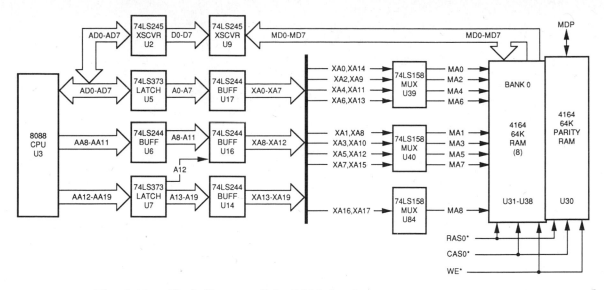

Fig. 3-12. Block diagram of the RAM circuitry.

most likely why the 74LS158 Multiplexer (U84) in Fig. 3-12 was not installed in the original XT systems.

Three active-low input lines are used to select and enable each RAM chip—row address strobe (RAS*), column address strobe (CAS*), and write enable (WE*). The logic condition of WE* determines if a read or write operation will occur. Sixteen address bits decode one of 65,536 storage cell locations in each RAM chip. The sixteen address bits are multiplexed into a bank of RAM by row (RAS0) and column (CAS0). The row address is multiplexed into the selected RAM bank first followed by the column address.

Refresh

The RAM chips on your XT system board are dynamic. A logic 1 is represented by a tiny electrical charge stored in a memory cell. However, since the charge in each cell leaks away with time, each memory location must be periodically accessed to restore the charge in cells that are in the logic-high condition. This periodic accessing of memory to restore charge is called "refresh." The refresh circuitry is shown in Fig. 3-13.

Each time a DRAM location is read, all the memory cells in the row of the selected bank are refreshed. Memory cells that held a logic-high are recharged to the full logic 1 charge. Depending on the manufacturer of the dynamic RAM, refresh must occur every 2–4 milliseconds. Refresh is accomplished by performing a memory access using only the row address to the ICs. Any cycle in which RAS* becomes active will refresh an entire memory bank row. Since the data output of the RAM bank being addressed is electronically disconnected from the memory data bus unless CAS* is applied, refresh is performed without ever

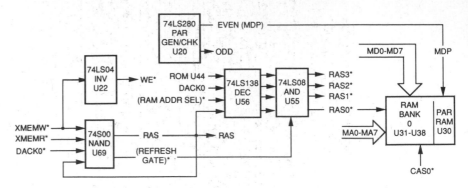

Fig. 3-13. RAM refresh circuitry.

activating CAS*. This RAS*-only refresh prevents data being output during refresh and conserves power during the memory cycle.

Refresh is initiated by OUT1 from the programmable timer. OUT1 produces a DRQ0 DMA request signal for 8237 DMAC U28. The (DACK0 BRD)* response from U28 becomes DACK0 and combines with RAS in Fig. 3-13 to produce (Refresh Gate)*. This causes 74LS08 AND gate U55 to generate an active row address strobe signal to one of the four banks of dynamic RAM memory. Since OUT1 occurs every 15 microseconds, the memory accesses caused by OUT1 are well within the 2–4 millisecond (2,000–4,000 microsecond) refresh requirement. Refresh affects the memory on the system board and on any I/O expansion cards.

Parity

Fig. 3-14 describes the memory error detection circuitry in an XT system. Each bank of RAM includes a ninth chip dedicated to storing a bit corresponding to the parity of the 8 bits stored for each byte or word of data. Each data word written into memory is evaluated to determine the number of binary 1s in the word. If the count of 1s is an odd number, a 0 memory data parity bit (MDP) is stored in a dedicated memory chip (parity RAM). If the number of 1s is even, a 1 parity bit is stored in the corresponding location in the parity memory chip causing the total (data word plus parity bit) to become odd.

When a word is read from memory, the parity of the word is checked by 74S280 9-bit odd/even parity generator/checker U20 and compared with the memory data parity bit (MDP) stored in the corresponding parity RAM chip. If the two parity values (computed and stored) are equal, the data word is accepted by the CPU or coprocessor and system operation continues. However, if the two values differ, a nonmaskable interrupt (NMI) occurs, causing the machine to halt with "PARITY CHECK" displayed on the screen.

Both even and odd parity outputs from U20 are used during memory writing and reading operations. Memory data bits (MD0 through MD7) being written into or read from RAM are also applied to U20. To ensure that parity checking occurs only during a read operation, one input to U20 is generated by

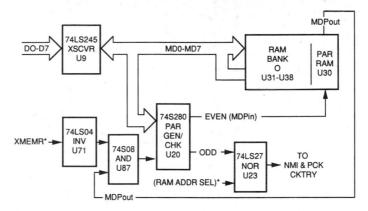

Fig. 3-14. Logic diagram of parity circuitry in the XT.

ANDing the parity bit read from memory (MDPout) with buffered memory read XMEMR*. The parity operation associated with RAM Bank 0 will be described.

During a write operation, the EVEN parity output becomes the memory data parity in bit (MDPin) that is written into the parity RAM of the bank selected (U30 in Fig. 3-14). The XT system is designed for ODD parity.

During a read operation, the eight bits of data (MD0 through MD7) and the corresponding parity bit (MDPout) are copied from RAM into U20. MDPout is compared with the parity value calculated by evaluating MD0 through MD7. Writing a data word with an even number of 1s should cause a high MDP value to be stored yielding an odd number of total 1s. Now, when the data and parity bit are read from memory and into U20, the stored MDP high value causes the number of 1s to be odd. This generates a high on the ODD PARITY output (input to U23). When this high (odd parity) signal is NORed with active-low (RAM ADDR SEL)* in 74LS27 NOR gate U23, its output goes low and all is well. However, if an even number of 1s is read into U20 while MDPout is low, the input to U23 from U20 produces a high output to the NMI and PCK circuitry indicating incorrect parity and a RAM memory error. This causes a nonmaskable interrupt to the CPU resulting in a halt to system operation.

Keyboard

Both the IBM PC and XT use the same type keyboard. Refer to Fig. 2-15 in the keyboard section of Chapter 2 for a description of how the keyboard circuitry functions. We will begin here with what happens to the scan code data once it exits the keyboard and enters the XT system board. Fig. 3-15 shows the system board circuitry that interfaces with the attached keyboard.

The scan code data (SERIAL DATA) passes through the keyboard cable to the input of 74LS322 serial-to-parallel keyboard buffer U27. In the meantime, the keyboard's 8048 microcomputer (M1) generates a signal that is passed

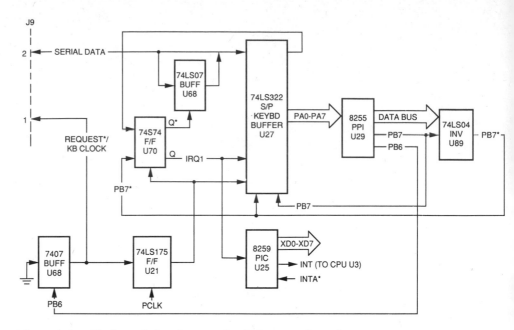

Fig. 3-15. Keyboard circuitry on the XT system board.

through keyboard connector J9-1 onto the system board to the D input of 74LS175 quad-D flip-flop U21. This signal is converted into a stream of clock pulses by a 2.386-MHz PCLK signal and caused to step the scan code data into U27.

Serial-to-parallel keyboard buffer U27 is configured to convert serial input scan code into a parallel data word for 8255 PPI U29 port A (PA0 through PA7). When the last of the 8-bit scan code has shifted serially into U27, a buffer-full signal is passed out of U27 into the D input of 74S74 dual-D flip-flop U70, generating IRQ1. IRQ1 causes U27 to pass the scan code contents of its parallel output register to port A of the 8255 PPI (U29). IRQ1 is also recognized by the 8259 programmable interrupt controller (U25), causing an INT signal to be passed to the 8088 CPU (U3). Servicing the keyboard interrupt causes BIOS to read the scan code and convert the code to an ASCII character using a ROM look-up table. An ASCII conversion chart can be found in Appendix B. The 8-bit scan code and the 8-bit ASCII character code are stored in 32 consecutive locations of a 16-character circular RAM buffer. The keyboard interrupt handler also clears the interrupt request so another keyboard interrupt can occur.

By capturing and translating keystrokes, BIOS can determine if the keyboard action included any special keys such as Ctrl, Alt, or Shift. The calling BIOS interrupt handler interprets the keystroke data as a software code character string or data input. BIOS then recognizes the character as a special password and uses it internally or passes it to an active output device (screen or printer) for positive feedback.

Video Display

The XT communicates with the user primarily by producing visible characters and shapes on an illuminated screen. Video signals are generated by the XT and passed to a display adapter board as ASCII code. The display adapter converts these signals into dot streams that the display monitor uses to produce tiny points of lighted areas on a screen.

Because the video signals for the PC family are produced on video adapter cards plugged into expansion slots on the system board, a separate chapter has been devoted to describing video displays. Refer to Chapter 5 for a description of video adapter board operation and video display monitors, including a description of how characters and graphic shapes are produced on the screen.

Floppy Disk Drive

The "standard" XT comes with two internal mass storage devices—a 360K floppy disk drive and a 10-Mbyte hard disk drive. The IBM 5.25-inch floppy disk drive adapter that plugs into one of the XT expansion slots is the same board as that used in the PC. Refer to Chapter 2 for a description of how this board works.

Hard Disk Drive

The internal 10-Mbyte hard disk drive in the IBM XT operates much like the floppy drive except the disks are sealed with the read/write heads in an airtight enclosure and rotated at 3600 rpm. This enables faster fixed disk accesses and far greater storage capability.

Like the floppy disk media, Track 0 represents the first track on a disk platter. Because hard disk platters are stacked in a fixed disk drive, the tracks are often called cylinders. The typical 10-Mbyte hard disk system consists of two platters with four read/write heads (one for each disk surface). Each disk surface is formatted for 305 or 306 track cylinders with 17 sectors per track. Each sector holds 512 bytes of data.

Sector allocation is similar to that for floppy disks except that hard disk platters can be partitioned to appear as several separate storage devices with each device containing a different disk operating system. Because the disk operating system (DOS) limits the size of disk storage to 32 Mbytes, the 10-Mbyte XT hard disk is usually configured as a single partition using PC- or MS-DOS as the operating system.

Also unique to hard disks is a formatting technique called "interleaving." Fixed disks rotate at ten times the speed of floppy disks making the system's hardware read/write time critical. It takes a finite amount of time to read a track and sector, buffer the data, and then transfer the data to the system unit RAM. As data is read from a sector, buffered, and then the head directed to read the next sector, the disk has rotated so fast that the next adjacent sector is no longer under the read head. Rather than wait for another rotation, designers spread out the sector allocation so Sector 2 is physically assigned several sectors away from Sector 1, and so on. The XT 10-Mbyte hard disk uses an interleave of six. This means that Sector 2 is six sectors removed from Sector 1. Thus, by the time the head is directed to read the next sector of data, the selected sector is just approaching a point beneath the read head.

Hard Disk Controller

Up to two hard disk drives can daisy chain to the adapter card through a flat control cable connection. Each hard drive uses its own data cable. Fig. 3-16 is a block diagram of the hard disk interface to the XT system board. Data and hand-shaking signals pass through the J8 expansion slot into the adapter card through an I/O buffer interface. (Slot 8 is recommended for the hard disk interface.) DMA is used to transfer data in 32K-byte blocks at a 5-Mbyte-per-second rate. The fixed-disk basic input/output system (BIOS) is stored in a ROM on the controller card (not in the ROM on the system board), causing the system to boot DOS from the hard disk drive if no disk is inserted in the floppy disk drive.

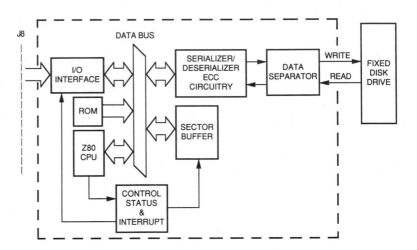

Fig. 3-16.   Block diagram of fixed disk drive interface to system board.

Controlled by a Z80 microprocessor and its associated control circuitry, the adapter board converts write data from parallel to serial in the serializer/deser-ializer error checking and correcting (ECC) circuitry and passes the data to the electronics in the fixed disk drive unit. The hard disk drive converts the digital data to reversing magnetic fields, using the same technique as that used for floppy disks.

Data Transfer

Fig. 3-17 shows the fixed disk drive adapter circuit. DMA control is achieved using DMA request 3 (DRQ3*) with a DACK3* response from the system board. For non-DMA data transfers such as status information, the interrupt request 5 (IRQ5) signal is used. (Recall that the floppy disk drive uses IRQ6 for the same purpose.)

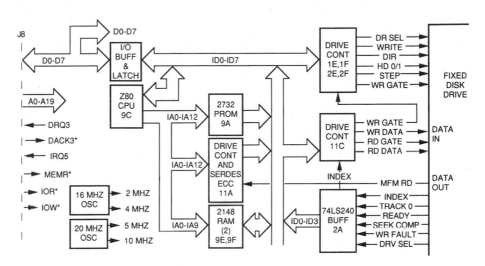

Fig. 3-17. Fixed disk drive adapter circuitry.

System data (D0 through D7) is buffered onto the adapter card and relabelled the internal data bus (ID0 through ID7). Under DMA control, write data is converted to a serial bit stream and passed to the fixed disk drive unit as WR DATA. The WR GATE signal positions the data in time during the write operation.

The drive controller circuitry (2E, 1E, 2F, and 1F) produces drive select, motor step, head number, and other signals similar to those described in the floppy disk drive section of Chapter 2.

Modified frequency modulation (MFM) coding is used to store data on the disk surface, providing more information on the disk surface (more tracks per inch). Since packing more information into a smaller disk surface area affects the integrity of the data (the accuracy), a lower write voltage is used to keep the write-data magnetic signals from interfering with each other on the disk surface. This makes the reading process critical. An error detection and correction scheme is used to assist in accurate write and read operations.

During a read operation, disk information is detected by the appropriate read head, converted to a digital signal, and transferred from the disk drive unit to the adapter card as MFM RD. The MFM RD data passes through a deserializer that performs error checking and correcting on the data before converting it into parallel data for transfer to the system board data bus (D0 through D7).

Then, using DMA, the data is transferred from the adapter card into the system board for use by CPU U3.

Two crystal oscillators are designed into the fixed disk drive adapter card to produce the necessary clock signals that move data through the adapter card. These clock signals are also used to synchronize and lock-step data being stored or retrieved from the hard disk media.

Other Input/Output Devices

Many different electronic and mechanical devices can connect to an XT system using specialized adapter cards. The devices include expanded and extended memory, a hard disk drive, hard disk card, modem, facsimile machine, printer, specialized display, mouse, joystick, trackball, light pen, plotter, graphics tablet, and other computers in small area, local area, or wide area networks. The open architecture of the PC provides ample opportunity to grow a system with the knowledge level of the user.

System Start-Up

Your system can be "started" in two ways. You can start the computer by turning the power on and allowing all the start-up tests to occur from a "cold boot," or you can simultaneously depress the Ctrl, Alt and Del keys with the computer already turned on, resetting the system. This is called a "warm boot."

In a warm boot, power is already present and the initial tests have been successfully performed. All you want to do is reset the system so you can start from a known condition and run an application program. This is the preferred method for restart because it bypasses the time-consuming memory tests common to cold start bootup.

When power is applied during a cold boot, a series of specific actions occur. The BIOS ROM U18 begins running a bootstrap program that loads and then pulls itself up to full readiness (the word bootstrap or "boot" refers to the computer pulling itself up by its own bootstrap). During this process, major system components are tested and the hardware is initialized to a known condition, ready to accept and respond to keyboard commands. The BIOS lets the hardware and software communicate. It also controls how the I/O will work and how the system board and CPU will communicate with the outside world (display, keyboard, and disk drives). In addition to the BIOS, ROM U18 also contains a power-on self test (POST) that checks major system components and then resets the system to a known start-up condition. It initiates the loading of DOS into RAM and then responds to your operator commands during system operation.

The name "boot-up" is an appropriate title for the start-up process. When the 512-byte boot record is copied from disk into RAM and then run, it begins loading the rest of DOS. First, it checks the directory for IBMBIO.COM and IBMDOS.COM. The former program contains the rest of BIOS and works in conjunction with ROM BIOS. The latter program, IBMDOS.COM, contains the disk operating system itself. Together, these programs are over 20K bytes long. If found in the directory, the boot record causes both programs to be loaded into RAM. If not found, a screen display will appear requesting you to insert and activate a system disk.

Control is then transferred to IBMBIO.COM. This program checks and initializes some equipment in the system and sets some interrupt vectors. Then it relocates and runs IBMDOS.COM, initializing DOS and setting up DOS interrupts in RAM. Finally, IBMDOS.COM invokes IBMBIO.COM, causing it to load COMMAND.COM from the hard disk. COMMAND.COM is a command processor program that provides the user an interface to DOS. It also generates the "A >" prompt you see on the screen. In this bootstrap process, each program element is used to pull up and activate a part of DOS until the system is fully operational. Without each part, the system cannot function.

Software Structure

Three primary levels of software can operate in your XT system. The lowest level (closest to and immediately understood by the 8088 CPU) is the system monitor hardware operating system (called "BIOS" for Basic Input/Output System). A major part of BIOS is permanently stored in 8K ROM U18; a part of BIOS associated with disk operation is loaded from a system disk during start-up.

The ROM-based BIOS is called "firmware" because it is software that is permanently written into hardware. BIOS is integral to communication between the components in the XT system. It also loads and runs other programs and causes the XT to start up in a known condition.

The next level of software is the disk operating system (DOS) that is loaded into RAM from the hard disk. When the XT was introduced in 1983, IBM also introduced its PC-DOS version 2.0 disk operating system. Besides providing data management utilities, partitioning ability for hard disk drives, multiple directories and subdirectories, DOS 2.0 changed the floppy disk drive configuration to a 9-sector formatting scheme, increasing the 160K/320K capability of the PC drives to 360K bytes per floppy disk. Together, BIOS and DOS oversee system operation and direct the flow of information between keyboard, screen, memory, and mass storage.

The highest level of software includes a language called BASIC for Beginner's All-purpose Symbolic Instruction Code. BASIC lets you generate custom programs using English language statements. BASIC is an interpretive language in that each instruction is interpreted and executed program line by program line. Like its PC predecessor, the XT includes BASIC in ROM.

You can also obtain and use other high-level languages such as FORTRAN, C, and Pascal. Programs written in these languages must be compiled before running. This means that the complete source code which you write must be converted to a machine executable object code before the program can be run. These languages allow faster execution time than the interpretive BASIC. Most commercial programs that you buy are written in one of the high-level languages. These programs are called *application* programs. Whenever you think about an XT computer system, you should view it as a combination of hardware, software, and firmware. All three of these parts are necessary for system operation.

Summary

This chapter provided a detailed analysis of the operation of the IBM XT system. This information lets you partition the XT into understandable building blocks for failure analysis and troubleshooting. As you recognized by studying this chapter, each building block is interconnected to form a complete XT computer system. By understanding how the computer hardware and software operate and interact, you are better equipped to quickly recognize and isolate trouble symptoms to one of these building block circuits.

Questions for Review and Discussion

1. Describe the primary differences between the IBM PC and the IBM XT.
2. Describe how stored data is checked for accuracy during a memory read operation.
3. Diagram the addressable memory in the XT. Include the address boundaries for RAM, ROM, and I/O.
4. How is the power supply in the XT different from that in the PC?
5. What signal causes the system board to clear and prepare for operation?
6. What signal causes the CPU to have BIOS read and translate a keyboard entry?
7. Why is interleaving important in a hard disk system?
8. What determines how many tracks will be formatted on a floppy disk?
9. Which 64K RAM chip contains bit D3 in address 10C2FH?
10. What signal controls when a memory refresh occurs?

4

Detailed System Operation of the IBM PC AT

Chapter 1 introduced the IBM PC family—the PC, the XT, and the AT personal computers. Chapter 4 describes the operation of the AT computer. In this chapter, as in earlier chapters, circuit schematics and block diagrams are included to enhance your understanding of signal and data flow.

The schematic symbols used in this book conform to the Howard W. Sams & Company COMPUTERFACTS labeling standard. A number enclosed in a box is used to represent a common voltage source. An active-low signal is normally represented by a signal label with a bar over the top. Because printing the "not" bar over signal labels is awkward in a text such as this, the active-low representation of a signal will be indicated by the symbol * following the label. Thus the active-low signal for reset will be represented as RESET*. Other symbols should be self-explanatory.

As shown in Fig. 4-1, power is applied to the AT through the ac power cord. The 192-watt switching power supply converts the ac input energy into the required voltage sources for the system board, the adapter boards in the expansion slots, and the floppy and hard disk drives.

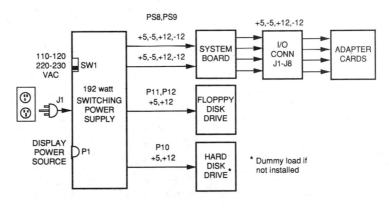

Fig. 4-1. System power requirements for the IBM AT.

Power Supply

Inside the AT system unit chassis is a rectangular metal box containing a switching power supply. The back of the supply is exposed through holes cut into the rear of the system unit chassis. A fan is mounted inside the power supply to remove heat generated by the supply and internal components.

The AT operates on either 115 volts or 230 volts ac power. Slide switch SW1 at the rear of the AT selects either 230- or 115-V ac as the source. The AT can also operate on either 50- or 60-hertz (Hz) alternating current (ac).

Fig. 4-2 is a block diagram of the switching power supply. When rocker switch SW2 is ON, line voltage is applied to the switching power-supply circuits. Switch SW2 also provides 0.75 amps of filtered power to display monitor receptacle P1 at the rear of the power-supply housing.

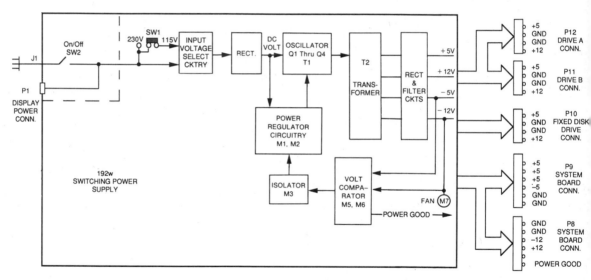

Fig. 4-2.   Switching power supply block diagram.

As current begins to flow into the power supply, ac power is provided to an input voltage selector and rectifier circuit that feeds the oscillator and special power regulator circuitry. Outputs from power transformer T2 and the rectifier and filter circuits provide clean direct-current (dc) voltage levels for the system components. The rectifier and filter circuits smooth the voltage levels and provide +5-V, +12-V, and −12-V dc. These voltages are connected to the AT system through five power cables (P8 through P12). The system board and the floppy and fixed disk drives are powered directly from the power supply. All other peripheral adapter boards receive their power from the expansion slots on the AT system board. The expansion slots receive dc power from power-supply connectors P8 and P9.

The +5-V dc connected to all five source connectors (P8 through P12) powers the ICs used throughout the AT personal computer system. The +12-V dc source is connected through P8, P10, P11, and P12 to the system board and both the floppy disk-drive and hard disk-drive motors. The fixed/floppy disk-drive adapter and EGA display adapter require +5-V, +12-V, and −12-V dc sources. These voltages are available on the system board expansion slot connectors.

As power reaches operating levels, the regulator circuitry in the power supply produces a POWER GOOD reference signal for the system board. The POWER GOOD signal is applied to an 82284 clock generator where it functions as the start flag for system operation.

The power-supply output voltages are monitored by internal circuitry to prevent catastrophic damage to the system or adapter boards should an overload or overcurrent condition occur. High voltages restrict troubleshooting and repair of the AT power supply to experienced technicians. Further discussion of the power supply is beyond the scope of this text. It is often more practical to replace a defective power supply when a failure occurs in this stage of the system.

When there is no fixed disk drive installed, a 5-ohm dummy load resistor is installed across connector P10 to prevent power-supply imbalance. This is done to keep the loading on the power-supply outputs nearly the same so no single part of the circuitry draws more current than another. Imbalance can cause excessive heating of components in the stages affected.

IBM AT System Board

Fig. 4-3 shows the component layout for the AT system board. This drawing will help you identify components as they are discussed. It also serves as a reference during troubleshooting. An alphanumeric identification code is printed on the system board near each component. This code identifies the components in block diagrams and schematics. The integrated circuits (ICs) are often called "chips." Chips are identified in this text and on schematics with a "U" prefix designator followed by a number. The chip in location U120 is labelled "74ALS00." The 7400 label identifies the IC as a quad 2-input NAND gate. The "ALS" indicates that this chip is an advanced low-powered Schottky type of IC. Other chips may have no center label designator, an "LS" for low-powered Schottky, "S" for Schottky, or other markings printed in the designator position.

When replacing a component, it is important to use the same type of device. Component characteristics including speed of operation are identified by the marking printed on the device. Using a 74S00 as a replacement when a 74ALS00 is intended can cause unpredictable operation after the repair. Speed is especially critical in memory chips. If the system needs a memory that can respond in 120 nanoseconds and you install a chip that can only respond in 200 nanoseconds, data will not be ready when needed. Remember to verify the

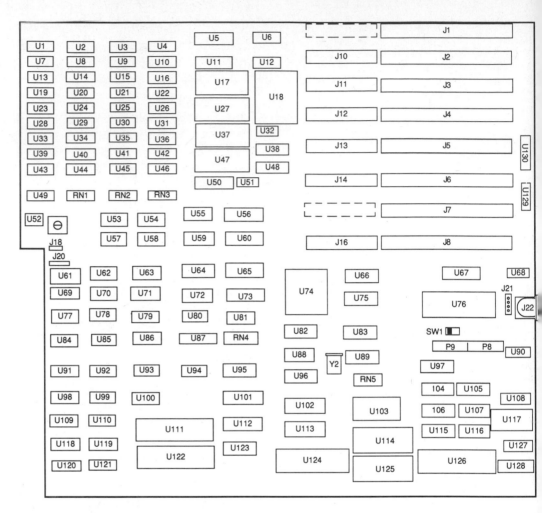

Fig. 4-3. IBM AT system board layout.

center designator whenever you replace a component. A list of the chips with their center designators can be found in Appendix B.

80286 Central Processing Unit

The AT personal computer was designed around the Intel 80286 central processing unit (CPU). The 16-bit Intel 80286 (U74) shown in Fig. 4-4 is upward compatible with the 8088 8-bit CPU in the PC and XT and with the 16-bit 8086 microprocessor. The bit size is determined by the number of binary digits in the data word. The 80286 works with 16-bit data both and outside the chip; the 8088 works with 16-bit data inside the chip but with 8-bit data external to it. Both the 80286 and the earlier 8086 have a 16-bit data bus; the 8088 used in the PC and XT has an 8-bit external data bus.

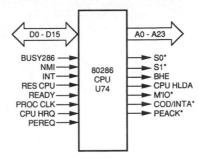

Fig. 4-4. Major control signals, data bus, and address bus used with the 80286 CPU (U74).

The 80286 can support both 8-bit and 16-bit operations including multiply and divide. Mounted in a large, square 68-pin package, U74 is powered by a single + 5-volt source.

With 24 address lines, the 80286 can directly access over sixteen million memory locations (two raised to the 24th power is 16,777,216). These address lines enable a physical memory address range between 000000H and FFFFFFH (the "H" means hexadecimal). Sixteen of the address lines are also used to access up to 64K of I/O. The I/O for the AT is memory-mapped, causing I/O devices to appear as memory locations to the CPU. Only a small fraction of the available I/O addresses are actually used by peripheral devices such as display, printer, and communication adapters.

Two 80286 operating modes are possible causing either 20 or 24 address bits to be active (1,048,576 or 16,777,216 addressable locations). In real address mode, the 80286 emulates the 8086 and 8088 with their 1-Mbyte memory space. In protected mode, the 80286 can use memory management circuitry to access up to 1 gigabyte (1,073,741,824 bytes) of virtual address space per task mapped into 16 Mbytes of physical address space. With the introduction of the AT came a dramatic improvement in addressable memory.

The AT's disk operating system (DOS 3.0) places the computer in the real address mode. The power-on self test (POST) shifts U74 into protected mode to check the CPU operation and to determine the existence of expansion RAM beyond 1 Mbyte. Then, at the end of initialization, the system is returned to real address mode, restricting the AT to the same addressable memory as the PC and XT. Later versions of DOS 4.0 and other operating systems were finally designed to drive the 80286 in protected mode with virtual memory capability.

As shown in Fig. 4-5, the 80286 is the central component in the IBM AT system. An 82284 clock generator provides clock pulses and special control signals, a pair of 8259 programmable interrupt controllers collectively provide an interrupt to alter program execution, and an 80287 coprocessor performs complex math processing for the 80286. Status signals S0*, S1*, and M/IO* are decoded by the 82288 bus controller (U83) to generate timed command and control signals. Access to system or I/O memory is achieved using memory read (MEMR*),

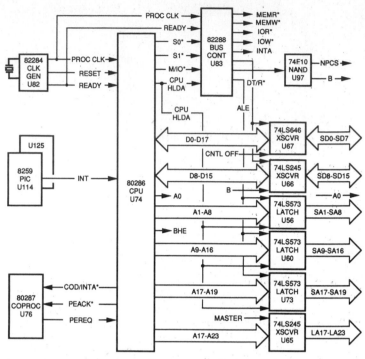

Fig. 4-5. 80286 system board configuration in the AT.

memory write (MEMW*), I/O read (IOR*) or I/O write (IOW*). MEMR* causes system memory to drive its stored information onto the data bus. MEMW* causes system memory to record the information presently on the data bus. Peripheral devices are controlled using IOR* and IOW* signals. These command signals instruct I/O devices to drive data onto or read data from the data bus.

The 16-bit local data bus is interfaced to the system data bus using two transceivers that route information in either direction. The 24-bit local address bus is routed through latch circuitry onto the system address bus.

When 80286 operations begin, the CPU places an address on its local address bus, accesses a memory location, fetches an instruction, interprets and executes the instruction placing the results in a location determined by the instruction, and then fetches another instruction to repeat the sequence. The 80286 can collect instructions in a queue; so while it's busy internally executing a current instruction, another part of U74 can be loading other instructions enabling maximum program execution speed.

80287 Math Coprocessor

The intel 80287 numeric processor extension math coprocessor was designed to support complex operations while residing in and using the same circuitry as the

80286 CPU. Both the hardware and the software interfaces for the 80287 are compatible with the 80286.

The 80287 coprocessor (U76) works much like the 8087 coprocessor option used in the PC and XT systems. It can handle number crunching applications using a wide range of data values including integer and noninteger numbers. It can produce precise results with many significant digits and can also handle calculations involving real and imaginary numbers. Integers up to 18 digits long and floating point numbers from 32 to 80 bits wide can be used. Coprocessor U76 has built-in math instructions for add, subtract, multiply, divide, absolute value, arctangent, tangent, square root, log base two and log base e.

A prewired 40-pin socket near keyboard connector J22 (Fig. 4-3) was designed to accommodate the optional 80287 math coprocessor. As shown in Fig. 4-6, the system board is configured so U74 and U76 share the data bus, clock, and S0*, S1*, and READY status signals. However, this is where the similarity between the 8088/8087 and 80286/80287 ends. In the AT, the coprocessor is treated as an I/O device.

The 80287 coprocessor (U76) is wired to function as a slave processor to the 80286 CPU. Three registers in U76, accessible through I/O addresses 00F8H, 00FAH, and 00FCH, receive instruction commands and operands from CPU U74 and store and provide results to numeric or logical operations. To access coprocessor U76, the 80286 CPU must send a status code to the 80288 bus controller causing it to generate an I/O read or write command. Then the address placed on the bus by CPU U74 is decoded and acted upon by coprocessor U76. Once a command is entered into the 80287, it takes charge and performs the instruction.

The coprocessor generates a busy signal to the 80286 CPU through PAL U130 that causes the CPU to wait for coprocessor execution before continuing. Thus, when CPU U74 tells U76 to perform a particular command, the coprocessor takes over the data bus using its busy handshaking line to keep control until the process is complete.

The 80287 math coprocessor runs at one-third the speed of the system clock. Running at only 4 MHz in a 12-MHz system, the 80287 in the IBM AT runs slower than the 4.77-MHz coprocessor on the PC and XT system boards. The 80287 doesn't improve the AT performance as much as might be expected.

The 80287 coprocessor (U76) can interrupt the 80286 CPU whenever U76 detects an error or exception. If an error condition occurs, U76 generates an ERROR* signal through PAL U130 into the IRQ13 input of 8259 interrupt controller U125. The resulting interrupt causes the system BIOS to read the status of the coprocessor to determine if the problem is in the 80287 or is a memory read error. The interrupt handler then takes action to service the interrupt or halt processor operations. A 7xx error code display indicates a problem with the 80287 math coprocessor (U76).

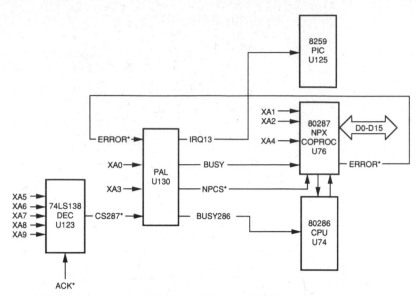

Fig. 4-6. 80287 coprocessor U76 and 80286 CPU U74 interface circuitry.

System Support Chips

The 80288 CPU on the IBM AT system board is configured to work with special system support chips. These chips include 82284 clock generator (U82), 8284 clock generator (U18), 8254 programmable interval timer (U103), 8259 programmable interrupt controllers (U114, U125), and 8237 programmable DMA controllers (U111, U122). Each of these chips and their associated circuitry are discussed in the following paragraphs.

Clock Generation Circuitry

Two clock generating ICs are designed into the AT system board—the 82284 system clock generator (U82) and the 8284 clock generator (U18). U18 is the same type clock generator IC used on the PC and XT.

82284 Clock Generator (U82)

Clock generator U82 uses the POWER GOOD signal from the power supply to develop a system reset signal (RESET) that initializes major components in the AT system. This reset pulse causes the 80286 to start program execution at location 0FFFF0H, the system initialization address.

As shown in Fig. 4-7, a 12-MHz crystal (Y2) causes U82 to generate a 12-MHz processor clock signal (PROC CLK) for the 80286 microprocessor and support components. PROC CLK is twice the CPU frequency of 6 MHz. PROC CLK is the basis for most of the clock signals on the system board.

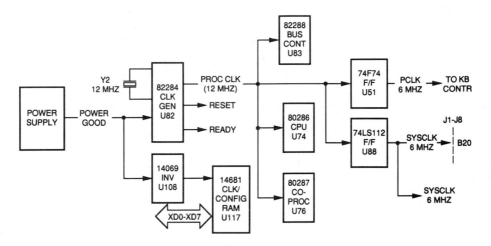

Fig. 4-7.   82284 clock generator U82 circuitry.

Two flip-flops (U51 and U88) divide the 12-MHz PROC CLK signal down to 6 MHz (PCLK and SYSCLK) for use in the keyboard circuitry, on the AT system board, and on expansion boards via pin B20 of expansion slots J1 through J8. External status signals also cause the 82284 to generate a ready signal that tells the 80286 CPU if slower components or devices have completed their processing and no longer need the CPU to hold in a wait condition.

8284 Clock Generator (U18)

The IBM AT uses a separate clock generator to develop video oscillator and 8254 programmable timer controller signals. As shown in Fig. 4-8, a 14.318-MHz crystal (Y1) provides the base frequency that 8284 clock generator U18 uses to generate two output clock frequencies (14.318 MHz and 2.386 MHz).

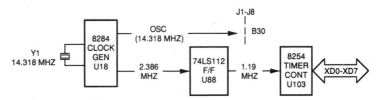

Fig. 4-8.   8284 clock generator U18 circuitry.

The 14.318-MHz video clock signal OSC is used to generate synchronization and horizontal scan signals on a video display adapter board. OSC is connected to pin B30 of expansion slots J1 through J8. The 2.386-MHz output from U18 is divided by 74LS112 flip/flop U88 to produce a 1.19-MHz clock for 8254 timer controller U103. The operation of U103 will be described next.

8254 Programmable Interval Timer (U103)

Fig. 4-9 shows the 8254 programmable interval timer (U103) and its associated circuitry. U103 performs three important functions. It generates a system time-of-day interrupt, it initiates a dynamic RAM refresh pulse, and it helps produce sound from the two-inch speaker mounted inside the system unit chassis.

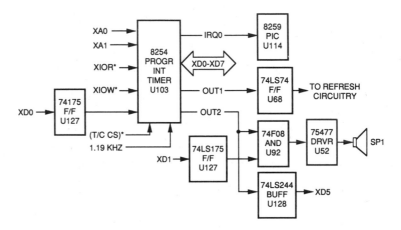

Fig. 4-9. 8254 programmable interval timer U103 and related circuitry.

Three independent, programmable 16-bit down counters inside U103 are driven by a 1.19-MHz clock signal input. Each counter is preset during start-up. Once programmed, the counters operate automatically. Upon count start, the 8254 programmable interval timer causes each counter to clock down from its preset delay value until the count reaches zero. At this point, the counter sends out a count-complete signal and rolls over backwards to its preprogrammed preset value so the countdown can begin once more. Depending on the setting of each counter, three timed outputs are generated—OUT0 (IRQ0), OUT1 (to U68) and OUT2 (to the speaker circuitry).

The first counter produces OUT0 (IRQ0) to request interrupt service through an 8259 programmable interrupt controller (U114). IRQ0 causes the time-of-day interrupt that occurs approximately 18.2 times each second. A second counter produces OUT1 66,287 times each second and causes the CPU to access the dynamic RAM every 15 microseconds. This periodic access is called "refresh." The third counter produces an 896-Hz square wave output (OUT2) that is ANDed in U92 with speaker data from data bus bit 1 (XD1). The audio output from U92 is applied to speaker driver U52. OUT2 can be varied by presetting its counter with different values, each producing a unique audio output frequency

8259 Programmable Interrupt Controllers (U114, U125)

The IBM PC, XT, and AT computers all use an Intel microprocessor as the CPU. Intel designed their 8088 and 80286 microprocessors to operate in an environment where interrupt signals are used to control input and output data transactions. Interrupts are also used to control the execution of CPU instructions.

When a program is running, external devices inform the CPU of a need for attention by generating interrupt signals. When the 80286 recognizes an interrupt, it transfers control to the location of an interrupt-handling subroutine that services the interrupt request. Then control is returned to the CPU or software program that was running when the interrupt occurred. Interrupts can be caused by the operator (e.g., pressing a key on the keyboard), by disk drives, displays, and other peripheral hardware, or by software instructions.

Interrupts can be classified as maskable (can be programmed out) or nonmaskable (must be recognized). Software interrupts are part of the program code and they occur as designed during program execution. Software interrupts and many hardware interrupts can be masked out. Memory read problems can cause a parity error nonmaskable interrupt (NMI) signal that is connected directly to the 80286 CPU. The IBM PC and XT also generate an NMI when a coprocessor error occurs. The AT uses custom programmable array logic (PAL) chip U130 to detect and convert a 80287 numeric coprocessor interrupt into a standard maskable hardware interrupt request.

The NMI input to the 80286 provides a way to interrupt CPU operation whenever a "catastrophic" event such as bus parity error occurs. An NMI is the highest priority hardware interrupt and causes system operation to stop. It cannot be masked or disabled. As soon as an NMI occurs, the 80286 CPU completes executing its current instruction and transfers control to a special interrupt service routine. No hardware interrupt acknowledge responses are generated. Execution is automatic.

Except for the parity NMI, all other hardware interrupts are recognized by two special interrupt control chips that are preprogrammed to accept interrupt requests in a priority order. These external interrupt-request signals are connected to 8259 programmable interrupt controllers (PIC) U114 and U125 as shown in Fig. 4-10. Controllers U114 and U125 are connected in a master/slave configuration. Although the output of each interrupt controller is a CPU interrupt signal (INT), the INT from U125 is connected to the IRQ2 input of PIC U114, effectively cascading IRQ8 through IRQ15 to U114. The INT output from U114 is then applied directly to 80286 CPU U74.

Interrupt controllers U114 and U125 each handle up to eight vectored priority interrupt requests and generate a logic high interrupt signal (INT) response. These controllers require no clock input and respond to any interrupt request once configured. Their ability to handle multilevel priority interrupts minimizes software and real-time system overhead.

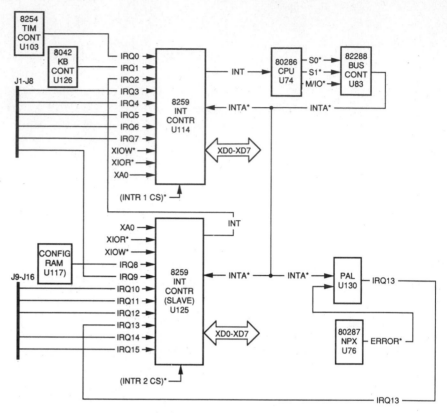

Fig. 4-10. 8259 programmable interrupt controllers (PIC) U114 and U125
with related circuitry.

During start-up, each 8259 PIC is tested and then preset to prioritize
interrupt-request inputs. Then when two devices send interrupt requests to
U114 and U125 at the same time, the device with the highest priority is serviced
first. Interrupt requests to U114 and U125 can be selectively masked without
affecting the interrupt-request lines of other priority request inputs. The INT
input to the 80286 can also be masked causing the system to ignore all hardware
interrupt requests except the NMI.

Interrupt-request 0 (IRQ0) has the highest priority. It causes a time-of-day
clock tick 18.2 times each second just as in the PC and XT. The second highest
priority interrupt (IRQ1) is used during keyboard entry. The next highest priority
of interrupt requests come from IRQ8 through IRQ15 because their INT output
connects to IRQ2 on U114 as shown in Fig. 4-10. Table 4-1 lists the assignments for
the interrupt-request inputs to U114 and U125. If two request lines become active
at the same time, the request whose number is closest to IRQ0 is serviced first.

When an interrupt-request signal is sensed, the affected interrupt control-
ler produces a corresponding interrupt signal. If the request comes into U125, its
INT becomes an IRQ2 signal applied to U114. U114 responds by generating an
INT which is sent to CPU U74, causing the 80286 to pull status outputs S0*, S1*

Table 4-1. Listing of Hardware Interrupt Requests to Controllers U114 and U125

Interrupt Request	Meaning
IRQ0	8254 timer 0
IRQ1	8042 keyboard controller
IRQ2	Slave interrupt controller
IRQ3	Serial communications 2, LAN adapter 2
IRQ4	Serial communications 1
IRQ5	Parallel printer port 2
IRQ6	Floppy diskette controller
IRQ7	Parallel printer port 1
IRQ8	Real-time clock
IRQ9	LAN adapter
IRQ10	Reserved
IRQ11	Reserved
IRQ12	Reserved
IRQ13	80287 error (redirect to NMI vector)
IRQ14	Fixed-disk controller
IRQ15	Reserved

and M/IO* active low. This status code is decoded by 82288 bus controller U83 which in turn generates a sequence of two active-low interrupt acknowledge (INTA*) signals that are passed back to both controllers.

The first INTA* communicates to the interrupt controllers that the INT signal has been recognized by U74, and that an interrupt acknowledge cycle is in progress. The 80286 locks out other peripheral devices from gaining access to the bus and then generates another S0*–S1*–M/IO* status code causing bus controller U83 to send a second INTA* signal to the interrupt controllers. When the affected interrupt controller senses this second interrupt acknowledge signal, it places a code on the buffered data bus XD0 through XD7. This code byte represents the interrupt type (Type 0 through 255) associated with the requesting device. The CPU uses this byte to develop an address pointer to an interrupt vector table containing the address of the service routine.

8237 Programmable DMA Controllers (U111, U122)

Like its predecessors, the IBM AT uses direct memory access (DMA) operations to transfer large blocks of data between mass storage and the system RAM. Two 8237 DMA controllers (U111 and U122) are used in the AT as shown in Fig. 4-11. These controllers allow external devices to transfer 8-bit or 16-bit information to the system board in up to 64K blocks.

Transfer occurs over seven DMA channels. Four DMA request channels come in on dedicated pins on expansion slots J1 through J8. The remaining three channels are used for 16-bit operation and connect to pins on slots J10 through

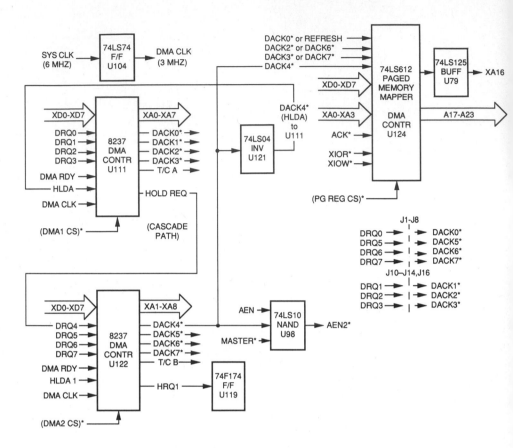

Fig. 4-11. 8237 programmable DMA controllers U111 and U122 with related circuitry.

J14 and J16. Each channel includes a DMA request input and a DMA acknowledge output.

The key to DMA activity is a dual DMA controller design with 8237 DMA controller U111 functioning as a slave to the master DMA controller U122. A DMA is initiated when an external device sends a DMA request (DRQ) via the system board expansion slots. DRQ0 and DRQ5 through DRQ7 connect to expansion slots J1 through J8. DRQ1, DRQ2, and DRQ3 connect to expansion slots J10 through J14 and J16. The system response is a DMA acknowledge back to the requesting device.

Each DMAC contains four independent request/acknowledge channels that can automatically reinitialize to a preprogrammed condition following a DMA process. Each channel has a 64K address and word count capability. Channels 0, 3, and 5 through 7 are not dedicated on the AT system board. Channels 0 through 3 are used for 8-bit data transfers. Channels 5, 6, and 7 handle 16-bit transfers. Channel 1 is used for synchronous data link control (SDLC) communication device data transfers. Channel 2 handles disk-drive data transfers.

Each DMA request signal is applied to one of the two 8237 DMA controllers causing the selected controller to generate a DMA acknowledge signal (DACK and a hold request to the CPU. Either DMA controller can take over the system and conduct a data transfer. When a DMA occurs, the CPU is suspended while a DMA controller takes over the address, control, and data buses. Once initiated, the transfer of information automatically continues until a predetermined amount of data has been moved. Then control is passed back to the CPU and normal system operations continue.

DMAC U111 is cascaded to U122 by connecting its hold request (HOLD REQ) output to the DRQ4 channel 4 input of master DMA controller U122. This lets DMA requests to either controller generate the hold request (HRQ1) that is converted into a CPU hold request signal (CPU HRQ). By cascading the controllers, the hold request from U111 results in the generation of DACK4* by U122. DACK4* is passed through 74ALS04 inverter U121 producing a hold acknowledge (HLDA) that is sent back to U111.

Internal DMA logic decodes the various commands sent to U111 and U122 by the 80286 CPU prior to servicing a DMA request. This logic also decodes a control word from the CPU that determines the type of DMA to be performed. Rotating encoder logic in each DMA controller resolves priority contention between several DMA channels requesting simultaneous service.

Timing for U111 and U122 is achieved using a 3-MHz DMA CLK signal from 74ALS74 flip/flop U104. In the idle state, both DMACs sample their four respective DMA request lines (DRQ0 through DRQ3 and DRQ4 through DRQ7) each time a DMA CLK pulse occurs to determine if any channel is requesting a DMA transfer.

Each DMA request line is an individual asynchronous channel input used by peripheral circuitry to obtain DMA service. A DMA request is not timed or preset, but occurs under control of the requesting device. However, the DMA request lines are in a fixed priority with DRQ0 holding the highest priority and DRQ7 the lowest.

When a DMA request line goes active, the DMA controller produces a hold request that results in a CPU HRQ input to CPU U74 from the 82284 clock generator. The CPU HRQ input causes the 80286 to give the requesting 8237 DMAC control over the address, data, and control buses. Once a DMAC has control, its circuitry produces the signals necessary for data transfer.

The DMA acknowledge signals produced by U111 and U122 are connected to the expansion bus and to the 74LS612 paged memory mapper DMA controller (U124). The DMA acknowledge signals on the expansion bus tell an individual peripheral that a DMA cycle has been granted. These acknowledge signals are typically used to produce I/O chip select signals, causing the requesting devices to place an input byte on the data bus. The DMA acknowledge signals applied to paged memory mapper U124 expand the transfer capability.

The 8237 DMACs (U111 and U122) can handle only one 64K memory page at a time. Therefore, U124 functions as a DMA page-register memory mapper to increase the DMA capability from 64K to the full 16-Mbyte available memory space (16 Mbytes in protected mode—1 Mbyte in real mode) while retaining the

64K page boundary. Paged memory mapper U124 generates a 12-bit address output. An internal 16-word by 12-bit RAM is loaded through the buffered data bus. Page register chip select (PG REG CS)* determines which of two inputs (the DACK inputs or XA0 through XA3) will be entered and decoded to select one of the sixteen particular page-memory address outputs. Only eight of the twelve available output address bits are used (XA16, and A17 through A23). With 256 possible address output combinations of the eight address bits, and with each word representing a 64K page boundary, a memory-mapped address space of 16 Mbyte is possible (256 × 64K = 16,384K).

Up to 16 of the 64K memory page boundaries are stored inside U124 and made available whenever a DMA operation is initiated. This causes the condition of four DMA acknowledge inputs (DACK3* or DACK7*, DACK2* or DACK6*, DACK0 or Refresh, or DACK4*) to select one of the 16 word locations inside U124, copying the data word out as A16 through A23. When the DMA operation is complete, address bits A16 through A23 electronically disconnect from the address-bus (go to the open-circuit tristate condition). This permits the same address-bus segment (A16 through A23) to be used by the CPU and DMA addressing circuitry.

During DMA data transfers, memory and I/O control signals are generated by the DMA circuitry. If more time is required to complete the DMA cycle (accessing a slow memory or I/O device), a ready signal (DMA RDY) to U111 and U122 causes the DMACs to wait in the current cycle until the memory or I/O device has completed its data transfer.

Data transfers occur in up to 64K blocks. Each time a word counter in an active 8237 DMAC reaches 64K (FFFFH), a terminal count signal (T/C A, T/C B) is generated indicating the completion of a DMA operation. These signals are used by the system board and adapter cards to keep track of DMA cycles.

Memory Configuration

The AT personal computer comes configured with up to 512K of system board RAM and can interface with additional memory on expansion cards. In its normal (real) mode, the AT is limited to a total of 640K of physical RAM memory like the PC and XT. This is unfortunate because the 80286 CPU can address up to 1 Mbyte of storage in real mode and up to 16 Mbytes within a virtual memory space of 1 gigabyte in protected mode. In real mode, the addressable memory space is from 00000H to FFFFFH. In protected mode, the memory space reaches from 000000H to FFFFFFH.

During system setup you tell the software how much base and expansion board memory is installed. This value is stored in a CMOS RAM that is kept active by a battery backup circuit. A jumper on the system board can be changed to allow the system to recognize up to 512K of system board RAM. There are also switches on the memory expansion adapters to allow up to five 512K adapters to work in the same system. When powering up your system, the operating system software reads the CMOS RAM to determine the total amount of available memory. Maintaining the system configuration in a RAM, which is backed up by a battery, provides quick system configuration recognition during start-up.

Memory Addressing Scheme

This section describes the memory allocation scheme for the system board and peripheral memory. Besides the 1-Mbyte or 16-Mbyte addressable main memory, the AT can address up to 64K of peripheral I/O in a memory-mapped design. Each installed peripheral device has a unique address (or set of addresses) that can be accessed using special I/O read and write commands. These devices include the floppy and hard disk drives and the video displays.

As shown in Table 4-2, the 16-Mbyte AT memory space is divided into dedicated, available, and reserved areas. All memory locations are expressed in hexadecimal. For convenience, a hex-to-decimal conversion table is included in Appendix B.

Within this memory space, certain locations are reserved for special CPU functions. As shown in Table 4-3, locations 000000H through 0003FFH are reserved for interrupt vectors. Intel specifically reserves addresses 00000H through 003FFH (1024 bytes) for specific interrupts.

In real mode, 80286 program interrupt vectors 00H through 1FH are contained in addresses 00000H through 0007FH. The next set of vectors (hardware, BASIC and DOS interrupt vectors 20H-FFH) are located between 00080H and 003FFH. DOS interrupt vectors are contained in locations 00080H through 0003FH. Addresses 00100H to 001BFH contain a reserved interrupt area and eight locations for user interrupt vectors 60H through 6FH. System interrupt requests IRQ8 through IRQ15 are stored in locations 001C0H through 001DFH, and locations 00200H through 003C3H contain BASIC interrupt vectors 80H through F0H. Special BIOS data is stored between 00400H and 004FFH. DOS uses locations 00500H through 00504H, and BASIC uses locations 00510H to 0051DH. The addresses from 0051EH to 07FFFFH provide approximately 510K of RAM memory space for the user.

Two read-only-memory (ROM) chips are standard on the AT system board, although two optional ROMs can be added. With a large address space allocation, ROM can also be designed into I/O adapter cards and still be directly accessed by the 80286 CPU.

As shown in Table 4-4, the AT read-only memory (ROM) is allocated to three separate memory areas with optional ROM in two additional areas. Area 1 maps up to 128K of I/O adapter card ROM to address space 0C0000H to 0DFFFFH. ROM areas 2 and 3 each contain 64K of addressable memory space. These areas (0F0000H to 0FFFFFH, and FF0000H to FFFFFFH) are coded the same. Optional ROM can be installed and accessed within the address space bounded by

Table 4-2. Memory Allocation for the AT

Address	Size/Function	
000000	**512Kb** System board RAM	
07FFFF		640Kb
080000	**128Kb** I/O channel expansion memory option	
09FFFF		
0A0000	**128Kb** Video RAM graphics display buffer	
0BFFFF		
0C0000	**128Kb** I/O expansion ROM	
0DFFFF		
0E0000	**64Kb** Reserved system board (duplicated at FE0000)	
0EFFFF		
0F0000	**64Kb** ROM on system board (duplicated at FF0000)	
0FFFFF		
100000	**15Mb** I/O channel memory—512Kb memory expansion options	
FDFFFF		
FE0000	**64Kb** Reserved on system board (duplicated at 0E0000)	
FEFFFF		
FF0000	**64Kb** ROM on system board (duplicate at 0F0000)	
FFFFFF		

0E0000H and 0EFFFFH. For protected mode addressing, these ROMs can be accessed via addresses FE0000H to FEFFFFH.

Locations 0FFFF0H through 0FFFFFH are reserved for 16 bytes of system initialization code. When power is applied, or the system is reset, the first address accessed by the 80286 is location 0FFFF0H. A jump instruction must be stored at 0FFFF0H shifting program execution to a special bootup routine. Note that this is the same address as that used by the 8088 and 8086 microprocessors. This consistency in Intel design is appreciated.

The AT can support both 8-bit and 16-bit peripheral devices mapped into special I/O addresses or addressable anywhere within the 16 million address locations of an 80286 in the protected mode. The system board is designed so that I/O devices are accessed using special commands within their own separate I/O memory space. I/O memory resides within addresses 0000H to FFFFH (64K bytes) although little of this addressable space is actually used. The allocation of I/O memory for the AT is shown in Table 4-5.

Table 4-3. Allocation of the Lower 64K of Memory

Hexadecimal	Memory Content
0000–03FF	Interrupt vector tables
0400–04A1	ROM BIOS data area
04A2–04EF	Reserved
04F0–04FF	Intra-application communication
0500	DOS
0504	DOS
0510–0511	BASIC segment address store
0512–0515	BASIC clock interrupt vector segment
0516–0519	BASIC break key interrupt vector segment
051A–051D	BASIC disk error interrupt vector segment
051E–05FF	DOS
0600–FFFF	I/O.COM, ROM BIOS interface, and user defined area

As shown in Table 4-5, some system board ICs are directly accessible using I/O write or read commands. Other I/O locations are reserved by IBM or a chip manufacturer. For example, Intel reserves addresses 0360H through 036FH (16 bytes) and 03C0H through 03CFH (16 bytes) for future hardware and software products.

Fig. 4-5 described how the four memory command signals (MEMR*, MEMW*, IOR*, and IOW*) are generated. These signals originate in the 82288 Bus Controller (U83) and are buffered to become XMEMR*, XMEMW*, XIOR*, and XIOW* signals used throughout the system board. IOR* and IOW* are also connected to specific pins of expansion connectors J1 through J8. MEMR* and

Table 4-4. ROM Memory Space Allocation

Area	Address	Application
1	0C0000 0DFFFF	28K For ROM on adapter cards
2	0E0000 0EFFFF	64K Reserved for optional ROM (duplicated at FE0000)
2	0F0000 0FFFFF	64K System board ROM (duplicated at FF0000)
	EDFFFF FE0000 FEFFFF	64K Reserved for optional ROM (duplicated at 0E0000)
3	FF0000 FFFFFF	64K System board ROM (duplicated at 0F0000)

MEMW* are also buffered to become the system memory read and write signals SMEMR* and SMEMW* that are also applied to the system expansion bus connectors J1 through J8.

Read-Only Memory (ROM)

The AT system board is designed to hold up to 64K of ROM using four sockets (U17, U27, U37, and U47). These sockets contain either two 32K by 8-bit ROMs or four 16K by 8-bit ROMs configured as 32K by 16 bits. In addition, 128K of expansion board ROM can be installed on adapter cards and accessed using addresses between 0C0000H and 0DFFFFH.

The AT system board ROM is designed to use the top 64K of the first 1 Mbyte of addressable memory (0F0000H to 0FFFFFH), or the last 64K of the 16-Mbyte protected mode memory space (FF0000H to FFFFFFH). In this way, the system can operate in either the real address mode or the protected virtual address mode using the same ROM BIOS.

The AT system board described here contains 64K of ROM installed in two 32K by 8-bit (U27 and U47). ROM pair U27 and U47 constitute a 32K by 16-bit

Table 4-5. The AT I/O Addresses Decoded by I/O Devices on the System Board and Certain Adapter Cards

Hexadecimal Address	Access Function
0000-001F	8237 DMA controller 1 (U111)
0020-003F	8259 master interrupt controller (U114)
0040-005F	8254 timer (U103)
0060-006F	8042 keyboard controller (U126)
0070-007F	Real-time clock, NMI mask (U117)
0080-009F	74612 DMA page register (U124)
00A0-00BF	8259 interrupt controller (U125)
00C0-00DF	8237 DMA controller 2 (U122)
00F0	Clear 80287 NPX busy (U76)
00F1	Reset 80287 NPX (U76)
00F8-00FF	80287 NPX coprocessor (U76)
01F0-01F8	Fixed disk adapter card
0200-0207	Game I/O adapter
0278-027F	Parallel printer port 2
02F8-02FF	Serial port 2
0300-031F	Prototype card
0360-036F	Reserved
0378-037F	Parallel printer port 1
0380-038F	SDLC, bisynchronous 2
03A0-03AF	Bisynchronous 1
03B0-03BF	MDA adapter card
03C0-03CF	Reserved
03D0-03DF	CGA adapter card
03F0-03F7	Diskette controller
03F8-03FF	Serial port 1
0400-FFFF	Open I/O addresses

module. ROM sockets U17 and U37, which are not used, are assigned to addresses E0000H through EFFFFH. Their protected mode addresses are FE0000H to FEFFFFH.

Short programs that provide an operational interface to the system are permanently stored in U27 and U47. These programs include routines for loading part of the disk-based BIOS down into RAM and for working with displays, printers, floppy and fixed disk drives, and various sizes of memory. ROM also contains code to control the time-of-day clock, the power-up self test, 128 character codes for keyboard/display operations, and disk bootstrap loading of the disk operating system (DOS).

The internal ROM-based power-up self test (POST) includes a series of diagnostics that occur each time power is applied. These tests check the 80286 CPU (U74), the keyboard, the video display adapter card, the floppy and fixed disk-drive interface, and the ROM and RAM. The RAM test contains five different write/read operations. Each memory test writes and then reads and checks a different bit pattern in memory. RAM testing time depends on the configuration of the AT system. A fully populated system board with 512K of RAM and full expansion-slot use will require more time to test during start-up. Restarting the AT system with power already on bypasses the memory-test part of the POST operation and significantly reduces system initialization time.

The ROM BIOS includes software to integrate ROM chips on adapter boards. During POST, BIOS interrupt vectors are copied down into the first part of RAM. Then the BIOS scans for more ROM out on the adapter cards. If found, the adapter-board interrupt vectors are also copied into user-reserved areas of system board RAM. If additional ROM modules are installed (U17 and U37), they are also recognized and integrated into the system during the POST operation.

Fig. 4-12 shows the circuitry associated with the ROM chips installed in the AT system board. Buffered addresses XA1 through XA15 and ROM select circuitry position the ROM modules in the memory space 0F0000H through 0FFFFFH and FF0000H through FFFFFFH. XA16 is used in conjunction with lower chip select ROM signal LCSROM* to produce ROM chip select signals Y0 and Y1 (Y0 for ROMs U17 and U37; Y1 for ROMs U27 and U47). Address bits A17 through A23 are used by PROM U72 and buffer U73 to develop LCSROM*.

Once enabled, address inputs XA1 through XA14 cause a memory byte or word to be read out from a ROM pair onto data bus MD0 through MD7 or MD0 through MD15. These signals are passed to 74ALS245 transceivers U5 and U11. Depending on the size of the data word, data passes through one or both transceivers to 74LS646 transceiver U67 and 74ALS245 transceiver U66 into the 80286 CPU.

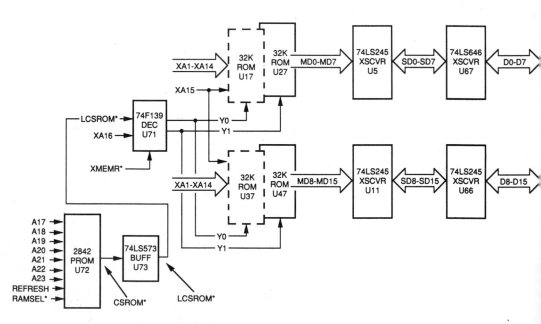

Fig. 4-12. The AT ROM circuitry.

Random-Access Memory (RAM)

Four banks of 128K by 1-bit dynamic RAM chips can be installed in the AT system board, providing up to 512K of system board RAM. An additional 128K can be installed on adapter cards expanding the total system RAM to 640K. Using memory management and the protected mode addressing, over 15 Mbytes of additional memory can be installed on expansion cards.

The first IBM AT personal computers had 64K by 1-bit RAM chips on the system board, so IBM offered a piggy-back version RAM chip where another 64K by 1-bit RAM chip was slipped over the board-mounted RAM, providing 128K by 1-bit in each memory socket. Single 128K by 1-bit dynamic RAM chips later replaced the piggy-back dual 64K by 1-bit versions on the system board.

The dynamic RAM chips on the system board are mounted in four rows, or banks, of nine chips each. The ninth chip is used to store a parity bit associated with each 8-bit word in that row of RAM. All of the RAM is parity checked during readout (ROM is not parity checked). RAM parity checking will be described later.

System board and expansion card RAM can be accessed as 8-bit bytes or 16-bit words. Therefore, Banks 0, 1, 2, and 3 can contain individual bytes or paired bytes of 16-bit words. The key to data size is the instruction decoded by the 80286 CPU (U74). The first bit in the first byte of an instruction defines a word or byte operation. If this bit is 1, then an instruction dealing with 16-bit words is intended. Thus, to move a single byte of information from memory into the CPU requires a MOV instruction whose first byte (of three bytes total in the instruction) is 1 0 1 0 0 0 0 0. Moving a 16-bit word of data requires the first instruction byte to be 1 0 1 0 0 0 0 1. Only the first bit is different.

When the 80286 decodes the instruction (with its accompanying low and high address bytes), it outputs two key signals: address bit 0 (A0), and bus high enable (BHE*). These two signals control transfers over the lower and upper halves of the data bus. Table 4-6 describes the function assumed by the system board for each combination of A0 and BHE*.

Table 4-6. Interpretation of Encoded Outputs on CPU Lines A0 and BHE*

A0	BHE*	Function
0	0	16-bit word transfer
0	1	Byte transfer on D0 through D7
1	0	Byte transfer on D8 through D15
1	1	Reserved

Fig. 4-13 shows the circuitry associated with a RAM read or write. For simplicity, only RAM Bank 0 is shown. Banks 0 and 1 each can handle 8-bit operations. Each ZA1250NL dynamic RAM chip has eight address lines (MA0

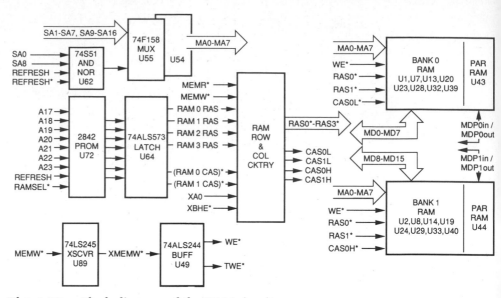

Fig. 4-13. Block diagram of the RAM circuitry.

through MA7), two row address strobes (RASn, RASn + 1), a write enable (WE*), and a column address strobe (CASnL* or CASnH*). Each chip has a single data input line (MDn), and a single data output line (MDn). The signals for RAM banks 0 and 1 will be described. Each bank has separate MD0 through MD7 and MD8 through MD15 input and output data lines. For simplicity, these lines are shown as bidirectional in Fig. 4-13.

Four control lines are used to select and enable each RAM chip—Row Address Strobe 0 and 1 (RAS0*, RAS1*), a low or high bit Column Address Strobe (CAS0L* or CAS0H), and Write Enable (WE*). The active row and column address strobe signals are determined by address bus bits A17 through A23 and the REFRESH and RAMSEL* signals. These nine inputs are applied to a TBP2842N 512-word by 8-bit PROM (U72) and the select outputs from U72 are latched in 74ALS573 latch U64. These outputs are passed through row and column select circuitry to develop the RAS0* through RAS3*, CAS0L*, CAS0H, CAS1L*, and CAS1H* select signals for the RAM banks.

Write enable (WE*) from 74ALS244 buffer U49 controls whether a Bank 0 or 1 read or write operation is intended. When WE* is HIGH, the read mode is selected. An active-low WE* input causes the chip to enter the write mode. TWE* is the write enable for Banks 2 and 3 on a 4-bank board.

Address bits SA0 through SA16 and special refresh signals are used to develop an 8-bit memory address to each byte of RAM. RAM data can be accessed as 8-bit bytes or as 16-bit words. Signals XA0 and XBHE* applied to the RAM row and column circuitry define how the system board memory will be used. XA0 qualifies signals CAS0L* and CAS1L* for 8-bit operation. XBHE* is used to produce the CAS0H* and CAS1H* signals for 16-bit data words.

RAM Memory Refresh

The RAM chips in Banks 0, 1, 2, and 3 are dynamic RAM with logic 1 represented by a tiny electrical charge stored in a memory cell. Since this charge leaks away with time, each memory location must be periodically accessed to restore the charge in cells that are in the logic-high condition. This periodic accessing of memory to restore charge is called "refresh." The dynamic RAM (DRAM) chips in your system must be periodically refreshed.

Each time a DRAM location is read, the same memory cell is accessed in all nine chips associated with a selected bank of memory. All the memory cells in that bank are refreshed together, and memory cells that held a logic high are recharged to a full logic 1 charge. Any memory-access cycle in which a row address strobe signal becomes active will refresh an entire row of memory cell locations. Each dynamic RAM chip is designed so its output is electronically disconnected from the memory data bus until the column strobe signal is applied. Therefore, refresh can occur without ever activating the column output. A simple memory read operation will achieve refresh of the memory cells.

Fig. 4-14 describes the circuitry responsible for periodically refreshing the dynamic RAM on the system board and on adapter cards installed in expansion slots.

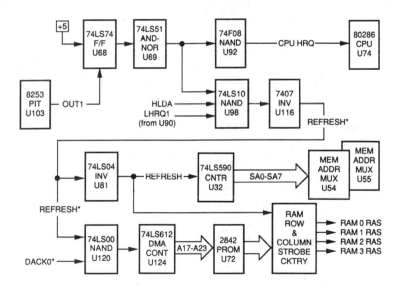

Fig. 4-14. The AT refresh circuitry.

Refresh is accomplished by performing a memory-access cycle at each of the row addresses within a bank of RAM every two to four milliseconds. Each OUT1 from the 8254 interval timer (U103) produces a CPU hold request (CPU HRQ) and a refresh signal (REFRESH*). REFRESH* is inverted and applied to a 74LS590 8-bit binary counter (U32) producing SA0 through SA7. REFRESH* is also NANDed with DACK0* in 74ALS00N NAND gate U120 and applied to 74LS612 DMA controller U124 to generate the upper address bits A17 through A23. The upper address bits are decoded by the TBP2842N 512-word by 8-bit PROM U72. Both REFRESH and the eight PROM outputs are decoded in the RAM row and column strobe circuitry to activate one of the four row address strobe signals. Since OUT1 occurs every 15 microseconds, the memory accesses caused by OUT1 are well within the two to four millisecond (2000 to 4000 microsecond) refresh requirement.

Parity

The IBM AT personal computer contains an error-detection circuit that checks memory data words for accurate storage and retrieval. Each of the four banks of system board RAM includes a ninth chip dedicated to storing a bit corresponding to the parity of each byte of stored data. Every byte that is written into memory is evaluated to determine the number of binary 1s in it. If the count of 1s is an odd number, a 0 parity bit is stored in a special parity RAM chip. If the number of 1s is even, a logic 1 parity bit is stored in the corresponding location in the parity memory chip causing the total (byte plus parity bit) to become odd.

When eight bits of data are read out of a memory bank, the parity bit for that byte is also read out. This data is checked by special circuitry on the system board and compared with the memory data parity bit (MDP) stored in the corresponding location in the parity RAM. If the two parity values (computed and stored) are equal, the data word is accepted by the CPU or coprocessor and system operation continues. However, if the two values differ, a nonmaskable interrupt (NMI) occurs, causing the machine to halt with "PARITY CHECK" printed on the screen.

As shown in Fig. 4-15, the key to memory parity error monitoring is a dedicated 74F280 9-bit odd/even parity generator/checker for each pair of lower byte and upper byte RAM banks. Parity generator/checker U6 handles RAM Banks 0 and 2 while U12 handles Banks 1 and 3. Accesses to the lower byte of a stored data word (Banks 0 and 2) cause U6 to monitor each 8-bit byte and generate a parity bit that is stored in a dedicated parity RAM chip (U43 for Bank 0, U45 for Bank 2). Accesses to the upper byte of a data word (Banks 1 and 3) cause parity generator/checker U12 to produce a parity bit for parity RAM chip U44 or U46.

The circuitry for Bank 0 will be described here. The parity process is the same for all four banks. The even parity output from U6 is used during memory write and read operations. Memory data bits (MD0 through MD7) are copied into U6 at the same time they are applied to RAM Bank 0. Parity generator/checker U6 calculates a parity value for the 8-bit input and produces output MDPin0 that is written into parity RAM U43.

Parity generator/checker U6 requires no clock signal to cause a timed operation. Its output (MDPin0) is always represented. During a write operation,

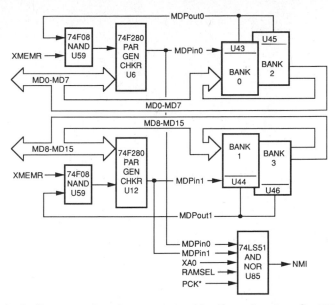

Fig. 4-15. Block diagram of parity generator/checker circuitry for IBM AT.

the memory data parity in bit (MDPin0) from U6 is copied into parity RAM U43. The system is designed to seek odd parity.

During a read operation, eight data bits (MD0 through MD7) and their corresponding parity bit (MDPout) are read from RAM into U6. The active high XMEMR input to NAND U59 enables U59 to pass the MDPout0 bit into U6 for parity checking. If MD0 through MD7 contained an even number of 1s during the write operation, the parity bit that was stored in U43 should be high causing an odd number of 1s in the combined MD0 through MD7 and MDP data. During a read operation, a new parity value is computed using MD0 through MD7 and the stored MDPout0 value. If the new parity value on MDPin0 is low, proper parity checking occurred and the read data matches the write data. The low MDPin0 signal is applied through 74LS51 AND/NOR U85 holding the nonmaskable interrupt (NMI) output of U85 low and indicating proper parity with no memory bit error. However, if an even number of 1s are read into U6 while MDPout0 is low, U6 will produce a high MDPin0 output to U85 indicating detection of a parity error. This results in a nonmaskable interrupt and system halt.

System Configuration and the Real-Time Clock

Jumper J18 on the left side of Fig. 4-3 enables the second 256K of system board installed RAM. In one position, only 256K of RAM can be accessed on the board, and additional system RAM must reside on adapter cards. With J18 in the other position, the system electronics will respond to a full 512K of system board installed RAM.

The switch blocks common to the PC and XT have been replaced in the IBM AT with an MC146818 real-time clock and CMOS configuration RAM (U117). U117 contains 64 bytes of storage. One quarter of this storage is dedicated to maintaining the seconds, minutes, hours, day, month, year, and alarm information for the clock circuitry. The rest of the RAM contains diagnostics, shutdown procedures, and information pertaining to floppy disk, hard disk, coprocessor, memory, and expanded memory information. As shown in Fig. 4-16, U117 is kept energized using a battery backup system connected to J21.

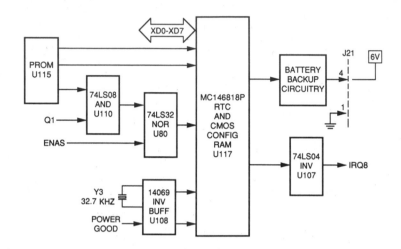

Fig. 4-16. Real-time clock and configuration RAM circuitry.

I/O addresses 070H and 071H provide read and write access to U117. An OUT to location 070H causes the bits on XD0 through XD7 to serve as an address into the RAM. An OUT to 071H copies the byte on XD0 through XD7 into U117 at the location specified by the earlier 070H out command. Table 4-7 describes the memory map of the RAM inside U117.

During system setup, the time, day, month, and year information are stored with the configuration information in U117. Once the configuration has been established and stored in RAM U117, a 6-volt lithium battery keeps the information active even when power to the AT is turned off. When the system is restarted, the POST procedure checks the physical setup on the system board and on the adapter cards and compares the actual configuration with that stored in U117. It also checks the voltage level of the battery itself. If a discrepancy is found, the BIOS displays an error code on the screen and prevents system execution until the discrepancy has been corrected. A dead battery will cause a "161" error-code display. A system configuration discrepancy will also cause a "161" error-code display. Errors in the time and date cause a "163" error code, and a memory-size error results in a "164" error code. If the configuration hasn't changed, BIOS initializes the motherboard and expansion cards based on the configuration values stored in U117 during startup.

Table 4-7. Real-Time Clock and Configuration RAM Address Map.

Hexadecimal Address	Function
00-0D	Real-time clock information
0E	Diagnostic status byte
0F	Shutdown status byte
10	Floppy disk drive A and B type
11	Reserved
12	Fixed disk drives C and D type
13	Reserved
14	Equipment configuration byte
15	Low base memory byte
16	High base memory byte
17	Low expansion memory byte
18	High expansion memory byte
19-2D	Reserved
2E-2F	CMOS checksum
30	Low expansion memory byte
31	High expansion memory byte
32	Data century byte
33	Information flags (set during power-up)
34-3F	Reserved

A 32.7-kHz crystal produces clock ticks through 14069 inverter buffer U108 that update internal timers inside U117. These timers can be read by the 80286 upon demand or during the time-of-day interrupt. Every 55 milliseconds, interval timer U103 generates interrupt request IRQ0 which results in a level 0 timer interrupt (INT 8) to the 80286 CPU. BIOS uses this interrupt to advance a time-of-day clock. INT 8 also maintains a count of interrupts since the power is turned on (used to help establish time of day) and turns the floppy disk-drive motor off after use. A related BIOS interrupt (INT 1A) lets the user read or set the real-time clock, date, and alarm features of U117.

In the meantime, real-time clock U117 generates an IRQ8 interrupt request 1024 times each second (approximately once every millisecond). IRQ8 is recognized by 8259 interrupt controller U125 and results in an interrupt to the 80286 CPU from master interrupt controller U114. This interrupt signals a timeout condition from an alarm clock counter in U117. IRQ8 can also be used as an event timer for special software or hardware functions.

The AT was one of the first computers to use a battery to power the real-time clock (RTC) and configuration RAM. The lithium battery that powers U117 attaches to the rear wall inside the AT system unit as shown in Fig. 4-17. The RTC in U117 requires at least three volts to maintain time and memory configuration. The lithium battery provides a continuous 6 volts to keep the real-time clock and configuration RAM in U117 operating whether the AT system power is on or off. A failure of this battery can cause the AT to function erratically. The clock and calendar may stop, and the formatting and configuration files may shut down

Fig. 4-17. Photograph of the backup battery in the rear of the AT
system unit.

preventing the system from recognizing the disk drives, memory, and printer.
The system will then lock up and refuse to function.

Battery manufacturers point out that the type of backup battery selected
and installed in the AT is important. The lithium thionyl-chloride (TCL) battery is
the best of all the backup batteries available for keeping time and maintaining
system configuration. The operating characteristics of less expensive alkaline
batteries can change as the internal AT temperature rises during operation. This
could cause premature battery failure. The internal heat of the AT has no effect
on the voltage or service life of a lithium TCL battery. Lithium TCL batteries also
contain internal components that safeguard against possible damage due to a
short circuit, inadvertent recharging, or exposure to temperatures above 212° F.

Lithium TCL batteries are not designed to be recharged. Their continuous
operation service life is between 5 and 6 years. By contrast, the service life of an
alkaline battery is slightly less than 3 years. Most personal computers with
battery backup use a lithium battery because of their long shelf life, high cell
voltage, high capacity, extremely long service life, and safety.

However, there are important safety considerations to remember regarding
the lithium TCL battery in the AT. These batteries should not be stored loosely or
in an unventilated area. The contacts on the battery should not be shorted.
Shorting causes excessive heat inside the battery resulting in pressure buildup
and possible case rupture. This is why safety glasses should be worn when
handling these batteries. Even a discharged battery may contain significant
unused energy. In addition, lithium TCL batteries should NEVER be charged.
These facts are not meant to frighten you. Used properly, backup batteries are
safe and will provide years of reliable power. But, like a car battery, they can be
misused.

Keyboard

Chapter 1 provided an overview of the new keyboards developed for the IBM AT. In this section, you will learn how the keyboard interfaces with the system board to produce characters and special symbols on the display screen.

The keyboard is just another I/O device to the AT. It appears as a data bus, with an interrupt request and two I/O addresses. However, there are two complex circuits associated with the keyboard—one on the system board and one out in the keyboard unit. Each circuit contains its own microprocessor (there are actually three microprocessors in the AT although the microprocessor in the keyboard unit is technically a single-chip microcomputer). Each of the keyboard processors is configured as a controller for a specific part of the keyboard electronics.

The keyboard circuitry is shown in Fig. 4-18. A capacitive key matrix is connected through sense amplifier Z1 to the keyboard controller and scan code buffer microcomputer (M5). Besides the arithmetic logic and control units, M5 contains a 2048 by 8 ROM, a 128 by 8 RAM, and its own timer/counter and clock. M5 is preprogrammed to function in the keyboard environment. It scans the key matrix producing a serial scan code for the make or break condition due to operator action. The scan code is transmitted to an 8042 8-bit slave micro-controller (U126) on the system board. M5 can also send status information to the system board. This data/status transfer occurs over a bidirectional data line that is one of the five wires in the coiled cable connecting the AT system unit and the keyboard.

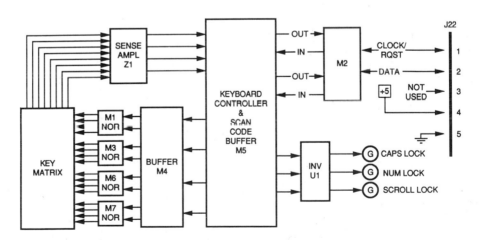

Fig. 4-18. The keyboard circuitry.

Data commands can also be sent from the microcontroller on the system board to M5 in the keyboard over the same serial line. Data is clocked each way using a timed signal generated in the keyboard. The J22 keyboard connector has two primary signal paths—clock and data. One of the five pins on keyboard connector J22 is not used by the system board.

The AT keyboard also contains three light-emitting diodes (LEDs) that are controlled by M5. These LEDs indicate when the keyboard letters are set to all caps (Caps Lock), when the numeric keypad has been switched from cursor control keys to numbers (Num Lock), and when the user or a software program locks the scrolling feature of the machine (Scroll Lock). Each LED is tested during power-up.

The AT keyboard is not compatible with the IBM PC and XT. Its design handles keypress information differently than the PC and XT keyboards. The keyboard detects all key actions and generates scan codes in the correct sequence for each key activated. A 16-character first-in/first-out (FIFO) buffer in M5 stacks key activation codes. The first code entered is the first code read out and sent across the keyboard cable. If the buffer fills and another key is pressed before a code can be withdrawn, an overrun code (00H) is generated. Additional key actions will not be recognized until the buffer starts to unload.

The keys produce a unique 8-bit scan code on both key closure (make) and key release (break). The keys are typematic in that the scan code for a key closure is continuously generated while key contact is being made. Both a 0.25-second and a 1.25-second delay between first keypress and repeat action can be programmed. The repeat rate (typematic rate) is also programmable between 2 and 30 characters per second. On start-up, the default delay is 0.5 second and the default repeat rate is 10 characters per second.

When power is first applied, keyboard controller M5 causes a keyboard logic reset. Then a program in the M5 ROM conducts a checksum of the ROM (adds up all the bytes in each location and compares the result with a stored value). A check is made for stuck keys and the program momentarily turns on and checks all three keyboard LEDs. After this, M5 sends a system-check completion signal to the system board indicating that it is ready to proceed. The keyboard acknowledges system board commands by pulling both the data and clock lines high for 500 microseconds.

Fig. 4-19 shows the system board circuitry associated with the AT keyboard. The 8042 keyboard controller (U126) plays a critical role in keyboard data recognition and operation. Both M5 in the keyboard and U126 on the system board communicate using the bidirectional clock and data lines.

Keyboard controller U126 appears as I/O addresses 60H and 64H to the 80286 CPU. When serial data is passed to U126 from the keyboard, it is translated into ASCII code by the 80286 CPU and passed to the display adapter or printer adapter for visual output.

Two switches are connected to keyboard controller U126. Switch SW1 selects color or monochrome as the display being used. The other switch can provide keyboard security by preventing keyboard entries from being recognized by the CPU. When the keyboard security switch is placed in the locked

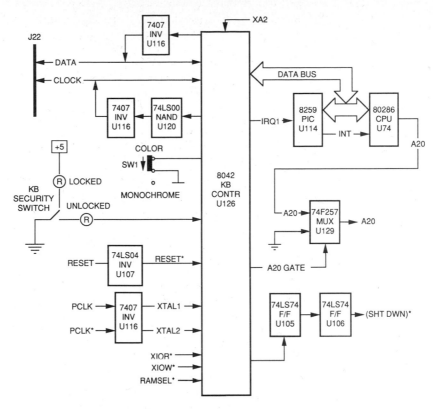

Fig. 4-19. System board interface to the AT keyboard.

position, key actions are allowed but keyboard controller U126 tests each data code to determine if it is a command response or a scan code. The command responses are placed in the U126 output buffer, but all scan codes are ignored.

A legitimate keyboard operation is recognized by the 80286 CPU after an IRQ1 interrupt request reaches the 8259 interrupt controller (U114). Each time an IRQ1 occurs, the BIOS causes U74 to read the U126 output buffer over the data bus.

Each key has a unique 8-bit scan code assigned to it representing the make (or break) condition for that key. Each scan code is combined with start, stop, and odd parity information before being transferred to the system board. The 11-bit frame of keyboard information is shown in Fig. 4-20.

START BIT	8-BIT SCAN CODE	PARITY BIT	STOP BIT

Fig. 4-20. Structure of an 11-bit frame of data.

Before sending data to the system board, the keyboard circuitry checks the clock line to see if U126 is trying to communicate. If not, M5 begins clocking the

11-bit serial data packet containing the scan code through the keyboard cable into the 8042 keyboard controller (U126). U126 strips off the start and stop bits, checks the parity, and reformats the serial scan code into an 8-bit wide, parallel system scan code. When conversion is complete, U126 generates IRQ1 causing the 80286 CPU to read U126 and convert the system scan code into an 8-bit ASCII code for the character selected. An ASCII conversion chart can be found in Appendix B.

The system scan code and its ASCII conversion are stored in two consecutive bytes of system board RAM with the high byte representing the scan code. A scan code of all zeroes means that a noncharacter key was pressed. BIOS reads the status of the data to determine if a special key such as Ctrl, Alt, or Shift was depressed. The low byte in RAM is zero if a special key has been pressed. If so, the ROM BIOS software takes specific action based on the key or keys pressed. The ASCII code for a character or symbol is sent to the display or printer adapter for conversion into dot-streams that produce the visual representation of the character.

Some keys, or key combinations, directly affect the ROM BIOS. Holding the Alt key down while typing three digits on the numeric keypad directly enters an ASCII character code from the keyboard into RAM. This is one way to generate graphic characters. Depressing Shift and PrtSc at the same time causes all the characters on the display screen to be sent to a printer.

Video Display

The PC family was designed with expansion slots to permit a wide variety of I/O devices to work with these microcomputers. Each major I/O device—display monitor, disk drive, and printer—can only be accessed and driven by the system board through adapter boards plugged into these expansion slots.

When the AT was introduced in 1984, IBM also introduced products that supported the enhanced graphics adapter (EGA) and professional graphics adapter (PGA) color display interface standards. EGA quickly became the most widely accepted and used display interface for the PC family. The EGA display can be used with the PC, XT, and AT computers.

Video display interfacing for the PC, XT, and AT is described in Chapter 5. Here you will find information on the MDA, CGA, and EGA adapter boards including a description of how characters and graphic shapes are produced on the display monitor screen.

Disk-Drive Interface

Magnetic disks drives and disk media were described earlier in Chapter 1. This section deals with the disk drives used with the AT and how they differ with those used on the PC and XT. With the introduction of the AT came the IBM blessing for microcomputer use of the mainframe computer acronym "DASD." Just when users became accustomed to the terms hard disk and fixed disk, the AT documentation began describing the same disk as a *direct access storage device* (DASD). Any storage device that can be directly accessed by the CPU using the address and data lines on the expansion bus can be called a DASD device. Both hard disk and floppy disk drives are DASD devices.

Each AT model comes with at least one 1.2-Mbyte, high-capacity, 5.25-inch floppy disk drive installed. The second disk-drive space is taken up with a standard 5.25-inch 360K double-sided disk drive or a 20-Mbyte or 30-Mbyte hard disk drive. If an IBM 360K floppy disk drive is installed, it can be distinguished from the IBM high-capacity floppy disk drive by the asterisk on the lower right front panel of the 360K drive.

The combination fixed and floppy disk drive adapter card used in the AT can support two floppy disk drives and two hard disk drives. However, the system unit can only hold three disk drives internally. Therefore, a "stuffed" AT will contain two floppy drives and a hard disk drive or two hard disk drives and a single floppy drive.

If a standard 360K floppy disk drive is installed, the operator should be aware that the design of the high-capacity 1.2-Mbyte floppy disk drive is different than that of the standard 360K double-density disk drive. The 1.2-Mbyte high-capacity disk drive uses newer technology and is designed to store over three times the information.

To achieve this higher storage capacity, a new disk media was designed with a harder oxide coating instead of the plain iron oxide of earlier disks. Since the high-density disk can store a binary message in less area, 96 tracks per inch are possible instead of the 40 tracks per inch common to standard drives. Higher current must flow through the write head to store this information, and the disk spins at a faster rate (360 rpm). All these factors—the improved disk surface, the faster spin rate, and the higher write current requirement, coupled with a smaller write/read head, enables more information to be stored in less space. This poses potential problems when users want to mix disk media.

The high-capacity drive can read or write 1.2-Mbyte high-capacity disks, 320/360K double-sided, and the older 160/180K single-sided disks. But disks written using an AT high-capacity drive cannot be reliably used in standard capacity drives (such as in the PC or XT). The best rule of thumb is to use the disk media designed for the type of drive installed. Use standard media in a standard drive and high-capacity media in a high-capacity drive.

The standard AT fixed disk rotates at 3600 rpm. The drive formats the disks to 17 sectors per track with a read/write head for each side of a platter. The number of track cylinders for the standard AT drive has been increased to 615 cylinders providing a storage capability of 20 Mbytes. The IBM AT is also available with a 30-Mbyte hard disk drive.

Fixed Disk and Floppy Disk Adapter

The AT system includes a combination fixed disk and floppy disk adapter card that controls both the 5.25-inch floppy drives and fixed disk drives. This adapter allows concurrent operations of one floppy disk drive and one fixed disk drive. Both the 36-pin and 62-pin expansion slot connectors are used by the combined floppy/hard disk adapter card. Ten address bits are used with IOR and IOW to access the disk data. The disk drive adapter card is a set of unique addresses to the AT as shown in Table 4-8. A jumper on the card selects one of two I/O address ranges, providing the capability to install two cards in the same system. However, BIOS only supports the first set of addresses.

Table 4-8.　I/O Address Map for the Combination Fixed Disk and Floppy Disk Adapter card

Primary Address	Secondary Address	I/O Read	I/O Write
3F2	372	Floppy Disk Section	Digital output register
3F4	374	Main status register	Main status register
3F5	375	Diskette data register	Diskette data register
3F6	376		Fixed disk register
3F7	377	Digital input register	Diskette control register
1F0	170	Data register	Data register
1F1	171	Error register	Write precomp
1F2	172	Sector count	Sector count
1F3	173	Sector number	Sector number
1F4	174	Cylinder low	Cylinder low
1F5	175	Cylinder high	Cylinder high
1F6	176	Drive/head register	Drive/head register
1F7	177	Status register	Command register

Floppy disk transfers are achieved using DMA signals DRQ2 and DACK2 and an interrupt signal (IRQ6). Fixed disk transfers are direct and use interrupt IRQ14. The system data bus connects through several transceivers to a 512-byte sector buffer RAM as shown in Fig. 4-21. During fixed disk-drive data transfers, RAM ICs U53 and U54 are accessed at 2 Mbytes per second using 80286 CPU string instructions. A portion of the address bus and IOW* and IOR* are passed through 74LS367 buffer U46 into one of several programmable array logic (PAL) devices on the card. PAL U19 generates a clock signal that steps 74LS393 counter U52. The RA3 output of U52 becomes the clock input to counter U62. Together, these two counters produce the RAM addresses that access U53 and U54.

Every adapter board uses a key controller to handle data and control signals between the adapter card and the peripheral device. The combination fixed and floppy disk-drive adapter card has one controller for floppy disk drives and another controller for fixed disk drives.

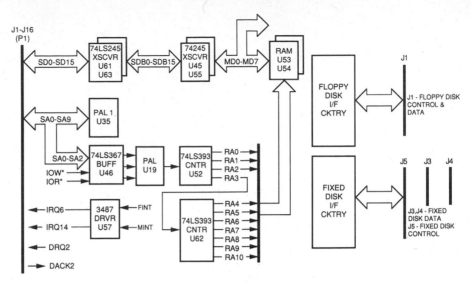

Fig. 4-21. Block diagram of fixed and floppy disk-drive adapter.

Floppy Disk-Drive Interface

The combination fixed and floppy adapter can support 160K, 320K, and 1.2-Mbyte floppy disk drives. The disk drive parameters are programmable during system start-up. The AT uses DMA transfer to move floppy disk data just as it does in the PC and XT. However, IBM designed the AT system with 5-MHz DMA controllers. Since the controllers cannot run at the 6-MHz system clock rate and because it's difficult to get clock rates that are not an integer division of a system clock rate, the AT is limited to a DMA rate of 3 MHz. Because of this limitation, the AT transfers data in 1.66 microseconds while the XT transfers the same data in only 1.05 microseconds.

Fig. 4-22 shows the floppy disk interface on the combination adapter. The 8 bits of the system data bus connect directly to a 765 floppy disk controller (U30). This is the same type floppy disk controller used in the PC and XT systems. DMA request (DRQ2) and DACK2 are associated with floppy disk transfers. An interrupt signal notifies the system board that CPU action is required. During a write operation, floppy disk controller U30 generates the control signals and serial data stream that are passed to floppy disk-drive connector J1.

During a read operation, the synchronization clock and data information are detected by the disk drive read heads and passed serially through connector J1 as READ DATA to controller U29 and into a 74LS221 multivibrator (U38). The output of U38 (FFD DATA) is passed back into FDC U30 for conversion from serial to parallel data and eventual transmission to the system unit. The floppy disk interrupt signal (FINT) from U30 is passed through MC3487 driver U57 (Fig. 4-21) onto the expansion bus and back to the AT system board as IRQ6.

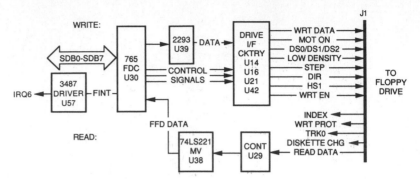

Fig. 4-22. Floppy disk-drive interface circuitry.

Hard (Fixed) Disk Interface

The construction and operation of a hard disk drive was covered in Chapter 1. This section focuses on the 20-Mbyte hard disk drive that is standard in some models of the AT. The internal 20-Mbyte hard disk drive operates much like the 10-Mbyte drive in the XT except it has twice as many tracks, and DMA is not used in the AT fixed disk interface. The AT system board BIOS has a parameter table allowing interface to 14 different hard disk types ranging from 10.6 Mbyte up to 117.5 Mbyte. The 20-Mbyte hard disk is standard.

The key component in the hard disk circuitry is hard disk controller U18 shown in Fig. 4-23. U18 causes the fixed disk interface (U24) to convert the 8-bit memory data bus (MD0 through MD7) into a serial data stream that is passed through PAL2 U19 and IC 9638 U5 to produce positive and negative modified frequency modulation (MFM) write data signals for the fixed drive selected. MFM was discussed in Chapter 3.

During a read operation, serial MFM data is sensed on the disk surface and converted to a digital pulse stream. The digital pulse stream is passed from the disk-drive unit into the adapter card where it is checked for errors and reformatted into parallel 8-bit data words. Instead of DMA data transfer, the fixed disk controller sends and receives data through a 512-byte sector buffer that is accessible to the 80286 CPU as a 16-bit device. Data transfer is controlled by the CPU. When the sector buffer on the adapter card is full or empty, the controller interrupts the 80286 CPU (IRQ14). The BIOS interrupt handler then uses programmed I/O instructions to read or write data to or from memory at 2 megabytes per second. Even without DMA, this is approximately twice the transfer rate of the XT.

The read operation begins with a command from the system board. The information stored on a disk track is detected by the appropriate read head and transferred from the disk drive unit to the adapter card as positive and negative MFM read data. This data enters operational amplifier U13 where it is converted into a digital signal and passed to hard disk controller U12. U12 generates a serial sequence of error checked/corrected 8-bit data words that are passed through

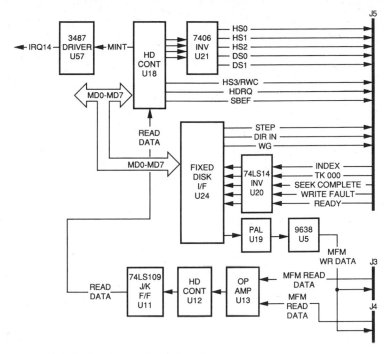

Fig. 4-23. Hard disk-drive interface circuitry.

flip-flop U11 into hard disk controller U18 as READ DATA. U18 converts these serial words into parallel 8-bits words and places them on memory data bus MD0 through MD7 for transmission back to the system board.

System Start-Up

You can start an AT from a cold, powered-down condition by switching the power on, or you can restart the system from an operating condition by causing a system reset to occur. A "cold boot" occurs when you first apply power to a deenergized computer. A "warm start" occurs when you simultaneously depress the Ctrl, Alt, and Del keys on an energized machine. The cold boot begins with a deenergized system—nothing operating. With a warm start, system board power is present and the initial boot-up tests have already been successfully performed at least once. All you want to do is reset the system so you can start from a known condition and run an application program.

When power is first applied during a cold boot, electrical power is applied to the motherboard causing the system clock to begin pulsing through the circuitry. The 80286 CPU accesses BIOS ROMs U27 and U47 and begins running a power-on self test (POST). During the POST diagnostic process, major system components are tested and the hardware is initialized to a known condition, ready to accept and respond to the operator keyboard commands. This process is completed when the BIOS loads the boot record stored on Track 0, Sector 1 of the disk drive. This bootstrap program loads into RAM and then pulls itself up to full readiness (the term bootstrap or "boot" refers to the computer pulling itself up by its own bootstrap). As mentioned before, the BIOS lets the hardware and software communicate. In conjunction with DOS, the BIOS also controls how the I/O will work and how the system board and CPU will communicate with the outside world (display, keyboard, and disk drives). Once boot-up has occurred, the control of the system is passed to the operation for command.

The start-up process for the AT is similar to that for the PC and XT. However, the enhanced power of the AT causes this process to be more complex and involved. The faster AT system clock causes the power-up cycle to occur with little apparent overhead time.

Software Structure

The physical hardware is important in any computer system, but it's of little use if it can't do functional work. A computer system is not complete without software. It takes software to make a computer generate a letter, to print a spreadsheet, or draw an image on the screen.

Three types of software programs can run in an IBM AT system—a low-level hardware operating system called BIOS, a disk operating system called DOS, and high-level languages such as BASIC, C, Pascal, FORTRAN, and others. Originally, a hardware operating system was called a system monitor because it monitored and controlled all the basic functions in the circuitry of a microcomputer. In the PC family, this monitor is called a basic I/O system (BIOS). BIOS gets the computer running the moment power is applied. It loads the boot-up program from the disk and begins the bootstrap process causing the AT to start up in a known condition. BIOS also tests the primary system components and lets the operator communicate with the computer. BIOS is what causes your keystrokes to be recognized and your commands to be accepted and acted upon.

Part of the IBM AT BIOS routines are stored in two 32K ROMs (U27 and U47). Programs that are permanently written into ROM are called "firmware." ROM BIOS is a firmware. Another part of BIOS is stored on the system disk. It is loaded into RAM during start-up.

The second type of software is the disk operating system (DOS). DOS is an extension of BIOS, but it's much more. It's a collection of utility programs that work with BIOS to handle interface communications and manage data in the AT system. Together, BIOS and DOS optimize the interface between the 80286 CPU and user programs. While BIOS keeps everything straight and responsive, directing the flow of information between keyboard, screen, memory, and mass storage, DOS contains more than 40 commands that access file management programs. These file management tools let you format disks, copy, erase, and rename files, generate a directory, and perform a myriad of other functions related to display and the mass storage interface. For example, it's DOS that creates the track and sector signature of the disk media used with the computer.

DOS is contained in three programs that are loaded into the AT system board RAM each time you conduct a boot-up process. First to be loaded by the boot record program on the hard disk is IBMBIO.COM. This program contains the interface routines between the high-level DOS functions and the low-level BIOS functions. It checks and initializes the display, keyboard, and disk drives. IBMBIO.COM also sets some interrupt vectors. Next, IBMDOS.COM is loaded. This program contains DOS itself. As IBMDOS.COM is first loaded into RAM, it sets up DOS interrupts and then invokes IBMBIO.COM to load the third DOS-related program—COMMAND.COM. COMMAND.COM is a command processor that provides a user interface with DOS. It generates the A prompt and enables recognition of special key-combinations such as Ctrl-Break (^C). While BIOS gives you low-level access to the display, keyboard, and disk drives (you can physically address the controllers in each peripheral), DOS is more convenient and easier to understand by nontechnical system users.

With the introduction of the AT in 1984, IBM also introduced PC-DOS version 3.0. This DOS version gave the AT the ability to use a 1.2-Mbyte high-capacity disk drive. It also provided an ability to recover "erased" data. In 1985, DOS 3.1 was introduced adding networking, file sharing, and data locking capability. Then in July 1988, IBM introduced DOS 4.0, taking a major step forward in user-to-computer interface. DOS 4.0 replaced the A command line with a menu screen and added cursor control using a mouse or the keyboard. More importantly, DOS 4.0 overcame the 640K limitation of usable RAM imposed by earlier versions of the operating system. Prior to DOS 4.0, users could only load and run application programs that required less than 640K of system memory. After loading earlier versions of DOS and then an application program, many users found little memory left for results and scratch-pad calculations. DOS 4.0 supports the Lotus/Intel/Microsoft (LIM) Expanded Memory Specification (EMS) allowing application programs access of up to 16 Mbytes of RAM.

Another enhancement provided by DOS 4.0 is the ability to use and recognize hard disk drives larger than 32 Mbytes. Earlier DOS versions could only support 32 Mbytes. This meant that a 40-Mbyte hard disk drive had to be partitioned into at least two segments (for example, two 20-Mbyte segments) so the full 40 Mbytes could be used. DOS 4.0 fixed all of this. There are those who insist that DOS 4.0 is the stepping stone to IBM's OS/2 Presentation Manager with its Microsoft Windows flavor. DOS 4.0 comes on five 360K diskettes and contains about 84 files. Now, rather than just booting up DOS as with earlier versions, you must install DOS 4.0. IBM threw a wrench in the machinery by constraining the hard disk drive environment to PC-DOS (not MS-DOS). When loaded on a hard disk, DOS 4.0 takes up about 1 Mbyte of storage.

With BIOS and DOS (initially 3.0) provided with the AT, all that remains to run your own or commercial program code is a high-level programming language. This third type of software is not provided by IBM. You must purchase it separately. Programming languages let you generate custom software code using near-English statements. The PC and XT computers included a BASIC interpreter stored in ROM, but the AT does not include either an interpretive or a compiler high-level programming language. You can purchase compiler BASIC, COBOL, APL, FORTRAN, or Pascal at additional cost. With these compiled languages, the entire source code listing is converted into executable object code instructions that can be readily recognized and implemented by the CPU.

Many companies sell commercial application programs written using these high-level languages. Examples include Word from Microsoft Corporation, Page Maker from Aldus Corporation, and WordStar from MicroPro, and others.

The key point to remember is that when you think of a computer system, think of it as a combination of hardware, software, and firmware. It takes all three parts to build a fully functional IBM AT system.

Summary

Chapter 4 provided a detailed description of the operation of the IBM AT computer system. The information presented in this chapter helps you partition the AT personal computer into simple building blocks for failure analysis. As you recognized by studying Chapter 4, each building block can be analyzed and then connected to the others to form the complete AT system. By knowing how the computer and software interact and function, you are able to quickly recognize and isolate trouble symptoms to a single stage in one of the building block circuits.

Questions for Review and Discussion

1. Describe the major differences between the IBM AT and the IBM XT personal computers.

2. When the letter "A" is pressed, describe how the AT converts the keyboard signal into an ASCII character that is sent to the video display adapter card.

3. What happens on the system board when an IRQ1 signal is received?

4. How does the addressable memory in the AT relate to the mass storage memory on the floppy disk drive?

5. What causes the clock signal to begin pulsing on the clock input of the 80286 CPU, U74?

6. Describe the different clock frequencies used in the AT.

7. How does the AT computer determine what size RAM is installed?

8. What is the function of the key lock on the front of the AT?

9. Which interrupt request is related to the hard disk drive?

10. Why can't the AT keyboard be used with the PC and XT personal computers?

5

Display Monitors and Adapters

The computer communicates with the operator by producing visible characters and shapes on an illuminated screen. Video signals are generated by the computer and passed to a display unit that converts these signals into tiny points of light on a screen.

The design of the IBM PC, XT, and AT system boards is such that all video signals are produced on expansion cards plugged into one or more slots. Signals available on the system board's expansion bus provide all the information and control necessary for software to generate character or graphics information that can be read and interpreted by an installed video adapter card. The video card receives the information and causes the connected display monitor to produce the correct alphanumeric character or graphic shape on the screen.

Video Signals

Three types of video signals can be produced by video adapter cards plugged into expansion slots in the PC, XT, or AT system board. One is NTSC (National Television Systems Committee) composite video comprised of horizontal and vertical synchronization signals combined with video information. For a color display, the composite signal includes color information. A second type of video signal is a radio frequency (rf) signal that can drive a standard television receiver. The third type signal is comprised of discrete video and synchronization signals that directly drive a special IBM display monitor. The monochrome digital signal, often referred to as a TTL signal, is the only signal produced by a monochrome adapter card. The color/graphics adapter card provides three video outputs—a direct drive digital RGB color signal at a 9-pin connector, a composite video signal at an RCA connector, and a composite video signal suitable for driving an rf modulator. All three signals will be described.

NTSC Composite Video

When standard broadcast television was in its infancy, government and industry teams worked hard to establish standard ways to transmit and receive video picture information. RCA and the National Television Systems Committee (NTSC) jointly developed a set of video standards in the mid-1950s. These video standards defined the way video information should be formatted for broadcast. The standards carry the initials of the developing government team (NTSC). The committee's goal was to pack all the necessary picture information into a single channel for use over a single wire.

The NTSC signal is a composite signal composed of video information (B&W or color), and the horizontal and vertical drive (H and V sync) signals to control where the video will be displayed on the screen. This composite video signal is combined into a simple 2-wire (signal and ground) RCA-type phono connector.

For color graphics, the composite NTSC signal is a mixture of red, green, and blue colors (RGB), luminance, and the H and V sync signals. The combining of this information into a single signal reduces the detail possible in a video image display. This limitation becomes critical when displaying color.

In the video display unit, the various components of the combined NTSC signal are stripped off and routed to appropriate circuitry to produce the screen display. This composite signal is analog (of varying amplitude) as opposed to digital with only two discrete conditions (binary high or low). Analog video has an almost infinite number of possible color combinations including shading by gradually varying the proportions of red, green, and blue.

One disadvantage of composite video is that the NTSC standard was designed to operate within a narrow frequency range (bandwidth). Modern communications systems crowd the available frequency bands, so the 4.5-MHz NTSC bandwidth does not allow enough resolution to display color characters well. However, it is satisfactory for black-and-white text and graphic shapes such as TV and VCR images.

RF-Modulated Signal

An rf modulator connection is provided on the color/graphics card. The rf modulator converts the video display adapter signals into frequencies compatible with standard television channels 3 or 4. If you've ever seen a computer using a TV for the display, you'll know why rf modulators are only used for low-resolution computer displays and VCRs. They simply cannot produce clear characters in an 80 column line.

Direct Drive Video

The best way to produce sharp, clear text and graphics is by developing and sending each major video signal component separately to the display unit as *direct drive video*. A direct drive monitor is similar to a television receiver except that it does not have a tuner or IF section. Because the IBM PC, XT, and AT computers have built-in speakers, the monitors usually do not include provisions for audio input. In direct drive video systems, separate wires (lines) carry the color (B&W or RGB), intensity, and horizontal and vertical synchronization signals. More wires or conductors are required, but the quality of the display is dramatically improved.

Since a computer is a digital machine, direct drive video data is usually digital. The number of bits used to specify color information determines the color palette available. If only R, G, and B are available, eight combinations (eight colors) are possible. Add an intensity bit (I) to the signals available and 16 colors are possible.

Each of the digitally generated colors is completely present or absent at any particular point on the screen. There are no in-betweens such as with analog direct drive video displays having infinite color-intensity combinations. However, direct drive digital displays can produce higher-resolution color than can NTSC or rf-modulated composite display monitors.

Screen Image Generation

A video screen image is composed of thousands of tiny picture elements (pixels) arranged in neat rows and columns. Each row is called a *raster line* and each column position in a raster line is called a *pixel* or *dot*.

Each type of display unit (monitor or television) contains a cathode ray tube (CRT). The face of the CRT is what you observe when you look at the display screen. The inside of the CRT screen is coated with a phosphor material that glows brightly when struck by high-intensity electron beams. A metal sheet called a *shadow mask* perforated with thousands of tiny holes is located just behind the phosphor screen of the CRT. The shadow mask defines the resolution of the display. Another way to relate resolution is by the number of dots on a horizontal screen line.

A stream of electrons is produced in the narrow neck area (gun) of the CRT as shown in Fig. 5-1. This beam passes through a set of magnetic beam deflection fields in the neck of the CRT. Electrical signals control the strength of the magnetic fields to direct the beam toward a specific spot on the phosphor screen. Each beam of electrons scans across the screen under control of horizontal and vertical drive signals that alter the magnetic fields surrounding the beam. As it is moved, the beam is turned on or off depending on which pixel or dot on the screen is to be illuminated.

As the electron beam passes through holes in the shadow mask it strikes a dot area on the phosphor screen causing the dot to glow. The areas that are made to glow define an image that we observe from the other side (outside) of the CRT. Only certain phosphor pixel positions are made to glow. In a color

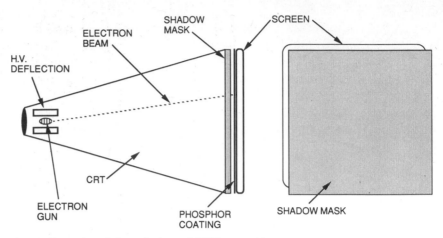

Fig. 5-1. Functional description of CRT operation.

display, three CRT *guns* produce three beams of electrons. The screen is comprised of *triads* (groupings of three) of red, green, and blue phosphor dots. Each dot in the triad glows a different color (red, green, or blue) when struck by an electron beam. The number of dots a display monitor can generate on a screen is critical to the amount of detail that can be seen on the screen.

The spacing of holes in the shadow mask determines the degree of possible image detail or resolution. This spacing is called *dot pitch*. Three dot pitch classes are used in color displays as shown in Table 5-1.

Table 5-1. Dot Size Determines Quality of Displayed Image

Class of Display	Dot Pitch
Standard television	.62 mm or larger
General-purpose monitor	.40 to .62 mm
High-resolution monitor	.40 mm and smaller

As a beam moves across the screen, its intensity may increase momentarily as it passes over specific pixel positions causing the dots to illuminate brightly. Upon reaching one side of the screen, the electron beam is turned off and is retraced back to its original column and then the horizontal scan is repeated. A second control signal is applied to the vertical circuitry to move the beam down one row (raster line). Therefore, the beam is moved across the CRT by a horizontal sweep signal, blanked out during retrace, and then shifted down a raster line by the vertical sweep signal. When the last row has been traced, the beam is blanked and returned to the upper left corner of the display area and then the scan process is repeated.

The dots of varying intensities form patterns on the screen. Since the screen is divided into dots, the activation of a pattern of dots produces characters and graphics shapes. The smaller and closer the dots, the greater the image detail that is possible. A 12-inch (diagonal) color monitor that is rated at 640 dots is typically 9.5 inches (240 mm) wide. If each character requires 8 dots and 80 columns of text are to be displayed, a maximum dot pitch of 0.375 mm (240/640) is required. This is why a high-resolution monitor is required to display 80 sharp, crisp characters on the screen. While our discussion will concentrate on screen displays up to 640 dots wide, current state-of-the-art monitors can have up to 8192 by 8192 dot pixels on the screen. This is ultrahigh resolution.

The pattern of dot intensity is determined by a sequence of binary values generated within the video adapter card plugged into the system board. These binary values are synchronized to the horizontal and vertical sweep frequencies of the display monitor. Each logic high in the video dot pattern causes a particular pixel position on the inside of the CRT phosphor screen to be illuminated by a high intensity electron beam.

The number of raster lines and the number of dot pixels on each raster line define the resolution of the display. The more raster lines and the more pixels in each raster, the higher the resolution. Horizontal resolution is defined as the number of dots (pixels) that can be displayed on a single raster line. Vertical resolution describes the number of visible raster lines per picture. Thus a 640 by 200 display mode would have a horizontal resolution of 640 pixels and a vertical resolution of 200 lines. The generation of color video works the same way as monochrome except that a monochrome monitor uses a single electron beam, while a color monitor requires three electron beams and a phosphor screen coated with a pattern of three color dots arranged in a three-pixel (triad) configuration. One of the three dots glows red when hit by an electron beam, another dot glows green, and the third dot glows blue. Combining these three primary colors produces the myriad of other available colors.

The alphanumeric characters or graphic shapes produced on the monitor screen are represented by closely spaced dot patterns that are drawn one raster line at a time. Characters are produced in a fixed matrix pattern within the dot array of the complete screen as shown in Fig. 5-2. The label "Cn" represents a screen character. Thus, in the example in Fig. 5-2, "C3" is the third character position at the top left of the screen and uses 14 raster lines of pixels. In this figure, R0 = 97 is the total character dot arrays provided, R1 = 80 is the number of characters displayed horizontally, and so on, as shown.

The IBM monochrome display produces a 7 by 9 dot matrix character contained within a 9 by 14 character box as shown in Fig. 5-3. The extra raster lines and columns of dots allow room for ascenders, descenders, and for spacing between characters and lines. To provide time for the horizontal retrace, 97 nine-dot sequences of data are sent to the display unit. Each nine-dot packet represents one raster line of the 14 needed to define a character box.

In the 7 by 9 dot matrix configuration, two blank raster lines appear above the character and three blank raster lines appear below the character. In addition, the first and last dot column of each character box is blank. This provides good separation between characters. The color/graphics adapter pro-

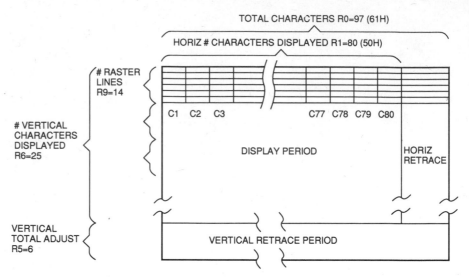

Fig. 5-2. The display screen is comprised of raster lines and pixels.

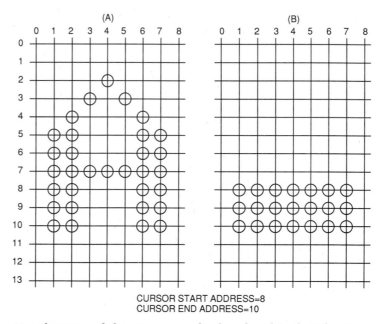

CURSOR START ADDRESS=8
CURSOR END ADDRESS=10

Fig. 5-3. How letters and the cursor are displayed within the 7 by 9 area of the 9 by 14 dot matrix.

duces characters in either a 7 by 7 or 5 by 7 dot pattern within an 8 by 8 box. The enhanced graphics adapter uses an 8 by 14 character box.

As previously mentioned, all the video signals required by the display monitor are produced by plug-in video display adapter boards. Address, data, and control signals are passed from the system board onto the expansion bus and into one of many types of video display adapter boards designed for the IBM PC family.

IBM Display Adapters

The four display adapters for the IBM PC family were described briefly in Chapter 1. These display adapters include MDA, CGA, EGA, and PGA. Although only one video adapter board is required to get video output from your computer, you can use a color display adapter and a monochrome display adapter in the same system to provide flexibility. As described in Chapter 1, a number of display boards are produced by IBM. Non-IBM display boards are also available including the popular Hercules adapters. However, since all display adapter boards operate in a similar fashion, only the Monochrome Display Adapter, the Color/Graphics Adapter, and the Enhanced Graphics Adapter will be discussed in this text. The concepts described for these three boards will help you understand the video adapter cards provided by other companies.

The IBM Monochrome Display Adapter can produce text-only display with 350 raster lines of vertical resolution and 720 dots of horizontal resolution. However, the IBM Color/Graphics Adapter can produce 200 raster lines of vertical resolution and 640 dots of horizontal resolution for both text and graphics. These pixel specifications define a screen display area of 720 dots by 350 raster lines or 640 dots by 200 raster lines in size. Each of these displays can easily fit within the 525 lines of horizontal resolution in a standard television receiver.

The horizontal and vertical sweep circuits in the display monitor are controlled by synchronization signals that cause the CRT electron beam to scan across and up and down the screen. Horizontal sync pulses lock the picture horizontally to the incoming video signal. Vertical sync pulses perform a similar role in the vertical sweep circuitry to prevent the display from rolling. The vertical sweep of the CRT gun is controlled by a vertical hold control on the back of the monitor.

Video monitors have wider signal bandwidths (10–20 MHz) than a standard television receiver (4.5 MHz) so they can display small details clearly. In a standard television receiver the horizontal sweep frequency is 15.75-kHz, so each scan line requires about 53.5 microseconds plus 10 microseconds for horizontal retrace. The television vertical sweep frequency is 60 Hz, which allows 262.5 horizontal scan lines during one vertical sweep period. It takes 16.7 milliseconds (one 60th of a second) to scan the entire screen area once (this is called one field), and 60 fields are displayed per second. However, since 1.25 milliseconds is required for the vertical retrace to bring the beam back to the top of the screen after a field has been completed, only about 245 of the horizontal lines are visible on the screen.

The IBM monochrome display monitor uses a higher-than-normal horizontal sweep frequency (18.432 kHz) and a lower-than-normal vertical sweep frequency (50 Hz) so 350 raster lines can be traced within one complete screen scan. The monochrome adapter produces 720 dots on each horizontal raster line to obtain the 80 characters per row. These dots are transmitted from the adapter board to the display monitor during the time required to scan a single raster line. This places strict performance requirements on the circuitry in the monitor and the adapter. The dot transmission rate requires a video bandwidth of more than 16 MHz for the video amplifiers in the monitor. Because of the high bandwidth and nonstandard sweep rates, only IBM monitors and IBM compatible monitors can be used with the monochrome adapter card. The monochrome adapter card provides a single direct drive video signal to the display monitor.

The color/graphics adapter (CGA) card has a horizontal sweep rate of 15.74 kHz and a vertical drive frequency of 60 Hz. This enables a horizontal resolution of up to 640 pixels and a vertical resolution of 200 lines with a video bandwidth of 14 MHz. This card provides direct drive RGB video for high-resolution monitors and composite video for low-resolution (monochrome or color) monitors and for television receivers via an rf modulator 4-pin Berg connector.

The enhanced graphics adapter (EGA) card can drive monochrome, standard color, or enhanced color display monitors. When configured for a monochrome or standard color monitor, the EGA card produces a 15.75-kHz horizontal drive frequency to enable CGA-type resolution. Configuring the EGA card for an enhanced color display causes the horizontal drive frequency to shift to 21.85 kHz. The EGA card provides direct drive video only. The video connections for the monochrome, color/graphics, and enhanced graphics cards are shown in Fig. 5-4.

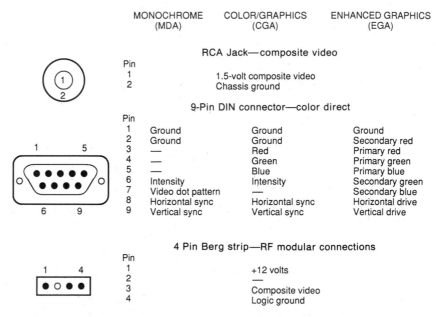

	MONOCHROME (MDA)	COLOR/GRAPHICS (CGA)	ENHANCED GRAPHICS (EGA)

RCA Jack—composite video

Pin			
1		1.5-volt composite video	
2		Chassis ground	

9-Pin DIN connector—color direct

Pin			
1	Ground	Ground	Ground
2	Ground	Ground	Secondary red
3	—	Red	Primary red
4	—	Green	Primary green
5	—	Blue	Primary blue
6	Intensity	Intensity	Secondary green
7	Video dot pattern	—	Secondary blue
8	Horizontal sync	Horizontal sync	Horizontal drive
9	Vertical sync	Vertical sync	Vertical drive

4 Pin Berg strip—RF modular connections

Pin			
1		+12 volts	
2		—	
3		Composite video	
4		Logic ground	

Fig. 5-4. The video connections on the monochrome, color/ graphics, and enhanced graphics adapter cards.

Monochrome and color video are produced in different ways, but each of these IBM display adapters uses a special CRT controller (CRTC) to generate the necessary signals. The Motorola 6845 CRT controller is used on both the monochrome and color/graphics adapter cards and its operation is similar on both cards. A custom CRTC IC is designed into the EGA card. The operation of the 6845 CRTC will be described in the next section. The operation of the EGA custom CRTC will be described in the section on the Enhanced Graphics Adapter.

Monochrome Display Adapter Card

The Monochrome Display Adapter generates monochrome video signals and parallel printer interface signals on a common circuit card. This text will cover the video portion of the board only. The direct drive video output from a 9-pin D-connector at the rear of the card produces 720 dots per raster line on a connected monochrome display monitor. The vertical sweep frequency generates 350 raster lines on the display. This produces a sharp 25-row display with 80 characters per row.

Only text characters are generated by the IBM monochrome adapter. No graphics are produced on this board. Each character is produced in a 7 by 9 dot matrix within a 9 by 14 dot array. The extra dots around the text character provide spacing between characters and lines and provide room for letters with ascenders (such as the letter t) and descenders (such as the letter g).

The horizontal and vertical sweep frequencies generated on this adapter card are not standard. The higher-than-normal video bandwidth requirement and nonstandard sweep rates limit the display options to IBM monitors and IBM compatible monitors. Most TTL monitors available today are IBM compatible. The video output is not a composite signal with the horizontal and vertical sync signals combined with the video dot pattern. Instead, the signals present on the pins of the output connector provide direct drive video. The video is comprised of separate sync signals, a video dot pattern signal, and an intensity (or highlight) signal that controls the brightness of the character.

6845 CRT Controller (CRTC)

The compact 40-pin 6845 CRT controller U35 shown in Fig. 5-5 provides an interface for the 8088 or 80286 CPU to a raster scan CRT display. The primary function of the 6845 is to generate timing signals necessary for raster scan displays under the control of the CPU. CRT controller U35 places keyboard functions such as cursor movements, editing, and read/write under control of the CPU while providing video timing and video buffer refresh memory addressing signals. U35 is fully programmable via the CPU data bus. Under software command, it generates a variety of character widths, display modes, and graphic shapes.

The chip can be programmed to generate a fixed-height cursor, blinking characters, and interlace or noninterlace scan. Noninterlace scan is used in the display monitors for IBM PC computers. Eleven of the 14 refresh memory address lines on U35 are used in the video adapter. Four pins generate an address into the character generator (U33). The 8-bit data bus is transferred between the expansion board backplane and U35 as buffered data bits BD0 through BD7. All the necessary control signals for raster scan display are produced by U35. Besides producing the refresh memory addresses MA0 through MA10 and character generator row raster addresses RA0 through RA3, U35 generates the horizontal and vertical sync, cursor, and display enable signals.

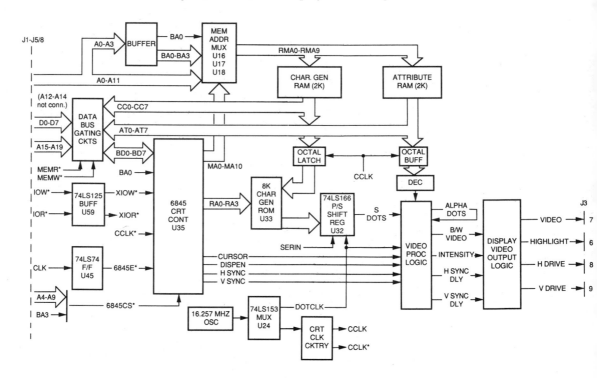

Fig. 5-5. The 6845 CRT controller video display circuitry.

The system reset signal and the application of +5 volts to the expansion bus starts the various clock signals on the video adapter card. The internal operation of the CRTC is synchronized by the control character clock signal CCLK*. The CPU uses CCLK to communicate with the 6845 CRTC over a buffered 8-bit data bus (BD0 through BD7). CCLK is generated by a 16.257-MHz crystal oscillator mounted on the adapter board. This same oscillator produces DOTCLK.

As the adapter board clock signals are started, and a 4.77-MHz CLK signal comes from the system board expansion bus, the monochrome adapter card is activated. The video adapter board looks like a set of I/O addresses to the CPU. It is accessed by addressing locations 3B4H, 3B5H, 3B8H, 3BAH, 3BCH, 3BDH, 3BEH, and 3D1H through 3D8H. Each address points to specific registers within the 6845 CRT controller, the printer port, or the CRT port.

Recall from earlier descriptions of the PC, XT, and AT RAM memory mapping that addresses A0000H to BFFFFH were reserved by IBM for display memory. Addresses B0000H to B8000H can be recognized by the MDA card when MEMR* or MEMW* are active. As shown in Fig. 5-5, system expansion board addresses A0 through A11 and A15 through A19 are connected to the MDA video card (A12 through A14 are not connected). Addresses A15 through A19 are applied to the data bus gating circuits. Decoders are included in this section that enable the transfer of character and attribute memories. Thus the MDA card's display memory can be accessed using the standard memory read and write control signals and by any address between B0000H and B8000H. However, control of the MDA card electronics is handled by I/O read/write commands using address bits A0 through A9 (3B4 through 3D8 address range).

Once reset, the video system is ready for the first command from the CPU. This command is an address to the CRTC at I/O location 3B8H. It causes the 6845 to set the monochrome board to the high-resolution mode. After initialization, sending a data word to U35 selects other modes of operation as shown in Table 5-2.

Table 5-2. 6845 CRTC Modes of Operation

Data Bit	Function
BD0	High-Resolution mode
BD1	(Not used)
BD2	(Not used)
BD3	Video Enable
BD4	(Not used)
BD5	Enable Blink
BD6	(Not used)
BD7	(Not used)

How Characters Are Produced

Both the Monochrome Display Adapter and the Color/Graphics Adapter define each character in two bytes of memory. The first byte is the ASCII code for the character. (A listing of the ASCII character codes is included in the Appendix.) The second byte is an attribute code that determines the video features of the character to be displayed. These features include background darkness, foreground darkness, brightness (intensity), and blink condition.

There are six possible combinations for the attribute byte. They are:

1. Normal video with light characters on a dark background,
2. Reverse video with dark characters on a light background,
3. Flashing light characters on a dark background,
4. Flashing dark characters on a light background,
5. Invisible light characters on a light background,
6. Invisible dark characters on a dark background.

The last two combinations have no practical use and exist only because the logic permits these codes. Two memories are installed on the monochrome display adapter board. One memory is an interlaced dual 2K by 8-bit display buffer RAM. The other memory is an 8K character generator ROM.

Display Buffer Memory

The codes for the characters produced on the screen are stored in 2K bytes of static memory (U12, U13, and U14) as shown in Fig. 5-6. U13 and part of U14 contain character codes for the top half of the display screen. The character codes for the bottom half of the screen are contained in U12 and the remaining part of U14.

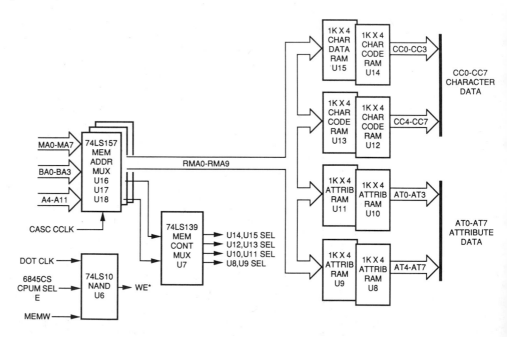

Fig. 5-6. Character and attribute circuitry.

The blink, highlight, reverse video, and underline attribute features are stored in another 2K bytes of static RAM (U8, U9, U10, and U11). Table 5-3 describes the memory allocation for monochrome display video attribute information. The blink feature for the top half of the screen (first 1024 characters) is stored in U9. The blink feature for the bottom half of the screen (976 characters) is stored in U8. Highlight and underline features for the top half of the screen are stored in U11 and for the bottom half of the screen these features are stored in U10. Reverse video information for the top half of the display screen is stored in U9 and U11, while reverse video for the bottom half of the screen is stored in U8 and U10.

Table 5-3. Memory Chip Allocation for Video Attributes

IC	Attribute	Screen Pixel Area
U8	Blinking	Bottom 976 character positions
U9	Blinking	Top 1024 character positions
U10	Highlight	Bottom half of screen
U10	Underline	Bottom half of screen
U11	Highlight	Top half of screen
U11	Underline	Top half of screen
U8, U10	Reverse Video	Bottom half of screen
U9, U11	Reverse Video	Top half of screen

Both 2K RAM arrays are collectively called a 4K display buffer. This static RAM display buffer holds the video information for one complete screen (25 rows by 80 columns). The first address in the display buffer (B0000H) corresponds to the upper left corner of the screen.

The 4K display buffer can store up to 256 different character codes. Each character is represented by a unique character and attribute code pair (CC0 through CC7 and AT0 through AT7) as shown in Fig. 5-6. Even address locations hold the character codes; odd address locations contain the attribute information. To support a 25-line, 80-column display (2,000 characters) requires 4,000 bytes of memory.

Combining the blink and intensity bits with the foreground and background bits produces other video features as described in Table 5-4.

Table 5-4. Attribute Feature Enhancements

Attribute Bits						
Background			*Foreground*			
Bit6	*Bit5*	*Bit4*	*Bit2*	*Bit1*	*Bit0*	Video Feature Achieved
0	0	0	0	0	0	Nondisplay
0	0	0	0	0	1	Underline
0	0	0	1	1	1	White character on black background
1	1	1	0	0	0	Reverse video

Character Generator ROM

The second video adapter board memory is an 8K character generator ROM containing the dot patterns (fonts) for 256 different character codes. The ASCII character code that enters the Monochrome Display Adapter board from the system board data bus cannot be directly displayed. It must be converted into rows of dot patterns that are sent serially out the video cable into the monitor. The conversion of ASCII code into dot patterns is accomplished by the MK-36906N-4 8K-by-6-bit ROM character generator U33.

When display data is required, the 6845 CRTC (U35) causes the ASCII code and attribute data stored in the RAM display buffer to be read out. The 8-bit character code is temporarily stored in an octal latch and then passed into character generator U33 (see Fig. 5-5). The other input into U33 is a 4-bit address (RA0 through RA3) defining which raster row of dots for the character to be displayed will be output from U33 into a 74LS166 parallel-to-serial shift register (U32) for conversion into a serial dot stream.

The attribute information is applied through an octal buffer and a decoder to video process logic where it is combined with the incoming serial dot patterns to produce a dot pattern modified with the desired attribute features. ALPHA DOTS is a select signal that enables a blink/no-blink intensity attribute signal, and a black-and-white video serial dot stream (B/W VIDEO). The B/W VIDEO signal passes through the display video output logic to become the VIDEO signal at video connector J3. ALPHA DOTS is used to disable the intensity signal and then blank out a dot or series of dots to prevent illumination of the display at specific pixel points.

An 8-bit code from character generator U33 is applied to the input of parallel-to-serial shift register U32. Once the character generator data has entered U32, DOT CLOCK shifts the 8-bit dot pattern code out of U32 beginning with the least significant bit as a sequence of serial dots (S DOTS). The character generator produces a row of 8 dots. The character box is 9 dots wide so a blank dot is inserted after each set of 8 dots between each character. SERIN is used to duplicate the 8th dot into the 9th dot position for ASCII characters whose codes are between B0H and DFH.

Bit stream S DOTS is combined with an attribute control signal and a delayed cursor to produce the ALPHA DOTS signal. ALPHA DOTS is Exclusive-ORed with a reverse video signal inside the video processing logic to become the black-and-white video signal B/W VIDEO. The video monitor direct drive output logic is shown in Fig. 5-5. B/W VIDEO is clocked through the display video output logic generating the VIDEO dot pattern information that is applied to pin 7 of connector J3.

Horizontal and Vertical Sync

As shown in Fig. 5-5, the horizontal and vertical sync (H SYNC, V SYNC), CURSOR, and DISPEN signals are applied to the video process logic. H SYNC and V SYNC are converted to H SYNC DLY and V SYNC DLY and then become the horizontal and vertical drive signals (H DRIVE, V DRIVE) at video output connector J3 as shown in Fig. 5-7.

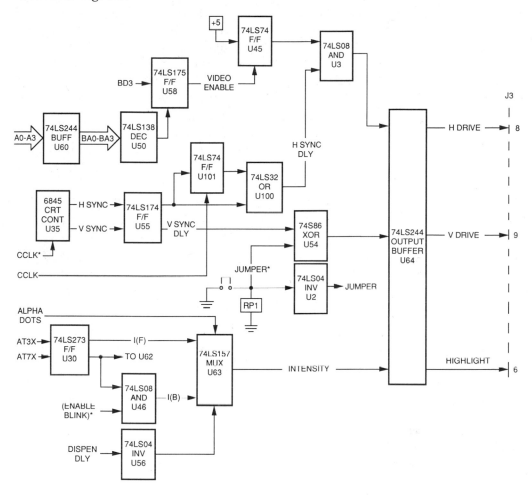

Fig. 5-7. Monochrome adapter horizontal and vertical sync circuitry.

The outputs from the 6845 CRTC U35 become inputs to 74LS174 hex-D flip-flop U55. H SYNC is passed through U55, delay-latched through 74LS74 U101, and then ORed in 74LS32 U100 to produce H SYNC DLY. A logic high at 74LS08 AND gate U3 when VIDEO ENABLE is active high is ANDed with H SYNC DLY and is buffered through 74LS244 tristate octal output buffer U64 to become a 15.75-kHz stream of active-low 5-microsecond horizontal drive (H DRIVE) pulses at pin 8 of video connector J3.

The V SYNC output from the 6845 CRTC U35 is latched through U55 and processed by 74S86 Exclusive-OR gate U54 to produce a 60-Hz stream of 190-microsecond pulses to U64 and output as V DRIVE on pin 9 of connector J3.

Besides VIDEO, H DRIVE, and V DRIVE, the fourth important output to the display monitor is the intensity signal (HIGHLIGHT) on pin 6 of J3. This signal originates from the high bit (AT7X) of the attribute byte coming out of the 2K attribute RAM. AT7X can be toggled to turn on and off the blink function. Bit 3 (AT3X) of the attribute word controls the intensity of the character being displayed. Buffered attribute bits AT3X and AT7X are latched in U30. The AT3X input to U30 results in a intensity control signal I(F). The AT7X input results in an output that is then ANDed with (ENABLE BLINK)* to produce a bright blinking character control intensity blink signal I(B). I(B) and I(F) are multiplexed through 74LS157 multiplexer U63 to produce an INTENSITY signal that is passed through U64 to pin 6 of output connector J3 as the signal HIGHLIGHT.

Thus a serial stream of video dot information is clocked out of pin 7 of video connector J3 into the monochrome display monitor (Fig. 5-5). Data in 6845 CRTC U35 determines how many characters are displayed (R1 = 80), the total character dot arrays provided (R0 = 97), the number of raster lines for each character (R9 = 14), the number of vertical characters displayed (R6 = 25), and the vertical total offset (R5 = 6). (See Fig. 5-2.)

Look at a single character position (for example, C1 in Fig. 5-2), and notice the 9 by 14 dot array (Fig. 5-3A). The serial VIDEO stream of dot pulses coming out of connector J3 are arranged such that each raster line is composed of 97 nine-dot packets. Each sequential nine-dot packet represents one raster line of the 14 lines needed to define a single character box. As shown in Fig. 5-3, two raster lines without dots appear above the character, and three raster lines without dots appear below the character. The additional raster lines below the "A" character provide room for an underline symbol (and for other characters that include descenders). One possible size of cursor display is shown in Fig. 5-3B. System board ROM BIOS software interrupt command INT 10 can be used to change the cursor size and position within the array box.

As the first raster line of dot information shifts into the display monitor, the horizontal and vertical drive signals move the electron beam to control when the serial dot stream for a particular raster line is complete and when the next raster line should begin. After 14 raster lines of video are shifted, one row of characters appears on the screen. The video circuitry then begins to produce the first raster line in the next row of characters. The process continues until the last raster line has been sent out to the monitor completing the last row of characters in the display. When the last line has been scanned, the electron beam is disabled (blanked), moved to the top left of the screen (retrace), and a new display is started.

Color/Graphics Adapter Card

Both alphanumeric characters (like those produced by the monochrome adapter card) and bit-mapped graphics can be generated by the IBM color/graphics card.

Designed to function with the an IBM or IBM-compatible color monitor, the CGA board can also drive other monitors and (with the addition of an rf modulator) standard television receivers.

Three video connections are mounted on the board: an RCA jack for composite video output, a 9-pin DIN connector for direct video drive to an RGB monitor, and a 4-pin Berg strip for composite video output to an rf modulator. A light pen input connection is also provided on the color/graphics adapter card.

The color/graphics adapter card looks like nine I/O addresses (3D0H, 3D1H, 3D4H, 3D5H, 3D8H, 3D9H, 3DAH, 3DBH, and 3DCH) plus 16K bytes of RAM addressable memory to the system board. Address bits A15 through A19 place the CGA board video RAM between B8000H and BBFFFH. Address bits A0 through A13 are used to access the video display memory on the CGA card and are used as I/O addresses to specific CGA components.

Color Adapter Board 6845 CRTC

A 6845 CRT controller is also used on the color/graphics adapter (CGA) card. However, unlike the monochrome adapter card, the CRTC on the color/graphics card must be reprogrammed each time graphics modes are changed. The CGA video circuitry is described in Fig. 5-8.

The 6845 CRT controller U38 is accessed using hex addresses 3D0H, 3D1H, 3D4H, and 3D5H. The P2 expansion bus connects the 8-bit data bus (D0 through D7) on the system board with the color adapter card.

A 14-MHz OSC signal from connector P2 is inverted on the color/graphics adapter card and applied to two 74S174 timing generator chips U4 and U5 producing special clock timing signals.

Selecting the Color/Graphics Mode

Sending a byte of information from the system board to I/O address 3D8H sets the color/graphics adapter board to one of two primary modes of operation. The selected mode is either a high-resolution (all points addressable, or bit-mapped graphics) mode, or a low-resolution (alphanumeric) mode like the monochrome card. Additional submodes are available within these two primary modes. Both 40-column by 25-line and 80-column by 25-line alphanumeric modes are available with characters defined in either a 7 by 7 dot pattern or a 5 by 7 dot pattern within an 8 by 8 dot matrix array. Both text modes can have up to 16 foreground colors and 8 background colors. Blinking, highlighting, and reverse video are available in the black-and-white mode only. Selective character blinking can be controlled. With either character font size, only a single line is available for descenders so the characters are not as well defined as those produced by the monochrome adapter card. Underlining is not used.

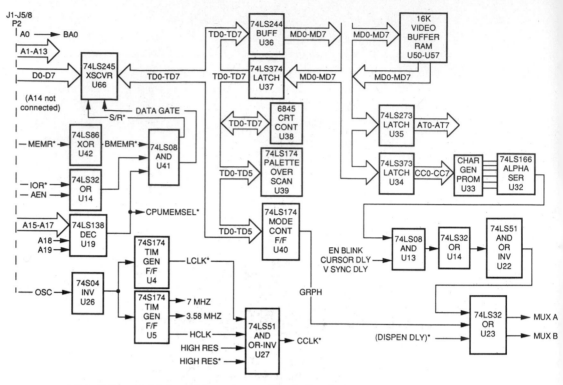

Fig. 5-8. Color/graphics adapter card circuitry.

Since each pixel is independently addressable in the graphics mode, many character shapes are possible. Three bit-mapped graphics modes are available: 1. a nonsoftware, operating-system-supported, low-resolution color graphics mode with 160-pixel rows and 100-pixel columns (pixels controlled in groups of two dots high by two dots wide); 2. a software-supported, medium-resolution color graphics mode with 320-pixel rows and 200-pixel columns (each pixel individually controlled); and 3. a software-supported, high-resolution, black-and-white-only graphics mode with 640 pixels in a row and 200 pixels in a column. In high-resolution graphics, each pixel is individually controlled.

Shifting to medium resolution lets each dot become one of four color configurations—one of 16 preselected background colors, and three other preselected colors. Two sets of three-color palettes are available: Color Set 0 (C0) with green, red, and brown, and Color Set 1 (C1) with cyan, magenta, and white. The background colors include the eight basic colors produced by combinations of red, green, and blue, and eight additional lighter versions of the same colors made possible by using the intensity control bit.

The color set is selected by sending a byte to the color-select circuitry at I/O address 3D9H. The first six bits of the data byte determine the background and foreground colors in the alphanumeric mode, and the medium- and high-resolution modes. Bit 5 selects the active color set in medium-resolution graphics.

Since the color/graphics adapter card is designed like the monochrome display adapter, the foreground (character) and background colors are defined by the attribute byte. With a CGA card, the display foreground and background colors can be preset. The combinations of red, green, and blue define the character background color. Sixteen colors are available for each character with blinking available on a per-character basis.

The condition of a light pen can be passed to the system board through the color/graphics adapter for status or action. The CPU can also read the status of the video card using data bus D0 through D7. The CPU program receives a byte of data and evaluates bits D0 through D3 to determine the status of the video circuitry. An active high bit 0 indicates that an I/O video memory access can be made without interfering with the video going to the display. Bit 1 high indicates that a positive light pen transition has set the light pen's trigger. This trigger is reset on power-up or with an I/O OUT command to 3DBH. Bit 2 reflects the status of the light pen switch. Bit 2 is low when the switch is on. A high bit 3 indicates that the raster is in vertical retrace and screen-buffer updating can be initiated.

Memory Utilization

The CGA card contains two types of memory. One is an 8K character generator ROM containing dot patterns for 256 different characters in three different font styles. Two of the three font styles are used on the color card: a 7-high by 7-wide double-dot font, and a 5-wide by 7-high single-dot font. The desired font is selected by a jumper on the adapter card. Inserting the jumper selects the single-dot 5 by 7 font. Removing the jumper selects the double-dot 7 by 7 font.

The other memory is a 16K byte dynamic RAM display buffer that stores character and color/attribute information. Table 5-5 describes the memory utilization for each of the video modes.

Table 5-5. RAM Utilization for the Color/Graphics Adapter Card Modes

Mode	Amount of Memory per Screen	Screens of Storage
Alphanumeric (40 by 25)	1000 bytes character 1000 bytes attribute	8 total
Alphanumeric (80 by 25)	2000 bytes character 2000 bytes attribute	4 total
Low-Resolution	(not supported in ROM)	
Medium-Resolution	200 rows of 320 pixels, 4 pixels defined per byte = 16,000 bytes	1 (memory-mapped)
High-Resolution	200 rows of 640 pixels, 8 pixels defined per byte = 16,000 bytes (pixel P0 - pixel P7 per byte)	1 (memory mapped)

The alphanumeric data and bit-mapped graphics information stored in the 16K dynamic RAM are accessed by the CPU using I/O addresses B8000H through B8FFFH. RAM ICs U50 through U57 store the information which eventually appears on the monitor screen. The color/graphics adapter video storage and access operations are similar to that on the monochrome display adapter card. The memory on the color/graphics adapter card is slower than the static RAM on the monochrome display adapter card so some blinking of the screen display can occur when performing a screen scroll function.

Video Output Signals

Three video outputs are available on the color/graphics adapter card. One is direct drive video on J2 and the other two are composite video outputs, one on RCA jack J1 and the other on Berg strip plug P1 (where an rf modulator is connected to drive a standard television receiver).

As shown in Fig. 5-9 (upper left), serializers convert graphic and alphanumeric information into a bit stream for the color encoder circuitry. This circuitry generates the direct drive red, green, blue, and intensity video signals that are available at connector J2.

Graphics serializers U7 and U8 generate C0 or C1 color set signals that determine which two sets of three color palettes will be displayed. The CPU selects the color palette by sending a byte of data to I/O address 3D9H. The first six bits determine the background and foreground colors in the alphanumeric mode, and the medium- and high-resolution modes. In medium-resolution graphics the fifth bit in this data word sets the active color set (C0 or C1). Parallel character data from the 8K character generator ROM U33 (Fig. 5-8) is converted into a serial bit stream by 74LS166 alpha serializer U32. The output from U32 is ANDed with blink and cursor signals in the color encoder circuitry and is used to produce the MUX A multiplexer control signal for the color encoder circuitry shown in Fig. 5-9. The MUX B signal is generated by mode control flip-flop U40. These two multiplexer signals determine which input will generate the color and intensity outputs from U9 and U10.

Once generated, the RGB and intensity signals are clocked through 74S74 quad D flip-flop U101 and 74LS244 tristate buffer U67 to J2 by a 14-MHz signal developed on the adapter board.

Composite Video

RGB and intensity signals are multiplexed from the color encoder circuitry and applied to a composite color generator circuit where the horizontal and vertical sync signals are added. This composite video signal is then clocked to RCA jack J1 or pin 3 on composite video connector P1.

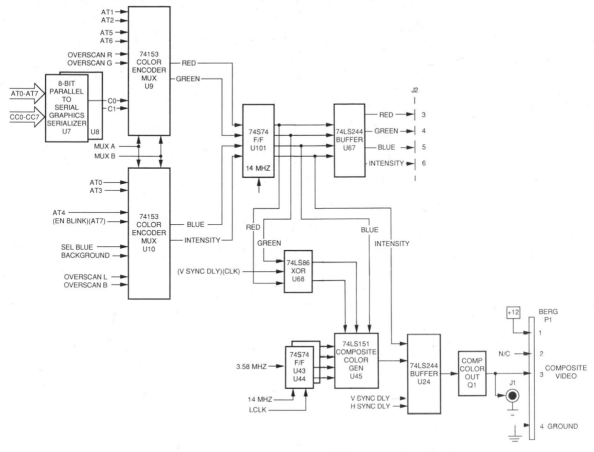

Fig. 5-9. Direct drive and composite video generation circuits.

Synchronization Signals

The color/graphics adapter board generates special pulses to synchronize the video signals with the horizontal and vertical sweep circuits in the display unit. The 15.75-kHz horizontal drive and 60-Hz vertical drive signals from the color/graphics adapter card are generated and passed to the direct drive video output connector J2 by the circuitry shown in Fig. 5-10.

The 6845 CRT controller U38 generates vertical and horizontal sync signals that are clocked through the 74LS174 D flip-flop U21 by HCLK. The Q outputs of U21 become vertical sync delay (V SYNC DLY) and horizontal sync delay (H SYNC DLY).

Horizontal Synchronization

U38 generates a 15.75-kHz horizontal synchronization signal H SYNC that is clocked by HCLK through U21 to become H SYNC DLY. This signal is applied to

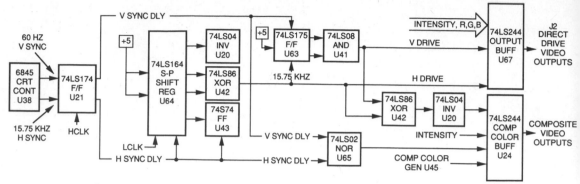

Fig. 5-10. Horizontal and vertical sync circuitry.

the active-low master reset input of 74LS164 serial-to-parallel shift register U64. Because both D inputs are strapped high (+5 volts), a logic high is clocked through the eight D-latches in U64 by LCLK. Outputs are taken from four of the eight stages. The outputs to 74LS86 XOR U42 are of particular interest because they eventually generate the V DRIVE and H DRIVE signals that are buffered through U67 to video connector J2. The clocking of a sequence of high inputs through U64 and the master clear control of H SYNC DLY produces a 15.75-kHz signal out of U42 through U67 to pin 8 of J2.

Vertical Drive Generation

The 60-Hz V SYNC signal from 6845 CRTC U38 is clocked through U21 to become V SYNC DLY. V SYNC DLY is applied to the master reset input of 74LS175 D flip-flop U63. Each time V SYNC DLY goes low, all the flip-flops in U63 are cleared and an output goes high applying a logic 1 to 74LS08 AND gate U41. One input pin of U63 is strapped to +5.00 volts causing the flip-flop to enter a high state upon the next low-to-high transition of the 15.75-kHz clock input. Two outputs of U63 connect to quad 2-input AND gate U41. A logic high on both inputs enables U41 generating V DRIVE out. V DRIVE is buffered through 74LS244 U67 to connector J2 as the vertical drive signal for the color monitor.

Enhanced Graphics Adapter Card

The IBM Monochrome Display Adapter (MDA) is well suited for word processing and spreadsheet applications. It produces 80 columns of text that is easy to read and can appear in several display modes including highlighted and blinking. However, the MDA cannot display graphics.

The IBM Color/Graphics Adapter (CGA) was designed to fill the need for color and graphics. It does produce color shapes, boxes, and even text, but the text is squeezed into an 8 by 8 dot array so the characters are deformed and difficult to read. A need still existed for a display adapter that could produce both good graphics and good quality text. The Enhanced Graphics Adapter (EGA) was introduced to fulfill this need.

The EGA card provides resolution and readability close to the Monochrome Display Adapter and has become the de facto standard display for all the PC family. The Enhanced Graphics Adapter can generate 16 simultaneous colors with a resolution of 640 dot pixels by 350 lines. The three types of display possible with the EGA card are: 350-line high-resolution monochrome; 200-line intensity-red-green-blue (IRGB) color; and enhanced color. The display modes include: four-color graphics (black, normal, bright, and blinking) in 640-by-350 resolution; 16 colors in 320-by-200 and 640-by-200 resolution for standard frequency IRGB displays; 350-line high-resolution 80-column alphanumeric characters; user-selected blink and highlight attributes on 16 color IRGB displays, 8-color RGB displays, or 16 colors on an IBM enhanced color monitor. The EGA circuitry also supports horizontal and vertical scrolling, split-screen displays, fast screen updates, and a light-pen interface. The possible display capability depends on the monitor used and the amount of memory installed on the EGA card.

The EGA board does not support a printer interface like the monochrome display, nor does it support composite monitors or TVs. The EGA board output is direct drive video with the primary R, G, B; secondary r, g, b; horizontal sync; and vertical sync signals applied separately to the display monitor.

Figure 5-11 shows the important components mounted on the IBM EGA board. These components include 51 ICs, a crystal oscillator, and a resistor network. Five of the ICs are custom large-scale integration (LSI) chips designed by IBM. By comparison, the CGA card has 69 chips without a crystal. The MDA card includes 66 chips and a crystal oscillator.

The primary components on the EGA card include eight 16K-byte by 4-bit display buffer RAM chips (U1, U2, U10, U11, U40, U41, U50, and U51) for 64K bytes of display RAM on the EGA board. Another 64K of RAM can be added on a memory expansion piggyback daughterboard that plugs into expansion socket J5. Other components on the EGA board include a custom CRT controller U32, two graphics controllers U21 and U31, an attribute controller U24, a sequencer U33, a two character set ROM U44, a 16.257-MHz crystal oscillator U7, and a video output buffer U36.

The display buffer memory is partitioned into four groups of two 4416 RAM chips. Each pair (U1, U10; U2, U11; U40, U50; and U41, U51) constitute a 16K-byte bit plane. Additional memory can be added in 64K-byte increments to increase the total display memory to 256K bytes. Only four of 16 colors can be displayed with an EGA card having 64K of memory. By adding 64K more memory, all 16 colors can be displayed in high-resolution graphics. Adding even more expansion memory (up to 256K total) provides the capability to run programs that require extra memory for multiple video pages.

The two graphics controllers (U21 and U31) on the left end of the EGA board are custom LSI chips dedicated to handling two of the four bit planes. Both

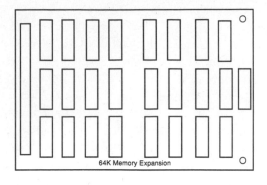

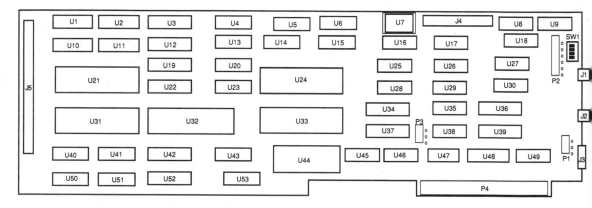

Fig. 5-11. Layout of the EGA card.

chips work in parallel and share common I/O addresses. They direct data from display memory to attribute controller U24 and main CRT controller processor U32.

The CRT controller processor U32 is a third custom LSI chip that functions similar to the Motorola 6845 CRTC. U32 generates addresses for accessing the display buffer, vertical and horizontal timing, cursor, underline, and dynamic RAM refresh signals.

A fourth custom LSI component on the IBM EGA card is the attribute controller U24. It provides a palette of 16 colors. Each color is set separately to control six direct drive color video outputs. U24 also controls the blinking and underlining functions as defined by the attribute bits in the display memory. Unlike the CGA card which sends attributes directly to the I, R, G, and B direct drive output pins, the attribute bits in the EGA circuitry become an index into the palette register array in U24. The contents of U24 are then sent to the display monitor. The color produced depends on the selected palette register rather than the actual attribute bits.

Below U24 is a custom LSI sequencer U33. U33 generates the basic memory timing pulses and a character clock for display refresh. It also coordinates memory access by CRTC U32. U24 includes a mask register that can be set to protect individual memory planes from access by U32.

U44 is a 16K-byte ROM containing a power-on adapter self test, the EGA BIOS and code to support video I/O, and character generator patterns for both alphanumeric and graphics modes. The IBM PC, XT, or AT using the EGA card must have a system board BIOS that will automatically scan for I/O control ROMs. Earlier PCs with system BIOS dated before 10/27/82 or with a 16K/64K system board having a serial number below 0300961 will not work with the EGA card unless the system BIOS is upgraded.

During initialization, the EGA procedure places its own address in the INT 10 vector after copying the original vector to the vector for INT 42. Then the EGA BIOS can call on the system BIOS for support. This is also how the fixed-disk adapter inserts itself into diskette service routines.

Two character patterns sets are contained in ROM U44. One is an 8 by 14 character array for high-resolution displays and the other is an 8 by 8 character set for TV frequency displays. Once an alphanumeric mode is selected (using function calls) BIOS copies the correct pattern from ROM into part of the display memory RAM. This pattern is then accessed like on earlier video adapter boards with character generator ROMs installed. However, with the EGA card the patterns can be ROM selected or user configured. The RAM character generator is loaded from the BIOS ROM or from user-specified memory. The same set of functions that loads the RAM character generator will also recalculate the number of rows that will fit on the screen. This causes BIOS to display text in the selected format.

The EGA card has five primary I/O connections. On the lower right is the 62-pin system board connector (P4) that fits in one of the expansion slots on the computer motherboard. Just above and to the right is a 9-pin D connector (J3) that provides direct drive video for the display monitor. RCA connectors J1 and J2 (above J3) are not used. Above and to the left of J1 is a 6-pin connector (P2) for interfacing a light pen to the EGA board. This connector is the same interface as found on the CGA board. On the top of the EGA card is the 32-pin video feature connector J4. This connector makes the six color bits, sync, and blanking signals available for external devices. By connecting external circuitry to the EGA card at J4, a video graphics generator system can be constructed. Finally, at the far left is a memory expansion connection, J5, which is used for piggybacking a 64K memory board. Up to three such daughter boards can be connected to the EGA card (assuming that you can fit them inside the system unit).

There are two jumpers on the EGA card. To the left of monitor connector J3 is jumper P1 for configuring the output for an enhanced display, or for a monochrome/standard color display. Another jumper, P3, located just above the system board connector is used to set the I/O address at 2xx or 3xx. Normally, the EGA card responds to I/O addresses in the range 3C0H to 3D9H (3xx). Jumper P3

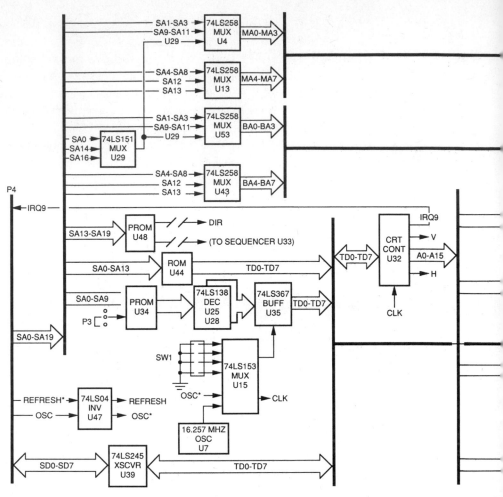

Fig. 5-12. Block diagram of the

enables more than one EGA board to be installed in the same PC system by selecting SA8 or SA8* as one of the decodable address bits. The SA8 bit location is the ninth bit in the address word. Since the system BIOS is coded to interface with I/O addresses 3xx, special software must be used to access an EGA board set to 2xx.

In addition to the two jumpers, a four-post switch block (SW1) is mounted on the upper right side of the EGA card, near the light pen I/O P2. During initialization, the EGA BIOS examines the EGA switches and jumpers. It is essential that the switch and jumpers be correctly set to prevent damage to the display monitor or to the EGA card itself. The IBM monochrome display is extremely sensitive to incorrect horizontal drive frequency or to incorrect polarity of the vertical retrace signal.

The monitor connected to the EGA card must be capable of recognizing and switching between a 15.75-kHz horizontal scan rate for the regular IBM

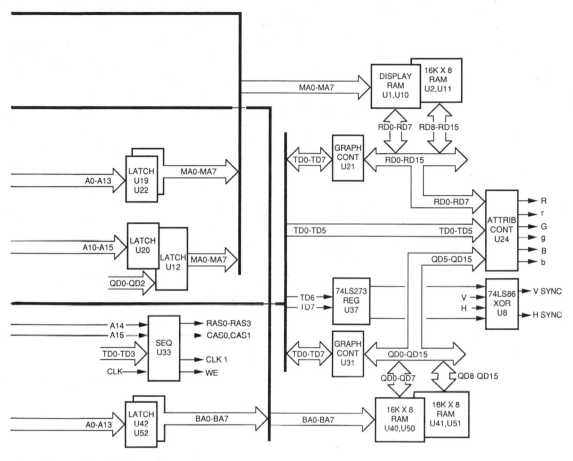

circuitry on the EGA card.

Color Display (CGA), and the 21.85-kHz horizontal scan rate for the EGA high-resolution modes. The horizontal frequency is determined by the polarity of the vertical sync signal. A vertical sync signal with negative polarity causes the circuitry to produce a 21.85-kHz EGA horizontal scan rate.

Fig. 5-12 is a block diagram of the circuitry on the EGA card. The address bus and data bus on the system board expansion slot connect to the EGA card via connector P4. In Fig. 5-12, the address bus is labeled system address SA0 through SA19. The data bus (D0 through D7) becomes SD0 through SD7 and is interfaced with the board through transceiver U39. The EGA side of the data bus is TD0 through TD7.

Display characters can be produced by addressing a RAM-based character generator that supports up to 512 character codes or by addressing a character generator ROM containing patterns for both alphanumeric and graphics modes. The EGA BIOS in ROM contains two character pattern sets—an 8 by 14 array for high resolution and an 8 by 8 array for medium resolution.

As shown in Fig. 5-12, the address bus connects with an array of multi plexers (U29, U4, U13, U53, and U43) that convert the input addresses into memory addresses MA0 through MA7 and buffer addresses BA0 through BA7 to access the display buffer RAM array. System address bits SA0 through SA13 are connected to ROM U44 to produce character generator patterns on TD0 through TD7, the EGA data bus.

EGA data bus (TD0 through TD7) can be driven by ROM U44, the 74LS367 buffer U35, 74LS245 transceiver U39, and CRT controller U32. As shown in Fig 5-12, TD0 through TD3 interact with A14 and A15 in sequencer U33 to produce the display RAM row and column address strobe signals. TD0 through TD7 are the primary interface with the display RAM via two graphics controllers (U21 and U31). Finally, TD0 through TD5 are used as an index code by the attribute controller U24, and TD6 and TD7 help generate vertical and horizontal sync signals via 74LS273 register U37.

EGA switch SW1 is set according to the type of display monitor used. The CRT controller U32 reads the setting of SW1 through U15 and U35 and then selects one of several clock inputs to 74LS153 multiplexer U15 as the source for CLK. CLK is used by sequencer U33 and the CRT controller to develop the correct horizontal sync signals for the type of monitor being used.

Data is transferred to the video RAM via graphics controller U21. RAM data bits RD0 through RD15 connect U21 with video display RAM pairs U1,U10 and U2,U11. Graphics controller U31 serves a similar function for data bits QD0 through QD15. Controllers U21 and U31 also direct data from the RAM display memory to the attribute controller and the main CRT controller processor.

The attribute controller U24 receives display RAM data RD0 through RD7 and QD5 through QD15, and EGA data bus bits TD0 through TD5. U24 uses these inputs to produce six output signals (R, r, G, g, B, b) that provide a palette of 16 colors. Each color is set separately using the six color outputs signals. A switch block on the IBM PC and XT system boards, and a single switch on the IBM AT system board, are used to configure the computer for a specific type of display monitor. The configuration switch on the AT system board is used to set the board for connection to a monochrome or color/graphics monitor. The switch has no function if an EGA card is installed because the EGA circuitry handles display configuration. Most people leave the AT system board switch in the monochrome position to cause the AT to default to monochrome if the EGA card is replaced. The documentation provided with the EGA card describes the correct EGA card switch and jumper settings for using various types of display monitors.

The attribute controller U24 in the output circuitry is key to the unique form of the EGA video output. Unlike the CGA circuit, in which the attribute bits are sent directly to the I, R, G, and B output pins producing the specified color with the specified blinking, underlining, etc., the attribute bits on the EGA card are used by U24 as an index. The primary and secondary color signals that come out of U24 collectively define the characteristics of the display. The EGA display is not defined directly by the attribute bits.

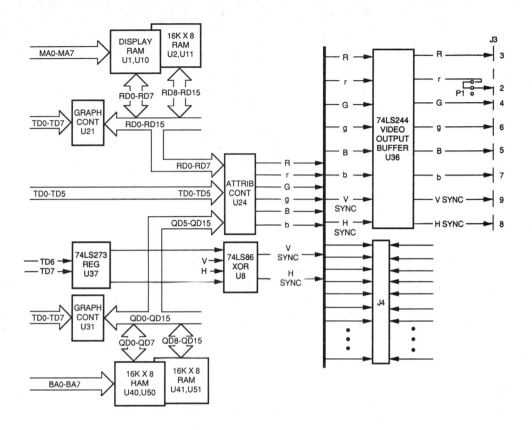

Fig. 5-13. EGA video output circuitry.

Note in Fig. 5-13 that the direct drive color information from video output buffer U36 is comprised of six signals. The primary R, G, and B represent dark, rich red, green, and blue. The secondary r, g, and b signals produce brighter red, green, and blue. Combining the primary and secondary signals produces even brighter colors. Thus, a primary R will produce a dark red, a secondary r will produce a brighter red, and combining R and r will produce an even brighter red. Combining r, g, and b produces a dim white. Each color pair (Rr, Gg, and Bb) has four combinations. With three color pairs, and four combinations each, any of 16 colors from a palette of 64 color combinations can be displayed simultaneously. In contrast, the CGA board produces 16 colors, but only those available by combining the red, green, blue, and intensity signals.

In enhanced mode (negative vertical sync signal), the IBM Enhanced Color Display monitor recognizes the six color inputs as a collective signal set defining the palette color to produce. In the compatible low-resolution mode, the display recognizes the R, G, and B inputs as the color select, and combines the r, g, and b inputs into a common intensity signal. This lets users install and operate the IBM Enhanced Color Display monitor with either the EGA card or the older CGA card. When standard color and monochrome monitors are used with the EGA card, jumper P1 is switched to ground pin 2 of connector J3.

When the EGA card is set to drive a standard color display, a 15.75-kHz horizontal sync signal is output on pin 8 of J3. The frequency of this signal becomes 21.85-kHz when an IBM Enhanced Color Display monitor is connected and the EGA card switches and jumpers are properly set.

In addition to being connected through U36 to monitor connector J3, all eight of the output signals to U36 are also wired to the video feature connector J4 (labels are not shown on connector).

Table 5-6 compares the features of the display monitors used with the IBM PC family of microcomputers.

Table 5-6.   Comparison of Display Monitors

	Monchrome	Standard	Enhanced
	Display	*Color*	*Color*
	5151	*5153*	*5154*
Text Resolution	25 by 80	25 by 80	25 by 80
Graphics Resolution	640 by 350	320 by 200	640 by 350
Text Character Box	9 by 14	8 by 8	8 by 8 or 8 by 14
Colors Possible (not attributes)	2	4 of 16	16 of 64

Professional Graphics Adapter (PGA)

The Professional Graphics Adapter (PGA) was designed to push the resolution limits for graphic applications. This adapter card can produce the 350-line vertical resolution of the EGA card or extend the vertical resolution to 480 lines.

Using an Intel 8088 on-board processor as the CRT controller, the PGA is best suited for graphic art, image processing, and computer-aided design (CAD) The board contains 320K bytes of display RAM enabling the generation of 256 colors out of a palette of 4,096 color combinations. Pixel crunching software helps to reduce the amount of memory required for advanced graphics applications. The PGA board can emulate the CGA video mode with its limited color capability or shift into a maximum-color PGA mode. Using two slots in the IBM XT and AT, or extra slots in an expansion chassis, the PGA card draws five amps of current from the power supply.

PGA has been criticized for being slow, kludgy, and expensive. Jim Seymour of *PC Magazine* once called the PGA "The Standard that Time Forgot." Acceptance of PGA has been limited to custom applications.

Questions for Review and Discussion

1. Why is a video adapter card required to connect a display monitor to an IBM PC, XT, or AT computer?

2. Which IBM video display is best suited for text?

3. Why is resolution an important consideration when choosing a display monitor?

4. What is the main advantage of a color/graphics display monitor?

5. Define the meaning of a 640 by 200 display resolution.

6. What are the advantages of a direct drive video signal over a composite video signal for a display monitor?

7. Why is a higher-than-normal horizontal sweep frequency used for the IBM monochrome display monitor?

8. What is the primary function of the 6845 CRT controller on the IBM monochrome display adapter card?

9. How many colors can be displayed by the IBM color/graphics adapter board in the medium-resolution mode?

10. What are the advantages of the IBM enhanced graphics display over the IBM color/graphics display?

6

Basic Troubleshooting Techniques

Verifying a real problem, analyzing symptoms, or isolating and correcting a failure in your IBM personal computer can be either a stressful hassle or a truly enjoyable rewarding experience, depending on your understanding of the machine and your ability to properly troubleshoot computer circuitry. Whether you're a hobbyist or a technician, this chapter will guide you through the troubleshooting process. It will provide you with the analytical tools and tips needed to localize a problem, identify the failed part, and then make the correct repair.

Introduction to Troubleshooting

PC problems will occur, but you need to know how to confirm that a failure symptom is really a failure and not just an operator error or a software bug. Software incompatibility can lead one to suspect a disk drive problem, even when it isn't. It's also easy to blame the computer, but the machine may not be at fault.

Imagine for a moment that you're in the midst of printing a lengthy report when suddenly the printer halts, the screen display goes blank, and your IBM PC ceases to function. What do you do? What failed?

This chapter is devoted to a subject we often wish we could pass off or ignore—trouble. Trouble is like a flat tire; no one wants one, but when it occurs, we all wish we could fix the problem quickly and get the experience behind us. However, knowledge and action are required to overcome trouble.

Static and Dynamic Failures

Integrated-circuit technology is advancing rapidly. Logic gates, on tiny chips of silicon, are getting smaller and faster. This has been welcomed by all of us, but with these advances in microelectronics comes the greater challenge of determining whether a chip, board, or the computer system is functioning correctly or not. Has the system been properly maintained? Faults, which are difficult to locate, can occur in the system.

A fault is any physical condition that causes an incorrect output when a circuit is exercised to perform a function. Faults can be classified as either static or dynamic. Static failures or faults include the stuck-at problems associated with open or shorted data paths in circuitry. These failures are typically catastrophic, causing system operation to terminate.

Shorts can be described as electrical conduction in the wrong place. Shorts are typically caused by a mechanical failure in a device or by a solder bridge during repair. *Opens* are characterized by a lack of electrical conduction when it should be present. Electrically open inputs can affect the switching speed of a device and can degrade the noise immunity of the component. Other catastrophic faults can be caused by a wrong component being installed on a board, an improperly installed component, a missing component, or a dead or partially dead device.

Dynamic failures include time-dependent errors, such as the loss of signal quality, which causes a circuit output to reach steady state too late to be properly used by another part of the system. The symptoms of dynamic faults include devices operating too slow. This failure is seen in setup-and-hold problems, data and addressing problems, machine cycle-time instability, and interactive problems between components. In the logic gate, dynamic faults are seen in propagation delay problems—there is a time delay in getting a signal from the input to the output. Flip-flops typically experience dynamic faults in their ability to capture and hold data after the inputs have dissipated. Dynamic faults in memory happen in the data/address relationships where timing problems arise between the occurrence of valid data and address information. Even an 8088 central processing unit (CPU) can experience dynamic faults in the cycle-time stability of the microinstruction function cycle. Component dynamic failures are more difficult to find than are static catastrophic faults. Locating static and dynamic faults will be covered in this chapter.

Logic Troubleshooting

The most effective way to locate a failure in an IBM computer is to approach the problem just as the machine operates—logically. Imagine the computer system as a human body. The timing and the timing circuitry represent the heart. The CPU and related circuitry are like the brain. Without the heart and brain, nothing in the body works. The keyboard and drives represent the eyes and ears. The display and printer act like the mouth. By viewing the computer system as a functioning body system, you can quickly determine which area is not working properly and home in on the malfunctioning part. You need to understand what should happen and compare the "shoulds," one by one, with what is really happening.

There are typically two ways to analyze electronic circuit failures: (1) classical troubleshooting incorporating the localizing and isolating of failures, using deductive reasoning and mental intuition; and (2) brute force troubleshooting utilizing flowcharts and the replacement of all suspected components. Both techniques will be addressed in this chapter.

Basic Troubleshooting

Solving computer system problems requires the application of a deductive technique called "troubleshooting." Effective and efficient troubleshooting involves gathering clues and applying the deductive reasoning needed to isolate a problem. Once you know the cause of a problem, you can follow a process of analyzing, testing, and substituting good components for each suspected bad component to find the particular part that has failed. Good deductive reasoning is used to isolate a failure to a particular group of components or chips. Then, circuit analysis is used to reduce the problem to a specific component.

In general, there are some optimum steps that you can follow to successfully troubleshooting and repair a computer.

1. Don't panic.
2. Observe the conditions.
3. Use your senses.
4. Retry.
5. Document.
6. Assume one problem.
7. Use correct technical reference data.
8. Diagnose to a section (fault identification).
9. Localize to a stage (fault localization).
10. Isolate to a failed part (fault isolation).
11. Use correct equipment to aid in the repair.
12. Repair.
13. Test and verify.

The following pages discuss in detail the steps necessary for troubleshooting success. But first, some cautions and warnings.

> **CAUTION**: Modifying or removing components from the circuit boards in your system may void the manufacturer's warranties.
> **CAUTION**: Discharge any static electricity present on your body before troubleshooting or repairing any part of the computer system.

> **WARNING**: High voltages are present inside the power supplies and display terminals. Unless you are trained in the repair of these units, you should not try to troubleshoot, or in any way open and work inside either the power supply or the display monitor.

Basic Steps

Now that you understand what is appropriate in troubleshooting and repairing the IBM personal computer family, let us proceed.

Every computer is composed of functional sections as diagrammed in Fig. 6-1. Any of these sections can fail. When something functionally goes wrong in the computer, the first step is to determine whether the trouble is from an actual failure, such as a loose connection, or from human error. To do this, you need to understand how the IBM system works and how it interacts with the other parts of the system. The earlier chapter(s) on the "operation" of IBM computers were written to support this requirement.

Once you're convinced that a true component failure has occurred, the next step is to determine which functional section of the system is not operating—disk drive, keyboard, display, or some other part. To do this, break each section of the computer or peripheral into stages and trace the trouble to a circuit stage within that section. If a display isn't working, for example, the problem could be in the display monitor itself, in the video cable, or in the video circuitry on the adapter card. Each of these can be considered a stage of the video-display functional section. Then, analyze the circuit to isolate the failed part, using the appropriate specific troubleshooting and repair procedures given in the following chapters.

When troubleshooting a computer, you must discipline yourself to always check that the power switch is in the correct position required at that time (usually OFF). Make it a practice to always place your hand over the power switch whenever you first start thinking about doing something inside the computer. Turn off the power, and then open the system unit.

Visual Inspection

There are several specific steps you should take when troubleshooting an IBM system. First, search out all the symptoms—the clues—that point toward the location of the failure. Make a visual and operational check of everything that is normally active during operation of the failing function. Look for loose or incorrectly connected cables and power cords, switches that are incorrectly set, disk drive doors inadvertently left open, de-energized wall sockets, and bad disks. Look for anything that appears out of place.

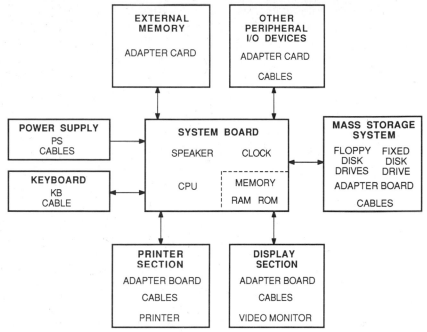

Fig. 6-1. The functional units of the IBM Personal Computer family of microcomputers.

Cleaning the Connections and System Unit

Turn off the computer and clean all the edge connectors on plug-in cards. Reseat the associated cables, making sure to look for bent pins. Examine the system board and related interface cards for discolored components or loose debris. You'd be amazed at what has been found inside computers, printers, and disk drives. During analysis, I've found pieces of bread, cigarette ashes, stains from coffee spilled in the keyboard, and even sticky soda pop all over the motherboard. Inside drives, I've found everything from pencils to carrots to dead mice! Don't be surprised by the things that somehow find their way into these machines.

After checking inside the computer system unit, disk drive, and any other associated equipment, close the system up and reboot. Check to see if the same failure occurs. If it does, shift to *symptom analysis.*

Symptom Analysis

This troubleshooting process involves the examination of symptoms to determine the area of system failure. If the display screen is black and shows no sign of video life, check the monitor and video circuitry and the interconnecting cables. If the program locks up in the middle of an operation, the failure is most likely in the CPU, ROM, RAM, or related circuitry. If the drive doesn't boot, then the drive, the drive circuitry, the disk-drive adapter board, and the related interface cables become suspect.

When checking symptoms, remember to evaluate all symptoms, not just ones that seem directly related to the problem. Often other clues are available.

Diagnose to a Section

Once symptom analysis is completed, narrow the failure down to a single section. Let's step through an actual problem example. Suppose you have an IBM PC that won't boot the disk in the disk drive. Making a visual check, you find that nothing looks amiss, so you analyze the failure symptom in depth. You notice that when power is applied to the system, the computer turns on and the power on self-test diagnostics run and pass without any error message or improper beep emitting from the speaker. You remember that even though the diagnostics pass, there can still be a problem in the circuitry tested by the BIOS POST. POST (Power-On Self Test) diagnostics do not test all types of "stuck-at" or improper signal conditions. In this example, the diagnostics run fine, but when the drive tries to boot a disk, the system just locks up and doesn't do a thing—yet no failure code is displayed on the screen.

Turn the computer off and, several seconds later, turn it back on. Closely watch the action of Drive A. When the BIOS reaches the program step that tries to load DOS from the disk, the drive light turns on and you can hear the drive head movement inside. However, several seconds later, the drive motor stops. The drive light remains on, but no data seems to be loading from the disk into the system board RAM. A curious fact. You try another known good disk. Same results. You swap disk drives and retest. Again, no change. You clean and reseat the drive adapter board. You also clean and reconnect the cable from the drive to the adapter board. Then you retest. The problem remains. What could be the cause for this behavior?

Removing the disk from the drive, you power the system down and back up, trying to boot the system up in BASIC. It does. Now that the system has been proven to work without the drives, you conclude that the CPU, the system board, the screen, and the keyboard sections are working properly. The problem has been reduced to the disk-drive portion of the system circuitry. Closing in on the failure, you decide that you have a choice to make. (If you have spare cables and adapter boards, you can swap out one at a time until the problem goes away. However, if you don't have spares, you must investigate further.)

Look at the magnetic head inside the failing drive as you reapply power to the system. Upon receiving electrical power, the head should immediately move to the "home" position farthest from the center of the hub. This is the location of Track 0. Disk-unique information, such as the boot record, file allocation table (FAT), and directory is located on this track. In our example, the head goes to the home position. Then, the head moves across the disk just as if it were reading data off a track cylinder but, a few seconds later, the head movement stops with the head positioned halfway over the disk surface.

Localize to a Stage

Check the cable. Then, check the disk-drive controller by swapping the adapter board with another. The problem goes away. The faulty part has been localized to a circuit stage on the adapter board. In most problem-analysis procedures, you normally find the problem by this time. At this point, you must decide if you have the technical experience to desolder and replace ICs and other components. Most PC operators do not have (or even want) this skill.

Isolate to a Failed Part

You've isolated the failure to the adapter board. Further tests reveal the failed part. If you don't feel comfortable desoldering and soldering components, the thing to do is purchase a trade-in replacement board. Or you can send the bad board to a repair shop having the capability to perform component exchange.

Replacing the part (by whatever means is appropriate), you restore proper system operation.

Summary of Problem

Note that the specific problem described in this example is not important. The value of the preceding problem analysis lies in the troubleshooting steps that were followed. The first step was a visual check (including swapping disks with a known good disk). Next, the problem was carefully examined and decisions were made specifying what was and was not occurring. Then the problem was reduced to a subsystem by checking symptoms, and a preliminary check was conducted on the circuitry in question. This was followed with a specific circuit analysis designed to isolate and identify a particular failed component.

Component Recognition

In the earlier chapters, we looked inside the hood of the IBM Personal Computers to see how these microcomputers are built. Now, we'll take a deeper look at the construction of these marvellous machines.

The strong housing (or case) and the detachable keyboard are made of high-strength, flame-retardant, molded plastic. These casings are not likely to fail under normal use. MAKE SURE POWER IS TURNED OFF. Now, open your IBM personal computer using the disassembly instructions found in the appendix of this book.

Inside the computer housing are a number of subassemblies, such as the system board (or motherboard), the disk-drive adapter card, the video display board, and the switching power supply. Let's concentrate on the system board at this time, since this is where most failures occur.

The IBM Personal Computer motherboard shown in Fig. 6-2 is made of fiber glass and has lots of colorful devices mounted on it—sockets, connectors, wire traces embedded into the board, integrated circuits (or chips), resistors, capacitors, and transistors. Fig. 6-3 illustrates some of the types of devices typically mounted on the motherboard.

Fig. 6-2. A system board.

Chips

The black-cased, centipede-looking IC chips, and the several square devices found on a PC AT board functionally contain hundreds (or thousands) of transistors. These cause the computer to work in a logical fashion, based on the binary system and using binary digits (bits), where all the conditions are either ON (logic 1) or OFF (logic 0), and all operations occur in sequence.

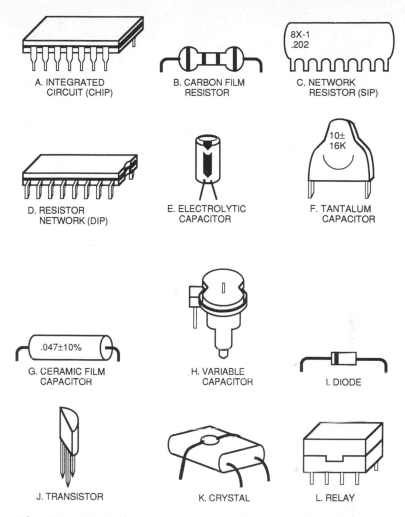

Fig. 6-3. Typical components on an IBM system board.

Depending on which personal computer you examine, there are about nine sizes of chips on your motherboard: eight dual-in-line (DIP) 8-pin, 14-pin, 16-pin, 18-pin, 20-pin, 24-pin, 28-pin, and 40-pin packages, and the large, square, 168-pin, leaded chip-carrier package of the 80286 CPU. The ROMs in all of the PC families and several special ICs in the IBM PC AT are custom chips. International Business Machines placed some of these chips in sockets, so repair is quick and easy, with no desoldering or soldering requirements.

As shown in Fig. 6-4, integrated circuits have a notch or groove at one end that physically marks the location for pin 1. Pin 1 is just to the left of the groove or notch as you look down upon the top of the chip. On the large 168-pin Intel 80286 chip illustrated in Figure 6-4, the lower left corner has been clipped off, signifying it as the pin 1 location. Some DIP ICs have a circle indentation at the left side of the notched end. This indentation marks pin 1.

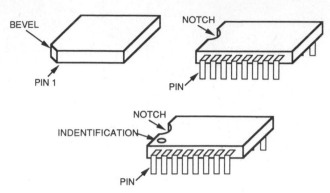

Fig. 6-4. Locating pin 1 on a typical IC.

The pins of an IC are numbered counterclockwise starting from pin 1, so that the highest-numbered pin is located directly across from pin 1. In chip replacement, you must always insert a new chip into its socket with pin 1 in the right place.

Component Markings

Integrated circuits have special markings that tell a lot about what's inside the chip. Look at the printing on the top of the ICs on your computer's motherboard. Many different companies make chips, and most companies place their logo on the chip (Fig. 6-5A). Some of these companies are outside the United States—in Brazil, El Salvador, Indonesia, Korea, Malaysia, Mexico, Singapore, and Taiwan, for example. You'll also notice letter-number combinations on the chips. Some chips have two sets of letter-numbers. One set identifies the type of device, and the other set tells when the chip was made (Fig. 6-5B).

The first, or primary, set of letter-numbers in Fig. 6-5B is called the manufacturer's type number or the manufacturer's device code. It appears in three sections. For example, the prefix "SN" in SN74LS244N is usually used to identify the manufacturer, although sometimes it is used to identify the device family (also associated with a manufacturer) or a temperature range. The prefix is sometimes omitted. The chips found on the IBM PC, PC/XT, and PC/AT motherboards, and the MDA, CGA, and EGA display adapters are listed in the appendix.

After the primary number or letter code comes a three- to six-digit core number. It indicates the basic type number (logic family). Most of the chips in the IBM Personal Computers are in the 74xx series, which represents TTL logic (transistor-transistor logic). The core number 74LS244 is the code for an octal buffer/line driver/line receiver. The letters in the middle of the core number describe the chip's logic series, such as speed or power. The LS stands for low-power Schottky, a particular type of TTL logic design. Other types are the S for Schottky, AS for advanced Schottky, ALS for advanced low-power Schottky, and H for high-speed TTL.

(A) Typical manufacturer markings on an IC.

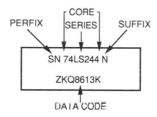

(B) Interpretation of the package markings on an IC.

Fig. 6-5. Photograph showing actual ICs in a PC system.

The suffix represents either the package type or the temperature range. Usually it describes the package type. For the 74LS244 IC, "N" denotes a plastic dual in-line (DIP) package. Other package types include flatpacks, single in-line packages (SIPs), and leaded or leadless chip carriers.

The second letter-number combination shown on a chip represents the manufacturer and the year and week that the chip was made. For example, the numbers 8613 printed below a manufacturer's device code represent the 13th week in 1986, the date of manufacture of the chip. Likewise, a chip marked 7 4 L S 7 4 and 8 3 4 7 is a quad 2-input NOR gate manufactured in the 47th week of 1983.

Resistors

Resistors are used to restrict or limit the flow of electrical current through a board's circuitry. Fig. 6-6 shows three of the primary types of resistors found in the IBM PC/XT/AT circuitry.

(A) Two standard carbon-film resistors used on the PC/XT system board.

(B) A single in-line package (SIP) resistor network found on the fixed disk–floppy diskette drive adapter card.

(C) A DIP resistor network used on the PC AT system board.

Fig. 6-6. Three primary types of resistors.

One type of resistor is the carbon-film device shown in Fig. 6-6A. Its value of resistance is given in ohms, and can be determined by comparing the color bands on the resistor with the color values given in Table 6-1. For example, resistor R2 in Fig. 6-6A is located next to keyboard connector J9 on the system board. It has a color code of green-brown-brown-gold. The first two bands describe the primary number 51. The third band represents the number of zeroes to add to the primary number—in this case, one. The last band is the tolerance value, or how close to the color band value the actual value must be. Thus, by using Table 6-1, the value of R2 is found to be 510 ohms. This matches the value given on the schematics of the IBM PC/XT. The gold band represents a 5% tolerance value. (This means the actual resistance value can be ±5% of the 510-ohm designed value.)

Table 6-1. Color Code Chart

Color	Digit	Multiplier
Black	0	
Brown	1	10
Red	2	100
Orange	3	1000
Yellow	4	10,000
Green	5	100,000
Blue	6	1,000,000
Violet	7	10,000,000
Gray	8	100,000,000
White	9	1,000,000,000
Gold	±5% tolerance	
Silver	±10% tolerance	

Fig. 6-6B shows a single in-line package (SIP) network resistor. It is labelled Z3 on the fixed disk–floppy diskette adapter card. A recently developed electronic device, the resistor network is actually a group of resistors built into a single in-line package (SIP) or into a dual in-line package (DIP). Several SIP resistor networks are mounted on the board. These resistors are designated "RNxx," "RMxx," or "Zx". Resistor network Z3 is used by several components on the board at the same time and contains 220- and 330-ohm resistors in a single package.

The resistor shown in Fig. 6-6C is a dual in-line package (DIP) network resistor. Labelled RN1, it is located near the RAM chips on the PC AT system board.

Network Resistors

The resistance designation of the resistors in a network is printed on the side of each package. DIP package RN1, on the AT system board, is marked 916C300X2SR. The "300" is a key to its resistance value in ohms. The first two numbers (3 and 0) indicate the significant figures. The third number (0) tells how many zeroes to add to the significant figures. Thus, 300 means 30 plus no zeroes, or 30 ohms.

Some network resistors are marked directly with the value of their resistance. Network RN2 on the PC system board is marked 898-1-R8.2K. The 8.2K labels the resistor network as a network of 8.2K-ohm resistors.

Several other resistor types can be found in the PC including metal-film resistors (resistor R15 in the AT), wire-wound resistors (resistor R6 in the XT), metal-oxide resistors (resistor R52 in the XT power supply), and temperature-sensitive thermistors (devices R1 and R99 in the AT power supply).

Capacitors

In addition to chips, your computer's system board contains a number of devices called capacitors. Capacitors come in four varieties:

1. Electrolytic.
2. Tantalum.
3. Ceramic Film.
4. Variable.

Each of these types of capacitors can be found on the motherboards and the adapter cards. Three of these are shown in Fig. 6-7.

Capacitors are measured in fractions of a farad. Capacitance values are labelled "μF" or "mfd" for microfarad (one millionth of a farad) and "pF" for picofarad (one trillionth of a farad). (The "mfd" is an old radio operator/

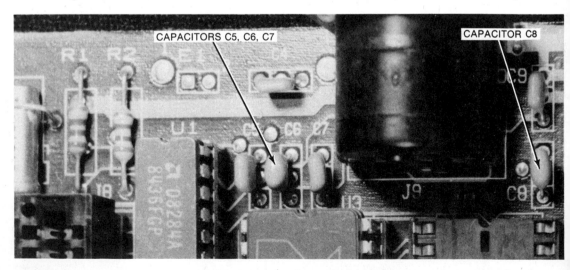

(A) Film capacitors on the PC/XT system board.

Fig. 6-7.

mechanic's term. It has been replaced with μF.) Thus 0.022 microfarad means 0.000000022 farad and 47 picofarads means 47 trillionths of a farad.

Capacitor value identification is one of the most challenging tasks you will encounter because most companies like to use their own identification standards. Fig. 6-7A shows three film capacitors mounted on the PC/XT system board. Capacitors C5 and C6 are rated at 0.047 microfarad. Capacitor C7 is rated at 56 microfarads.

Ceramic film capacitor C8, between the J3 and J4 slots on the PC system board, has the value "0.047 ± 10%" stamped on it. It's easy to see that this is a 0.047-μF capacitor. Other ceramic film capacitors are color-banded and can be decoded using a color chart similar to that given for resistors. A capacitor color chart is shown in Table 6-2. These color-banded capacitors have two additional bands added, which specify the capacitor's temperature dependence and tolerance. Capacitance varies with temperature (and to some extent with size and

ELECTROLYTICS

(B) Electrolytic capacitors on the fixed disk–floppy diskette drive adapter card.

C22

C37

(C) Variable capacitor C22 on the fixed disk–floppy diskette drive adapter card.

(D) Variable capacitor C37 on the fixed disk–floppy diskette drive adapter card.

Capacitors.

applied voltage.) The temperature dependence of the capacitance value is given as the coefficient parts per million per degree Centigrade (PPM/°C). Tolerance defines how much variation is permissible between the actual value of the capacitance and the nominal capacitance value.

Table 6-2.   Capacitor Color Codes*

Color	Digit	Multiplier	Tolerance
Black	0	1	
Brown	1	10	
Red	2	100	
Orange	3	1,000	
Yellow	4	10,000	
Green	5	100,000	
Blue	6	1,000,000	
Violet	7		
Gray	8		
White	9		10%
Gold			5%
Silver			10%

*Indicating capacitance in picofarads.

The third type of capacitor is called an electrolytic capacitor (Figure 6-7B). This capacitor has its polarity marked on its case. Usually, the negative pole is indicated with an arrow marking. Electrolytic capacitors C45 and C46 on the fixed disk–floppy diskette adapter card each have a rating of 22 microfarads.

Variable capacitor C22 is located at the upper right side of the Diskette adapter card (Fig. 6-7C). Capacitor C22 is used to adjust the voltage-controlled oscillator signal in VCO U16. Varying the capacitance from 7 to 60 picofarads changes the VCO frequency. Variable capacitor C37, on the lower left side of the same adapter card (Fig. 6-7D), varies the frequency of VCO U51. This capacitor can be set to any value between 4 and 20 picofarads.

Diodes

Diodes are tiny (usually glass) devices shaped like resistors. They are marked with identification printing on their sides (although most of the time you'll have a tough time reading it). There are several diodes on the motherboard. The key to determining if the device in question is a diode or something else is the glass construction and the label on the side. A "1Nxxxx" label denotes a diode. Near the top of the PC system board, right above the expansion slots, is diode D1. D1 is a standard diode, much like a 1N4001 diode. It's part of the voltage-regulation circuitry for the cassette data in signal (CASS DATA IN) being applied to the input port of the 8255 PPI.

Transistors

The half-moon-shaped device on the system and adapter boards is a transistor. The key to recognizing a transistor is its shape and its "2Nxxxx" designator. Fig. 6-8 is a drawing of the transistor. On its flat side is printed "2N3904." The "2Nxxxx" label tells us it's a transistor. If we look this transistor up in a parts catalog, we will find that the 2N3904 transistor is a general-purpose device. It sells for about 35 cents.

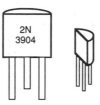

Fig. 6-8   Representation of the 2N3904 transistor.

In electronic parts catalogs, you'll find several lists of circuit-board components, with prices that will pleasantly amaze you. Since most microcomputer discrete-component failures involve ICs, introducing the capacitors, the resistors, the diodes, and the transistors serves only to familiarize you with what is on your IBM motherboard. These devices are soldered onto the board and should be replaced only by those experienced in electronics repair. Socketed chip replacement is probably as far as you'll want to go in repairing a computer. Usually you'll let a repair technician replace the soldered-in components.

Why Components and Devices Fail

Many failures can be found using deductive reasoning and understanding. However (for those who know how to use such equipment), the use of troubleshooting equipment makes it easier to analyze and isolate computer problems associated with timing, frequency, and intermittent operation. Fortunately, most troubleshooting and repair can be relatively simple if you know how the system should operate and understand why electronic components fail.

Failures generally occur in the circuits that are used or stressed the most. By stressed, I mean subjected to heating up when data or control signals pass through, then cooled down, and then heated again. These include the RAM and ROM memory chips, the 8088 and 80286 CPUs, and the input/output (I/O) chips between the motherboard and the peripherals. The CPU is highly reliable and seldom fails (although many pseudo-technicians replace the CPU first when system board failures occur). Most failures involve the other chips, particularly the I/O circuits. Except for the ROM chips, which are programmed by IBM, and the PAL (programmable array logic) chips, which are fabricated to IBM design requirements, most of the other chips on the system board and adapter cards are standard, off-the-shelf devices. They are so common that they've earned the nickname "jelly beans"—inexpensive, easy-to-replace products. They can be obtained at a relatively low cost from almost any electronics store or IC distributor.

Integrated Circuits (Chips)

An integrated circuit, or chip, is constructed typically of silicon with tiny particles of certain impurities imbedded in the silicon. By selective doping and metallization of the silicon during manufacture, tiny transistor-type circuits, or "gates," can be formed. Applying a voltage to selected locations on the chip allows the device to invert a voltage level (+ 5 volts, logic 1, to 0 volts, logic 0) and perform other logic functions. The chips can be made with silicon/metal junctions so tiny that hundreds of thousands transistors can be placed on one chip. A memory chip the size of a fingernail can hold over 500,000 transistors.

One problem that chip manufacturers encounter is how to get voltages and signals on and off such a tiny device. Very thin wires are used as inputs and outputs to the chip. These wires are bonded to tiny pads on the chip. The other end of each wire is bonded to a larger pad on a supporting material (the big part of what we call the integrated circuit, as shown in Fig. 6-9).

Fig. 6-9.   Photo shows the chip pad-to-package interconnect leads.

The chip's supporting structure includes the plastic package in which the chip is mounted and the pins that are used in mounting the IC onto our printed-circuit boards.

The material used in the manufacture of ICs has much to do with how long a chip will reliably operate. Integrated circuits are designed to operate for many hours, as shown in Table 6-3.

Table 6-3. Life Test Data for Various IC Technologies

Technology	Operational Hours Before Failure
Bipolar	6 million
CMOS	55 million
NMOS	100 million
NMOS microprocessors	40 million
PMOS	10 million
PMOS microprocessors	35 million
8080 microprocessor	16 million
4K SRAM	10 million

From Table 6-3, one would think these ICs almost never fail. On the contrary, the use we make of these components and how we physically handle the chips has a tremendous impact on their operational life. These tiny silicon and metal chips are placed in environments that put them under continuous thermal stress (heating up, cooling down, heating up, etc.) during normal operation. Thermal stress affects those tiny strands of wire, or leads, going between the chip and the supporting structure, including the large pins inserted or soldered into sockets. After a period of time, the thermal stress can cause the bonding of the wire lead to break away from the pad on the chip. This disconnect causes an input or output to become an "open" circuit, and chip replacement is then required. These interconnection failures are principally caused by electromigration. Silicon aluminum and copper aluminum were invented to replace the older pure aluminum interconnection wiring because these composite metals can tolerate higher current.

Chip failure is also caused by a phenomenon called "metal migration." An IC can be compared to an ocean of atoms. Some tiny particles of metal float about in this sea, migrating in directions perpendicular to electrical current flowing through the chip. Problems occur when these metal particles begin to collect in localized areas of the chip. If the concentration is in the middle of one of the microelectronic transistors, these concentrations cause the transistor to operate differently (or not at all). If the resistance of these collected metals gets high enough, it causes the device to operate intermittently or to simply refuse to work. Since a transistor is part of a logic gate, the gate malfunctions and the output may become "stuck at 1" or "stuck at 0," no matter what the input signal is.

Theoretically, a wearout failure won't occur until after several hundred years of use. We shorten the life span of our chips by placing them in high temperature, and high voltage or power cycling environments. These cause the devices to fail sooner. This is an acceptable reality when we desire performance from our electronic circuitry. Thus, there is a practical limit to how long your system and adapter boards can operate without failure.

Any event that acts to break down the material composition of a chip can become a failure mechanism. A number of effects can weaken the breakdown strength of the chip including its operational time (time-dependent breakdown).

In bipolar and MOS technologies, the most important failure mechanisms in failed parts returned from the field can generally be attributed to poor assembly procedures and poor chip packages.

The second most important failure mechanism in ICs is caused by electrical overstress. Approximately one fourth of the returned parts tested, demonstrated failures caused by operating the device in high temperature or high humidity.

The remaining cause of failures found in returned parts was a physical malfunction caused by pinholes in the chip die and by broken interconnections.

In the manufacturing process, the major contributing factor to failure was dust particles. In fact, dust particles are believed responsible for 80% of all fabrication-line failures in today's MOS chips.

I/O buffers have a higher failure rate than the internal logic cells because they experience higher currents and consume more power. Most bipolar parts have high power dissipation at the interconnection of the chip to the leads. Other problems occur outside the chip package, between the chip pad wires and the support structure pin leads—the physical inputs and outputs of the device.

These types of failures include inputs or outputs shorted to ground, pins shorted to the +5-volt supply, pins shorted together, open pins, and connectors with intermittent defects. Under normal use, chips finally fail because of an input or output shorted to ground.

I/O pins and the bonding wires that connect the package pins to the pads on the IC die inside the package have a higher failure rate than the chip devices because the interconnections are susceptible to environmental stress, such as temperature variations, vibration, and improper handling and operation. Historically, only 2% of all IC failures occur in the silicon of the chip. Usually, 98% of all IC failures occur in the interconnects—the bonding wires and the leads of the package, and the interface cables.

The classical "stuck-at" faults typical of early IC logic devices, have been joined by nonclassical faults, such as shorts between adjacent signal paths, which cause changing functions in an IC circuit. A "stuck-open" fault in a CMOS transmission gate, or a reduction in performance caused by electrostatic discharge (ESD) damage, can cause slow chip operation. There are several other causes for slow independent changes in a logic level. For instance, a logic high simply drifts down to a logic low. Some typical IC failure mechanisms are summarized in the following list.

► Improper fabrication techniques.

► Contaminants in the IC material.

► Broken wires.

► Bond wires lifted from chip pad.

► Deformed layout of IC circuits.

► Mechanical defects.

► Poor metal alloys in wires and leads.

► Chip die separation inside the package.

► Loss of hermetic seal on the package.

Diodes and Transistors

The diodes and transistors on your computer's system board and adapter cards are made of solid materials that act much alike, whether used in a diode or in a transistor. In fact, a transistor can be considered as being constructed of two diodes.

Diodes are one-way valves for electric current that allow current flow in only one direction. Typically made of either silicon or germanium, they are used in power supplies as rectifiers or in circuits that maintain a constant voltage level. Other specialized diodes are made of gallium arsenide and produce light when energized in a certain way. These are called light-emitting diodes, or LEDs. LEDs are used as power-on indicators for switches and keyboard key-use switches.

Transistors are used in the IBM microcomputer circuitry as amplifiers or electronic switches. Transistors and diodes usually fail because their outputs short together, or because a connection inside the device disconnects causing an open or break in the circuitry. Either failure will cause a total loss of signal (and the usefulness of the component).

Diodes and transistors fail in the same ways and for the same reasons as IC chips, but chips fail more often than do diodes or transistors. One reason is that there are many more tiny transistors on a chip (and thus more pn junctions) than on a single (discrete) diode or transistor. This produces more heat and hence more thermal wear in the chip. In addition, the tiny transistor pn junctions of an IC make it more susceptible to electrostatic discharge effects. Thus, when we touch a component (or even the keyboard), we can zap a static charge off our body into the computer.

Capacitors

Several types of capacitors are mounted on the system board and adapter cards. Understanding how a standard capacitor is constructed will aid in understanding how these devices fail. The capacitor is constructed of two plates, separated by a dielectric. A voltage is placed across the plates and, for a short instant, current flows across the dielectric gap. But soon electrons build up on one plate matching the number of electrons on the other plate; this causes the current flow to stop. The capacitor is then considered charged to some voltage potential. Capacitors are used to store a potential charge and, due to this ability, they can filter unwanted signal spikes (sharp, quick peaks of voltage) to ground. An electrolytic capacitor is constructed as shown in Fig. 6-10.

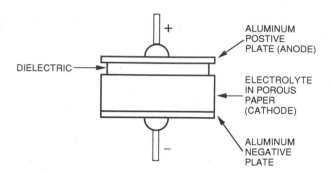

Fig. 6-10. A diagram of an electrolytic capacitor.

An electrolytic capacitor consists of two aluminum foils, sheets, or plates separated by a layer of porous paper soaked with electrolyte (a conductive liquid). On one plate (the positive plate) a thin layer of aluminum oxide is deposited by applying a dc voltage to the two aluminum plates. This oxide layer is called the dielectric of the capacitor because of its insulating ability. A capacitor has an anode (the positive plate with the oxide layer) and a cathode or negative capacitor plate (the electrolyte). The second aluminum foil (plate) connects the cathode to the external circuits. In operation, electrons build up on one plate causing it to become so negative that further current flow is prevented (remember that electrons have a negative charge). An electrical potential (charge) is stored.

Film capacitors, such as C5, C6, and C7 in Fig. 6-7A, are constructed of alternating layers of aluminum foil and a plastic (usually polystyrene) insulation. The metal foil acts as the plates and the plastic insulation acts as the dielectric between the plates. Film capacitors are coated with epoxy and have tinned copper leads.

Capacitors open or short, depending on the operating conditions and their age. Capacitors fail when they short internally or when one of the leads disconnects, causing an open. Again there is a loss of signal.

Electrolytic capacitors are especially susceptible to the aging process. One effect of aging is the "drying out" of the electrolyte. The capacitance value increases and circuit performance decreases. Finally the capacitance value drops dramatically as the plates fold toward each other, gradually shorting the plates together.

Another type of failure occurs when some of the dielectric oxide insulation dissolves into the moist electrolyte, causing the thickness of the dielectric to shrink. This usually occurs when the electrolytic capacitor sits for a long time without any applied voltage. In this case, the capacitance value increases and a high leakage of electrons occurs across the plates, making the capacitor useless.

The leads of a capacitor can also become physically detached from a plate, causing an open in the circuit. Also, the plates can short together if a large area of one plate is stripped of its dielectric oxide layer by the application of too much voltage.

Resistors

Resistors are current-limiting, voltage-dropping devices that are quite reliable and which should function properly for the life of a computer. However, the same factors that shorten the useful life of ICs also act to reduce the operational life of resistors—high temperatures, high voltage, and power cycling. Such stresses cause breaks in the carbon, resistive paste, or resistive layers that comprise the resistor, producing an open conduction path in the circuit. Excessively high voltages can produce an electrical current so large that it actually chars resistors to burnt ash, although this is rare in digital circuits where the highest voltage on a board is normally 12 volts (usually 5 volts), and the currents are very tiny indeed (in milliamperes).

The failure of a circuit-board resistor is almost always associated with a catastrophic failure of some other circuit component. Resistor failures, when they occur, are usually located in the printer electronics rather than on the system board or adapter cards of the personal computer. However, like capacitors, resistors seldom fail. Excessive temperatures will also damage resistors.

Resistors can be subjected to too much current and can actually bake in the circuit. The result is usually an open circuit with shorting during the "meltdown." All the devices mentioned so far are of the solid-state type. These components are built to rigid specifications but are constructed of materials (metals, plastics, oxide, etc.) whose electronic performance changes as the components age. This process can be accelerated by placing excessive voltages on the board circuitry, or by allowing the system to operate without adequate cooling. Severe temperatures or high voltages can cause the device and the circuit or system to behave strangely. Fortunately, the motherboards of the IBM PC, XT, and AT are not normally exposed to high voltages. But they can get pretty hot (especially if you plug a lot of adapter cards into the expansion slots, or cover the ventilation slots around the system unit chassis), and this will affect the operation of the components.

During normal operation, circuit components (especially the chips) are subjected to thermal stress. They heat up when the machine is energized and cool down when the PC is turned off. They then heat up again when we turn the machine back on. This heating up and cooling down weakens the ICs and eventually causes failures. Thermal stress can produce a break in a wire connection leading from inside the chip to a pin, causing an "open" circuit and the need for a chip replacement.

Lengthy exposure to high voltages or high temperatures can change the operating characteristics of a device even if no break in the chip or lead connections occurs. When the performance of these devices degrades enough, the system starts to fail. A chip may work intermittently or may simply refuse to work at all. An output can become stuck at "1" or stuck at "0," no matter what input signal is applied. Theoretically, such a wear-out failure won't occur until after several hundred years of use, but we typically shorten the life span of the chips by placing them in high-temperature, high-voltage, and power-cycling environments. This causes early failures.

Problems between the chip internal leads and the support structure pins that connect the device to the rest of the computer can cause failures, such as inputs or outputs shorted to ground, pins shorted to the + 5-volt supply, pins shorted together, and bent or broken pins and connectors. Most failures result from opens, or shorts to ground. Chips fail far more often than do diodes or transistors, because the chips contain hundreds or thousands of tiny circuits that are each susceptible to failure.

Disk-Drive Failures

Disk drives provide the ability to save data to disk and load programs and data into and out of the computer at almost unbelievable speeds. These drive "boxes" contain some of the most complex collections of electronics and mechanical components/hardware ever constructed. Thousands of tiny magnetic signals can be stored on a diskette when the diskette is inserted into one of these drives. Also, on command, the drive can load the stored data back into the computer.

We expect the disk drives to save all of our programs and data accurately and quickly, and, then, accurately load the information back into our IBM Personal Computer without losing a single number or letter. And they usually do. Disk drives will provide months of faultless service if you do your part, by operating them carefully and providing periodic cleaning and adjustments.

But, users tend to operate drives while smoking. They slam the drive door closed. And, they "save" money by buying and using the least expensive disks they can find. Finally, one day, the DOS ERROR message appears and the drive "gives up the ghost." Now what? What kind of failure occurred to the floppy disk drive(s)? Is the failure due to "heavy handed" handling, cigarette smoke contamination, or is the cause oxides from the cheap disks? Both smoke and oxides can clog the read/write heads.

Consistent heavy use of these electromechanical disk drives causes them to be involved in most of the common computer problems. Not only is the circuitry active much of the time, but, by definition, any machine with a mechanical movement, will require periodic alignment. The moving parts in a disk drive will gradually drift out of their very strict operating range.

Typically, drive failure is usually a change in the drive rotation speed that affects the reading and writing of information on a diskette. Floppy disk rotation speed is adjusted for approximately 300 revolutions per minute, or 200 milliseconds per revolution. As the speed varies from this optimum, disk read and write errors begin to occur. Both drive speed and tracking must be within prescribed limits for proper disk data storage and retrieval. Therefore, both the drive speed and tracking must be periodically checked and adjusted, because age and movement of equipment can cause the settings to drift off. However, you needn't worry about relocating your system as long as you carefully lift up and set down all of the computer equipment. Don't jar it.

However, even when a drive sits in one place and simply operates day-in and day-out, the drive and tracking can drift outside the proper write/read specifications. Every time you energize the computer, the system runs a diagnostic test and then commands the magnetic head in the drive to seek the home (Track 0) position. When it senses home, it moves back and forth from track to track, writing or reading data. The movement of the mechanical parts in the drive can affect the tracking a tiny bit with each disk access. Many drives compensate for speed loss due to the aging of components, but compensation can only work so far. After a period of use, depending on the amount of use and care given the equipment, the tracking can be barely within limits. So periodically check and adjust tracking and speed to keep them in "tune." The steps required to make tracking adjustments require the use of oscilloscopes and special diagnostics diskettes. Therefore, we do not recommend that you attempt these procedures yourself. The speed adjustment also requires a special program diskette. However, a method for adjusting the speed on some drives is outlined in the troubleshooting section detailing the procedures for your PC model type.

Rough handling in disk insertion and removal can cause misalignment of the read head. Head misalignment is not an easy thing to fix. It usually requires special software and head alignment tools, including an oscilloscope. Therefore, head alignment should be done by an authorized service department.

Video Display Failures

Like a television set, a display monitor will sooner or later develop a problem and need repair. One reason for the failure of a display is that this output device is the only "new" electronic unit that still uses a form of vacuum tube. As mentioned in earlier chapters, the cathode-ray tube (CRT) is the screen you look at when you work with your computer. It displays video information. The CRT is probably the only modern electronic component that is guaranteed to wear out.

Also, in the discussions pertaining to PC operation, you learned that the letters and numbers you see on your screen are produced by electrons striking the back side of the CRT face. The electron streams get weaker as the CRT ages, but you can correct some of the effects of age if you possess knowledge and experience in television and monitor repair. Unless you're so trained, DO NOT open the monitor and expose yourself to dangerous high voltages.

The following are some possible video display failures:

▶ *Short inside the CRT*—This can result in an audible "hum" and a visible bar across the screen, very poor contrast, a bright beam on the screen, or even diagonal lines on the screen.

▶ *Open or disconnected wiring inside the CRT*—No characters are displayed on the screen.

▶ *Bright "bloomy" letters; poor intensity control*— This is caused by tube age. The center of the CRT has worn so that you can get normal brightness with the intensity turned down as far as possible, but black is really black, and the gray shades are poor or not displayed.

▶ *Screen edge won't display; picture fuzzy*—A deposit has formed on the inside of the screen (tube face) causing reduced brightness and a fuzzy display. The deposit is thicker at the outer edge of the CRT.

▶ *No picture*—Brightness and intensity controls have no effect.

▶ *Marginal performance*—Display monitor performance is less than optimal. Monitors, like computers, printers, and other electronic equipment, are affected by dust and dirt. These pollutants coat the components inside the chassis and cause a heat buildup.

In general, CRT failures cannot be corrected by anyone other than a trained service technician. The voltages inside the chassis of your monitor reach as high as 25,000 volts. These levels can be lethal if you make a mistake.

Unless you are trained to repair video displays, the only adjustments you should attempt are those that can be accomplished from outside the chassis. If you see alignment holes in the back of the chassis, you'd be better off keeping out of these, too. But if you feel experimental, be sure that you use a plastic alignment tool (it looks like a thin pen with screwdriver-shaped ends). The first action for a dull, low-intensity display is to clean the screen.

Repairs Can Generate Failures

Some people have a knack for fouling up whatever they try to "repair." These folks should keep their hands out of the equipment, bite the bullet, and take their system into a repair shop. Overzealous or undertrained repair personnel, and those novice techs who are in a hurry or do not understand the system being analyzed, can introduce more trouble than they can correct.

Bent or Broken Pins

Watch the way you put those chips in. You can only straighten the pins on an IC so many times before they break off completely.

All too often, IC pins bend while being inserted into the board during repair procedures. One of the most frustrating experiences is to replace an IC only to discover much later that you bent a pin under the chip, thus creating symptoms that cause you to believe something else was bad. Imagine replacing a chip that caused a speaker failure and then having the disk drive fail to boot. You could spend hours searching for a failure that you created yourself! To avoid this, be alert and careful when conducting repairs. Above all, don't rush when "fixing" the problem. Take your time and make sure the job is done right. And check your work after making a component replacement.

Electrostatic Discharge (ESD)

Devices can be damaged or destroyed by improper handling. ESD, or electrostatic discharge, occurs when someone picks up an electrostatic-sensitive IC, such as a RAM, ROM, or CPU, without first grounding himself or herself to dissipate any static electricity which that person might be carrying.

Self-repair enthusiasts aren't the only ones who err when it comes to ESD. Many technicians consistently and improperly ground themselves when trying to remove static electricity. People and objects, such as desks and benches, can accumulate a substantial electrical charge. Your body can actually accumulate static charges up to 25,000 volts. It's not unusual to build up and carry charges of 500 to 1500 volts. When you touch a computer or a component inside the unit, the potential you are carrying will discharge to ground. This discharge will find the shortest path to ground and, if it's through a chip, it can damage or destroy the IC. Many types of ICs are extremely sensitive to static electricity. A discharge of only 3 volts into a chip can cause malfunctions and wild screen displays.

The ICs in your IBM were designed to withstand a certain amount of low-voltage electrostatic discharge. Latch-up (sticking at a logic high or low) and the destruction of the transistors in a chip can both occur when excessive ESD is passed through the chip. To prevent ESD problems from affecting electronic circuitry, you should discharge any potential on your body to ground before touching anything inside the machine. This can be accomplished by touching a grounded object before touching the computer. I instinctively touch a metal desk lamp near my computer before reaching for the computer's power-on switch. Inside the system unit, you can touch the power-supply case. The better service technicians use a grounding strap, which they attach around one wrist. The other end of the strap is connected to system ground. This frees them to move about and touch components without fear of zapping something.

Some chips, such as the bipolar TTL ICs, are more susceptible to static than others. The chips produced in metal-oxide semiconductor (MOS) technology are the most susceptible. These chips include the following:

► 8088/80286 CPU.

► ROM memory chips.

► 8237 DMA controller.

► 8253/8254 programmable interval timer.

► 8255 programmable peripheral interface.

► 8259 programmable interrupt controller.

► 8284/82284 clock generator.

► 8288/82288 bus controller.

Improper Soldering/Desoldering

A self-generated failure can also be caused by improper desoldering and soldering. NEVER ATTEMPT TO UNSOLDER OR SOLDER A PC BOARD IF YOU DON'T KNOW HOW! Soldering and desoldering is a skill that every technician needs to know, but one that self-repair users need only know if interested. If you're a novice, for goodness sake don't learn by practicing on a $500 system board. Practice on wires, on a board containing cheap components, or on devices that won't cost much to replace. A typical solder-related problem is that of a novice solderer holding the solder iron or pencil to the board for so long that it melts the etches and pads on the board. This can introduce many more hours of repair work than you expected. Also, NEVER use the device called a "soldering gun" on a PC board. The high heat of a soldering gun cannot be controlled and you will destroy more than you fix.

Solder splashes can also raise havoc on a component board when too much solder is used to fuse a connection. Then, when the soldering pencil is removed, a tiny ball of molten solder can drop from the end of the soldering pencil right onto the board, shorting out parts of the circuit. Solder balls are so tiny that they are not usually noticed when falling into the circuitry.

Oversoldering can also occur. This is when the soldering pencil is held too long to the point being soldered and too much solder flows to the connection. The solder can flow through the spacing in the hole around an IC pin and start building up on the other side of the board. It may flow back through the board and then start climbing the pin. When the pin is all covered with solder, a big solder ball builds under the chip, shorting the soldered pin to other pins and to the board etches around it. This is a sure indication that the repair person doesn't yet understand how to solder properly. Soldering is an art. If you haven't mastered this art, don't fret, let someone else do it.

Incomplete soldering (or cold-solder joints) can also introduce failure problems. I remember one repair where a resistance test from one IC pin to ground measured nearly infinity instead of close to zero. There was continuity across the component, but from one side of the component to the next component in the circuit path, an infinitely high open resistance was measured. A visual inspection revealed a cold-solder connection at the component wire lead. The wire end was cleaned, retinned, and resoldered, eliminating the problem and completing the repair.

In yet another case, many hours of alternately applying canned coolant, followed by hot air, to various areas of the suspected circuit failed to locate the problem. More time was then expended pulling on wires and prodding joints with a plastic screwdriver blade, but to no avail. Finally, when moving one wire, the problem disappeared. The pins were resoldered correctly, removing the cold solder joints and eliminating the problem.

If a component is desoldered during a test, or if a new part is installed, it must be placed in the correct board holes or on the correct pads, and then soldered in carefully. Careless or improper desoldering and resoldering procedures can create troubles and multiply the difficulties, thus converting a typical simple repair into a tough "dog" repair. Soldering and desoldering techniques are covered later in this chapter.

Using the Wrong Replacement Part

Installing a wrong replacement part can change problem symptoms without correcting the failure. The following discussion illustrates how even some repair techs get snookered into using the wrong replacement part.

I remember being told of an unusual problem observed by a service technician while repairing a broken machine. During the visual inspection, the service tech noticed fresh solder flux around a diode and a nearby transistor on a circuit board. Someone had replaced the original diode and transistor in a vain attempt to correct the malfunction. Both the diode and transistor tested good. Then he noticed that the previous "repair tech" had installed a universal transistor in place of the device called for on the schematic and in the parts list. Replacing the universal transistor with the specified original-type part didn't correct the failure symptom, however. Since the transistor replacement was improper, the tech also suspected the replacement diode. He checked it carefully and discovered that this component too was not as recommended by the manufacturer. The correct diode was installed and the system was restored to proper operation.

In an April, 1987, issue of *Electronics Servicing & Technology*, Max Goodstein described a difficult troubleshooting incident in which a malfunction occurred about 30 minutes after circuit activation. The components in the suspected circuit were sprayed with cooling spray, hoping to identify a heat-sensitive device. Cooling one IC seemed to help, so the IC was replaced, but the problem remained. All the components in the malfunctioning stage, both in and out of circuit, were tested. No bad components were found. Then the repair person noticed two parts in a related stage that were connected to the suspected stage. Conducting ohmmeter tests of the resistors, capacitors, and diodes in this stage, a shorted diode was discovered. The diode was replaced, but the symptom remained. Removing a transistor from its mounting, the device was tested with a meter and discovered to be bad. Not having a direct replacement in stock, a "similar" transistor was substituted into the circuit. The malfunction was not corrected. However, when the proper type replacement transistor was later installed, the problem went away.

Although you will most likely limit your repairs to IC replacement, be very careful to use the correct replacement parts for failed components. Both the manufacturer's code and the series of the replacement should be the same as that of the failed part.

Improper Cable Hook-Up

The improper connection of cables can not only cause nonoperation, it can also damage components. Plugging cables into sockets or connectors, with the connector one pin-position off, has destroyed plenty of ICs. This is why many cable manufacturers key their plugs and sockets so mating can only occur one way. On adapter cards where keyed connection is not provided, a danger exists in improper mating, thus placing the signals and voltages on the wrong pins.

Another typical error occurs when cable connections are not tightly made. The interface may look fine, but only some of the signals can get through. This can also happen if you haven't kept the connectors clean. Corrosion on the pins and in the socket holes builds up, blocking signal flow. If cable connectors are not fully made or if they become corroded, no signal, or at best, intermittent signal action can occur.

Noise Interference

Ribbon cables don't have much protection from radio-frequency interference or from magnetic fields produced by high-voltage machines (or even power cords). Electronic signal noise can be introduced into computer circuitry when cables are placed near sources of radio-frequency interference (RFI) or electromagnetic interference (EMI). These interference noises are typically due to being in close proximity to CRTs and to power cables. Even a nearby vacuum-cleaner motor can interfere with proper computer operation. Data can be changed or lost during transmissions between the computer and a disk drive or printer when in a high-noise interference area. Don't place cables near the CRT or pass them through loops of power cable.

Printers may either print garbage or nothing at all, if the ribbon cable connecting the computer to the printer runs alongside or through a loop in an energized power cord. Loops of cable and power cords are particular sources of unwanted signal noise. Most quality-type interface cables are insulated from this type of noise interference, but you can defeat the cable's shielding by placing it in a strong magnetic or electrical field. This can produce weird symptoms or even an apparent system failure. Noise interference is a major cause of intermittent failures. This will be discussed in detail later.

Other Common Repair-Generated Failures

When it comes to repair-generated failures, if it can be done, someone has probably done it.

Take "liquid fry" for example. "Liquid fry" occurs when someone brings a liquid too close to the computer and then accidentally spills the liquid into the top of the keyboard while the machine is running. Besides having a real mess to clean up, you also get to replace lots of components.

Blocking the computer's ventilation openings or stuffing the computer with piggyback expansion boards can produce unwanted heat. Such asphyxiation of the circuitry "kills" components, introducing unnecessary headaches to computer users.

How to Localize Failures

There are two ways to localize failures and determine which computer part has malfunctioned: the *software approach* and the *hardware approach*.

The software approach is a troubleshooting method used widely by most IBM repair technicians and system self-repair users. As long as the disk drive will boot up properly, we can often find the failure using diagnostic software. As you know, your PC has a built-in diagnostic power-on self test (POST) program that checks out the machine each time you apply power. This program is well written and does much to ease your mind that all is well inside the computer. But it doesn't check everything. We'll discuss this in greater detail later.

In the hardware approach, physical tests are conducted on the system and its components to isolate, localize, and identify failure sources. Often troubleshooting tools are used to measure the voltage (logic) levels in the circuitry. These tools can include the logic probe, the logic pulser, the current probe, the oscilloscope, the multimeter, the logic analyzer, and the signature analyzer. While this text provides a minimum hands-on way to find most hardware failures, this approach can get involved. Detailed analysis requires a knowledge of electronics and test equipment. Both the hardware and software approaches are important in their own right, so each will be covered separately in the following paragraphs.

The Hardware Approach

Usually when a chip comes to the end of its useful life, a catastrophic failure occurs—it cooks itself internally. Although your eyes can't always see the chip defect, you can find the problem without much effort. (But don't think that every time your IBM personal computer quits working, you've just had a catastrophic failure.) For those problems that are not easy to identify, let's refer again to our guidelines for success.

1. Don't panic.
2. Observe.
3. Use your senses.
4. Retry.
5. Document.
6. Assume one problem.
7. Use correct service data.
8. Use the proper test equipment.
9. Diagnose to the section.
10. Consult your index of symptoms.
11. Localize to a stage.
12. Isolate to the failed part.
13. Test and verify proper operation.

Don't Panic

Besides your user's and reference manuals, you now have a book that will help

Observe

What are the symptoms? What conditions existed at the time of failure? What actions were in progress? What program was running? What was on the display screen? Was there an error message? What functions still work?

Use Your Senses

Look and smell. Is there any odor present that suggests overheated components? Does any part of the system feel hot? Do any components look charred or broken?

Retry

If the display monitor is dark, check its brightness control, the power plug, and the power cord. Is the plug inserted snugly into the back of the computer? Is the other end of the power cord plugged into a wall socket? Is the wall socket working? One AT system "failure" turned out to be the 115/220 switch on the computer. If any of these items aren't all right, fix them and try again.

If the problem involves an external display, the printer, or other I/O peripheral equipment connected to the computer by cable, confirm that the power to the system is turned off. Then disconnect the power plug from the computer and retighten all of the connector cables associated with the failure. Cables have a habit of working loose if they aren't clamped down. Most cables have screw-in hold-downs, or the socket may have clips to hold the cable plug securely fastened. However, many computer users ignore these helpful clamps and just plug the cable into the socket without making sure that it stays mated. Once you've checked the cable connections, reconnect the power plug, power up, and retry.

If a disk won't boot, try booting the disk in the other drive (if there is another floppy drive), or try booting another copy of the program disk. You could also try booting the disk in another compatible PC. (Always use a copy of the program disk. Then, any disk-drive failure won't cause as much frustration if it destroys the data on the backup disk as it would if the disk in use were the program master. Also, if data are altered by a malfunctioning drive, the disk can be recopied again from the program master once the drive problem is resolved.)

If the system still won't work, disconnect all the external equipment except the display monitor, and try to operate the system alone (this is tough if you're using an AT). Sometimes, the failure in a peripheral device appears in another functional part of the computer. If the computer works by itself, the problem is probably in an external device or in the connecting interface (cable or adapter card) to the device. If the computer still doesn't work, refer to step 9 (Diagnose to the section).

Document

Document everything you see, sense, and do. Write down all the conditions observed at the time of failure, or when you verified a reported failure. Write down the conditions that exist now.

- ► What is the PC doing?
- ► What is it not doing?
- ► What is being displayed on the monitor?
- ► Is there an error message?
- ► What is still operating with everything connected? With everything but the monitor disconnected?
- ► Is power still indicated on each part of the system?

Assume One Problem

In digital circuitry, the likelihood of multiple simultaneous failures is low. Usually a single chip malfunctions, causing one or more symptoms. However, if you've shorted something in the circuitry, all bets are off.

Use Correct Service Data

Even a do-it-yourselfer needs good information. You'd be amazed at how many "Mom and Pop" service centers try to run repair operations with little or no technical information on the equipment they claim to support. In one case, a service center covering an entire state was conducting repair activities on a myriad of personal computers, using a 20-page "Technical Manual" and one of my troubleshooting and repair guides. The manufacturer's technical manual was so poor, it was essentially useless. And, while the Howard W. Sams & Company micro-maintenance series of troubleshooting and repair guides are good, they are high-level overview descriptions of personal computer equipment and do not provide information on measurements, waveforms, dc voltages, and in-depth technical theory of operations. This information can be found in advanced types of troubleshooting and repair manuals, the manufacturer's technical repair manuals, and the Howard W. Sams & Company COMPUTERFACTS on the IBM PC, IBM PC/XT, and IBM PC AT.

You can go only so far using this book. Don't attempt a detailed repair without additional service data. If this is your intent, make sure that you have the appropriate Sams COMPUTERFACTS and an advanced troubleshooting and repair manual on hand, and also anything the manufacturer can or will provide. The use of correct and complete service information can prevent moderately difficult repair jobs from becoming "tough dogs." If you value your time, prepare before you repair.

Use Proper Test Equipment

If you intend to go after the "dogs," use the right test equipment. Just like the proper technical documentation, the right test equipment can change difficult repair jobs into routine activities. Going after a failure in electronic circuitry when you are inadequately prepared is like tracking a rabbit through your carrot garden with your eyes blindfolded. Your actions make little difference and, all the while, that rabbit eats more and more of your garden away. The use of proper equipment will be discussed in greater detail later in the book.

Diagnose to the Section

If the system worked when the peripherals were disconnected (step 4), turn the power off and reconnect one of the peripherals. Power up and test. If the unit still works, turn the power off, and reconnect another peripheral. Again, power up and test. Follow this procedure until the unit fails. The built-in diagnostic tests are a big help here. Once a failure occurs, you know what device and what interface section has the problem.

If you disconnected all the peripherals in step 4 and tested the computer alone, and it still didn't work, try to determine what section or division of the machine failed. Describe the failure in simple terms—Drive B won't read a disk, Drive A will.

Consult the Symptom Index

The machine-specific troubleshooting procedures in the following chapters contain an index or chart of the most common failure symptoms associated with the IBM Personal Computers. Each of these chapters includes a section on system error displays. If any error codes are displayed, translating these codes properly can guide you to the correct area of the problem. If the trouble symptoms match a problem described in the pertinent troubleshooting index, turn to the referenced page and follow the instructions given.

CAUTION: Any time you open the computer, ensure that the power is off. Then, touch a metal lamp, or other grounded object, to remove any stray static electricity that might be on your body.

Localize to a Stage

Turn off the power to the computer, and disconnect the power plug. Disassemble the computer. Follow the detailed circuit troubleshooting and analysis steps and procedures given in the following chapters to localize to the failed stage.

Isolate to the Failed Part

Closely following the detailed circuit troubleshooting and analysis procedures given in the following chapters should guide you to the failed part.

Test and Verify Proper Operation

This is an important step. We need to know that all is well with the system. After booting up and testing the system using a copy of your DOS program disk, run the same program that was in the machine at the time of failure to verify that the system is fixed and operating properly.

Replacing IC Chips

Many things can cause an improper system operation, including socketed IC chips. Chips have a tendency to work themselves out of their sockets under normal operation. Thus, a loose RAM chip could be your whole problem.

Replacing IC chips that are installed in sockets may look easy, but there are some pitfalls to recognize and avoid. IC pins are fragile and bend easily, and it doesn't take very many straightening actions to break a pin completely off. It takes a little practice before you can remove a socketed chip without causing it to jump out, flip in midair, and stick you right in the thumb or index finger with that double row of tooth-like pins. Fortunately, there are several devices that make the job much easier. These are the tiny screwdriver or "tweaker," and the IC extractor tool. Fig. 6-11 shows how such tools can aid in removing stubborn chips from their sockets.

Fig. 6-11.　ICs can be removed with a chip extractor or by gently prying up with a screwdriver.

Getting the old chip out is only part of the repair challenge. Now you have to put the new chip in the socket. Here's how to do it:

1. Line up the Pin-1 end of the IC (the end with the notch or dot) with Pin 1 slot on the IC socket. (Note how all the other chips around this socket are mounted.)

2. Place the chip over the socket, lining up the row of pins on one side of the IC with their socket holes. With the chip still at a slight angle, press down gently, causing the row of pins in contact with the socket to bend slightly, which lets the other row of pins slip easily into their sockets, as shown in Fig. 6-12.

3. Press down on the top of the chip firmly with your thumb to seat it completely into the socket. Be careful not to flex the circuit board too much. If necessary, support the motherboard with the fingers of your other hand as you press the chip into place.

Fig 6-12. Start one row of pins into the IC socket. Then press down gently to complete the chip insertion.

Now, that wasn't too bad, was it? Well, there is something else. It is pretty easy to make mistakes in replacing a chip. Here's a few:

► Make sure you don't put the chip in backwards. The notch or dot that marks the Pin 1 end of the chip is intended to help you correctly line up Pin 1 on the chip with Pin 1 on the socket.

► Don't offset the chip in the socket by one pin as shown in Fig. 6-13.

► Don't force the chip down so one of the pins actually hangs out over the socket or is bent up under the chip. Fig. 6-14 is a photograph of a "hang-out" discovered during a system board removal. Pin 1 on this RAM is a data line.

Fig. 6-13. Be careful not to offset the chip by one pin.

Soldering in Chips and IC Sockets

If the chip to be replaced is soldered into the motherboard, always replace the chip with an IC socket (not something you can do if the chip is surface mounted). Then, plug the new IC chip into the socket.

Fig. 6-14. An improperly installed RAM chip discovered on an AT motherboard.

Removing and reinstalling chips that are soldered into the motherboard are actions that require more than a passing knowledge of soldering techniques. Only attempt this part of the test/repair procedure if you have experience in soldering and desoldering multilevel printed-circuit boards. If you don't have the experience, get it before you try to work on an expensive system or adapter board.

Noise

Sometimes a problem is caused simply by nearby noise. Not audible noise, but electrical noise, the kind that produces "static" on your radio. This noise also affects computers. Noise in a computer system can cause data to be lost or wrong data to be stored and displayed. (*NOTE*: To avoid noise problems, keep cables clear and away from power cords, especially coiled power cords.)

It's appropriate, here, to add an admonition: Don't try out your new drill set next to your computer while computing the effect of your recent pay raise. Your calculations might prove unbelievable.

Testing the Repair

Good cleaning, pin and board reseating, and inside-the-case temperature control will prevent the occurrence of most random failures. Board reseating is not usually a problem on the IBM Personal Computer, since the boards can be secured down with screws.

After each repair action, test the system for correct operation. In some cases, the substitution of a good chip corrects the problem. After each substitution, reassemble the system enough to power up and test the repair. This process will very likely locate the trouble. Test and verify. This is an important step. We need to know that all is well with the system. After booting up and testing using a copy of your DOS program disk, run the same program that was in the machine at the time of failure to verify that the system is operating properly. *NOTE*: It's a good idea to log the repair action in a record book to develop a history of the maintenance conducted on the machine and each peripheral.

The Software Approach

Diagnostics and Special Tests

Watching strange and undesirable things happen to your computer system can be frustrating. Often you can't be sure if you caused those weird characters on the screen or if your machine is truly sick. You'd rather not start taking the system apart for failure analysis if the machine isn't really broken.

A way does exist to learn if failure symptoms are caused by some step you performed improperly or are caused by a bug in the software program you're trying to run. Try a different program, using a backup disk of the program, if possible. (If the disk is ruined, your program master disk is safe.) If the error is repeatable and the system drive still boots up, you can also insert a diagnostics disk into your system and run it. This type of disk will run a series of programs that test the condition of the computer. These self-test routines can give you a 95% or greater confidence indicator that your system is working properly and that you need to check your software.

Diagnostic programs can also indicate possible faults before they become hard problems. For example, some diagnostic software tells if the disk speed is too fast, too slow, or within a speed range where reading and writing data can occur without errors. These diagnostics measure the mechanical operation of the disk drives and are helpful during periodic preventive maintenance.

The effectiveness of self-test packages is measured by the level of confidence one can have that the component identified as bad by the software is indeed faulty. Some diagnostics are advertised as only 60% accurate; other companies say that their software test packages have an 85% confidence factor.

Most minicomputer diagnostics only identify faults to the board or module level. That's because most of the customers, in companies that own mini- and microcomputers, usually depend on the computer manufacturer's field service representatives for repair support. In this case, the diagnostic is used as an improved user interface. The user can relay to the computer service center what the diagnostic tests have determined, thus helping the field service technicians get to the problem quicker, shortening the repair visit, and theoretically mini-mizing maintenance costs. This is exactly the situation with the POST diagnostic stored in that ROM of your IBM Personal Computer. If it fails during diagnostic testing, a number is printed on the screen that is a key to help you identify a bad part. Fortunately, most of the PC diagnostics can call-out faults to the chip level (especially faults in memory).

Between 30% and 70% of all IBM Personal Computer failures can be detected by diagnostics programs. Diagnostics programs can be purchased from mail-order companies and many IBM-support computer stores. The IBM Advanced Diagnostics program is the best documented of them all. It comes with a hardware maintenance and service manual that contains a complete listing of all the Power-On Self Test error codes that could be displayed when energizing your IBM. (Of course, it costs an arm and a leg; but value has value.) There is a similar list in the later chapters of this book.

The IBM Advanced Diagnostic package also contains a switch configuration chart and a problem isolation chart to help you quickly get to the failing module. The diagnostics don't contain maximum stress tests for the floppy disk drive, the memory, or any hard disk drives, however. Therefore, if marginal systems problems exist, these diagnostics will probably not catch them. The diagnostics software that comes with each IBM system is much like the Advanced version, but doesn't contain the option to format the hard disk drive, or the wrap plugs to test the asynchronous and printer adapter. In addition, little documentation is provided with the basic system.

Besides the diagnostic software provided with the machine, several com-panies provide diagnostic programs for the IBM PC. These programs test the main memory, the system read-only memory (ROM), the CPU, the monitor, the keyboard, the disk drive speed, and many peripherals. The most common diagnostic programs only check the system random-access memory (RAM) and some of the input/output. Some routines check the operation of the CPU itself, but these usually locate only minor errors. It's difficult for a CPU like the 8088 or the 80286 to run a test on itself (although the PC AT POST takes a good shot at this). Most diagnostics assume that the CPU is working properly.

In this text, I don't recommend a specific product, but the following describes some of the support available. One company advertises software, alignment disk-ettes, parallel/serial wrap-around plugs, and ROM POSTs that they claim will isolate problems to the board and chip level. Their product prices range from

$50.00 for an alignment disk to $495 for the complete service kit. Another product is a $300 software diagnostic tool comprised of a replacement BIOS ROM and an instruction book. The POST test in the replacement ROM performs 36 diagnostic tests and can locate about 70% of the problems in a dead board. And yet another product is a $600 to $800 diagnostic board that plugs into any PC expansion slot (except slot 8). It conducts a self-test, then tests BIOS ROM, the 8253 timer, the 8237 DMA controller, the 8259 interrupt controller, the 8255 I/O chip, all system board and expansion board RAM (up to 1 Mbyte), the keyboard interface, and communication interfaces LPT1/2 and COM1/2. It comes in one version for the PC and the XT, and another for the AT. These products are often well worth the investment if you plan to maintain a quantity of IBM computers or begin your own repair business. The disk-drive support diagnostics are a bargain. Be aware that alignment disks require the use of an oscilloscope.

Testing the Microprocessor

Testing a microcomputer must begin with a thorough analysis and test development related to each component in the system. The logic of this approach is that verification of satisfactory component performance must be assured before a test is conducted on the whole system.

There are three widely used methods for testing a microprocessor. These are:

1. Actual use.
2. Stored response from a known good system board.
3. Algorithmic pattern generation.

In actual use testing, a very limited subset of the CPU's capability is tested under generally ideal conditions. This testing technique is satisfactory for non-critical applications, but is not suitable when the CPU is used for critical applications, such as braking systems on cars or medical monitoring and controlling systems. This testing is done every time you run a program.

Storing a set of response vectors derived from testing a known good board also has some limitations. How was the functionality of the reference system board verified? Another limitation is the large amount of memory required to store simulation and response patterns.

Generating an algorithmic pattern gets around much of the large storage requirement. A test vector compaction technique, such as signature analysis, further reduces the memory requirements of the tester.

Without automatic test equipment, the CPU is usually tested by executing a software program that exercises the nonmemory parts of the chip, such as the data path, the peripheral I/O logic, and the sequencer. During the execution of the program, the test results are compared with a pattern of expected results after every stimulus is applied to these functional blocks. Typically, an external tester monitors the output pins and compares the readings measured with stored expected values.

Testing the I/O Logic

The I/O logic in the IBM Personal Computers consists of latches and transceivers that enable 8- or 16-bit data and 20- or 24-bit addresses to move about on the system board. A test program can be written that exercises individual ports in a predetermined manner. By monitoring the port, and knowing what information should be present on the pins, the output signals can be validated.

Testing the Interrupt Logic

The interrupt signal and interrupt-enable latches are controllable and observable. Therefore, functional test patterns can be generated and applied to this circuitry via a test program written specifically for this purpose. Verification of the proper interrupt sequence can be easily made, but, to check the priority logic, an external tester will likely be required so that the output signals can be indirectly verified by checking whether or not a proper interrupt service routine was executed.

Bus Testing

The various buses in a computer (local, system, I/O, etc.) connect many devices on common interconnect lines. The first step in functionally testing a system board is to make sure each bus structure is free of defects.

Two types of problems are associated with a bus. First, devices connected directly to the bus can exhibit leaky outputs associated with weak internal diodes. These can introduce noise on the bus. Second, input problems occur in connected devices that have internal shorts, which overdraw current from the bus.

The IBM PC, XT, and AT microcomputers use many buses for data communication, including the control bus, the operand and result buses in the data path, the memory address and data buses, and a number of buffered buses on the system board and on each of the peripheral boards.

By controlling and observing a bus, all the logic connected to it can be easily accessed, improving testability. No special test points are needed to access bus-connected devices. In addition, all registers connected to a bus can be accessed from the bus. One good access point on the system board is the expansion-slot backplane. By inserting an extender card into one of these slots, many bus signals are readily accessible. Accessing one bus line at a time and observing the results can confirm a bad bus line.

Memory Tests

Some memory diagnostics test the computer's ability to properly set and clear individual bits in memory. Its ability to check if Store or Write operations affect more than one memory address location at one time is also tested. Other diagnostics test the permanent memory (ROM) by first reading every location and then computing a final signature, such as a checksum or a cyclic redundancy check code.

Both the Read-Only and Read and Write memories on the IBM system board are tested during the boot-up process. Each type of memory test is a part of the ROM BIOS power-up program.

ROM Diagnostics

In the IBM Personal Computers, each ROM is tested using the checksum technique. Initially, the ROM containing the BIOS is read and its contents summed. The final summation is compared with a stored value. If an error occurs, the system halts with an error message displayed on the screen.

RAM Diagnostics

Testing RAM memory is more involved than the testing of ROM because RAM requires the Write operation in addition to a memory cell Read. The main memory tests assume that the CPU is fine and conduct some pretty fancy tests on the RAM. This form of testing finds out if test data can be correctly loaded into one and only one location in memory. If a "storage error" occurs—that is, the test data stored are not the same as the test data sent—a message is printed on the screen. If the correct data gets stored but into several different memory locations at the same time, an "addressing error" has occurred and this too is noted on the screen.

Many algorithms (routines) test memories. Typical RAM tests are machine-language programs that implement RAM write/read algorithms. RAM is typically checked using a conventional memory testing program that writes a pattern of data into memory, and then reads the value out and compares it with an expected value. Because the test results are compared after each write/read operation, a RAM test takes time to complete. In addition, by implementing a machine-instruction write/read algorithm, the RAM cannot be exercised at its full-speed capability. Therefore, the test, while verifying the ability to write and read properly, does not guarantee that the same performance is assured at full operating speed. The following is a list of the most common memory tests:

► Common memory tests.

► Simple store and read test.

► Sequential numbers test.

► Rotating bit test.

► Walking bit test.

► Dual address test.

► Butterfield test.

► Sum test.

A "simple store and read test" writes a known value to every location in a selected block of memory. Then, it reads the contents of each location to ensure that the value was correctly stored. This is a quick-and-easy rough test.

A "sequential numbers test" involves loading all the binary number combinations for an 8-bit word sequentially into a block of 256 memory locations. Then, starting at the first address location, it reads out the data word stored and compares it to the value that should be there. If the data are correct, the routine displays an "ALL OK," and the test moves on to the second location. If an error is found, the program displays an "error" symbol on the screen and the test starts over at the next (third) address location. The test repeats until you reset your system.

A better memory test is the "rotating bit test." It checks each address location to see if a binary bit stored in any one of the eight positions in a binary 8-bit data word will falsely set another bit in the same word. This test starts by loading the binary number 0000 0001 into the lowest RAM address. The contents of this address are then read back out and verified. If the 0000 0001 was correctly stored, the bit is shifted one place to the left to 0000 0010 and the test is repeated. After the set bit (the "1") is shifted through all of the binary combinations, stored in that same address location, read out, and verified, the entire tests starts over at the next memory-address location.

The "walking bit test" improves slightly on the rotating bit test. All eight bits in a starting location are set to 0, or "cleared." Then the first bit is set to "1" (0000 0001), as in the rotating bit test. The program tests all seven other bits to see if they have changed from 0 to 1. Then the second bit position is set to 1 and all other positions to 0 (0000 0010). Again, all seven of the other bit positions are tested. This process walks through each bit in that memory location, setting each bit to 1 and testing all seven of the other positions.

Then the values are all reversed; all the cleared bits are set to "1" and the set bits are cleared to "0," and the entire process begins once more, but now as a rotating zero test.

This test is quite time-consuming. Apparently, it can take over 13 hours to check a 16-Kbyte area of RAM. And it can take over 52 hours to test 32K bytes of memory! You can just imagine how long it would take to test a fully packed IBM Personal Computer.

A "dual-address test" provides a more thorough addressing check. Starting with the lowest memory address in a selected block of memory, the program stores all zeroes into the area (clears it to zero). It then stores all ones (1111 1111) into the first location and checks all other locations to see if any other memory address falsely received any ones. If all other locations are still "zero-loaded," the test location is cleared (written into with all zeroes), and the test shifts to the next higher address, storing all ones in this location and again testing all other memory locations for their contents. This test repeats until the program reaches the end of the selected memory area.

Jim Butterfield wrote a program that is a variation of the dual-address test and is in the public domain. In the "Butterfield test" program, all 1s are stored in every location of the selected memory area. Then, all 0s are stored in every third address location, starting with the first address. The algorithm then checks the contents of every memory address to make sure the values have been stored correctly.

Next, the program shifts the position of the "all zeroes" word twice, using the second and then third locations in the memory as starting points. After the three-pass test using 0s in a memory field of all 1s, the bits are reversed and all 1s are stored in every third location of an all 0s memory field.

If an error is found, the program stops and the address of the error is displayed. If no error is detected, the program ends and the top address plus one is displayed on the monitor screen.

The "sum test" is probably the most sophisticated memory diagnostic test. It generates a unique data word for storing in each location of memory that is to be checked. The data word is the sum of the two bytes that comprise that memory address. (Recall that it takes 16 bits to address 64K bytes of memory; 16 bits are two 8-bit bytes.) Since each succeeding address is one location higher, the value stored increases, and each value is unique to an address. A variation on this scheme can be used with the 20- and 24-bit address word in the Personal Computer.

The algorithm then checks for correct value storage. If an error is found, the program displays the error and its location on the screen. This diagnostic test is also time-consuming. It's a good idea to run these types of dual-address tests on small blocks of memory rather than testing all of the RAM. It has been determined that the testing time quadruples for each doubling of the amount of memory tested.

The RAM memory test in the IBM PC, PC/XT, and PC AT is a Write/Read/Verify operation in which the patterns AA, 55, FF, 01, and 00 are written into the first bank of memory. After each Write, a Read is executed, and the value fetched is compared to verify proper storage and retrieval.

Self-Diagnosis

There is a trend toward building diagnostic capability into peripheral equipment, like printers and plotters. A strong incentive exists to place diagnostics in CRT displays and disk drives as well as the personal computers, because so many of these devices are being sold.

Disk drives and printers function both electronically and mechanically. The electronic controller portions of these machines can contain their own diagnostics and, indeed, many controllers now do some form of self-diagnosis each time the system is powered up. These tests check for faults in the electronics.

Mechanical components are inherently less reliable than electronics, so peripherals containing mechanical parts need diagnostics that regularly check their internal operation. Most of the conditions monitored are operator related, for example, "paper out" or "ribbon out." Disk-drive diagnostics measure the mechanical parameters like speed and head alignment.

All of the "canned" diagnostic packages use some version of the seven test algorithms described above. Each diagnostic program is a valuable addition to your "troubleshooting toolbox," but no software diagnostic can help if your system won't boot or display. The point is: "There are many ways to skin a computer cat. Know them all."

How to Specify Your Particular Problem

Trying to decide which section of the computer has failed can sometimes be confusing. The following paragraphs will help you narrow your problem to a section by describing what the symptoms might look like if a particular section were failing.

Memory Failure Symptoms

If a component in the memory subsection fails, strange things can happen and weird symptoms can surface, which apparently are not related to a failing POST boot-up diagnostics test. The computer can lock up in the middle of program execution. Or, operations can falter, pointing to a malfunction everywhere but in the memory.

For example, one morning you decide to turn on your computer and write a letter. Upon booting up, you get an error that detects a bad DMA chip. To verify the problem, you turn the machine off and back on again to see if the failure is consistent or is intermittent. This time, the POST test passes all boot-up diagnostics and the machine seems to run fine. Later, while you're typing in your letter, the system locks up and the keyboard refuses to accept key actions. The symptom now looks like a keyboard malfunction. So you press CTRL/ALT/DEL to reset the computer and see if the POST diagnostics picks up a keyboard failure, or if it gets the DMA failure again. However, the start-up tests again pass. You begin to get worried. This time, you insert your diagnostic disk into the drive and attempt to load. The disk starts to load but then stops. Disk problem? No, a memory problem.

The memory is used by so many functions and devices in your IBM that a failure in one of the RAM ICs can affect almost every other part of the system.

The boot-up diagnostics will usually catch hard RAM failures. However, if the failure is timing related (the RAM is slow under heavy use), the diagnostics will probably not catch it. If you get symptoms that point everywhere, then suspect a bad memory chip.

By logging what happened each time you experience a failure, a pattern can be developed, highlighting the main clue to the problem source. In this example, the memory is being accessed each time the failure appeared.

Here's another hint that might help if you get a PARITY CHK 1 or PARITY CHK 2 error message on your monitor. PARITY CHK 1 means that the problem is in RAM on the motherboard and PARITY CHK 2 means the trouble is in RAM on an expansion card. One of these types of failures in a PC AT results in an error display that provides more information than a PC or PC/XT RAM failure. See "Run Problems" in Chapters 7 and 8.

System Boards

A system board problem or support circuitry malfunction will usually result in a catastrophic failure that can either be detected by the POST diagnostics at boot-up or will prevent the boot-up from completing. If the power supply seems to work (the fan is running and the screen "blinks" when system power is applied), the failure is likely on the system board. See "Start-Up Problems" in Chapters 7 and 8.

Power Supplies

Two types of power-supply failures can occur: hard failures and short-term power fluctuations. A hard failure prevents any output to one or more power pins on the system board. Power-surge or suppression failures occur when a power supply puts out too much or too little voltage.

Hard failures are the easiest to diagnose. When a hard failure occurs, normal power is prevented (usually from the start). The fan fails to start spinning, no message comes up on the screen, and you don't hear the familiar beep from the speaker.

Besides floppy disk drives, the item with the next highest failure rate in the IBM Personal Computer system is the ON/OFF switch. This component gets a lot of use (often rough use). If the ON/OFF switch goes bad, you would probably think that the system had just suffered a major power-supply breakdown. The switch can be tested either with an ohmmeter or by replacement, but to change the switch requires access to the power supply, and this repair should only be done by an experienced repair person. The failure record of this component is one reason that many people connect their system to a surge-protected power strip that has an ON/OFF switch on it. Using the switch on the power strip saves wear and tear on the computer power switch. Just remember to energize the computer before powering up the printer or the external peripheral devices not directly connected and powered from the system-board expansion slots.

Once you've concluded that your power supply is bad, you have an important decision to make. Do you feel qualified to analyze and repair the problem?

WORKING ON POWER SUPPLIES CAN BE DANGEROUS.

You will be exposed to capacitors that are charged to high voltages when working inside a power supply. This is one time that repair techs really earn their money. In addition, power problems can result in capacitors, resistors, and even ICs, literally blowing up, throwing tiny pieces of the component everywhere. If the power plug is still connected to the wall socket, there are sources of dangerous high voltage in the supply. Unless you're a trained and certified power-supply repair tech, we do not recommend that you try to fix your own supply. It's better to take your power supply to an authorized service center for repair, and avoid the hassle and concern connected with repairing it.

Keyboards

Keyboard failures can be frustrating, especially when a key works right part of the time, but not all of the time. (Murphy's law holds true all too often; the key you need the most is the key that will break.)

The most common cause for keyboard failure is the heavy-fingered user. The heavy-fingered user is the person who thinks that computers are really just souped-up typewriters. This person treats the keyboard as if it were an old manual typewriter and imagines the proper way to type is to strike the keys hard and firm. But banging the keys in doesn't make the letters appear any better on the screen. Instead, beating the keys deforms the mechanical parts of the key mechanism, bending the connection inside the key lower and lower until connection can no longer be made WITHOUT beating. Finally, the connection just can't be made in a proper way and the key stops working.

Another common keyboard failure is caused by soft drink and coffee enthusiasts who spill liquid into the top of the keyboard. Now there's a real mess to clean up.

The remaining keyboard failures are much easier to handle. To localize a failure to the keyboard, carefully examine the clues. For a single key not working, the trouble is obviously in the keyboard, but with no key working can be caused by more than just the electronics in the keyboard. The challenge is to determine if the keyboard or the system has locked up—perhaps the coiled keyboard cable just isn't making correct contact.

The easiest way to confirm that the keyboard is bad is to try another keyboard. However, if this isn't an available option, don't despair. Check the keyboard connector cable to see if it is properly mated at both ends. If every thing looks all right, try to boot a program that doesn't require keyboard action to see if the program runs. If you have a program that goes through a long sequence of events without keyboard intervention, try that. If it works fine and the diagnostics at system boot-up pass muster, then suspect a keyboard failure. The keyboard on the PC AT has its own start-up diagnostics, so just rebooting an AT will check the keyboard for you. Once you've localized a problem to the keyboard, refer to "Keyboard Problems" in Chapters 7 and 8 for corrective action.

Displays

Most display problems are caused by bad connections and cables. If your display starts "acting up," try wiggling the cable to see if it affects the symptom.

Display problems are usually easy to spot. If you have no display at all, try to reboot to see if the POST test will catch a failure in the adapter card. If the boot seems to work, but you still have no display, type DIR and press the ENTER key to see if a drive will activate. Command your system to output something to the printer to verify that the printer I/O is functional. If everything seems to operate normally except for the display, then the malfunction is between the adapter board and the display circuitry.

Display problems in the monitor itself are like failures in the power supply—high voltages are involved. Don't try to fix them yourself. Problems inside the monitor are usually associated with the vertical and horizontal signals. A failure in either of these circuits can prevent the electron beam from sweeping across the screen. This could result in a pinpoint of light off the visible part of the screen. This appears as a complete shutdown (no display at all). Try another cable and then another monitor to isolate the problem to a board or component. An extensive list of display problems and solutions is provided in Chapters 7 and 8.

Floppy Disk Drives

Floppy disk-drive repair is one of the most difficult corrective actions for a self-servicer to make on a Personal Computer system. The mechanical and electronic components in a disk drive must operate within extremely strict tolerances. If these specifications drift out of acceptable limits, the drive may not function properly. It may not function at all.

Drive problems usually show up as "Not Ready" errors or "General Failure" errors during a disk read action. The disk Read function may not start, or it may start and then stop. A good way to localize functions to a drive problem is to enter ROM BASIC and try typing something. If the POST diagnostics pass the system and you can enter ROM BASIC, then chances are good that you have a bad disk drive or a bad disk-drive interface, rather than a failure on the system board.

To localize to the adapter card or the drive itself, swap the A and B drives and again try to boot a disk. If the problem remains, you have a bad cable or adapter card. If the alternate drive corrects the original problem, you've found the bad drive. (The failure followed the drive.)

One of the first things to do when a drive problem occurs is to clean the read/write heads and check the drive speed. Avoid disk-drive cleaning disks, even the ones that claim to be ideal for your system. All disk-drive cleaning disks are abrasive and may be harmful to the read/write heads inside the drive.

The drive that usually fails first is the A drive (unless you or someone else switched Drive A for the B drive sometime earlier). The A drive is usually the first to go because it's the most heavily used electromechanical I/O device (especially in the PC). For more disk-related tests and detailed corrective action, refer to Chapters 7 and 8.

Hard Disk Drives

Hard disk drives operate under very strict tolerances. If their alignment or speed settings drift out of specification, the drives may function erratically, or may not function at all. Hard disk-drive problems, like floppy disk-drive problems, appear as "Not Ready" or "General Failure" errors when you try to read a track and sector on one of the disk platters.

The disk may read erratically or may start to read and then stop. To localize these problems, conduct the same tests that you did for floppy disk drives. Reboot the system to see if you can get a bad drive error code. If the boot works, the analysis gets interesting. If you're using an XT (or a beefed-up PC), try to boot from a floppy disk. Try to get into ROM BASIC and try to type something for display on the screen to determine if the problem is disk-related or a failure on the system board.

To isolate the drive from the interface card and cable, swap the cable with a known good cable. If you still haven't isolated the problem, swap interface cards. You could try your drive in another known working machine, but removing the hard disk takes more time than removing the adapter card. See if the failure follows the drive, the cable, or the adapter card (or remains in your system). More preliminary checks as well as detailed repair steps can be found in Chapters 7 and 8.

Locating Replacement Parts

Once you've expended the effort necessary to localize and isolate a computer breakdown to a failed component, nothing will frustrate you more than to discover that your problems aren't over. Now you can't find a replacement part. Or, a vendor says he carries the part, but the minimum order amount is $50.00.

Standard off-the-shelf 7400-series ICs can be readily found. Unfortunately, as we demand more and more computing power in our machines, and the manufacturers introduce newer and higher-performance PCs, the standard part count begins to reduce. In place of a dozen ICs, the manufacturer designs in a custom chip. IBM uses a number of custom programmable array logic (PAL) chips in the PC AT. These parts (and the ROM chips) are proprietary to IBM, and thus the distribution is controlled by IBM. Such a reality means that you must go to IBM (or an authorized IBM service representative) to obtain a part (if they'll sell it to you).

Before you go to the original manufacturer, you might want to check the magazines for ads regarding chip parts. About a half dozen companies sell IBM parts and supplies through magazine ads. Give them a call. If they don't have the part you need, see if you can purchase it from (or have it installed by) an IBM authorized repair center.

If the cost is too high for your pocketbook, consider swapping out the complete board. A PC system board can be exchanged for around $200 (and an AT board for under $300). A color/graphics adapter can be swapped out for slightly over $100, and a power supply can be exchanged for between $85.00 and $225 (depending on the model and make of the IBM PC). Don't discount the swap-out process. Once you've isolated the problem to a board, the next best solution to a chip replacment may likely be a board replacement.

When dealing with a parts supplier, remember that most parts vendors are catalog-type operations. You want to deal with only reputable and stable companies. Here are some suggestions to help you so that your purchases will be rewarding instead of humiliating. Deal with the companies who:

1. Offer toll-free numbers.
2. Offer fast delivery.
3. Provide on-line information about their stocking conditions.
4. Offer easy return privileges for unacceptable and defective parts.

A lot can be said about a company from the professional look of their catalog, from the way the products are packaged on receipt (paper bag, wrapped in newspaper, in reused cardboard), from the accuracy of the order received, and from how much of your order actually arrived.

Horror stories abound about customer ripoffs. Internet, an international telecommunications network, often carries discussions about unprofessional or downright dishonest mail-order houses. If you can, deal with a parts supply company in your home town or deal directly with IBM. At least, when you deal directly with IBM, you can feel comfortable that Big Blue will stand behind their parts sales-and-repair actions.

Self-Repair or Service Center Action

You've localized the problem to the system board, and you've a pretty good idea which IC is bad. But it's soldered into the board. You have two choices. If you feel competent in circuit-board repair, you can break out the test equipment, confirm that the component is bad, and replace it. Should this be your intent, I strongly urge that you obtain the appropriate Howard W. Sams & Company COMPUTERFACTS (CSCS2 for the IBM PC, CSCS10 for the PC/XT, or CSCS17 for the PC AT). This technical data includes complete schematics, preliminary service checks, pin logic measurements, waveforms, and parts lists with a replacement cross-reference where possible. For those of you with technician genes in your blood, this book and the Sams COMPUTERFACTS are an important part of your system maintenance workbench.

If you're like 95% of the rest of the PC-using community, and don't want to tackle soldered-in component replacement, you should opt for repair center support. Given that a repair can cost over $70.00 an hour, anything you can do to reduce the repair time will benefit you directly in money not spent. Here are some things you can do to help keep the repair bill down:

1. Very clearly state the problem. (Answer these questions.)
   A. What is affected? Is there an error code?
   B. What is not affected? (It is not software related, not noticed on Drive B, not an intermittent failure, etc.)
   C. Where does it occur?
   D. When does it occur? (What was the system doing when it failed?)
   E. How much of the system/unit/component is affected?
2. Describe anything that you feel is new or distinctive about the problem. For example, what has changed about the system/unit/component? Did you change any system configuration? Did you make any recent adjustments or alignments?
3. Write down a complete description of the symptoms and your specification of the problem. Indicate what you think it might be. Describe why you feel this way. Now you're ready to find a repair shop to fix your machine.
4. First, check to see if your machine is still under warranty. You may be able to take it back to where it was purchased and let someone else worry about how costly the repair will be. If it's not under warranty, call your local PC user group representative. Ask for suggested repair centers. Who received the best support? Where?
5. Log the serial numbers of all the major system components that you'll be turning over to the repair facility (system unit, external drives, display unit, etc.).

6. Request a written estimate of repair time and charges.

7. Determine the warranty time for the repair.

8. Ask for a listing of what was repaired. Ask to have the bad components returned to you.

9. Finally, test the unit functional actions and the problem corrected action(s) before you pay the repair fee and leave the shop.

Summary

This chapter contains a lot of information and a lot of sage advice. After an in-depth look into basic troubleshooting, including component identification, failure mechanisms, and problem analysis, the world of troubleshooting and repair should have opened up to you. Recognizing that you needn't fear the machine or need to stand back, staring in awe at repair technicians, you now possess knowledge to make any IBM Personal Computer failure easier to find and easier to fix. The PC, PC/XT, and PC AT machines are tools. Now that you understand how they work and how to approach problem analysis, you are ready to tackle most personal computer failures.

Questions for Review and Discussion

1. You're operating your computer and you try to boot up a new program. The disk drive won't turn on. What should you do?

2. You try to print a document, but your printer just sits and ignores your commands. What should you do?

3. You move your computer system to the other side of the office. When you turn the system on, nothing happens. What should you do?

4. You're merrily typing away on your keyboard when the display stops echoing your keystrokes. What should you do?

5. What is the most important thing to remember when a failure occurs?

6. What are the two most common failures in an IBM personal computer?

7. Describe the RAM memory test performed by the POST test during boot-up.

8. Which ICs in a PC system are the most likely to fail?

9. Why is electrostatic discharge ignored by most people, yet is the potential cause of more trouble than any other failure mechanism?

10. Why should you not attempt repairs in the power supply or display unit?

Specific Troubleshooting and Repair Procedures: IBM PC and PC/XT

This chapter covers the detailed analysis of failures associated with the IBM PC and PC/XT. The chapter is divided into six parts as follows:

1. Start-up problems.
2. Run problems.
3. Keyboard problems.
4. Display problems.
5. Disk-drive problems.
6. Other I/O problems.

Each computer malfunction can be associated with one of these areas. A key problem index covering each of these general areas (Chart 7-1) is included to provide both preliminary checks and flowchart troubleshooting support. (Using the index, you can quickly locate a particular problem area for analysis. Each section part is subdivided into individual unique failures and provides symptoms for each.)

Part 1 covers the symptoms that can occur during initial power-up, including no power and no disk boot-up operation. Each PC and PC/XT comes with a built-in diagnostic test program, and most owners also have a diagnostic disk to use in conjunction with the built-in diagnostics. It's possible to get a system error number printed on the screen during start-up that will help localize a malfunction to a particular part of the machine.

Part 2 discusses the failure symptoms that can occur after initial boot-up—during system operation. These malfunctions include a bad memory and program lockup.

Keyboard problems are detailed in Part 3. This section covers such faults as single- and multiple-key operation failures, and unwanted "repeat" action.

Part 4 addresses those difficulties associated with the display portion of the computer. These problems include no display, no text mode, no HiRes or no LoRes, video synchronization failures, character faults, bad graphics, and other problems.

Then, Part 5 details troubleshooting the disk-drive failures. This includes Read/Write operations as well as access problems.

Finally, Part 6 encompasses other input and output problems, including speaker faults, cassette I/O failures, and light pen malfunctions.

These data are followed by preliminary checks, hints for repair ideas, and step-by-step flowchart troubleshooting instructions. In the flowcharts, ICs that are to be replaced will be listed in order of their priority. Therefore, the ICs at the beginning of the list are the ICs that are most likely to be bad. Occasionally, in the step-by-step flowchart troubleshooting instructions, a statement is made suggesting to the reader that "service center" action is advised. This statement is made to let you know that you need test equipment to solve this problem, which we are assuming you don't have. (It is too expensive, too technical, etc.) Therefore, the proper way to fix the problem is to take the system to an authorized service center. This chapter will help you describe your problem and equipment symptoms to the technician at the service center, so that his troubleshooting time (and your bill) is kept to a minimum.

As you use this manual, you will discover many useful hints for both troubleshooting and repair. Be especially alert to the caution notices, since further system degradation can occur if you do not follow those procedures exactly as listed.

Make sure you've read and understand the preliminary checks that can be made, before you deal with the step-by-step instructional flowchart. Few things are as humbling as disassembling a system for troubleshooting and repair, and then discover that the problem was caused by a bad cable between the system unit and the monitor.

This chapter will not directly discuss the malfunctions of resistors and capacitors because catastrophic failures of these passive devices are usually quite visible during the examination of the system board and peripheral cards. If you feel that a resistor or capacitor has failed, check the component resistance (out of the circuit) with a ohmmeter. The resistance value should closely approximate that of the value color code printed on the resistor; the capacitor should not register a short. Most capacitor failures are obvious because the capacitors usually blow apart or char in the circuit. A preliminary check statement, which refers to "visually examining" a board or card, means you should look for charred, hot, or physically broken parts.

NOTE: The troubleshooting problems and techniques given in the following pages may require soldering. Be sure that you are proficient in this technique before you proceed.

> **CAUTION**: Replacing components or otherwise modifying the IBM PC, the IBM PC/XT, or the IBM PC AT System Unit may void its warranty.

> **WARNING:** Before doing anything inside the System Unit, make sure that the power is in the correct condition (for example, *OFF* when removing or inserting any components).

Chart 7-1.   Troubleshooting Index

Start-Up Problems

Four types of error indications can occur during the initialization or start-up process—beep indicators from the built-in speaker, system error-code displays, I/O error-code displays, and other error displays. These indications will assist in isolating a failure to a module, subunit, or peripheral.

If the system won't boot, the IBM DOS manual suggests that you reread the manual. A number of things can cause the computer to either boot improperly or not boot at all—wrong diskette in the drive, no operating system on the diskette, cables loose, adapter card not fully seated, disk-drive failure, memory chip bad, no clock pulses, or even an unplugged power cord. You can probably deduce a particular problem faster by noting the conditions of the machine at the time of "failure" and following the troubleshooting steps outlined in this chapter.

Select the problem from the following list that best describes your PC's symptoms, and then turn to the appropriate page in this chapter for the proper troubleshooting procedures.

1. Self-test error displayed.
2. System won't boot, no fan, and screen is blank.
3. System won't boot, fan works, but screen is blank.
4. System won't boot, but both drive lights are on.

Problem 7-1

Self-test error displayed.

Symptom Described:

When the self-test is running, either a beep is heard from the speaker or an error code is displayed on the monitor.

Preliminary Checks:

1. Check all cables for continuity and proper mating.
2. Clean the edge connectors on the adapter cards.
3. Reseat the CPU (U3) on the system board.

Hints:

When an error is detected during boot-up, either a code is displayed on the screen (Table 7-1) or an audible beep sequence is heard (Table 7-2). From this error information, you can proceed to the correct section in this chapter. For example, if code 101 appears on your screen, you know (from Table 7-3) that there is a problem on the system board. The system will lock up and there will be no response to keyboard action. From this information, you can go to the "Run Problems" subsection discussed later in the chapter, and follow the procedures given there.

If the system detects a RAM failure, a four-character error code, followed by the number 201, will appear in the top left corner of the screen (Table 7-3). The value 201 identifies a RAM failure; the four-character code defines the bank and row of memory ICs in which the bad RAM was detected. The first two characters refer to the bank of memory in which the failure occurred (Table 7-4). The last two characters refer to the bit position of the RAM bank that failed. For example, if a failure occurs in the Bit 5 position of Bank 1, a 0420 201 should appear as the failure code.

Table 7-4 describes the RAM error codes. If the third and forth characters of the error code don't match the codes in Table 7-4, swap the entire bank of RAM chips and try again. A cost-saving way to find the bad RAM is to power-

Table 7-1.   I/O Error Codes

Code	Problem Area
199	Printer adapter or Printer.
432	Printer adapter or Printer.
7xx	System Unit I/O.
9xx	System Unit I/O (parallel printer adapter).
901	Printer adapter card or Printer itself is bad.
11xx	System Unit.
12xx	System Unit.
13xx	Game control adapter card.
14xx	Printer interface.
15xx	System Unit or communications adapter cable.
18xx	Expansion Unit or cable to expansion unit.
1819	Expansion Unit.
1820	Expansion Unit cable.
1821	Expansion Unit cable.
20xx	System Unit or communications adapter cable.
21xx	System Unit or communications adapter cable.

Table 7-2.   Beep Indicator Codes

Indicator	Problem Area
No beep, nothing happens.	Power, Power supply.
Continuous beep.	Power, Power supply.
Repeating short beep.	Power, Power supply.
1 long, 1 short beep.	System board.
1 long, 2 short beeps.	Display circuitry.
1 long, 3 short beeps.	EGA card.
1 short beep, blank or incorrect display.	Display circuitry.
1 short beep, Cassette BASIC displayed, no disk boot.	Diskette, Drive.

down the system and swap each chip, one at a time, with the corresponding bit in an adjacent row. Then power up and retest. See if the failure has moved to the new bank. The last chip that was swapped when the failure changes is the bad RAM.

A four-character code is also displayed when a ROM failure occurs. The self-test program resides on ROM U33 (U18 in PC/XT). ROM U33 does not get tested by the Power-On Self Test (POST) program. Table 7-5 will direct you to the ROM that is suspected (by the test) to be bad.

Table 7-6 lists other error-code displays and their meanings.

The tables in Appendix A provide further information on error codes, error-code displays, and their meaning. These tables are basically the same codes as are listed here in Chapter 7, but they provide more detailed listings.

Table 7-3. System Error Codes*

Code	Problem Area
02x	Power-supply problem.
100	Option configuration wrong.
199 100	Software option configuration wrong. Check switches.
101	System board malfunction.
131	Cassette port error.
201	RAM failure.
xxxx = 201	Memory failure.
1055 = 201	DIP switches set wrong.
2055 = 201	DIP switches set wrong.
xxxx = 201 PARITY CHECK X	RAM chip malfunction.
301	Keyboard malfunction. Keyboard cable disconnected.
xx301	Keyboard circuitry malfunction (xx is the Hex value representing the scan code of the malfunctioning key.)
401	Monochrome adapter card.
501	Color/graphics adapter card.
601	Diskette or disk-drive interface malfunction.
606	Drive assembly or adapter.
607	Disk is write-protected, disk not inserted properly, Write-Protect switch is bad, or analog card malfunction.
608	Diskette is bad.
611	Drive data cable or disk-drive adapter card is bad.
612	Drive data cable or disk-drive adapter card is bad.
613	Drive data cable or disk-drive adapter card is bad.
621–626	Drive assembly is bad.

*These error codes can appear alone or in conjunction with other numbers.

Problem 7-2

System won't boot. No fan. Screen is blank.

Symptom Described:

When the ON/OFF switch is moved to the ON position, nothing happens. No fan sound can be heard. (Refer to Flowchart 7-1.)

Table 7-4.   RAM-Memory Failure Error Codes*

X Y Z Z 201 PARITY CHECK 1	
System Board Memory Bank (X Y)	**Failed Chip (Z Z)**
16K RAM Chip System Board	00 = Parity
	01 = D0 chip
00 = Bank 0	02 = D1 chip
04 = Bank 1	04 = D2 chip
08 = Bank 2	08 = D3 chip
0C = Bank 3	10 = D4 chip
	20 = D5 chip
	40 = D6 chip
64K RAM Chip System Board	80 = D7 chip
0Y = 1st 64K Bank (0–64K)	
1Y = 2nd 64K Bank (64–128K)	
2Y = 3rd 64K Bank (128–192K)	
3Y = 4th 64K Bank (192–256K)	
4Y = 5th 64K Bank (256–320K)	
5Y = 6th 64K Bank (320–384K)	
6Y = 7th 64K Bank (384–448K)	
7Y = 8th 64K Bank (448–512K)	
8Y = 9th 64K Bank (512–576K)	
9Y = 10th 64K Bank (576–640K)	
(The Y value has no meaning in 64K RAM chip systems.)	

For example, in a 64K RAM chip system, the error code 4810 201 would be interpreted:

4 = 5th 64K Bank.   If the system board has 256K installed, the 5th Bank is the first on an expansion board.

8 = Don't care.   Applies only to 16K RAM-populated PC-I motherboards.

10 = Data Bit 4.   Fifth chip after the parity chip.

Table 7-5.   ROM Error Codes

Display	Problem ROM
F600 ROM	Cassette BASIC ROM (U29)
F800 ROM	Cassette BASIC ROM (U30)
FA00 ROM	Cassette BASIC ROM (U31)
FC00 ROM	Cassette BASIC ROM (U32)

Preliminary Checks:

1. Check that the external power cable is plugged into the system unit and into a wall socket.

2. Check that the fuse (F1) in the power supply is good.

3. Check the power-supply cables are properly seated on the system board: P8, P9, P10, P11 for the PC, and P8, P9, P11, P13 for the XT).

4. Remove all the peripherals including the disk-drive adapter cards. Power up and note if the fan energizes. If it does, turn off the system and plug each peripheral in, one at a time, powering up and testing each time to see if a failure on one of the adapter cards is causing the system to malfunction. When failure occurs, the last card plugged in is bad and most likely has a short between power and ground.

Table 7-6.   Other Error Displays

Display	Meaning
Blank display; beep; drive starts to boot, but no cassette BASIC message on screen.	System Monitor BIOS ROM (U33) failure/8284 clock generator is bad.
Keyboard not functional.	Keyboard problem.
PARITY CHECK 1	Power supply problems.
PARITY CHECK 2	Bad memory on expansion card.
PARITY ERROR 1	Bad or incorrectly seated RAM.
PRINTER PROBLEMS	Printer problem; check interface.

Hints:

A study by the Computer Center at the University of Iowa discovered that the part with the highest failure rate among PCs is the ON/OFF switch. If you need to replace your ON/OFF switch, you can do so without going into the power supply. Check the appendix for switch removal instructions.

If the ON/OFF switch is functional (not bad), the problem is most likely in the power supply itself. If the power-supply fuse is blown, make sure and replace it with a fuse that has the same rating and current level as the one that is being replaced. If the fuse keeps blowing, there is a short in the supply and you should take the power supply to a service center.

When replacing fuse F1, be sure the power cable to the wall socket is disconnected before opening the power-supply case.

BE EXTREMELY CAREFUL WHEN WORKING AROUND THE POWER SUPPLY.

Flowchart 7-1

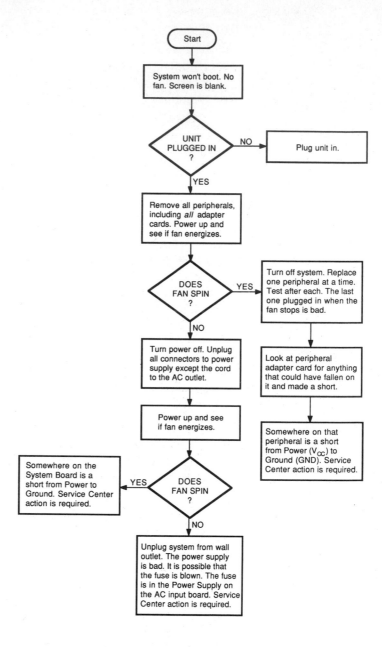

Problem 7-3

System won't boot. Fan works. Screen is blank.

Symptom Described:

There is no cursor, no screen display, no keyboard response, but you can hear the fan running in the power supply. (Refer to Flowchart 7-2 and Figs. 7-1 and 7-2.)

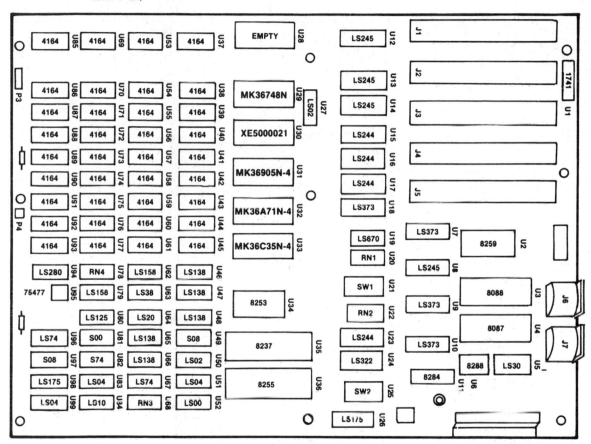

Fig. 7-1.   IC layout of the IBM PC system board.

Preliminary Checks:

1. Check cables for proper mating.
2. Clean all edge connectors on the adapter cards.
3. Reseat the CPU chip (U3).
4. Visually inspect the system board.

5. Remove all peripherals except the keyboard and the monitor (with its adapter card). Power up. Does the system boot to ROM BASIC? If it does, turn the machine off, and reinstall one adapter card at a time, testing after each installation. When the system fails to boot to ROM BASIC, the last card installed is bad.

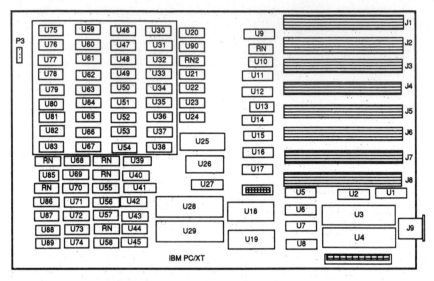

Fig. 7-2.   IC Layout of the IBM PC/XT system board.

Hints:

Many times, a problem of this sort is confused with a problem in the video circuitry. To avoid this, check that the keyboard seems to make the system do functions—like get a directory from the drive or print out a word. Even if the video circuitry is bad, you will see the drive get accessed and look (and sound) like it is getting the information.

For a description of the circuitry involved, refer to the discussion on system operation in the earlier chapters. If any of the ICs listed are not in the drawing, then assume that they are in the support circuitry.

Problem 7-4

System won't boot. Both floppy drive lights are on.

Symptom Described:

When the system is turned on, the access indicators of Drives A and B light and remain on. Drive A won't boot a disk. (Refer to Flowchart 7-3 and Fig. 7-3.)

Flowchart 7-2

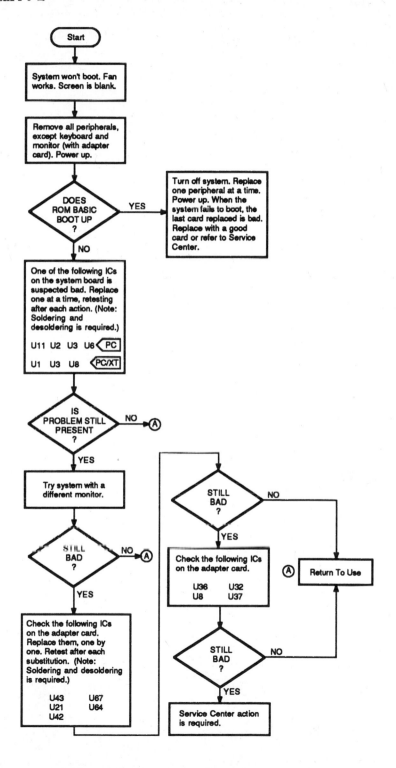

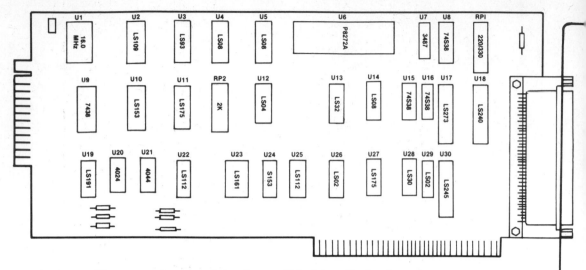

Fig. 7-3. Layout of the floppy disk-drive adapter board.

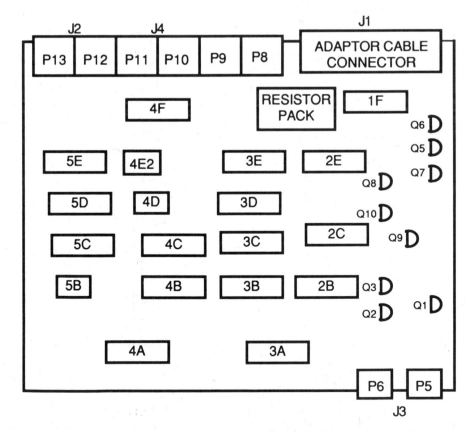

Fig. 7-4. Layout of the floppy disk-drive analog board.

Preliminary Checks:

1. Check that all drive cables are installed correctly.
2. Clean all board header connections, especially on the disk-drive adapter card.
3. Check that the resistor pack at 2F on the drive analog card is set for the correct drive.
4. Visually inspect the system board, disk-drive adapter card, and disk-drive analog card.

Flowchart 7-3

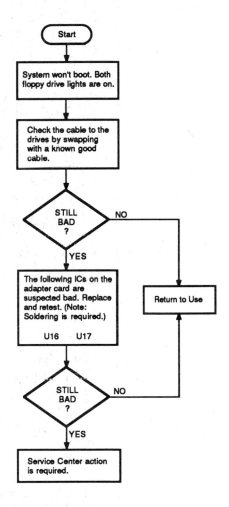

Hints:

Both drive lights coming on is a sign that both drives are being considered the primary boot drive. If the preliminary checks didn't solve the problem, check that the drive cables are good. For a description of the circuitry involved, refer to discussion on system operation given in the earlier chapters. If any listed ICs are

not in the drawings, assume they are in the support circuitry. IC U16, which is
not in Fig. 2-44, is located between the drive connector and IC U17.

Run Problems

This section covers those problems you might encounter while your system is
running. For example, you attempt to do something and get a response entirely
different from what you expected. The following sections cover broad malfunc
tions, such as display failure, keyboard failure, floppy drive failure, and input
output failures (although these may also occur during the time you start up your
system).

1. While running, the computer locks up. There is no keyboard response.
2. Power turns off after system runs for a while.

Problem 7-5

While running, the computer locks up. There is no response from keyboard.

Symptom Described:

During operation of a known good program, the computer locks up, the
display freezes, and the keyboard inputs have no effect. (Refer to Flowchart 7-4
and Fig. 7-1.)

Preliminary Checks:

1. Try a different program disk.
2. Check all cables for continuity and proper mating.
3. Clean the edge connectors on the adapter cards.
4. Reseat the CPU (U3) on the system board.

Hints:

This problem can be caused by a failure in the nonmaskable interrupt
circuitry, the Ready circuitry, the bus control circuitry, the Reset circuitry, the
timing circuitry, or the processor circuitry. There are so many areas of the
system board that could cause this problem that it is one of the hardest to solve.
Many times, a heat-related problem in an IC can cause this failure.

When the system locks up, turn it off, and after several seconds, power up again and see if an error code is displayed. If an error code is displayed, take note of it, for it can be a good hint for later troubleshooting. Also, write and run a short looping program to see if you consistently get the same failure. If so, you can use this program to monitor when corrective action has been successful.

Also check that your power supply is not overloaded and trying to drive too many power-hungry peripheral boards. If your system uses too many adapter cards and peripherals, the supply may need upgrading to a higher wattage. For a description of the circuitry involved, see the discussion on system operation given in the earlier chapters.

Problem 7-6

Power turns off after system runs for a while.

Symptom Described:

After the system has been running correctly for approximately a minute, the power shuts down and the operation stops. (Refer to Flowchart 7-5.)

Preliminary Checks:

1. Check to see if the fan is running when the system is first powered up.
2. Check all cables for continuity and proper mating.
3. Refer to the appropriate section in Chapter 2.

Hints:

Check that the fan is turning on when the system is first powered up. If it spins correctly, let the system heat up until the power fails. If the fan didn't turn on at system power-up, refer to Problem 7-2 and its associated text and flowchart. For a description of the circuitry involved, see the discussion on system operation given in the earlier chapters. If any listed ICs are not in the drawings, assume they are in the support circuitry.

Keyboard Problems

This section examines some of the keyboard problems you might encounter with your system.

Flowchart 7-4

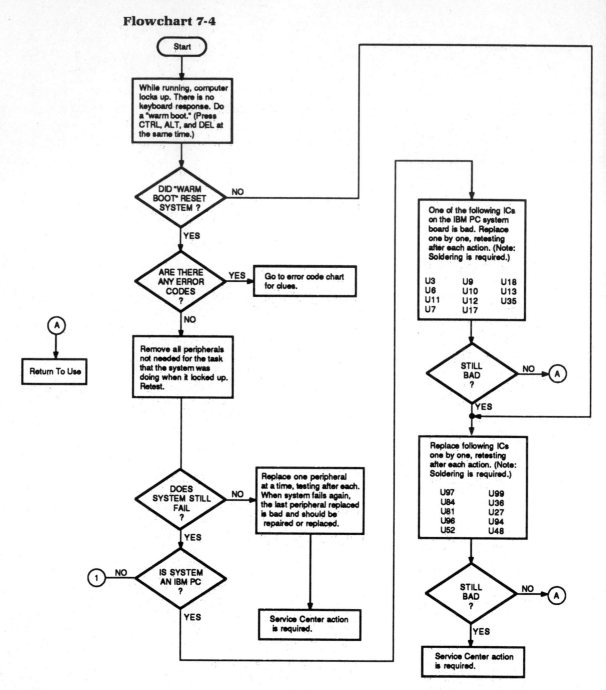

1. Keyboard won't respond at all, or a wrong character is produced.
2. Bad key action; one or more keys won't work.
3. You have key bounce, producing an unwanted repeat action.

Flowchart 7-4 *(continued)*

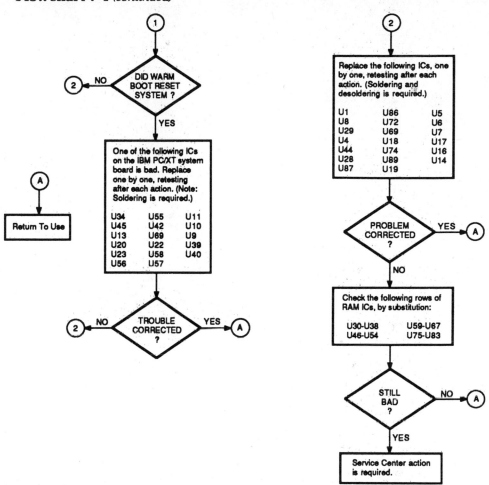

Problem 7-7

Keyboard won't respond at all, or a wrong character is produced.

Symptom Described:

When key is pressed, no display response occurs, or a wrong character is displayed on the monitor. (Refer to Flowchart 7-6 and Fig. 7-5.)

Preliminary Checks:

1. Check the keyboard cable for continuity and proper mating.
2. Clean the keys with a tuner cleaning spray.

Flowchart 7-5

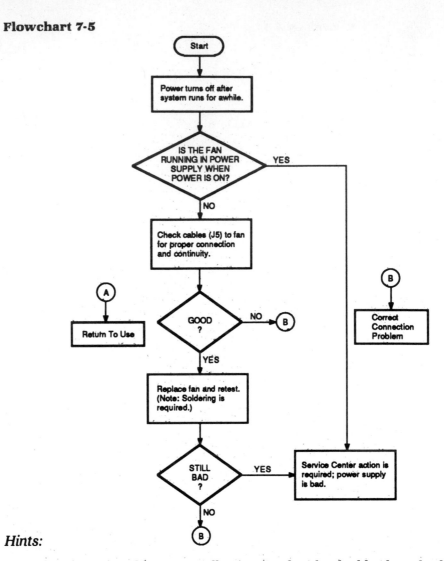

Hints:

This type of problem is usually associated with a bad keyboard cable. For a description of the circuitry involved, refer to the discussion on circuit operation given in the earlier chapters. If any listed ICs are not in the drawings, assume that they are in the support circuitry.

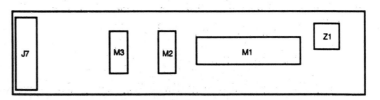

Fig. 7-5. IC layout of the IBM PC Type 2 keyboard circuit card.

Flowchart 7-6

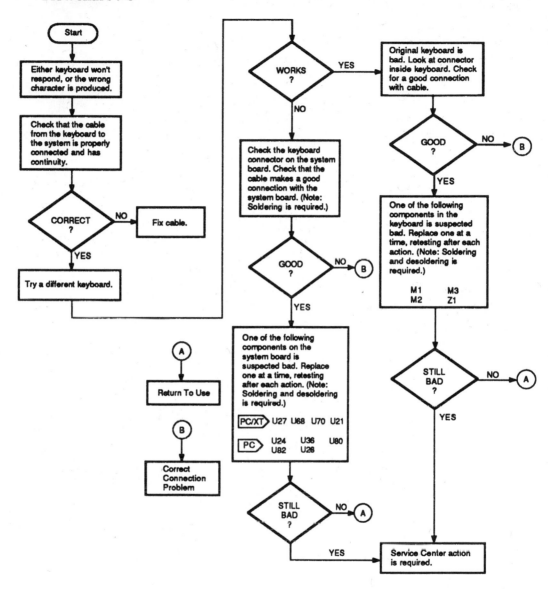

Problem 7-8

Bad key action; one or more keys won't work.

Symptom Described:

The boot-up operation occurs properly, with correct display action, but when a key is pressed, no display response occurs. (Refer to Flowchart 7-7 and Fig. 7-5.)

Flowchart 7-7

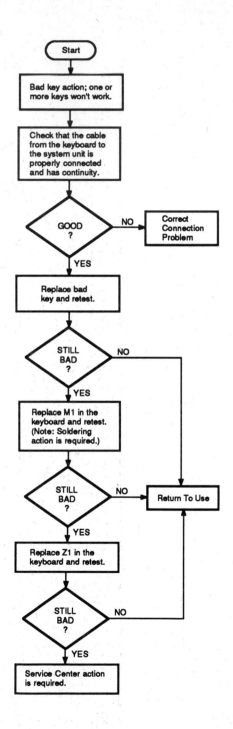

Preliminary Checks:

1. Verify that the keyboard/system-board cable has continuity and is properly connected.
2. Clean the keys with a tuner cleaner spray.

Hints:

The problem is usually a bad key, although occasionally, a good cleaning of the keyboard mechanism will solve the problem.

If only one key is failing, and you are good at soldering and desoldering, you can fix the problem without replacing the key. First, open the keyboard unit and locate the two switch contacts of the bad key. Then strip the insulation from the ends of two short wires, which are just long enough to get from the contacts on the bottom of the board to the key, when going through the center screw hole. Solder one end of one wire to one contact point and one end of the other wire to the other keyboard contact point. Run the wires to the top of the keyboard through the center screw hole. Attach one wire to a small metal washer that can slide over the spring shaft of the key that is bad. Loop an exposed bare section of the second wire around the top of the keyswitch slider and replace the key-switch cap. Reassemble the keyboard (see the appendix), minus the center screw. There you have it, a "new" key. For a description of the circuitry involved, see the discussion on system operation given in the earlier chapters. If any listed ICs are not in the drawings, assume that they are in the support circuitry.

Problem 7-9

You have key bounce, producing an unwanted repeat action.

Symptom Described:

When a key is pressed, more than one image of the same character is displayed on the screen. This occurs even when the key is not held down for an intended repeat action. (Refer to Flowchart 7-8 and Fig. 7-5.)

Preliminary Checks:

1. Check the cable for continuity and proper mating.
2. Clean the keyboard keys with a tuner spray.
3. If only one key fails, replace the key.

Hints:

Suspect the 8048 microprocessor (M1) in the keyboard chassis. If replacing M1 doesn't correct the problem, the problem could be Z1 (the decoder sense amp). Either Z1 is bad or a signal trace on the keyboard circuit board has been damaged. For a description of the circuitry involved, see the discussion on system operation given in the earlier chapters. If any listed ICs are not in the drawings, assume they are in the support circuitry.

Flowchart 7-8

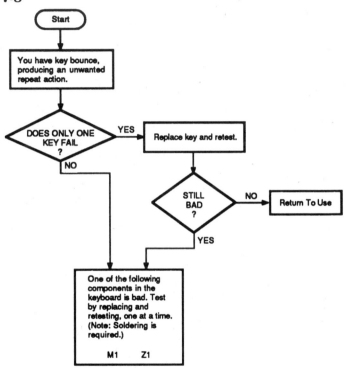

Display Problems

Display problems are similar for the IBM PC, the XT, and AT. Each of these machines use the same adapter cards to produce video signals. In order to save repeating the same troubleshooting procedure in each chapter, the procedures for all three IBM models are given here, under the appropriate display symptom category.

Monochrome Monitor Adapter

Problem 7-10

No display.

Symptom Described:

No graphics or text characters can be produced on the display monitor. (Refer to Flowchart 7-9 and Fig. 7-6.)

Flowchart 7-9

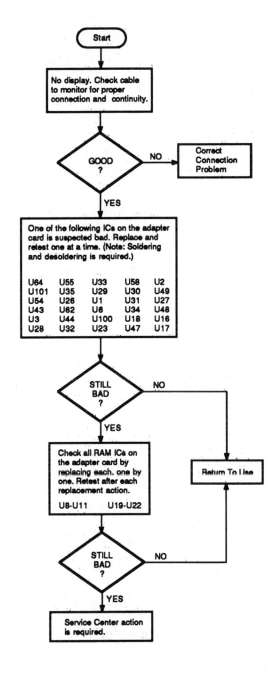

Preliminary Checks:

1. Check the video cable for continuity and proper mating.
2. Try another monitor.
3. Clean the monochrome display/printer adapter edge connector and reseat the board.
4. Check that the system is properly switch-configured.

Hints:

If there is no display, the problem is almost always the monitor cable or the monitor itself. A problem in the adapter card is very difficult to troubleshoot without the proper equipment. Taking the adapter card to a Service Center may be better than trying to fix it yourself. In some cases, it is more economical to purchase another adapter card. For a description of the circuitry involved, see the discussion on system operation given in the earlier chapters. If any listed ICs are not in the drawings, assume that they are in the support circuitry.

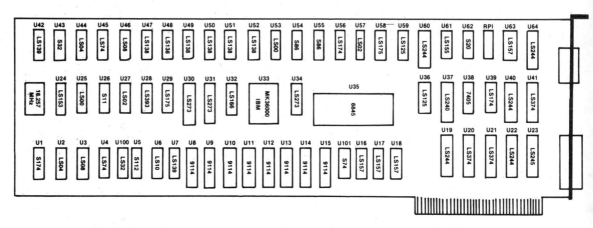

Fig. 7-6. IC layout of the IBM Monochrome Display Adapter Card.

Problem 7-11

No horizontal synchronization.

Symptom Described:

The display is unreadable due to a lack of horizontal sync signals. (Refer to Flowchart 7-10 and Fig. 7-6.)

Preliminary Checks:

1. Check the video cable for continuity and proper mating.

2. Clean the monochrome adapter-card edge-connector pins.

3. Try a different, known-good monitor.

Hints:

First, make sure that the problem is not in the monitor itself. Check the monitor on another system or try another monitor on your system. For a description of the circuitry involved, see the discussion on system operation given in the earlier chapters. If any listed ICs are not in the drawings, assume that they are in the support circuitry.

Flowchart 7-10

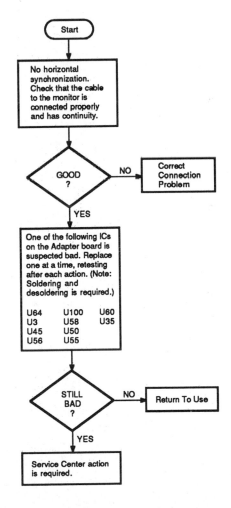

Problem 7-12

No vertical synchronization.

Symptom Described:

The display rolls without stopping, due to the lack of a vertical sync signal. (Refer to Flowchart 7-11 and Fig. 7-6.)

Preliminary Checks:

1. Check the video cable for continuity and proper mating.
2. Clean the monochrome adapter-card edge-connector pins.
3. Try a different, known-good, display monitor.
4. Check that jumper (J1) is properly connected.

Flowchart 7-11

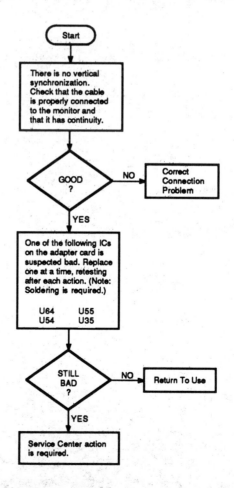

Hints:

Verify that the problem is not in the monitor itself. Check the monitor on another system or try another monitor on your system. For a description of the circuitry involved, see the discussion on system operation given in the earlier chapters. If any listed ICs are not in the drawings, assume that they are in the support circuitry.

Problem 7-13

No LoRes or HiRes display.

Symptom Described:

The text works, but there is no LoRes (low-resolution) or HiRes (high-resolution) display capability.

Preliminary Checks:

1. Check all cables for continuity and proper mating.
2. Clean the adapter-card edge-connector pins.

Hints:

Refer to Flowchart 7-12 and Fig. 7-6. For a description of the circuitry involved, see the discussion on system operation given in the earlier chapters. If any listed ICs are not in the drawings, assume that they are in the support circuitry.

Problem 7-14

Bad characters.

Symptom Described:

There is garbage on the screen (illegal characters and strange shapes) in both the graphics and text modes. (Refer to Fig. 7-6 and Flowchart 7-13.)

Flowchart 7-12

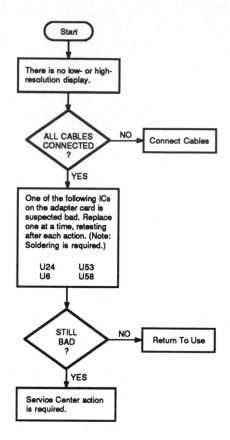

Preliminary Checks:

1. Verify that the cables are connected correctly.
2. Clean the adapter-card edge-connector pins.
3. Check that the system is configured properly.
4. Try a different known-good monitor.

Hints:

This type of problem is difficult to troubleshoot without the proper equipment. Taking the adapter card to a Service Center may be better than trying to fix it yourself. In some cases, it is more economical to just purchase another adapter card. For a description of the circuitry involved, the discussion on system operation given in the earlier chapters. If any listed ICs are not in the drawings, assume they are in the support circuitry.

Flowchart 7-13

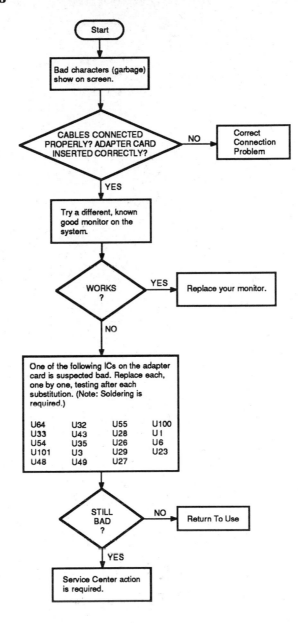

Color/Graphics Monitor Adapter

Problem 7-15

No display.

Symptom Described:

There is no screen display, no graphics, and no text. (Refer to Fig. 7-7 and Flowchart 7-14.)

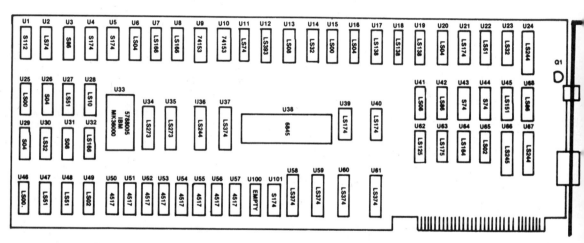

Fig. 7-7. IC layout of the IBM Color/Graphics Adapter card.

Preliminary Checks:

1. Check the cable for continuity and proper mating.
2. Try another, known-good, display monitor.
3. Clean the adapter-card edge-connector pins.
4. Check for proper system configuration.

Hints:

If there is no display, the problem is almost always in the cable to the monitor or in the monitor itself. If the problem is in the adapter card, it will be difficult to troubleshoot without the proper test equipment. Taking the adapter card to a Service Center may be better than trying to fix it yourself. In some cases, it is more economical to just purchase another adapter card. For a description of the circuitry involved, see the discussion on circuit operation given in the earlier chapters. If any listed ICs are not in the drawings, assume that they are in the support circuitry.

Flowchart 7-14

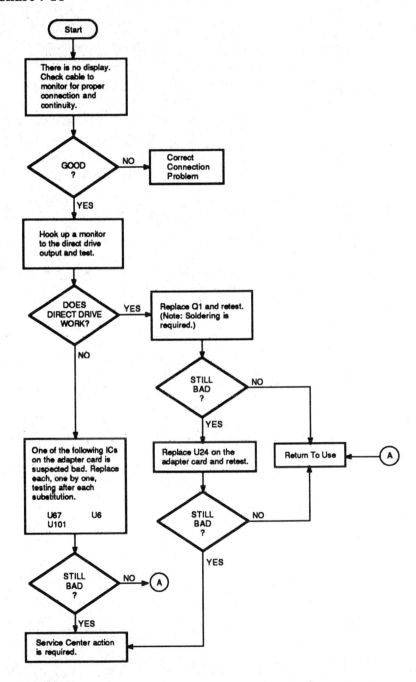

Problem 7-16

No horizontal synchronization.

Symptom Described:

Display is unreadable, due to lack of horizontal sync. (Refer to Fig. 7-7 and Flowchart 7-15.)

Preliminary Checks:

1. Check the cable for continuity and proper mating.
2. Clean the adapter-card edge-connector pins.
3. Try a different, known-good, display monitor.

Hints:

Make sure that the problem is not in the monitor itself. Check the monitor on another system, or try another monitor on your system. For a description of the circuitry involved, see the discussion on system operation given in the earlier chapters. If any listed ICs are not in the drawings, assume that they are in the support circuitry.

Problem 7-17

No vertical synchronization.

Symptom Described:

Display rolls due to the lack of a proper vertical sync signal. (Refer to Fig. 7-7 and Flowchart 7-16.)

Preliminary Checks:

1. Check the cable for continuity and proper mating.
2. Clean the adapter-card edge-connector pins.
3. Try a different, known-good, display monitor.

Hints:

Make sure that the problem is not in the monitor itself. Check the monitor on another system, or try another monitor on your system. For a description of the circuitry involved, see the discussion on system operation given in the earlier chapters. If any listed ICs are not in the drawings, assume that they are in the support circuitry.

Flowchart 7-15

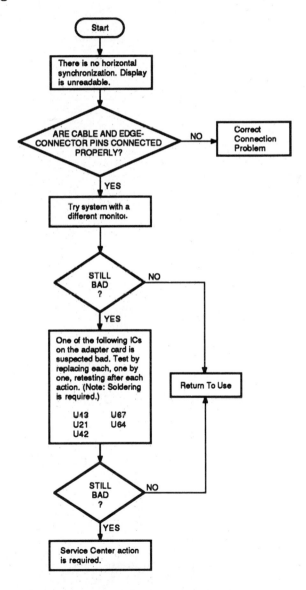

Flowchart 7-16

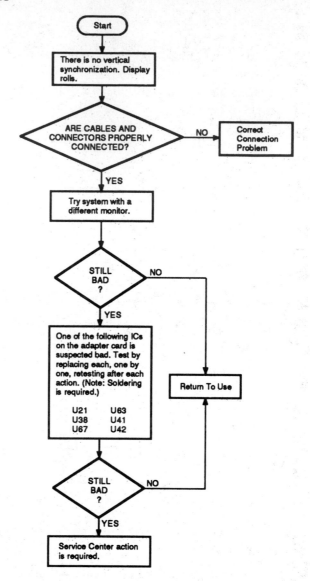

Problem 7-18

No text; graphics work.

Symptom Described:

When running a graphics program, the display is fine, but when running in text mode, either no display, or a garbage display, is produced.

Preliminary Checks:

1. Clean the adapter-card edge-connector pins.
2. Try a different, known-good monitor.
3. Verify that the system is configured properly (switches on system board correctly set, etc.).

Hints:

See Flowchart 7-17 and Fig. 7-7. For a description of the circuitry involved, see the discussion on system operation given in the earlier chapters. If any listed ICs are not in the drawings, assume that they are in the support circuitry.

Flowchart 7-17

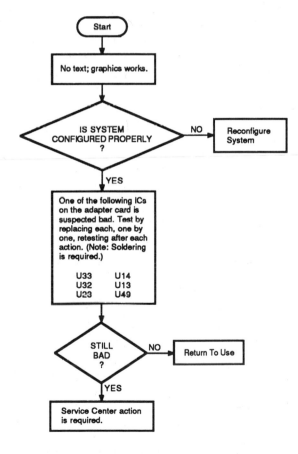

Problem 7-19

No graphics; text display works.

Symptom Described:

When trying to run a graphics program, either garbage is displayed or no display is produced. However, when running a text program, the display looks fine.

Preliminary Checks:

1. Verify the system configuration. Check the switches on the system board.
2. Clean the color/graphics adapter-card edge connector.

Hints:

See Flowchart 7-18 and Fig. 7-7. For a description of the circuitry involved, see the discussion on system operation given in the earlier chapters. If any listed ICs are not in the drawings, assume that they are in the support circuitry.

Flowchart 7-18

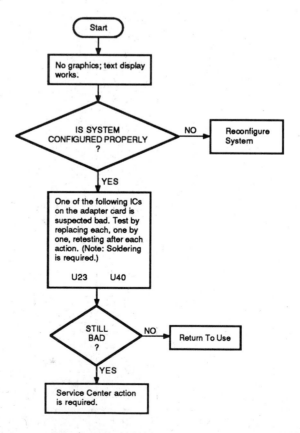

Problem 7-20

Bad characters.

Symptom Described:

There is garbage on the screen (illegal characters and strange shapes) in both the graphics and text modes. (Refer to Fig. 7-7 and Flowchart 7-19.)

Preliminary Checks:

1. Check the monitor cable for continuity. Ensure that it is firmly connected at both ends.
2. Clean the color adapter-card edge connector.
3. Verify that the system is configured correctly (check the switches on the system board).
4. Eliminate the monitor as the problem by substituting it with a known, good, display unit.

Hints:

This type of problem is difficult to troubleshoot without the proper equipment. Taking the adapter card to a Service Center may be better than trying to fix it yourself. In some cases, it is more economical to just purchase another adapter card. For a description of the circuitry involved, see the discussion on system operation given in the earlier chapters. If any listed ICs are not in the drawings, assume that they are in the support circuitry.

Problem 7-21

Bad or no color; image correct.

Symptom Described:

Text and graphics work fine, but the color is either wrong or no color is produced.

Preliminary Checks:

1. Clean the color-card edge-connector pins.
2. Try a different, known-good, display monitor.

Flowchart 7-19

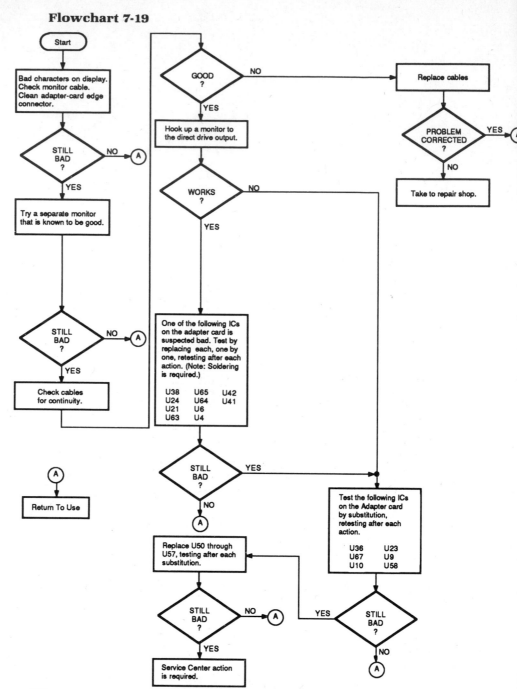

Hints:

See Flowchart 7-20 and Fig. 7-7. For a description of the circuitry involved, see the discussion on system operation given in the earlier chapters. If any listed ICs are not in the drawings, assume that they are in the support circuitry.

Flowchart 7-20

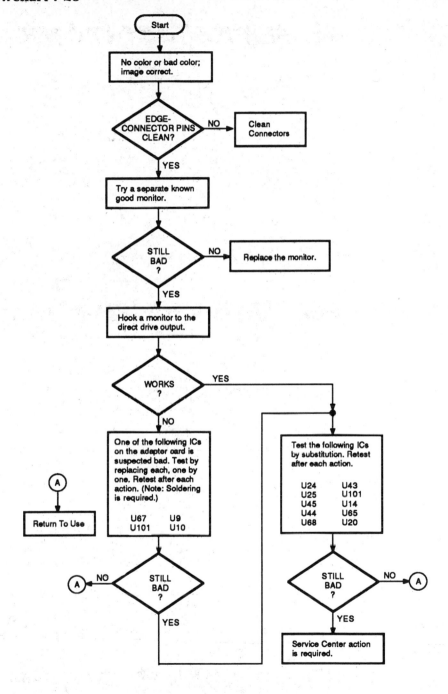

Problem 7-22

Cursor missing or not blinking.

Symptom Described:

No cursor shows on display, or the cursor is present but is not blinking.

Preliminary Checks:

1. Clean the color-card edge-connector pins.
2. Try a different, known-good, display monitor.

Hints:

See Flowchart 7-21 and Fig. 7-7. For a description of the circuitry involved see the discussion on system operation given in the earlier chapters. If any listed ICs are not in the drawings, assume that they are in the support circuitry.

Flowchart 7-21

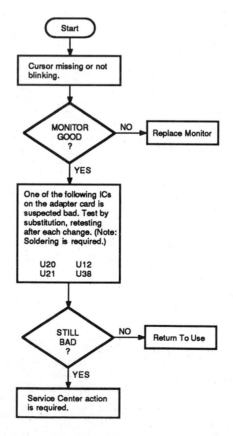

Enhanced Graphics Monitor Adapter

Problem 7-23

No display.

Symptom Described:

There is no screen display: no graphics or text. (Refer to Flowchart 7-22 and Fig. 7-8.)

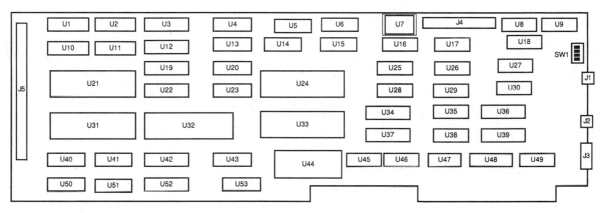

Fig. 7-8. IC layout of the IBM Enhanced Graphics Adapter board.

Preliminary Checks:

1. Check the cable for continuity and proper mating.
2. Try another, known-good, display monitor.
3. Clean the adapter-card edge-connector pins.
4. Check for proper system configuration.

Hints:

If there is no display, the problem is almost always in the cable to the monitor or in the monitor itself. If the adapter card is the problem, it will be very difficult to troubleshoot without the proper equipment. Taking the adapter card to a Service Center may be better than trying to fix it yourself. In some cases, it is more economical to just purchase another adapter card. For a description of the circuitry involved, refer to the discussion on system operation given in the earlier chapters. If any listed ICs are not in the drawings, assume that they are in the support circuitry.

Flowchart 7-22

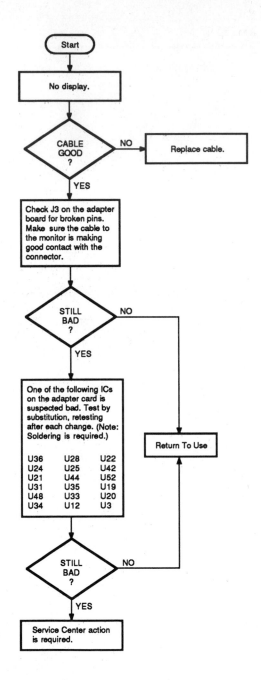

Problem 7-24

No horizontal synchronization.

Symptom Described:

Display is unreadable due to lack of horizontal sync.

Preliminary Checks:

1. Check the cable for continuity and proper mating.
2. Clean the adapter-card edge-connector pins.
3. Try a different, known-good, display monitor.

Hints:

Refer to Fig. 7-8 and Flowchart 7-23. Make sure that the problem is not in the monitor itself. Check the monitor on another system, or try another monitor on your system. For a description of the circuitry involved, see the discussion on system operation given in the earlier chapters. If any listed ICs are not in the drawings, assume that they are in the support circuitry.

Problem 7-25

No vertical synchronization.

Symptom Described:

Display rolls due to a lack of proper vertical sync signal.

Preliminary Checks:

1. Check the cable for continuity and proper mating.
2. Clean the adapter-card edge-connector pins.
3. Try a different, known-good, display monitor.

Hints:

Refer to Fig. 7-8 and Flowchart 7-24. Make sure that the problem is not in the monitor itself. Check the monitor on another system, or try another monitor on your system. For a description of the circuitry involved, see the discussion on system operation given in the earlier chapters. If any listed ICs are not in the drawings, assume that they are in the support circuitry.

Flowchart 7-23

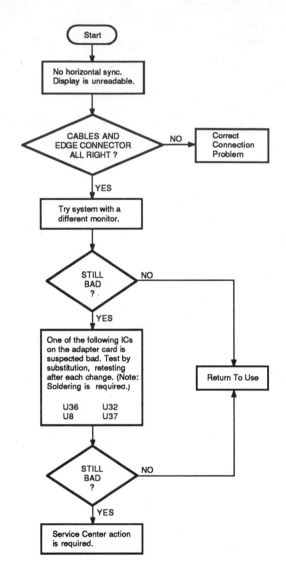

Problem 7-26

No text; graphics works.

Symptom Described:

When running a graphics program, the display is fine, but when running in text mode, either no display, or a garbage display, is produced.

Flowchart 7-24

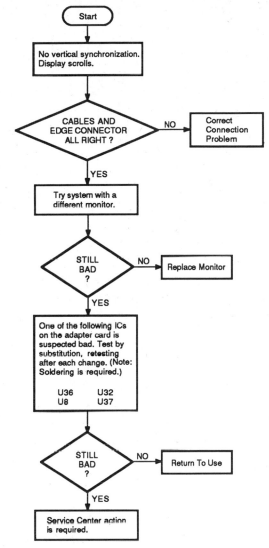

Preliminary Checks:

1. Clean the adapter-card edge-connector pins.

2. Try a different, known-good monitor.

3. Verify that the system is configured properly (switches on system board are correctly set).

Hints:

Refer to Flowchart 7-25 and Fig. 7-8. For a description of the circuitry involved, see the discussion on system operation given in the earlier chapters. If any listed ICs are not in the drawings, assume that they are in the support circuitry.

Flowchart 7-25

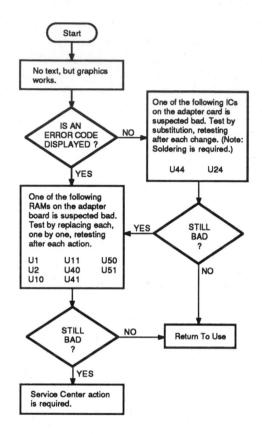

Problem 7-27

No graphics; text displays works.

Symptom Described:

When trying to run a graphics program, either garbage is displayed or no display is produced. When running a text program, the display looks fine.

Preliminary Checks:

1. Verify system configuration. Check switches on the system board.

2. Clean the color/graphics adapter-card edge connector.

3. Try a different monitor.

Hints:

Refer to Flowchart 7-26 and Fig. 7-8. For a description of the circuitry involved, see the discussion on system operation given in the earlier chapters. If any listed ICs are not in the drawings, assume that they are in the support circuitry.

Flowchart 7-26

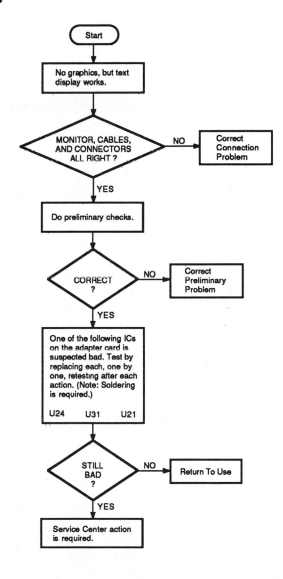

Problem 7-28

Bad characters.

Symptom Described:

There is garbage on the screen (illegal characters and strange shapes) in both the graphics and text modes.

Preliminary Checks:

1. Check the monitor cable for continuity and ensure that it is firmly connected at both ends.
2. Clean the adapter-card edge connector.
3. Verify that the system is configured correctly (check the switches on the system board).
4. Eliminate the monitor as the problem by substituting it with a known-good display unit.

Flowchart 7-27

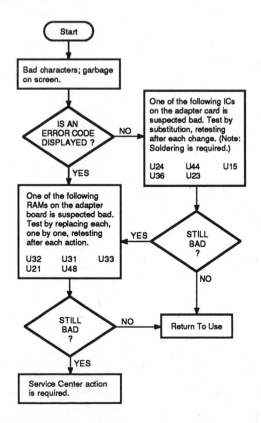

Hints:

Refer to Flowchart 7-27 and Fig. 7-8. A problem of this type is difficult to troubleshoot without the proper equipment. Taking the adapter card to a Service Center may be better than trying to fix it yourself. In some cases, it is more economical to just purchase another adapter card. For a description of the circuitry involved, see the discussion on system operation given in the earlier chapters. If any listed ICs are not in the drawings, assume that they are in the support circuitry.

Problem 7-29

Bad or no color; image correct.

Symptom Described:

Text and graphics work fine, but either the color is wrong or no color is produced.

Preliminary Checks:

1. Clean the color-card edge-connector pins.
2. Try a different, known-good, display monitor.

Hints:

Refer to Flowchart 7-28 and Fig. 7-8. For a description of the circuitry involved, see the discussion on system operation given in the earlier chapters. If any listed ICs are not in the drawings, assume that they are in the support circuitry.

Problem 7-30

Cursor missing or not blinking.

Symptom Described:

Either there is no cursor on the display screen, or the cursor is present, but it is not blinking.

Flowchart 7-28

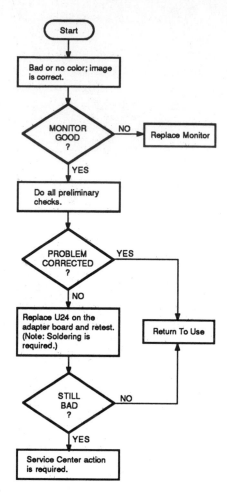

Preliminary Checks:

1. Clean the color-card edge-connector pins.
2. Try a different, known-good, display monitor.

Hints:

Refer to Flowchart 7-29 and Fig. 7-8. For a description of the circuitry involved, see the discussion on system operation given in the earlier chapters. If any listed ICs are not in the drawings, assume that they are in the support circuitry.

Flowchart 7-29

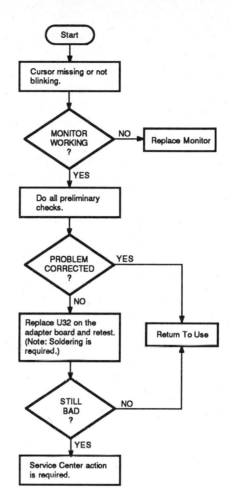

Disk-Drive Problems

There are many problems that can cause disk-drive failures. The following list contains just a few of these possible problems.

1. Can't read from one floppy drive.
2. Can't read from either floppy drive.
3. Can't write to one floppy drive.
4. Can't write to either floppy drive.
5. Can't access either floppy drive. No drive access lights. Drive motor is not energized.
6. Floppy drive destroys data on a Write-Protected disk.
7. Floppy drive accesses only one half of the space on the disk.

8. Can't read from the fixed disk drive.

 9. Can't write to the fixed disk drive.

 10. Can't access the fixed disk drive. No drive access lights. Drive motor is not energized.

Problem 7-31

Can't read from one floppy drive.

Symptom Described:

The drive spins continuously, trying to load data from the disk into the computer. An error display might occur.

Preliminary Checks:

1. Check the cables for proper mating.
2. Try another (known good) backup copy of the program disk.
3. Shift the bad drive to position A (if not already installed as Drive A).
4. Check for disk spinning action during the disk Read sequence. If no drive motor activation is observed, refer to Flowchart 7-30 and Fig. 7-9.
5. With system turned off, move the drive head towards the center of the disk. Turn the system on and note if the head moves back towards Track 00. If it doesn't, again refer to Flowchart 7-30.
6. Check that E1 on the analog card is properly jumpered.
7. Clean the drive Read/Write heads. (See Chapter 10.)

Hints:

A drive that will not read is one of the most common failures. Seek out the clues. Conduct the preliminary service checks. A good "suspect" in this problem is the cable from the adapter card to the drive. If the drive that is not functioning is the "A" drive, try swapping it with the "B" drive; change the jumpers and resistor pack from "A" to "B." If Drive B doesn't work either, then the problem is in the adapter card or the cable. If Drive B (when used as "A") does boot, then the problem is in the "A" drive. For a description of the circuitry involved, see the discussion on system operation given in the earlier chapters. If any listed ICs are not in the drawings, assume that they are in the support circuitry.

Flowchart 7-30.

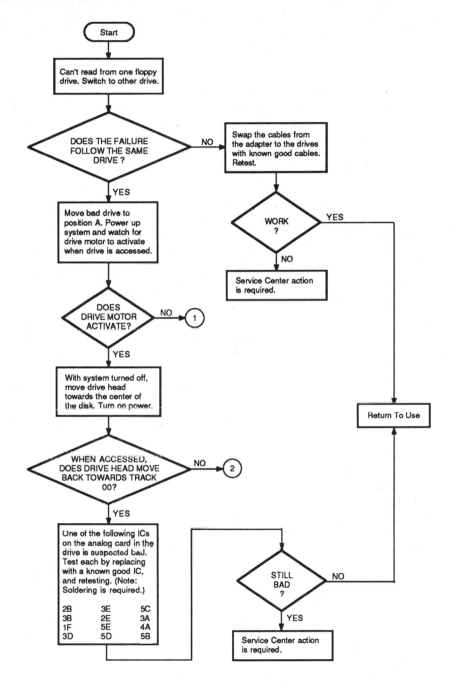

Flowchart 7-30 *(continued)*

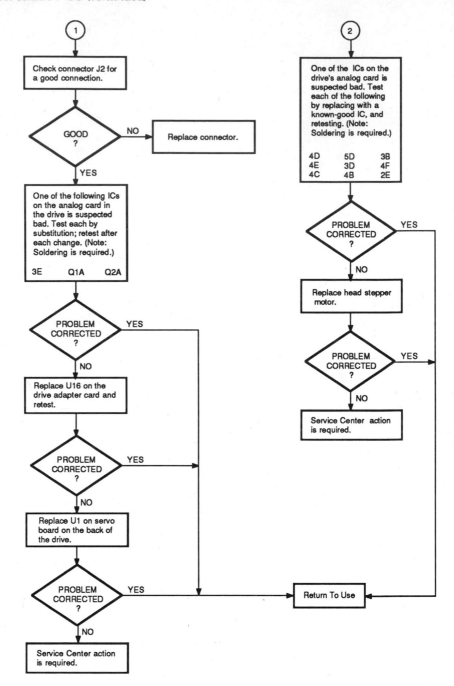

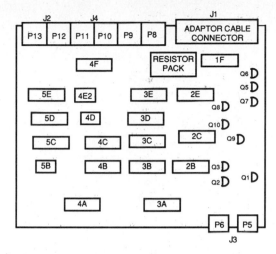

Fig. 7-9. IC layout of the analog board in the IBM floppy disk drive.

Problem 7-32

Can't read from either floppy drive.

Symptom Described:

During the power-up sequence, the system goes into ROM BASIC. When trying to load from either drive, an error message occurs.

Preliminary Checks:

1. Check that all cables are properly connected and have continuity.
2. Clean the edge connector on the disk-drive adapter card.

Hints:

Refer to Flowchart 7-31 and Fig. 7-9. During a Read sequence, note if the drive access light comes on. If it doesn't, go to Problem 7-35. If the drive access light comes on during a Read operation, check that the motor is rotating the spindle shaft. If it isn't, the problem may be in the +12-volt power supply. Check connector P10 in the power supply for proper mating. For a description of the circuitry involved, see the discussion on system operation given in the earlier chapters. If any listed ICs are not in the drawings, assume that they are in the support circuitry.

Flowchart 7-31

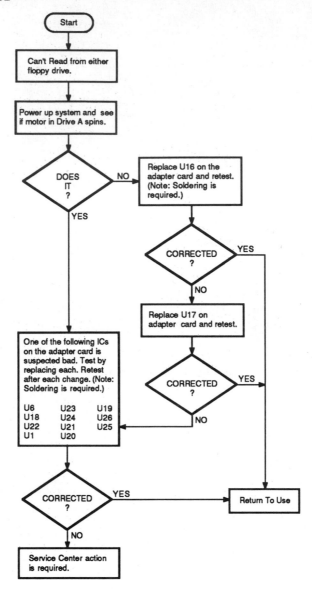

Problem 7-33

Can't write to one floppy drive.

Symptom Described:

Drive reads properly, but won't write to disk. The error message "DISK WRITE-PROTECTED" may be displayed.

Preliminary Checks:

1. Verify that there is no Write-Protect tab on the diskette being used in the drive.
2. Try a different disk.
3. Check the speed and tracking of the drive in use.
4. Check that all cables are properly connected and have continuity.

Hints:

Refer to Flowchart 7-32 and Fig. 7-9. If you keep getting a message that the drive is Write-Protected, there may be a problem with the switch that checks for the Write-Protect tab on the disk. Sometimes this switch can be moved out of position just enough to not read correctly. Try listening for the switch to click (softly) when you insert the disk all the way into the drive. Try both drives, if one works, to get an idea of the sound to listen for. If there is no click, then a quick adjustment of the switch's position should solve the problem. For a description of the circuitry involved, refer to the discussion on system operation given in the earlier chapters. If any listed ICs are not in the drawings, assume that they are in the support circuitry.

Problem 7-34

Can't write to either floppy drive.

Symptom Described:

When writing to a drive, either an error message occurs and the operation terminates, or the data written to the disk are not present during a later Read operation.

Preliminary Checks:

1. Check all cables for continuity and proper mating.
2. Clean the disk-drive adapter-card edge connector.
3. Configure the system as single drive, and test each drive individually.
4. Verify that no Write-Protect tabs are on the disks being used.

Hints:

Refer to Fig. 7-9. This problem is likely in the cables between the drive and the adapter card. If not, refer to Flowchart 7-33. For a description of the circuitry involved, refer to the discussion on system operation given in the earlier chapters. If any listed ICs are not in the drawings, assume that they are in the support circuitry.

Flowchart 7-32

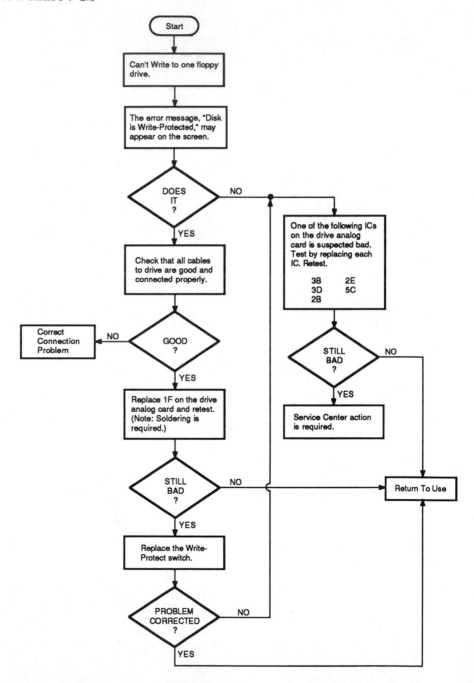

Flowchart 7-33

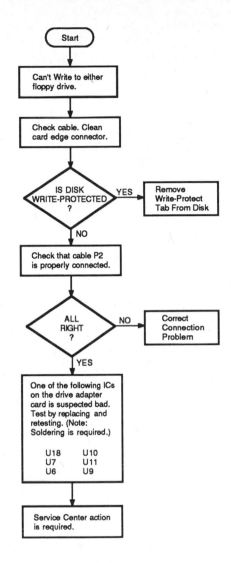

Problem 7-35

Can't access either floppy drive. No drive access lights. Drive motor is not energized.

Symptom Described:

Both drives fail to react to any Read or Write operation.

Preliminary Checks:

1. Check that all of the drive data and power cables are properly connected and have good continuity.
2. Clean the edge connector on the drive adapter card.

Flowchart 7-34

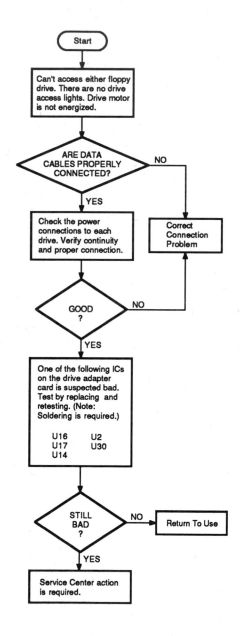

Hints:

Refer to Flowchart 7-34 and Fig. 7-9. This type of problem usually occurs when the cable between the adapter card and the drives is bad. For a description of the circuitry involved, see the discussion on system operation given in the earlier chapters. If any listed ICs are not in the drawings, assume that they are in the support circuitry.

Problem 7-36

Floppy drive destroys data on a Write-Protected disk.

Symptom Described:

While inadvertently trying to write to a disk that has a Write-Protect tab installed, data are written on the disk. The Write-Protect feature is not functioning.

Preliminary Checks:

1. Check the drive cables for proper mating and continuity.
2. Clean the adapter-card edge connector.

Hints:

Refer to Flowchart 7-35 and Fig. 7-9. Insert a disk, without a Write-Protect tab, into the bad drive slowly, while listening for the switch to "click" when it is activated by the Write-Protect tab opening on the diskette. If no click is heard, check the alignment of the Write-Protect switch. Another strong possibility is the cable going from the switch to the analog card in the drive. It may be bad. For a description of the circuitry involved, see the discussion on system operation given in the earlier chapters. If any listed ICs are not in the drawings, assume that they are in the support circuitry.

Problem 7-37

Floppy drive accesses only one half of the space on the disk.

Symptom Described:

An error display occurs. The drive seems to have only one half of the space it really has. Directory shows the total drive space to be only 180K bytes.

Flowchart 7-35

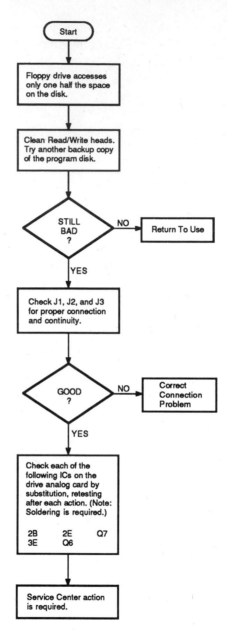

Preliminary Checks:

1. Check cables for proper mating.
2. Try another (known-good) backup of the program disk.
3. Clean the drive Read/Write heads. (See Chapter 10.)

Hints:

Refer to Flowchart 7-36. Also, see Figs. 7-9 and 7-10. A drive that will not read more than one half of the space on a disk will have something wrong in the Read/Write-head circuitry. This problem may be just that the heads need cleaning, or it could be a bad head. Replacement heads are expensive. However, the heads are probably the main suspect. For a description of the circuitry involved, see the discussion on system operation given in the earlier chapters. If any listed ICs are not in the drawings, assume that they are in the support circuitry.

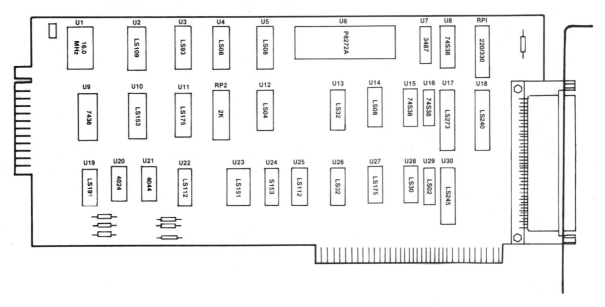

Fig. 7-10. IC layout of the IBM Floppy Disk Drive adapter card.

XT **Problem 7-38**

Can't read from the fixed disk drive.

Symptom Described:

Either an error display occurs, or the drive spins continuously, while trying to load data from the disk into the computer. (Refer to Flowchart 7-37 and Fig. 7-11.)

Preliminary Checks:

1. Check the cables for proper mating.

Flowchart 7-36

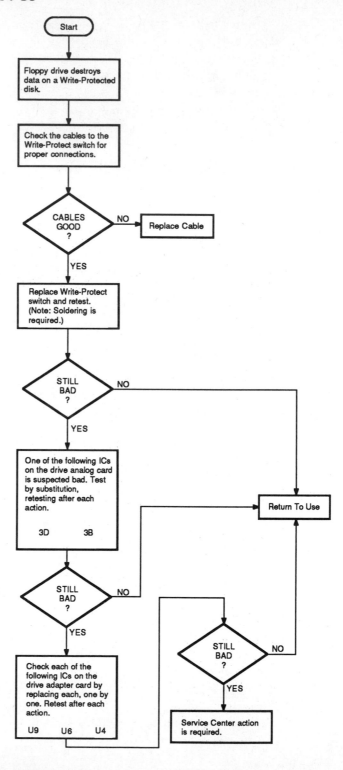

2. Try to format and configure the fixed disk to see if the software is causing the problem.

3. Try the fixed drive on another system to verify that the drive is good.

Hints:

A drive that will not read is a common failure. Watch for clues. Conduct the preliminary service checks. A good "suspect" is the cables from the adapter card to the drive. Try the drive on another system. If it works, then the problem is in the adapter card. If the drive doesn't work in another system, then the drive is bad and will need to be taken to a Service Center. Fixed drives are very hard to work on. The heads themselves are inside a vacuum and, therefore, cannot be adjusted or worked on without special equipment. For a description of the circuitry involved, refer to the discussion on system operation given in the earlier chapters. If any listed ICs are not in the drawings, assume that they are in the support circuitry.

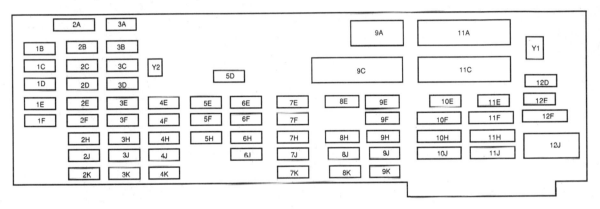

Fig. 7-11.   IC layout of the IBM PC/XT Fixed Disk Drive adapter card.

    Problem 7-39

Can't write to the fixed disk drive.

Symptom Described:

Drive reads properly, but won't write to disk. The error message "DISK WRITE-PROTECTED" may be displayed.

Preliminary Checks:

1. Check that all cables are properly connected.
2. Check that all cables have continuity.

Flowchart 7-37

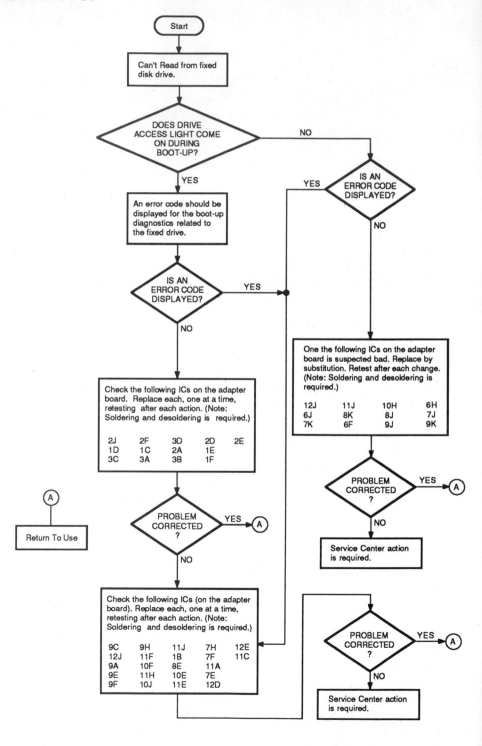

Hints:

Refer to Fig. 7-11 and Flowchart 7-38.

Watch for clues. Conduct the preliminary service checks. A good item to "suspect" is the set of cables running from the adapter card to the drive. Try the drive on another system. If it works, the problem is in the adapter card. If the drive doesn't work in the other system, then the drive is bad and will need to be taken to a Service Center. Fixed drives are very hard to work on. The heads are enclosed inside a vacuum and, therefore, cannot be adjusted or worked on without special equipment (and a clean room facility). For a description of the circuitry involved, refer to the discussion on system operation given in the earlier chapters. If any listed ICs are not in the drawings, assume that they are in the support circuitry.

Flowchart 7-38

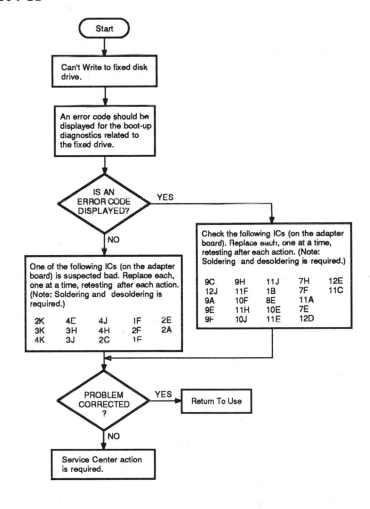

Problem 7-40

Can't access the fixed disk drive. No drive access lights. Drive motor is not energized.

Symptom Described:

Drive fails to react to any Read or Write operation.

Preliminary Checks:

1. Check that all of the drive data and power cables are properly connected and have good continuity.
2. Clean the edge connector on the drive adapter cards.

Hints:

Refer to Fig. 7-11 and Flowchart 7-39.

Look for clues. Conduct the preliminary service checks. A good item to "suspect" is the set of cables running from the adapter card to the drive. Try the drive on another system. If it works, then the problem is in the adapter card. If the drive doesn't work in the other system, then the drive is bad and will need to be taken to a Service Center. Fixed drives are very hard to work on. The heads are enclosed inside a vacuum and, therefore, cannot be adjusted or worked on without special equipment (and a clean room facility). For a description of the circuitry involved, refer to the discussion of system operation given in the earlier chapters. If any listed ICs are not in the figures, assume that they are in the support circuitry.

Input/Output Problems

In troubleshooting the IBM Personal Computers, you may encounter input/output problems of varying difficulties. The following are six of the most common problems.

1. Cassette recorder can't write data to tape.
2. Cassette player can't load data from tape.
3. Light pen won't work.
4. Printer won't print.
5. Printer either locks up or prints garbage.
6. Speaker doesn't work.

Flowchart 7-39

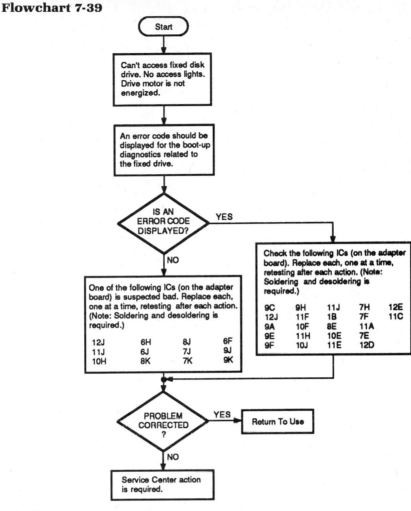

Problem 7-41

Cassette recorder can't write data to tape.

Symptom Described:

When trying to write to the tape, either an error occurs or nothing is written.

Preliminary Checks:

1. Check that the cables to the cassette recorder/player are connected properly and have good continuity.

2. Try another tape.

3. Try another recorder/player.

Hints:

Refer to Fig. 7-12 and Flowchart 7-40.

Most often this problem turns out to be in the recorder itself. Be sure that you are using a good recorder. For a description of the circuitry involved, see the discussion of the system operation given in the earlier chapters. If any listed ICs are not in the drawings, assume that they are in the support circuitry.

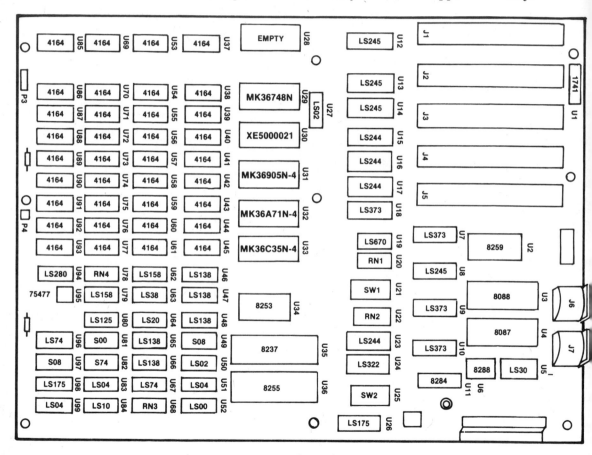

Fig. 7-12.　IC layout of IBM PC system board.

Flowchart 7-40

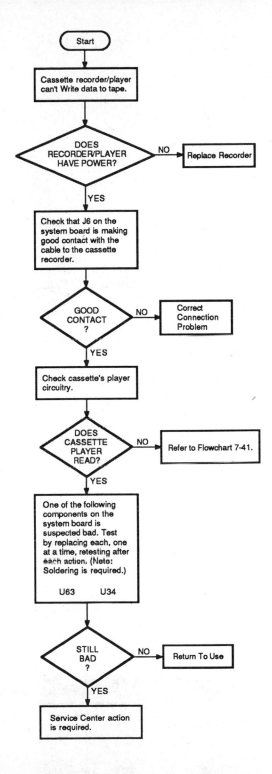

Problem 7-42

Cassette player can't load data from tape.

Symptom Described:

When trying to load data from a cassette, either an error occurs or no data get loaded into RAM memory.

Preliminary Checks:

1. Check that the cables to the cassette recorder/player are properly connected and have good continuity.
2. Try another tape.
3. Try another recorder/player.

Hints:

Refer to Fig. 7-12 and Flowchart 7-41.

The cable is the typical cause of this type of failure, followed closely by the recorder itself. For a description of the circuitry involved, see the discussion of the system operation given in the earlier chapters. If any listed ICs are not in the drawings, assume that they are in the support circuitry.

Problem 7-43

Light pen won't work.

Symptom Described:

No system response occurs when using the light pen.

Preliminary Checks:

1. Check the light pen cable for continuity and proper mating.
2. Test the light pen on another system.

Hints:

Refer to Fig. 7-13 and Flowchart 7-42.

The light pen cable is typically the cause of this problem, followed closely by the light pen itself.

Flowchart 7-41

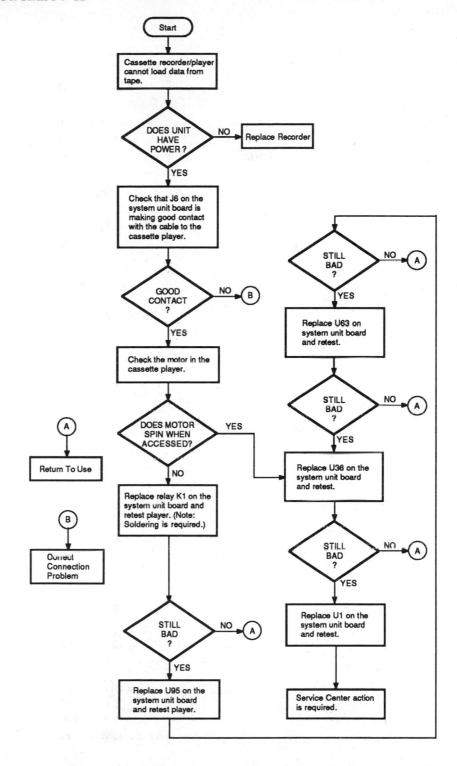

Flowchart 7-42

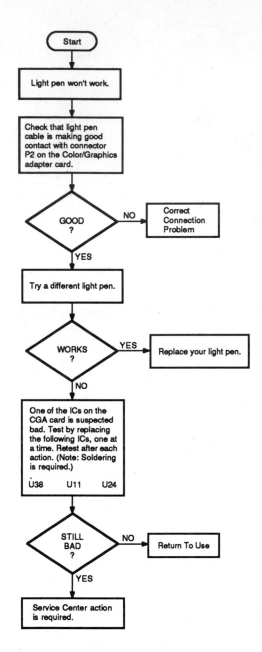

Problem 7-44

Printer won't print.

Symptom Described:

　When the command is given to print, nothing happens.

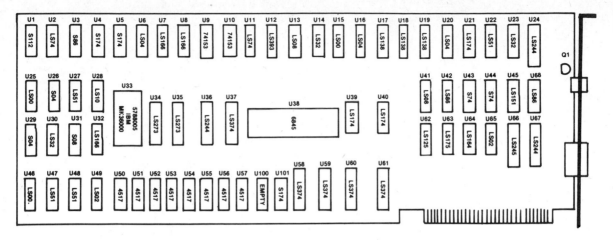

Fig. 7-13. IC layout diagram of the IBM Color/Graphics Adapter board.

Preliminary Checks:

1. Check that the cables are connected properly and have good continuity.
2. Clean the printer adapter-card edge-connector pins.
3. Verify that the printer is properly configured and working properly. Conduct a printer self-test.

Note:

The following description assumes a monolithic printer adapter card is in use. For the monochrome monitor/printer adapter card, map the ICs as follows:

Printer Adapter	Monochrome Monitor/Printer Adapter
U1	U23
U6	U61
U7	U39
U8	U38

Hints:

Refer to Flowchart 7-43 and Fig. 7-14.

Then, run the printer's self-test program. If it fails, the printer is bad. Even if the self test passes, the printer may still be bad. Printer self tests check only the system board logic and not the I/O. This problem is usually associated only with the printer circuitry.

Flowchart 7-43

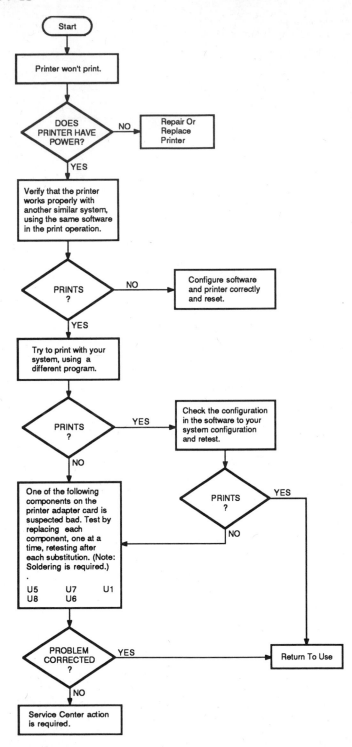

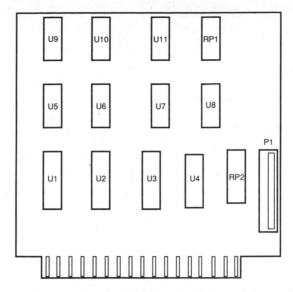

Fig. 7-14.   IC layout diagram for the IBM Parallel Printer Adapter board.

Problem 7-45

Printer either locks up or prints garbage.

Symptom Described:

When beginning, or while in a print operation, the printer either stops or begins printing garbage.

Preliminary Checks:

1. Check that the cables are properly connected and have good continuity.
2. Clean the printer adapter-card edge-connector pins.
3. Verify that the printer is configured properly and operates properly. Conduct a printer self test.

Note:

The following description assumes a monolithic printer adapter card is in use. For the monochrome monitor/printer adapter card, map the ICs as follows:

Printer Adapter	Monochrome Monitor/Printer Adapter
U2	U37
U3	U40
U4	U41

Flowchart 7-44

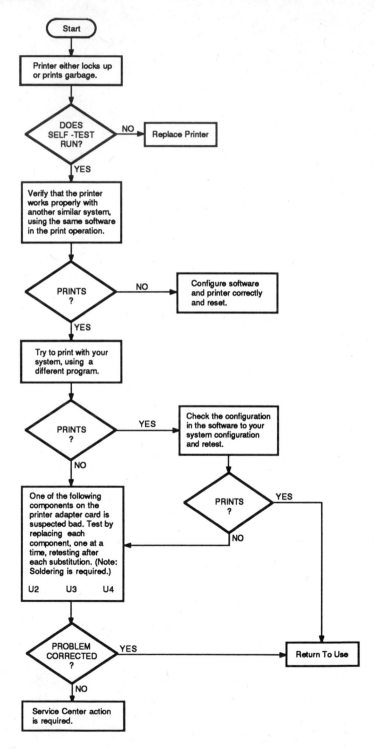

Flowchart 7-45

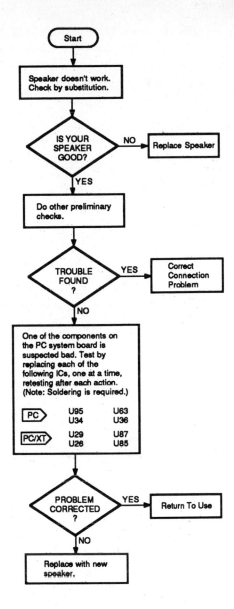

Start

Speaker doesn't work.
Check by substitution.

IS YOUR SPEAKER GOOD? — NO → Replace Speaker

YES

Do other preliminary checks.

TROUBLE FOUND ? — YES → Correct Connection Problem

NO

One of the components on the PC system board is suspected bad. Test by replacing each of the following ICs, one at a time, retesting after each action. (Note: Soldering is required.)

PC   U95   U63
        U34   U36

PC/XT   U29   U87
        U26   U85

PROBLEM CORRECTED ? — YES → Return To Use

NO

Replace with new speaker.

Hints:

Refer to Flowchart 7-44 and Fig. 7-14.

Then, run the printer's self test program. If it fails, the printer is bad. Even if the self test passes, the printer may still be bad. Printer self tests check only the system board logic and not the I/O. This problem is usually associated only with the printer circuitry.

Problem 7-46

Speaker doesn't work.

Symptom Described:

There is no sound from the speaker. (Refer to Figs. 7-12 and 7-15.)

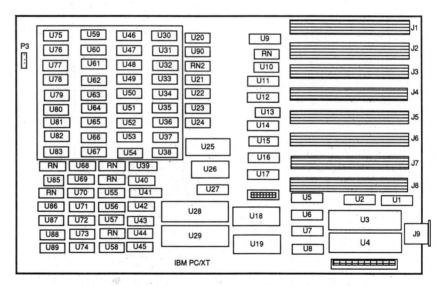

Fig. 7-15.   IC layout diagram of the IBM PC/XT system board.

Preliminary Checks:

1. Check the speaker cable for continuity and proper connection.
2. Check for damage to the speaker.

Hints:

Refer to Flowchart 7-45.

A bad speaker or speaker cable is usually the cause for this failure. For a description of the circuitry involved, see the discussion of system operation given in the earlier chapters. If any listed ICs are not in the drawings, assume that they are in the support circuitry.

Specific Troubleshooting and Repair Procedures: IBM PC AT

This chapter covers the detailed troubleshooting analysis associated with the IBM PC AT. Many of the failures discussed in these pages are the same as those analyzed in Chapter 7 for the IBM PC and PC/XT. This chapter is divided into six parts:

1. Start-up problems.
2. Run problems.
3. Keyboard problems.
4. Display problems.
5. Disk-drive problems.
6. Other I/O problems.

Each computer and peripheral malfunction in the IBM PC AT can be associated with one of these six areas. A key problem index (Chart 8-1) covering each of these general areas is included to provide both preliminary checks and flowchart troubleshooting support. Using the index, you can quickly locate a particular problem area for analysis and find specific sets of failures and symptoms for each.

Part 1 covers the symptoms that can occur during initial power-up, including no power and no disk boot-up operation. Each PC AT comes with a built-in diagnostic test program, and most owners also have a diagnostic disk to use in conjunction with the built-in diagnostics. It's possible to get a system error number printed on the screen during start-up that will help localize a malfunction to a particular part of the machine.

Part 2 discusses the failure symptoms that can occur after initial boot-up—during system operation. These include both bad memory and program lockup.

Keyboard problems are detailed in Part 3. This section covers such faults as single- and multiple-key operation failures, and unwanted "repeat" action.

Part 4 addresses those difficulties associated with the display portion of the computer. These problems include no display, no text mode, no Hi-Res or no Lo-Res, video synchronization failures, character faults, bad graphics, and other problems.

Then, Part 5 details troubleshooting faulty disk drives. This includes Read/Write operations to the floppy disk drive(s), as well as to the fixed drive.

Finally, Part 6 covers any other input and output problems, including speaker faults and light pen malfunctions.

These data are followed by preliminary checks, hints for repair, and step-by-step flowchart troubleshooting instructions. In the flowcharts, ICs that are to be replaced will be listed in order of their priority. Therefore the ICs at the beginning of the list are the ICs that are most likely to be bad. Occasionally, in the step-by-step flowchart troubleshooting instructions, a statement is made suggesting to the reader that "Service Center" action is required. This statement is made to let you know that to solve this problem you will need test equipment, which we are assuming you don't have. Therefore the proper way to fix the problem is to take the system to an authorized Service Center. This chapter will help you describe your problem and equipment symptoms to the technician at the Service Center, so that the Center's troubleshooting time (and your bill) is kept to a minimum.

As you use this manual, you'll discover many useful hints for both troubleshooting and repair. Be especially alert to the caution notices, since further system degradation can occur if you do not follow those procedures exactly as listed.

Make sure you've read and understand the preliminary checks that can be made before dealing with the step-by-step instructional flowchart. Few things are as humbling as disassembling a system for troubleshooting and repair, and then discovering that the problem was caused by a bad cable between the system unit and the monitor.

This chapter will not directly discuss the malfunctions of resistors and capacitors because catastrophic failure of these passive devices are usually quite visible during an examination of the system board and the peripheral cards. If you feel that a resistor or capacitor has failed, check the component resistance (out of the circuit) with an ohmmeter. The resistance value should closely approximate that of the code printed on the resistor, and the capacitor should not register a short. Most capacitor failures are obvious because capacitors usually blow apart or char in the circuit. A preliminary check statement, which refers to "visually examining" a board or card, means you should look for charred, hot, or physically broken parts.

NOTE: The troubleshooting problems and techniques given in the following pages may require soldering. Be sure that you are proficient in this technique before you proceed.

> **CAUTION**: Replacing components or otherwise modifying the IBM PC AT system unit may void its warranty.

> **WARNING**: Before doing anything inside the System Unit, make sure that the power is in the correct condition (for example, OFF when removing or inserting any components or adapter cards).

Chart 8-1. IBM PC AT Troubleshooting Index

Start-Up Problems

Four types of error indications can occur during the initialization or start-up process—beep indicators from the built-in speaker, system error-code displays, I/O error-code displays, and other error displays. These indications will assist in isolating a failure to a module, subunit, or peripheral.

If the system won't boot, the IBM AT DOS manual suggests that you reread the manual. A number of things can cause the computer to either boot improperly or not boot at all—wrong diskette in the drive, no operating system on the diskette, cables loose, adapter card not fully seated, disk-drive failure, memory chip bad, no clock pulses, or even an unplugged power cord. You can probably deduce a particular problem faster by noting the conditions of the machine at the time of "failure" and following the troubleshooting steps outlined in this chapter.

Select the problem from the following list that best describes your PC's symptoms, and then turn to the appropriate page in this chapter for the proper troubleshooting procedures.

1. Self-test error displayed.

2. System won't boot, no fan, and screen is blank.

3. System won't boot, fan works, but screen is blank.

4. System won't boot, but both drive access lights are on.

Problem 8-1

Self-test error displayed.

Symptom Described:

When the self-test is running, either a beep is heard from the speaker or an error code is displayed on the monitor.

Preliminary Checks:

1. Check all cables for continuity and proper mating.

2. Clean the edge connectors on the adapter cards.

3. Reseat the CPU (U74) on the system board.

Hints:

When an error is detected during boot-up, either a code is displayed on the screen (Table 8-1) or an audible beep sequence is heard (Table 8-2). From this error information, you can proceed to the correct section in this chapter. For example, if the code 101 appears on your screen, you know (from the Table 8-3) that there is a problem on the system board. The system will lock up and there will be no response to keyboard action. From this information, you can go to the "Run Problems" subsection discussed later in the chapter, and follow the procedures given there.

If the system detects a RAM failure, a four-character error code, followed by the number 201, will appear in the top left corner of the screen (Table 8-3). The value 201 identifies a RAM failure; the four-character code defines the bank and row of memory in which the bad RAM IC was detected. The first two characters refer to the bank of memory in which the failure occurred. The last two characters refer to the bit position of the RAM bank that failed (Table 8-4).

Table 8-4 describes the RAM error codes. If the third and fourth characters of the error code don't match the codes in Table 8-4, swap the entire bank of RAM chips and try again. A cost-saving way to find the bad RAM is to power-down the system and swap each chip, one at a time, with the corresponding bit in an adjacent row. Then power up and retest. See if the failure has moved to the new bank. The last chip that was swapped when the failure changes is the bad RAM.

Table 8-5 lists other error-code displays and their meanings, and Appendix A contains a more detailed description of the various error indicators.

Table 8-1. I/O Error Codes

Code	Problem Area
199	Printer adapter or Printer.
432	Printer adapter or Printer.
7xx	Math coprocessor.
9xx	Serial/Parallel adapter—Parallel port.
10xx	Alternate Serial/Parallel adapter—Parallel port.
11xx	Serial/Parallel adapter—Serial port.
12xx	Serial/Parallel adapter—Serial port.
13xx	Game control adapter card.
14xx	Graphics printer.
15xx	System Unit or Communications adapter cable.
20xx	BSC adapter.
21xx	Alternate BSC adapter.
2200	Cluster failure.
29xx	Color printer.
3000	Network failure.
3100	Network failure.

Table 8-2. Beep Indicator Codes

Indicator	Problem Area
No beep, nothing happens.	Power, Power supply.
Continuous beep.	Power, Power supply.
Repeating short beep.	System board.
1 long, 1 short beep.	System board.
1 long, 2 short beeps.	Display circuitry.
1 short beep, blank or incorrect display.	Display circuitry.
1 short beep, Cassette BASIC displayed, no disk boot.	Diskette, Drive.

Table 8-3. System Error Codes*

Code	Problem Area
02x	Power supply problem.
101	System board malfunction/Interrupt failure.
102	System board error/Timer failure.
103	System board error/Timer interrupt failure.

(continued)

Table 8-3. System Error Codes* *(continued)*

Code	Problem Area
104	System board error/Protected mode failure.
105	System board error/Command not accepted.
106	System board error/Converting logic test (NMI).
107	System board error/Hot NMI test.
108	System board test/Timer bus test.
109	System board error/Low meg chip select test.
121	System board error.
151	Defective battery, or new battery installed.
152	System board error.
161	System options not set, or dead battery.
162	System options not set.
163	Time and date not set.
164	Memory size error.
199	Option set-up error.
201	RAM failure.
xxxx = 201	Memory failure.
xxxx = 201 PARITY CHECK X	RAM chip malfunction.
202	Memory address error.
203	Memory address error.
301	Keyboard malfunction. Keyboard cable disconnected.
xx301	Keyboard circuitry malfunction. (xx is the Hex value representing the scan code of the malfunctioning key.)
302	System Unit keylock is locked.
303	Keyboard or System Unit malfunction.
304	Keyboard or System Unit malfunction.
401	Monochrome adapter card.
501	Color/Graphics adapter card.
601	Diskette or disk-drive interface malfunction.
602	Diskette boot record error.
1780	Fixed disk drive failure.
1781	Fixed disk drive failure.
1782	Disk controller error.
1790	Fixed disk drive error.
1791	Fixed disk drive error.

*These error codes can appear alone or in conjunction with other numbers.

Table 8-4. RAM Memory Failure Error Codes

System Board Memory Bank (XX)	Failed Chip (XX 201 Parity Check 1)
00 = Bank 0	00 = Parity
01 = Bank 0	01 = D0 chip
02 = Bank 0	02 = D1 chip
03 = Bank 0	04 = D2 chip
04 = Bank 1	08 = D3 chip
05 = Bank 1	10 = D4 chip

(continued)

Table 8-4. RAM Memory Failure Error Codes *(continued)*

System Board Memory Bank (XX)	Failed Chip (XX 201 Parity Check 1)
06 = Bank 1 07 = Bank 1	20 = D5 chip 40 = D6 chip 80 = D7 chip 100 = D8 chip 200 = D9 chip 400 = D10 chip 800 = D11 chip 1000 = D12 chip 2000 = D13 chip 4000 = D14 chip 8000 = D15 chip

Table 8-5. Other Error Displays

Display	Meaning
Blank display; beep; drive starts to boot, but no BASIC message shows on screen.	System monitor BIOS ROM failure/8284 clock generator is bad.
PARITY CHECK 1	Power supply problems.
PARITY CHECK 2	Bad or incorrectly seated RAM.
PRINTER PROBLEMS	Printer problem, check interface.
ROM ERROR	System ROM failure.

Problem 8-2

System won't boot, no fan, screen is blank.

Symptom Described:

When the ON/OFF switch is moved to the ON position, nothing happens. No fan sound can be heard.

Preliminary Checks:

1. None.
2. This problem was described for the IBM PC and PC/XT in Chapter 7.

Hints:

Refer to Problem 7-2 and Flowchart 7-1 in Chapter 7.

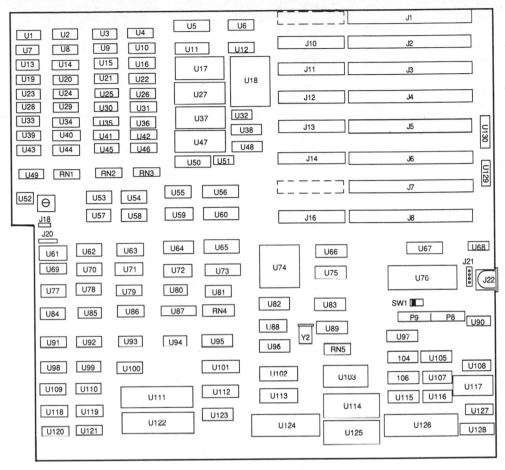

Fig. 8-1. IC layout of the IBM PC AT system board.

Problem 8-3

System won't boot, fan works, screen is blank.

Symptom Described:

There is no cursor, no screen display, no keyboard response, but you can hear the fan running in the power supply.

Preliminary Checks:

1. Check cables for proper mating.

2. Clean all edge connectors on the adapter cards.

3. Reseat the CPU chip (U74).

4. Visually inspect the system board.

5. Remove all peripherals except the keyboard and monitor (with its adapter card). Power up. Does the system boot to ROM BASIC? If it does, turn the machine off, and reinstall one adapter card at a time, testing after each installation. When the system fails to boot to ROM BASIC, the last card installed is bad.

Hints:

Refer to Fig. 8-1 and Flowchart 8-1.

Flowchart 8-1

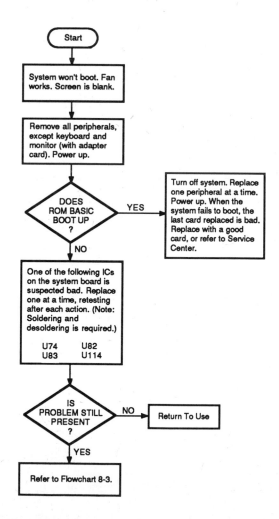

Many times, a problem like this is confused with a problem in the video circuitry. To avoid this, check that the keyboard seems to make the system do functions—like get a directory from the drive or print out a word. Even if the video circuitry is bad, you will still see the drive get accessed and look (and sound) like it is reading data. For a description of the circuitry, refer to the discussion on system operation given in earlier chapters. If any listed ICs are not in the drawing, assume that they are in the support circuitry.

Problem 8-4

System won't boot, but both drive access lights are on.

Symptom Described:

When the system is turned on, the access indicators of Drives A and C light and remain on. Drive A won't boot a disk. (Refer to Fig. 8-2 and Flowchart 8-2.)

Preliminary Checks:

1. Check that all drive cables are installed correctly.
2. Clean all board header connections, especially on the disk-drive adapter card.
3. Check that that select jumper on the drive analog card is set for the correct drive.
4. Visually inspect the system board, disk-drive adapter card, and disk-drive analog card.

Hints:

Both drive lights coming on is a sign that both drives are being considered as the primary boot drive. If the preliminary checks didn't solve the problem,

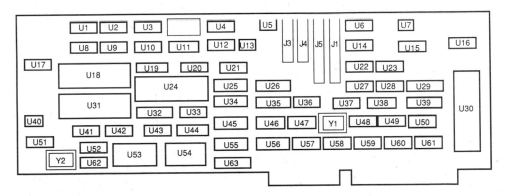

Fig. 8-2. IC layout of the IBM Fixed Disk/Floppy Disk Adapter board.

Flowchart 8-2

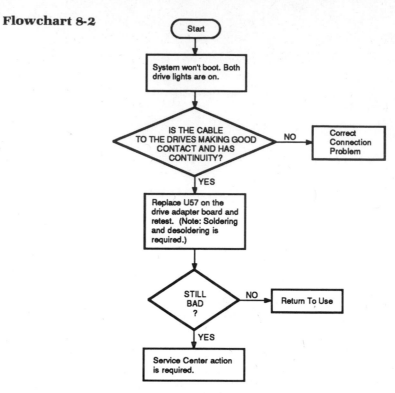

check that the drive cables are good. For a description of the circuitry, see the discussion of system operation given in the earlier chapters. If any listed ICs are not in the drawing, assume that they are in the support circuitry.

Run Problems

This section covers those problems you might encounter while your system is running. For example, you attempt to do something and get an entirely different response from what you expected. The following three sections will cover such broad malfunctions as display failure, keyboard failure, floppy drive failure, and input/output failures (although these may also occur during the time you start up your system).

1. While running, the computer locks up. There is no keyboard response.
2. Power turns off after system runs for a while.

Problem 8-5

While running, computer locks up. There is no response from keyboard.

Symptom Described:

During operation of a known-good program, the computer locks up, the display freezes, and the keyboard inputs have no effect.

Preliminary Checks:

1. Try a different program disk.
2. Check all cables for continuity and proper mating.
3. Clean the edge connectors on the adapter cards.
4. Reseat the CPU (U74) on the system board.

Hints:

Refer to Fig. 8-1 and Flowchart 8-3.

This problem can be caused by a failure in the nonmaskable interrupt section, the Ready circuitry, the bus control circuitry, the Reset circuitry, the timing circuitry, or the processor circuitry. There are so many areas of the system board that could cause this problem that it is one of the hardest to solve. Many times, a heat-related problem in an IC can cause this failure.

When the system locks up, try to turn it off, and after seven seconds, power up again and see if an error code is displayed. If an error code is displayed, take note of it, for it can be a good hint for later troubleshooting. Also, write a short looping program to see if you get the same failure consistently. If so, use the program to monitor when corrective action has been successful.

Also check that your power supply is not overloaded and driving a lot of peripheral boards. If your system uses a lot of adapter cards and peripherals, the supply may need upgrading to a higher wattage. For a description of the circuitry involved, refer to the discussion of system operation given in the earlier chapters.

Flowchart 8-3

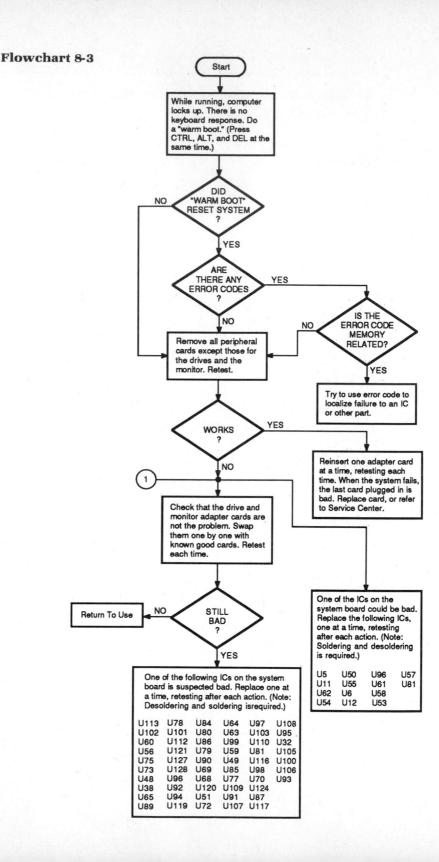

Flowchart 8-3 *(continued)*

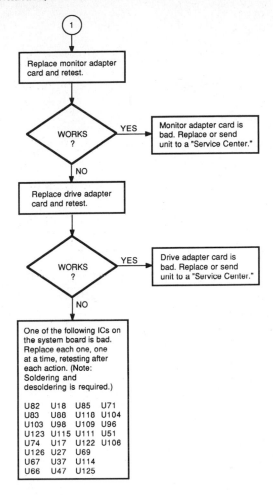

Problem 8-6

Power turns off after system runs for a while.

Symptom Described:

After the system has been running correctly for approximately a minute, the power shuts down and the operation stops.

Preliminary Checks:

1. None.
2. This problem was described for the IBM PC and PC/XT in Chapter 7.

Hints:

Refer to Problem 7-6 and Flowchart 7-5 in Chapter 7.

Keyboard Problems

This section examines some of the keyboard problems you might encounter while operating your system.

1. Keyboard won't respond at all, or the wrong character is produced.
2. Bad key action—one or more keys won't work.
3. You have key bounce, producing an unwanted repeat action.

Problem 8-7

Keyboard won't respond at all, or the wrong character is produced.

Symptom Described:

When a key is pressed, no display response occurs, or the wrong character is displayed on the monitor. (Refer to Flowchart 8-4 and Fig. 8-3.)

Preliminary Checks:

1. Check the keyboard cable for continuity and proper mating.
2. Clean the keys with a tuner cleaning spray.

Hints:

This type of problem is usually associated with a bad keyboard cable. For a description of the circuitry involved, refer to the description of system operation given in the earlier chapters. If any listed ICs are not in the drawings, assume that they are in the support circuitry. For more information, see Chapter 6.

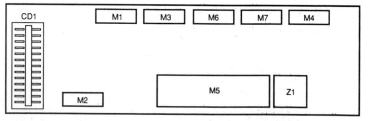

Fig. 8-3. IC layout of the IBM PC AT keyboard circuit board.

Flowchart 8-4

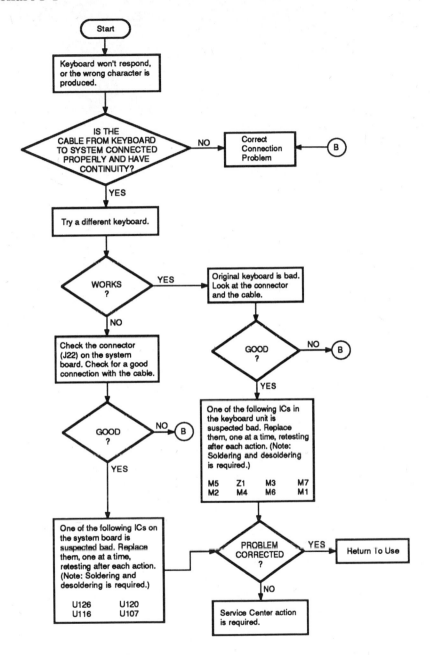

Problem 8-8

Bad key action—one or more keys won't work.

Symptom Described:

The boot-up operation occurs properly with correct display action, but when a key is pressed, no display response occurs. (Refer to Flowchart 8-5 and Fig. 8-3.)

Flowchart 8-5

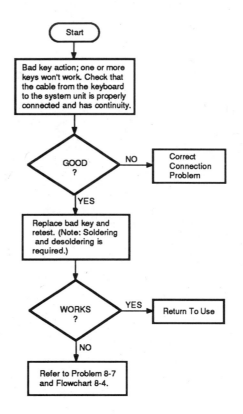

Preliminary Checks:

1. Verify that the keyboard/system-board cable has continuity and is properly connected.
2. Clean the keys with a tuner cleaner spray.

Hints:

This problem almost always turns out to be a bad key. Sometimes a good cleaning of the keyboard mechanism will solve the problem. For a description of the circuitry involved, refer to the discussion of system operation given in the earlier chapters. If any listed ICs are not in the drawings, assume that they are in the support circuitry.

If only one key is failing, and you are good at soldering and desoldering, you can fix the problem without replacing the key. First, open the keyboard unit and locate the two switch contacts of the bad key. Then, get two small wires that have the insulation stripped from just the ends. Ensure that they are long enough to get from the contacts on the bottom of the board to the key, when going through the center screw hole. Solder one end of one wire to one contact point and one end of the other wire to the other keyboard contact point. Run the wires to the top of the keyboard through the center screw hole. Attach one wire to a small metal washer that can slide over the spring shaft of the key that is bad. Loop an exposed bare section of the second wire around the top of the key-switch slider and replace the key cap. Reassemble the keyboard, minus the center screw. There you have it, a "new" key.

Problem 8-9

You have key bounce, producing an unwanted repeat action.

Symptom Described:

When a key is pressed, more than one image of the same character is displayed on the screen. This occurs even when the key is not held down for an intended repeat action. (Refer to Fig. 8-3 and Flowchart 8-6.)

Preliminary Checks:

1. Check the cable for continuity and proper mating.
2. Clean the keyboard keys with a tuner spray.
3. If only one key fails, replace the key.

Hints:

Suspect M1 in the keyboard chassis. If M1 isn't bad, the problem could be Z1. For a description of the circuitry involved, refer to the discussion of system operation given in the earlier chapters. If any listed ICs are not in the drawings, assume that they are in the support circuitry.

Flowchart 8-6

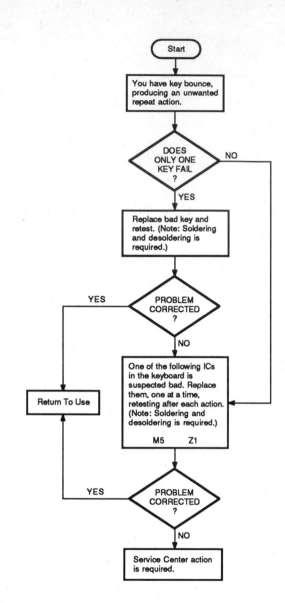

Display Problems

The display problems experienced with the IBM PC AT are similar to those for the IBM PC and PC/XT microcomputers. Each of the machines use the same adapter cards to produce video signals. Refer to the specific symptoms and problem(s) given in Chapter 7 for a solution to your troubleshooting problem(s).

Disk-Drive Problems

There are many problems that can cause disk-drive failures. Several of those pertinent to the AT are similar to the problems experienced by PC and XT owners. The following lists just a few of these problems.

1. Can't read from the floppy drive.
2. Can't read from any drive.
3. Can't write to the floppy drive.
4. Can't write to any drive.
5. Can't access either drive. No drive access lights. Drive motor is not energized.
6. Floppy drive destroys data on a Write-Protected disk.
7. Floppy drive accesses only one half of the space on the disk.
8. Floppy drive doesn't recognize when a disk has been changed.
9. Can't read from the fixed disk drive.
10. Can't write to the fixed disk drive.
11. Can't access the fixed disk drive. No drive access lights. Drive motor is not energized.

Problem 8-10

Can't read from the floppy drive.

Symptom Described:

The drive spins continuously, trying to load data from the disk into the computer. An error display might occur.

Preliminary Checks:

1. Check the cables for proper mating.
2. Try another (known-good) backup copy of the program disk.
3. Check for disk spinning action during the disk Read sequence. If no drive motor activation is observed, refer to Flowchart 8-7.
4. With system turned off, move the drive head towards the center of the disk. Turn the system on and note if the head moves back towards Track 00. If it doesn't, refer to Flowchart 8-7.

5. Check that the select jumper on the analog card is properly jumpered.

6. Clean the drive Read/Write heads. (See Chapter 10.)

Hints:

Refer to Fig. 8-2, Fig. 8-4, and Flowchart 8-7.

A drive that will not read is one of the most common failures. Look for the clues. Conduct the preliminary service checks. A good "suspect" is a cable from the adapter card to the drive. Try swapping the drive with a known-good drive or test your drive on another known-good system. This way you can localize to either the drive or the adapter card. If your drive works on another system, your adapter is bad. If your drive does not work on another system, then the drive is bad. For a description of the circuitry, refer to the discussion of system operation given in the earlier chapters. If any listed ICs are not in the drawings, assume that they are in the support circuitry.

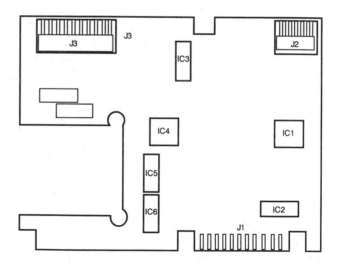

Fig. 8-4. IC layout of the IBM floppy disk-drive analog board.

Problem 8-11

Can't read from any drive.

Symptom Described:

During the power-up sequence, the system goes into ROM BASIC. When trying to load from either drive, an error message occurs.

Preliminary Checks:

1. Check that all cables are properly connected and have continuity.
2. Clean the edge connector on the disk-drive adapter card.

Hints:

Refer to Fig. 8-2 and Flowchart 8-8.

During a Read sequence, note if the drive access light comes on. If it doesn't, go to Problem 8-14. If the drive access light comes on during a Read operation, check that the power-supply cables to the drives are properly mated and not

Flowchart 8-7

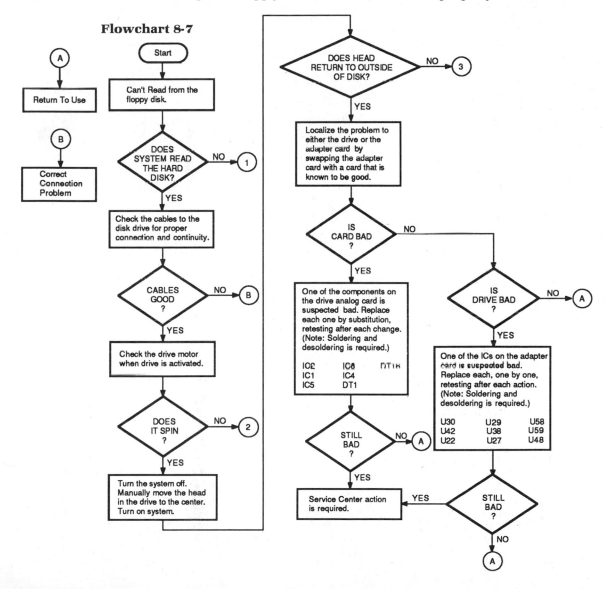

Flowchart 8-7 *(continued)*

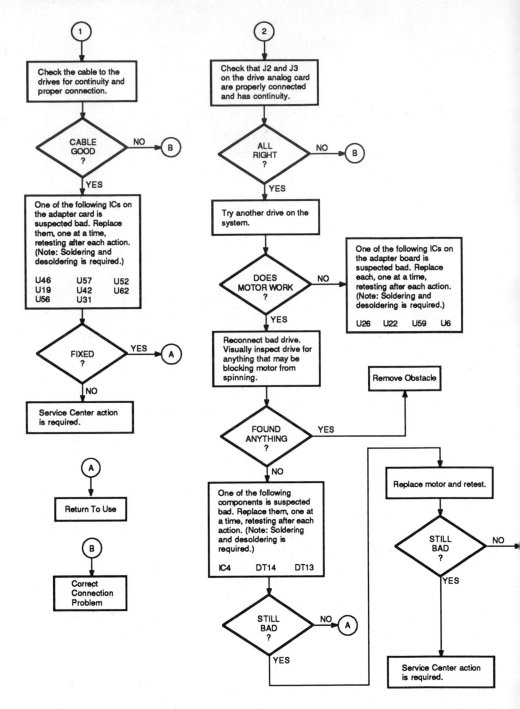

Flowchart 8-7 *(continued)*

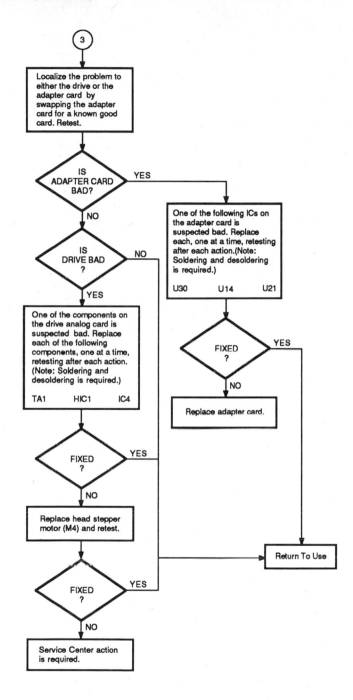

broken. For a description of the circuitry involved, refer to the discussion of system operation given in earlier chapters. If any listed ICs are not in the drawing, assume that they are in the support circuitry.

Flowchart 8-8

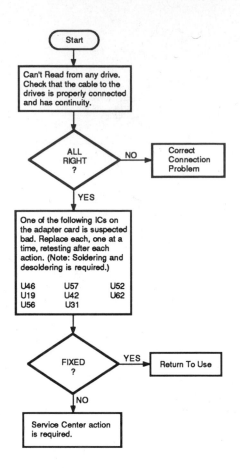

Problem 8-12

Can't write to the floppy drive.

Symptom Described:

Drive Reads properly, but won't Write to disk. The error message "DISK WRITE-PROTECTED" may be displayed.

Preliminary Checks:

1. Verify that there is no Write-Protect tab on the diskette being used in the drive.
2. Try a different disk.
3. Check the speed of the drive in use (see Chapter 10).
4. Check that all cables are properly connected and have continuity.

Hints:

Refer to Fig. 8-2, Fig. 8-4, and Flowchart 8-9.

If you keep getting the Write-Protect message, there may be a problem with the switch that checks for the Write-Protect tab on the disk. Sometimes this switch can be moved out of position just enough to not read correctly. Try listening for the switch to click (softly) when you insert the disk all the way into the drive. Try both drives, if one works, to get an idea of the sound to listen for. If there is no click, then a quick adjustment to the switch's position should solve the problem. For a circuit description of the circuitry involved, see the discussion of system operation given in the earlier chapters. If any listed ICs are not in the drawings, assume that they are in the support circuitry.

Problem 8-13

Can't write to any drive.

Symptom Described:

When writing to either drive, either an error message occurs and the operation terminates, or the data written to the disk are not present during a later Read operation.

Preliminary Checks:

1. Check all cables for continuity and proper mating.
2. Clean disk-drive adapter-card edge connector.
3. Configure the system as single drive, and test each drive individually.
4. Verify that no Write-Protect tabs are on the disks being used.

Hints:

Refer to Fig. 8-2.

Suspect and check the cables between the drive and the adapter card. If this doesn't solve the problem, refer to Flowchart 8-10. For a description of the circuitry involved, refer to the discussion of system operation given in the earlier chapters. If any listed ICs are not in the drawing, assume that they are in the support circuitry.

Flowchart 8-9

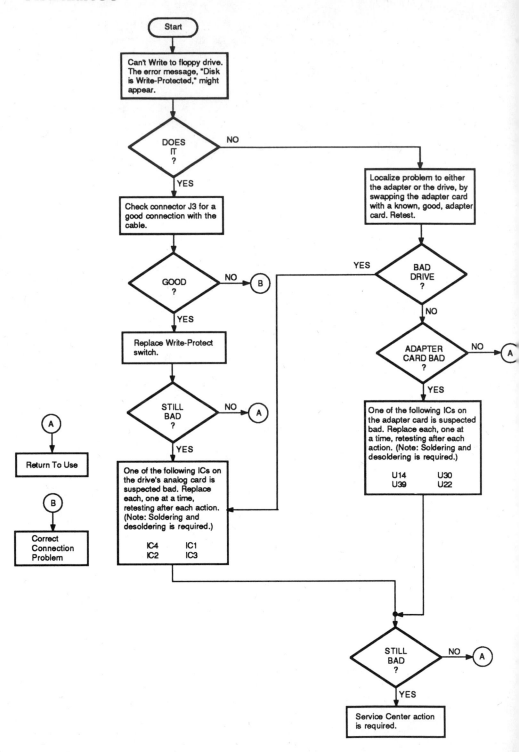

Flowchart 8-10

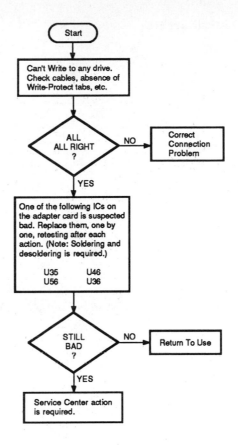

Problem 8-14

Can't access either drive. No drive access lights. Drive motor is not energized.

Symptom Described:

Both drives fail to react to any Read or Write operation.

Preliminary Checks:

1. Check that all drive data and power cables are properly connected and have good continuity.
2. Clean the edge connector on the drive adapter card.

Hints:

Refer to Fig. 8-2 and Flowchart 8-11.

Flowchart 8-11

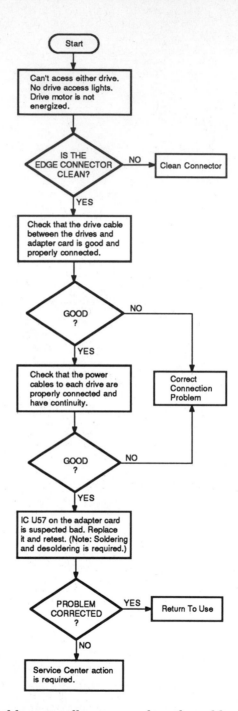

This type of problem usually occurs when the cables between the adapter card and the drives go bad. Refer to Flowchart 8-11 for the troubleshooting steps. For a decription of the circuitry involved, see the discussion of system operation given in earlier chapters. If any listed ICs are not in the drawing, assume that they are in the support circuitry.

Problem 8-15

Floppy drive destroys data on a Write-Protected disk.

Symptom Described:

While inadvertently trying to write to a disk that has a Write-Protect tab installed, data are written on the disk. The Write-Protect feature is not functioning.

Preliminary Checks:

1. Check the drive cables for proper mating and continuity.
2. Clean the adapter-card edge connector.

Hints:

Refer to Flowchart 8-12 and Figs. 8-2 and 8-4.

Insert a disk, without a Write-Protect tab, slowly into the bad drive while listening for the switch to "click" when it falls into the Write-Protect tab opening on the diskette. If no click is heard, check the alignment of the Write-Protect switch. Another strong possibilty is the cable going from the switch to the analog card in the drive. It may be bad. For a description of the circuitry involved, see the discussion of system operation given in the earlier chapters. If any listed ICs are not in the drawing, assume that they are in the support circuitry.

Problem 8-16

Floppy drive accesses only one half of the space on the disk.

Symptom Described:

An error display occurs. The drive seems to have only one half the space it really has. Directory shows the total drive space to be 180K bytes.

Preliminary Checks:

1. Check cables for proper mating.
2. Try another (known-good) backup of the program disk.
3. Clean the drive Read/Write heads. (See Chapter 10.)

Flowchart 8-12

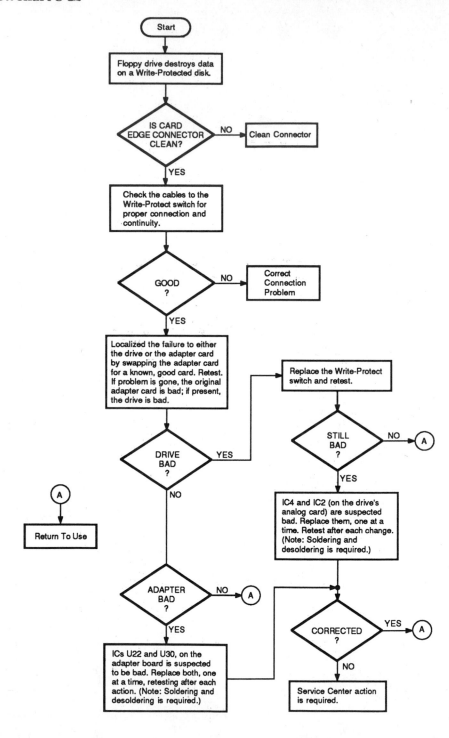

Hints:

Refer to Fig. 8-4 and Flowchart 8-13.

A drive that will not read more than one half of the space on a disk has a Read/Write-head circuitry problem. This problem may be solved by head cleaning; however, the heads are the main suspect. Replacement heads are expensive. For a description of the circuitry involved, see the discussion of system operation given in the earlier chapters.

Flowchart 8-13

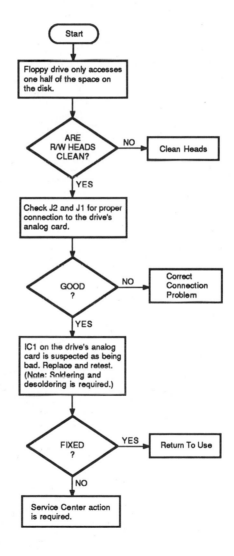

Problem 8-17

Floppy drive doesn't recognize when a disk has been changed.

Symptom Described:

When a disk is exchanged in the floppy drive and the directory is called up, the drive doesn't recognize the disk change and lists the old directory.

Preliminary Checks:

1. Check cables for proper mating.
2. Try another known-good backup copy of the program disk.
3. Open the drive and look visually at switch JJ for anything that may be blocking the switch or may be stuck in it.

Hints:

Refer to Fig. 8-4 and Flowchart 8-14.

This type of problem can be very frustrating. Check the door switch on the drive for anything that could possibly be getting in the way of the switch. This is a rare problem that has in the past always turned out to be the switch. For a description of the circuitry involved, refer to the discussion of system operation given in earlier chapters.

Problem 8-18

Can't read from the fixed disk drive.

Symptom Described:

Either an error display occurs, or the drive spins continuously, while trying to load data from the disk into the computer.

Preliminary Checks:

1. Check the cables for proper mating.
2. Try to format and configure the fixed disk to see if software is the problem.
3. Try the fixed drive on another system to verify that the drive is good.

Flowchart 8-14

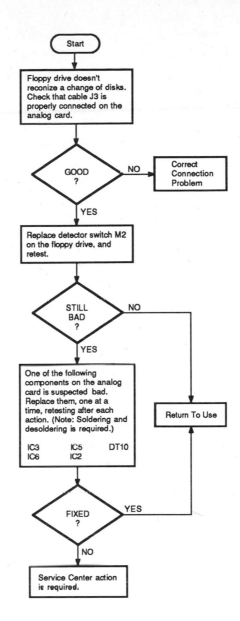

Hints:

Refer to Fig. 8-2 and Flowchart 8-15.

A drive that will not read is one of the most common failures. Look for clues. Conduct the preliminary service checks. A good "suspect" is a cable from the adapter card to the drive. Try swapping the drive with a known-good drive, or test your drive on another known-good system. This way, you can localize to either the drive or the adapter card. If your drive works on another system, then your adapter is bad. If your drive does not work on another system, the drive is bad and will need Service Center attention. Fixed disk drives are hard to work on. The heads are inside a vacuum and cannot be adjusted or repaired without special equipment. For a description of the circuitry involved, see the discussion of system operation given in earlier chapters. If any listed ICs are not in the drawings, assume that they are in the support circuitry.

Flowchart 8-15

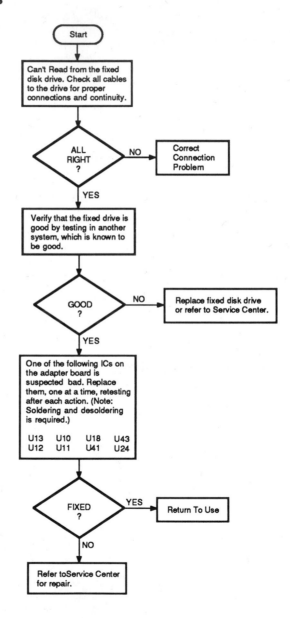

Problem 8-19

Can't write to the fixed disk drive.

Symptom Described:

Drive reads properly, but won't write to disk.

Preliminary Checks:

1. Check that all cables are properly connected.
2. Check that all cables have continuity.

Hints:

Refer to Fig. 8-2 and Flowchart 8-16.

Look for the clues. Conduct the preliminary service checks. A good item to "suspect" is the cable from the adapter card to the drive. Try swapping the drive with a known, good drive, or test your drive on another known, good system. This way, you can localize the problem to either the drive or the adapter card. If your drive works on another system, then your adapter card is bad. If your drive does not work on another system, the drive is bad and will need Service Center attention. Fixed disk drives are difficult to repair. The heads are enclosed inside a vacuum and cannot be adjusted without special equipment. For a description of the circuitry involved, refer to the discussion of system operation given in the earlier chapters. If any listed ICs are not in the drawings, assume that they are in the support circuitry.

Problem 8-20

Can't access the fixed disk drive. No drive access lights. Drive motor is not energized.

Symptom Described:

Drive fails to react to any Read or Write operation.

Preliminary Checks:

1. Check that all drive data and power cables are properly connected and have good continuity.
2. Clean the edge connector on the drive adapter card.

Flowchart 8-16

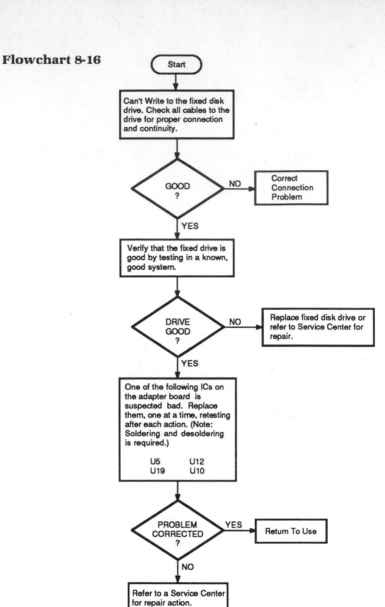

```
                    ┌─────────┐
                    │  Start  │
                    └─────────┘
                         │
        ┌──────────────────────────────┐
        │ Can't Write to the fixed disk │
        │ drive. Check all cables to the│
        │ drive for proper connection   │
        │ and continuity.               │
        └──────────────────────────────┘
                         │
                    ╱─────────╲         ┌───────────┐
                   ╱  GOOD      ╲   NO   │ Correct   │
                  ╱     ?        ╲──────▶│ Connection│
                   ╲            ╱        │ Problem   │
                    ╲─────────╱          └───────────┘
                         │ YES
        ┌──────────────────────────────┐
        │ Verify that the fixed drive is│
        │ good by testing in a known,   │
        │ good system.                  │
        └──────────────────────────────┘
                         │
                    ╱─────────╲         ┌──────────────────────┐
                   ╱  DRIVE     ╲   NO   │ Replace fixed disk   │
                  ╱   GOOD       ╲──────▶│ drive or refer to    │
                   ╲    ?       ╱        │ Service Center for   │
                    ╲─────────╱          │ repair.              │
                         │ YES           └──────────────────────┘
        ┌──────────────────────────────┐
        │ One of the following ICs on   │
        │ the adapter board is          │
        │ suspected bad. Replace        │
        │ them, one at a time, retesting │
        │ after each action. (Note:     │
        │ Soldering and desoldering     │
        │ is required.)                 │
        │                               │
        │   U5        U12               │
        │   U19       U10               │
        └──────────────────────────────┘
                         │
                    ╱─────────╲         ┌──────────────┐
                   ╱ PROBLEM    ╲  YES   │ Return To Use│
                  ╱ CORRECTED    ╲──────▶│              │
                   ╲    ?       ╱        └──────────────┘
                    ╲─────────╱
                         │ NO
        ┌──────────────────────────────┐
        │ Refer to a Service Center     │
        │ for repair action.            │
        └──────────────────────────────┘
```

Hints:

Refer to Fig. 8-2 and Flowchart 8-17.

Look for the clues. Conduct the preliminary service checks. A good item to "suspect" is the cable from the adapter card to the drive. Try swapping the drive with a known-good drive, or test your drive on another known-good system. This way you can localize the problem to either the drive or the adapter card. If your drive works on another system, then your adapter card is bad. If your drive does not work on another system, the drive is bad and will need Service Center attention. Fixed disk drives are difficult to repair. The heads are enclosed inside a vacuum and cannot be adjusted without special equipment. For a description of

Flowchart 8-17

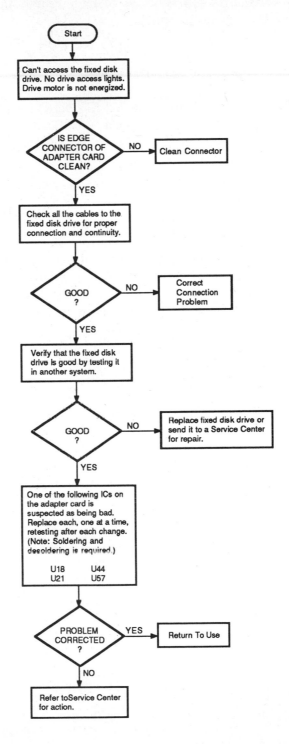

Start

Can't access the fixed disk drive. No drive access lights. Drive motor is not energized.

IS EDGE CONNECTOR OF ADAPTER CARD CLEAN?

NO → Clean Connector

YES

Check all the cables to the fixed disk drive for proper connection and continuity.

GOOD ?

NO → Correct Connection Problem

YES

Verify that the fixed disk drive is good by testing it in another system.

GOOD ?

NO → Replace fixed disk drive or send it to a Service Center for repair.

YES

One of the following ICs on the adapter card is suspected as being bad. Replace each, one at a time, retesting after each change. (Note: Soldering and desoldering is required.)

| U18 | U44 |
| U21 | U57 |

PROBLEM CORRECTED ?

YES → Return To Use

NO

Refer toService Center for action.

the circuitry involved, refer to the discussion of system operation given in the earlier chapters. If any listed ICs are not in the drawings, assume that they are in the support circuitry.

Input/Output Problems

In troubleshooting the IBM AT microcomputer, you will encounter several input/output problems of varying difficulties. The following problems are four of the most common:

1. Light pen won't work.
2. Printer won't work.
3. Printer either locks up or prints garbage.
4. Speaker doesn't work.

Problem 8-21

Light pen won't work.

Symptom Described:

No system response occurs when using the light pen.

Preliminary Checks:

1. None.
2. This problem was described for the IBM PC and PC/XT in Chapter 7.

Hints:

Refer to Problem 7-43, Fig. 7-13, and Flowchart 7-42 in Chapter 7.

Problem 8-22

Printer won't print.

Symptom Described:

When the command is given to print, nothing happens.

Preliminary Checks:

1. None.
2. This problem was described for the IBM PC and PC/XT in Chapter 7.

Hints:

Refer to Problem 7-44, Fig. 7-14, and Flowchart 7-43 in Chapter 7.

Problem 8-23

Printer either locks up or prints garbage.

Symptom Described:

When beginning, or while in a print operation, the printer either stops or begins printing garbage.

Preliminary Checks:

1. None.
2. This problem was described for the IBM PC and PC/XT in Chapter 7.

Hints:

Refer to Problem 7-45, Fig. 7-14, and Flowchart 7-43 in Chapter 7.

Problem 8-24

Speaker doesn't work.

Symptom Described:

There is no sound from the speaker. (Refer to Fig. 8-1 and Flowchart 8-18.)

Preliminary Checks:

1. Check the cable to the speaker for continuity and proper connection.
2. Check for damage to the speaker.

Hints:

A bad speaker or speaker cable is usually the cause of this problem. For a description of the circuitry involved, refer to the discussion of system operation given in the earlier chapters. If any listed ICs are not in the drawing, assume that they are in the support circuitry.

Flowchart 8-18

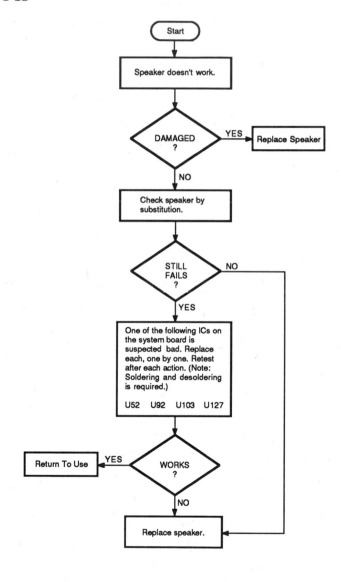

Advanced Troubleshooting Techniques

In the earlier chapters, you learned the basic techniques for troubleshooting most of IBM failures. You found that there are eleven optimum steps to successful fault identification and correction. You also learned how to recognize the various components of your computer, and you discovered how to find failures.

Then, in the hardware approach, you learned to use troubleshooting tools, such as logic probes and logic pulsers, to step through a circuit. This required test equipment and some knowledge of digital electronics. You were told that the software approach is a troubleshooting method used widely by IBM repair technicians (those out in the retail stores), and as long as the disk drive boots up properly, diagnostic software is effective at finding chip failures.

Next, you have learned of another option—the use of troubleshooting guides (in Chapters 7 and 8) to quickly pinpoint potential chip failures. If you concluded that the problem was not a chip and you still wanted to locate the failed part, you found that you needed more information. Now, you can use the techniques discussed in this chapter to test the rest of the components in the computer, and fully check the suspected failure area.

Here in Chapter 9, you will learn advanced troubleshooting techniques. You'll be introduced to the repair technician's "tools of the trade." Like other parts of this book, Chapter 9 is chock full of the "meat and potatoes" information needed to keep your system in peak operating condition.

Tools of the Trade

When the problem can't be solved using flowcharts and pictures, repair technicians reach for help—they reach for their "tools." These tools are not only the tiny screwdrivers (tweakers), the diagonal cutters (dykes), and the soldering pencil. They also include electronic test equipment, such as the various measurement meters (VOMs, DVMs, DMMs), logic probes, logic pulsers, current tracers, clips, oscilloscopes, and logic and signature analyzers.

Meters

Electronic measurement equipment has improved a great deal over the years, markedly improving your ability to test and locate circuit troubles. Ten years ago meters such as the vacuum-tube voltmeter (VTVM) and the volt-ohm-millimeter (VOM) were used to measure the three parameters of an electric circuit: voltage, resistance, and current. It wasn't long, however, before digital circuits replaced analog circuits, and new meters were needed for troubleshooting. The digital voltmeter (DVM) and the digital multimeter (DMM) quickly became the preferred measurement devices for technicians because they offer capabilities better suited for electronic circuit testing, including increased accuracy (Fig. 9-1). These meters have characteristically high input impedances (resistances) and so don't load down or draw down a digital circuit (where the voltages and currents are far lower than those found in analog circuits).

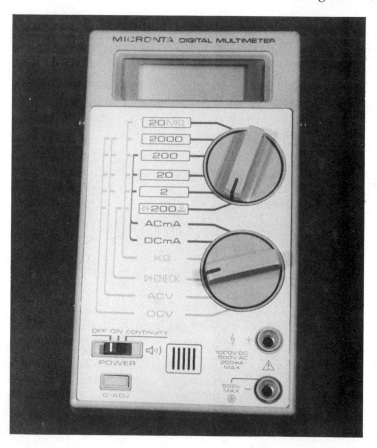

Fig. 9-1.   The multimeter is one of the most common tools of the technician's trade.

Two changes affected the types of tools used in troubleshooting and repair. First, vacuum tubes were replaced by solid-state devices, such as transistors and the integrated circuit (IC). Second, the circuits themselves became smaller, with more and more components packed compactly into less and less board area. One need only compare the early radio and television sets (standing about 4-foot tall and weighing at least 40 pounds) to the wrist radios (and now, the wrist televisions) of today to recognize that electronic circuits are smaller, more complex, and more difficult for test-probe access.

Electronic advances always lead to electronic opportunities, and clever test equipment designers soon came up with devices that enabled the technician to do digital circuit testing without fear of inaccurate readings (caused by circuit overload), or circuit failure (caused by bulky test probes shorting out two pins or wires on a packed printed-circuit board).

Logic Clips

One digital circuit-testing device is the logic clip shown in Fig. 9-2. This handy tool fits over an IC and has exposed pins at the top. Measuring or monitoring probes, or tiny test clips, can then be attached to the exposed pins to measure the logic level on any pin of the device under test. Logic clips can be obtained in several varieties, to work with almost all logic families (including TTL and CMOS), and in voltages up to 30 volts DC.

Fig. 9-2.   A logic clip.

Another type of logic clip has a built-in monitoring capability (Fig. 9-3). Instead of exposed pins, the top of the clip is lined with two rows of light-emitting diodes (LEDs) which continuously display the logic condition of each pin on the chip. The LEDs are turned on (indicating a logic 1) by power from the circuit under test. All the pins are electrically buffered so the clip doesn't load down the circuit being tested.

Fig. 9-3.   A logic clip with monitoring capabilities.

> CAUTION: When using a logic clip, turn the power to the circuit off, attach the clip, and then turn the power back on. This helps prevent accidentally shorting out the chip.

To use the clip, squeeze the top (LED) end to spread the pin contacts, and then slip the clip over the top of the chip to be tested. When power is applied to the circuit, the LEDs will indicate the logic level at each pin on the chip.

Logic clips can be used on ICs with up to 16 pins, or 80% of the ICs you will find on your IBM PC system board.

Logic Probes

When you really want to "get into" your circuit, you can use a logic probe. A blown chip can't be repaired, but a logic probe can tell you which chip has failed so you can replace it.

The logic probe shown in Fig. 9-4 is the most widely used tool for this kind of analysis. It can't do many of the things that complex test equipment, such as logic analyzers, can do, but the simplicity of the probe and the ability to rapidly troubleshoot a printed-circuit board make this tool ideal for 90% of your fault-isolation needs.

Fig. 9-4. A logic probe.

When the tip of the probe is placed against a pin of a suspected bad chip, a test point, or even a trace on a circuit board, an indicator light on the body of the probe tells you the logic state (level) at that point. The metal tip on most logic probes sold today is protected against damage caused from accidentally touching a source of voltage higher than the +5 volts of logic gates (to 120 volts AC for 30 seconds).

Some probes have two built-in lights near their tips—one for logic HIGH and the other for logic LOW. The better probes can also tell you whether the test-point signal is pulsing. They can also store a short pulse burst to tell you if a glitch or spike has occurred at that point. If you're planning to buy a logic probe, be sure it will work with the logic chip families you plan to analyze.

The ability to touch a point with the probe tip and directly determine the condition at that point, and the ability to store pulses, make this device easy to use and universally accepted as the proper diagnostic tool for all but the most complex digital troubleshooting. Other tools force you to attach the measurement probe and then look at some display to read the condition. The logic probe displays the condition near the tip of the probe or on the body of the probe itself.

The logic probe shown in Fig. 9-4 provides four indications:

► Lamp OFF for logic LOW (logic 0).

► Lamp ON bright for logic HIGH (logic 1).

► Lamp DIM for floating or tri-state logic.

► Lamp FLASHING for pulsing signals.

Power for the probe comes from a clip attached to a voltage point on the circuit under test. Another clip attaches to ground, providing improved sensitivity and noise immunity.

Probes are ideal for finding short-duration, low-frequency pulses which are difficult to see on an oscilloscope, but more often, probes are used to quickly locate logic gates whose output is hung, or locked, in a HIGH or LOW condition.

A useful method of circuit analysis, using the probe, is to start at the center of a suspected circuit (Fig. 9-5) and check for the presence of a signal. (This, of course, assumes that you have and can use a schematic of the circuit.) Move backward or forward toward the failed output. It doesn't take long to find the faulty chip whose output isn't changing.

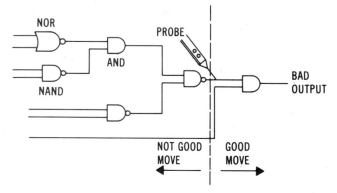

Fig. 9-5.   Problem analysis starting at the center of a suspected circuit.

The only limitation of logic probes is their inability to monitor more than one line at a time.

Logic Pulsers

If the circuit under test doesn't have a pulsing or changing signal, you can inject controlled pulses into the circuit using a logic pulser (Fig. 9-6). These handy devices are portable logic generators.

Fig. 9-6. A logic pulser.

When activated by a push-button or slide switch, the pulser will sense the logic level present at the point touched by the tip and will automatically generate a pulse or series of pulses of the opposite logic level. The pulses can be seen on an LED lamp built into the handle of the pulser.

The ability to introduce a changing signal into a circuit without unsoldering or cutting wires makes the logic pulser an ideal companion to the logic probe and the logic clip. These two tools, used together, permit step-by-step stimulus/ response evaluation of sections of a circuit.

Fig. 9-7 shows a way of testing logic gates using the probe and pulser. Assume that the output of the NAND gate is HIGH. Testing inputs 1, 2, and 3, you find them all HIGH. This condition should cause the AND gate output to go high, producing a LOW out of the NAND gate. Something is wrong. Placing a probe at the AND gate output, you discover the level is LOW. It should be HIGH. Now, which gate is bad?

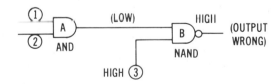

Fig. 9-7. Testing logic gates.

To find out, place a probe on the NAND gate (B) output and the pulser on the AND gate (A) output (one of the NAND gate inputs). Pulse this line. The probe should blink, indicating a change at the input to the NAND gate. If it doesn't blink a change, the NAND may be bad. But what if the LOW was caused by a short to ground at the AND gate output or the NAND gate input?

Place the probe and the pulser on the AND output and trace and pulse this line. If the pulse blinks, the NAND gate is bad; its input changed state, so its output should have changed state also.

If the probe doesn't blink, you know the line is shorted to ground. One way you can determine which chip is shorted is by touching the chip case. A shorted chip gets pretty hot, while a chip that is hung at one level seems to be normal, but just won't change state.

Current Tracers

A fourth handy troubleshooting tool is the *current tracer*. This portable device lets you precisely locate shorts on your computer's motherboard (or peripheral card). The current tracer senses the magnetic field produced by the flow of electrical current in the circuitry. The logic pulser can be used to generate a pulsing signal that will make the current tracer LED blink, indicating the presence of current.

If you set the tip of the tracer on a printed-circuit line and slide the tracer along the line, the LED in the tip end of the tracer will pulse as long as there is a current present. When you slide past a shorted point, the lamp will dim or go out, clearly marking the short.

Fig. 9-8 shows an easy way to determine which logic gate is shorted to ground. Assume gate B has a shorted input. Place the pulser and the tracer midway between the two gates. Adjust the LED in the current tracer so that it just lights. Pulse the line as you place the tracer on the output of gate A and then on the input to gate B. The gate with the short to ground will pulse brightly because most of the current is going to ground there. Therefore, the input to gate B causes the tracer lamp to pulse brightly, while the gate A side of the line doesn't cause the LED to light. Following the LED light with your tracer will lead you to where the current is going.

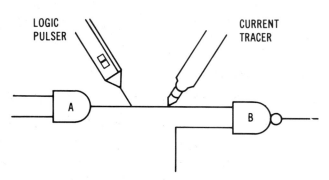

Fig. 9-8. Finding a short to ground.

IC Testers

Advanced troubleshooting equipment is becoming very sophisticated (and expensive). Today, you can buy equipment that tests almost every chip in your system for between $1000 and $2000. For $10,000, you can even conduct your tests from a remote location.

Several companies manufacture IC testers that can test all the 7400 TTL and 4000 CMOS series devices. Options include RAM and ROM tests. One tester can do complete functional pin tests of all 900 devices in the 54/74 TTL series chips, while displaying the condition of the chip under test on a liquid-crystal display (LCD). It uses LEDs to signal Go/No-Go test results.

Another company markets an in-circuit component tester and a 50-MHz CRT that displays voltage versus current characteristics for virtually all electronic components, including capacitors, diodes, integrated circuits, resistors, and transistors. With this tester, the condition of the component under test is determined by the shape of the CRT display. Using this test equipment, you can easily pick out open circuits, shorts, leaky diodes, leaky transistors, and marginal ICs. The tool is valuable because it can test a wide selection of components while they're still mounted in the circuit.

Oscilloscopes

The oscilloscope has been with us for years, although recent advances in the state of the art have added a great many capabilities to the instrument.

The oscilloscope is an electronic display device that draws on a CRT screen a graph of signal-voltage amplitude versus time or frequency. A "scope" is used to analyze the quality and characteristic of an electronic signal, using a probe that touches a test point in a circuit. It is also used as a measuring device to determine the voltage level of certain signals. An excellent example is shown in Figure 9-9.

Scopes come in all sizes, shapes, and capabilities. Prices vary between $500 and $20,000. Some scopes use a single test probe for displaying and analyzing a single trace signal. Others have two probes and display two different signals (dual trace) at the same time. As many as eight traces can be analyzed at the same time on some oscilloscopes. There is even a seven-color digital scope for the discriminating troubleshooter. Colors make it possible to compare signals at different locations in the circuitry very rapidly.

Besides sensitivity and trace display, one of the major distinguishing characteristics of oscilloscopes is the ability to allow a great range of frequencies to be observed on the CRT screen as frozen images. We call this "bandwidth." Bandwidths will vary between 5 MHz and 300 MHz, and price is proportional to frequency.

Oscilloscopes are useful tools for freezing an analog or varying signal, and displaying its static waveform on the face of a CRT screen which is covered with a measurement grid. While it is time-consuming to learn how to use an oscilloscope, the analytical rewards are substantial. Not only can you measure the voltage amplitudes and frequencies of test signals, you can also measure delay times, and signal rise and fall times, and often locate the intermittent glitch.

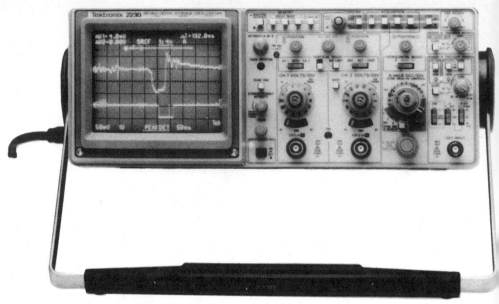

Fig. 9-9.   A digital storage oscilloscope. *(Courtesy Tektronics, Inc.)*

Some scopes have built-in memories to let the instrument store a signal of interest for future evaluation.

If you're not trying to set the world on fire as a system designer, you can probably get along fine with a dual-trace, 25–30-MHz scope. Investment in an oscilloscope is not cost-effective if you intend to use it only for analyzing your PC system board during troubleshooting of a component failure. You'd be better off saving the money and spending a comparatively small portion of it to have a Service Center fix your machine.

The nice thing about dual-trace, quad-trace, and even eight-trace machines is the ability to look at different signal paths or different signals simultaneously. For example, you could look at the input and output of a gate, and actually see and be able to measure the delay time for the signal passing from input to output of the chip. Another useful technique is simultaneously displaying all or parts of the data bus, or part of the address bus, to see what the logic level (high = +5 V, low = 0 V) is and what binary number it represents.

Logic Analyzers

A companion device to the oscilloscope, the logic analyzer is a multichannel oscilloscope with a memory. It captures and stores a number of digital signals, letting you view the signals simultaneously. If each signal is a "bit" on the data bus, you can see the entire data bus at one time. This means that you can analyze the logic level for each bit on the bus for any instant in time. The bus signals are frozen for your display and analysis. The ability to freeze a single event or data pattern, so you can determine the information present on a digital bus at any moment in time, is a distinct advantage for troubleshooting.

Logic analyzers, like oscilloscopes, cost between $500 and $20,000. And, again like the scopes, logic analyzers work at frequencies from 2 MHz up to 200 MHz.

These analyzers can display many signals (channels of input) simultaneously. A current product handles 32 channels of input data, at frequencies up to 100 MHz. Another product is a 48-channel, 200-MHz analyzer with a built-in microcomputer and dual, double-density, floppy disk drives. Each channel has a dedicated probe clip for connecting to some test point in the circuitry. Fortunately, the clip probes are tiny and easy to install.

Further sampling of the capabilities currently available in logic analyzers revealed one configuration that provides 104 channels at 25 MHz, another with 32 channels at 100 MHz, and yet another with 16 channels at 330 MHz. A final configuration has 8 channels of input and can operate at 600 MHz!

Where would logic analyzers be useful? One place is in debugging software circuits. You can read the data in machine code and trace the data flow through the circuit. By simultaneously analyzing the input and output of memory, you can quickly locate a bad RAM chip. Or, you could uncover intermittent glitches—those phantom spikes that can raise havoc with your system. Other uses for logic analyzers include the monitoring of floppy and fixed disk I/O operation.

The logic analyzer has been called the oscilloscope of the digital domain. It can be a valuable tool for the software or hardware designer. But for the home or small business computer owner who simply wants to fix his or her own computer, the logic analyzer is an expensive overkill.

Signature Analyzers

Logic probes can be effective in detecting logic levels and pulses at single points. Oscilloscopes extend the number of points to be monitored even though the data pulses all tend to look alike. And logic analyzers extend the number of test points even further to include groups of signals the size of the data and address buses. However, as the sophistication and capability of the measurement device increases, so does the expertise required to operate the test tool. Logic analyzers, in particular, can be very capable but they can also be difficult to understand and operate. The signature analyzer was developed to allow easy detection of hardware failures.

Signature analysis is a comparison method of troubleshooting. It works by running a diagnostic program, in the system being tested, and evaluating a coded signal at specific test points in the circuitry. If the coded signal matches the code observed when the system was running properly, the malfunction is not in that part of the circuitry. When a test-point signature fails to match the base-line correct code, it indicates that you have located the faulty area. Then you can probe backwards or forwards from that point to isolate and locate the component(s) that has failed.

The first codes were developed by Hewlett-Packard and, with slight modification, are still being used today. The key to the success of this test technique is in the signature code. It is a 16- or 24-bit repeatable value that represents a stream of data passing a test point during an interval of time. This known stream of data, when sampled at different places on a good circuit board by a signature analyzer, produces a unique 16- or 24-bit code at each test point. These codes can be documented or stored in a Programmable Read-Only Memory (PROM) and recalled later for comparison during troubleshooting. The PROM then becomes a custom memory module, containing every signature sampled from a properly working system that was being stimulated or pulsed with a known data stream.

Signature analysis has not been a popular troubleshooting tool because it takes lots of time to identify the test points or nodes, probe the nodes, produce a signature, and then document the code. Once this task is completed, however, the task of locating a failure becomes a breeze. And the introduction of PROM modules has made the setup task much easier. More improvements in this analysis technique can be expected in the near future.

One analyzer on the market uses a mode called "backtrace" to prompt the troubleshooter through a series of test points, guiding the tester to trace bad signatures back to the failed part.

The investment for a signature analyzer is between $400 and $10,000. Signature analysis uses a simple, nontechnical approach to troubleshooting, so even untrained people can use the equipment and the technique.

Using Special Tools to Find Failed Components

Most chips on the IBM PC/XT and PC AT motherboards are Transistor-Transistor Logic (TTL) devices. If you know the logic gates in a chip to be tested (NAND, NOR, OR, AND, etc.), you can test for opens or shorts by applying a known logic level to the inputs, while monitoring the output. For example, if you were to place a slowly pulsing 0-volt to +5-volt signal on the input to an AND gate with both inputs shorted, you should see the output voltage level change (pulse) along with the input. Whenever the input is a logic "1," the output becomes a logic "1" (between +5 volts and +2.4 volts).

The tool you use on the input is a logic pulser. The monitor tool on the output is a logic probe. The pulser places a cyclical logic level on the input to the device and the probe measures the presence or absence of a logic signal on the output of the chip.

If the input to the AND gate becomes shorted to ground, the pulser cannot cause the gate to react to its signal and the output remains at a logic zero, or LOW (about 0 volts). Even if just one of the inputs shorts to ground, the output cannot change and it will remain at a logic 0.

A short to the gate supply voltage (+5 volts) will have the effect of qualifying or enabling one input to the gate all the time. This means that each time the second input receives a logic 1, the input set is correct and causes the output to change to a logic 1 even though only one input signal was actually correct. This produces an incorrect circuit operation and strange results. This is the kind of problem that shows up in memory circuits. Only one of the inputs to a particular gate is shorted or opened. Whenever this gate is used, the resulting output may or may not be correct—a difficult problem to trace down.

Shorting an input pin to +5 volts can have potentially disastrous results. When the previous gate tries to deliver a logic 0, or LOW, a huge current is produced which usually causes catastrophic failure of the driving chip. The same result occurs when the input pin is shorted to ground and the previous gate tries to deliver a logic 1, or HIGH. The +5-volt logic HIGH is shorted directly to ground, producing an unusually high current with equally disastrous results.

Open connections prevent logic levels from being transferred and prevent the affected gate from being able to respond. If one input of a two-input NAND gate is open at the input, all but one of the four possible input combinations will be correct. This means that with this type of failure, the system could operate correctly most of the time with only half of the inputs good. The failure would be intermittent.

If the device being tested is a NOR logic gate, the output would be a logic 1, or HIGH, only when both inputs are at logic 0, or LOW. Should one of the inputs become open, it would float to logic 1, and cause none of the input conditions to produce a logic 1, or HIGH output. Thus, the output would be low all the time—just as though the output were shorted to ground.

If the chip has an open pin at its output, it cannot deliver a logic 1, or 0, to the next gate. You can measure a voltage at the input to the next gate since it is providing the potential—a logic 1, or HIGH level (something around +4 volts). The key here is that any time an input to a TTL gate opens (a condition we call "floating"), the gate will act as though a logic 1 were constantly applied to that input. The voltage on this floating input will drift between the high supply voltage of +5 volts and a level (about 1.5 volts) somewhere between a valid "HIGH" and a valid "LOW." (A valid HIGH is usually above +2.4 volts; a valid LOW is below +0.4 volt.)

A voltmeter reading of about +1.7 volts at the output pin of a gate on a chip is a clue that the output is floating open and the voltage is actually being provided by the next chip or the following gate.

All these kinds of failures can be located using a logic pulser and a logic probe, with backup from a DMM for voltage measurement.

Since the system board is flexible at certain points, a user who is replacing chips, or depressing the board without supporting it from beneath, could cause a break to occur, opening a trace on the circuit board. A hairline crack, such as this causes, is often difficult to find but looking at the board with a magnifying glass and under a strong light (or a magnifying lamp) can sometimes reveal a suspected failure. A resistance test can be conducted with a DMM by placing a probe at either side of the suspected bad trace, as shown in Fig. 9-10, and observing whether a 0-ohm reading is measured. Another way to ascertain if an open trace is present is to compare the logic states at either end of the trace.

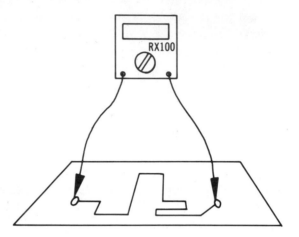

Fig. 9-10. Testing for a open circuit.

Keep in mind when testing for individual shorted or open gates in the system-board circuitry that more than one gate may use the same input or output lines to or from another gate. This is called "fan-in" or "fan-out." When studying the gate circuitry, remember, the failure could be located at the other end of the board. One long trace from it to the chip you are looking at may be shorted or open at that end. The schematics in the Sams COMPUTERFACTS® and the IBM PC Technical Reference Manual will be of value here.

Advanced Troubleshooting Techniques

There are some interesting tricks you can use as aids in finding chip failures.

Use Your Senses

Look, smell, and feel. Sometimes failed components become discolored; or, they may develop bubbles or charred spots. Blown devices can produce some distinctive smells—the odor of a ruptured electrolytic capacitor, for example. Finally, shorted chips can get really hot. By using a "calibrated finger," you can pick out the hot spots on your board.

Heat It, Cool It

Heating and cooling is a fast technique for locating the cause of intermittent failures. Frequently, as an aging device warms up under normal operation, it becomes marginal and then intermittently quits working. If you heat the energized area where the suspected bad chip is located until the intermittent failures begin, and then methodically cool each device with a short blast of canned coolant spray, you can quickly cause a marginally defective chip to function again. By alternately heating, cooling, heating, and cooling, you can pinpoint the trouble in short order.

You can heat the area with a hair dryer or a focused warm-air blower designed for electronic testing. Be careful using this technique since the thermal stress you place on the chips being tested can shorten the life of good components. A 1- or 2-second spray of freeze coolant is all you should ever need to get a heat-sensitive component working again.

Most coolant sprays come with a focus applicator tube. Use this to pinpoint the spray. And avoid spraying electrolytic capacitors, because the spray soaks into the capacitor, destroying the electrolyte in some aluminum capacitors. Also, be careful not to spray your own skin. You could get a severe frost burn.

Another technique for locating the source of intermittents is to give the area under suspicion a vibration test. Take a screwdriver and, using the handle, lightly tap the board while it is in operation. Any components with opens or shorts that are all right most of the time, and only fail occasionally, will usually make themselves known by failing when tapped.

Piggybacking

There is a way you can chase down those failures which are caused by a break in a chip bond (wire) inside the chip housing, and which allow a good contact only when the chip is cool.

Place a good chip over the top of the suspected chip, piggyback fashion, and energize the circuitry. You may need to squeeze the pins of the good chip inward slightly so they make good contact with the pins of the suspected device.

If the failure is caused by an open connection, the new chip will react to the input data and will cause its output to act accordingly. Use your stock of spare parts as your piggyback source.

The Easter Egg Approach

Quite often we can quickly locate a fault to a couple of chips, but, then, further testing is needed to determine which chip is the culprit.

When time is of the essence, take the "Easter Egg" approach. Just as a youngster picks up and examines Easter eggs one at a time to see if his/her name is marked on it, you can try replacing the chips one at a time to determine which chip replaced is causing the problem. You have a 50–50 chance of selecting the right chip first time. If it didn't work, replace the other chip.

If the chips involved are inexpensive, why not replace them both? For thirty cents more, go ahead and splurge. If the problem's gone, but you're still curious, you can always go back later and test each chip individually.

Microvolt Measuring of a Piece of Wire

If you have a meter with microvolt sensitivity and have isolated a "stuck LOW" problem to two chips, you can try the technique shown in Fig. 9-11. Measure the voltage drop between input pin 1 of gate B and output pin 3 of gate A. Now this means that you are measuring the opposite ends of the same trace or piece of wire! You're interested in determining which end of that trace is the more negative. The end nearest a bad chip will be more negative as the defective chip will short the trace voltage to ground causing this point to be more negative than at pin 3.

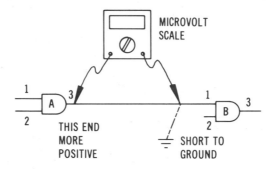

Fig. 9-11. Measuring for a microvoltage voltage drop.

Testing Capacitors

How do you check out a capacitor that you believe has failed? If the device has shorted, resulting in severe leakage of current, it can easily be spotted by placing an ohmmeter across the capacitor and reading the resistance. At first, you'll notice a low reading, because the capacitor acts as a short until it charges. Then, if the capacitor is working properly, it will charge, and the resistance will rise to a nominally high value. If the device is shorted, the capacitor won't charge, and the initial low-resistance reading continues.

Should the component be open, you'll not see the instantaneous short at time zero, the moment the charge starts to build. An open circuit has infinite resistance. An in-circuit capacitance tester is helpful here.

Total failure to a condition of a short or open is pretty easy to find. But how about the device whose leakage depends on the temperature, or the device whose dielectric has weakened, changing the capacitance value? To test these capacitors requires a different level of analysis.

Capacitance Measuring

If you have an older needle-scale ohmmeter, whose faceplate has the number 10 in the middle of the scale, you can use it to approximate the capacitance of a device, using the time-constant formula, $T = RC$, where the time in seconds (for a capacitor to charge to 63.2% of supply voltage) is equal to the resistance in ohms times the capacitance in farads. Using a 22-μF (0.000022 farad, or 22 microfarad) capacitor and a 1-Megohm (1,000,000 ohm) resistor, the charge time for one time constant is 0.000022 $\times$ 1,000,000 = 22 seconds.

Transposing the formula to read:

$$C = T/R$$

you can determine the value of capacitance by knowing the resistance and then counting the seconds required for the charge to cause the meter needle to reach 63.2% of full scale (infinite resistance). This point is at about 17 on the meter's scale.

To do this, disconnect one end of the capacitor from the circuit, turn on your meter, and let it warm up for a minute. Zero-adjust the OHMS-scale reading. Then, estimate the OHMS-scale multiplier needed to let the capacitor charge in some acceptable time period. For microfarad capacitors, use the $\times$100K scale, because this will let the capacitor charge in less than one minute. The 17 on the scale represents 1.7 Megohms on the $\times$100K scale.

Short a low-ohm-value resistor across the two capacitor leads for several seconds to thoroughly drain off any charge. Then connect the meter's ground lead to the negative side of the capacitor (either side if the capacitor is not an electrolytic), and touch the positive probe of the meter to the other lead of the capacitor. Using a stop watch to count seconds and tenths of a second, watch the faceplate of the ohmmeter as the capacitor charges, moving the resistance needle up scale. When the needle gets to 17 on the scale, stop the clock and read the time. This will give you the value of capacitance in microfarads.

This technique will give you a close enough approximation of the capacitance value to determine if the device is good or if it should be replaced.

Replacing Capacitors

Always try to use the same type and value of capacitor as the one being replaced.

Keep the leads as short as possible and solder the capacitor into the board, using the proper-type soldering iron. The soldering process should not exceed 1.5 seconds per lead (to prevent heat damage to the component).

To speed the solder bond process, tin the capacitor leads just before soldering them to the board.

Testing Diodes

If you have a digital multimeter (DMM) with a diode test capability, you can quickly determine whether a suspected diode is bad or good. Placing the meter on the ohmmeter setting, and the probes across the diode, causes the meter to apply a low current through the diode, if the diode is forward biased. (The voltage drop across a diode is normally 0.2–0.3 volt for germanium diodes and 0.6–0.7 volt for silicon diodes.) Reversing the leads should result in no current flow through the diode, so a higher reading should be observed. A low-voltage reading, when biasing the diode in either direction, indicates that the device is leaking or shorted. A high-voltage reading in both directions indicates the diode bond has opened. In either case, replace the diode immediately.

In-circuit tests of diodes can also be done by desoldering one end (lifting a lead) and then using an ohmmeter to check the resistance across the diode in both directions. With one polarity of the meter probes, you should get a reading different from that obtained when the probes are reversed—not just a few ohms different but several hundred ohms different. For example, in the forward-biased direction, you could read 50–80 ohms; in the reverse-biased direction, 300K ohms. This difference in readings is called *DE*, for "diode effect," and is also useful for evaluating transistors. When diode readings in both directions show a low resistance, you can be sure the leaky short is present and the diode is bad.

Testing Transistors

It's no fun to desolder a transistor to test it for failure, and then finding it good, solder it or a new device back into the circuit board. Fortunately, there is a way to determine the quality of silicon transistors without removing them from the circuit. In 90% of the tests, this procedure will accurately determine whether a device is bad or not.

Transistors operate in the same way as a configuration of diodes. PNP and NPN transistors have opposite-facing diodes. The transistor functions by biasing certain pins and applying a signal to one of the leads (usually the base), while taking an output off the collector or emitter.

These tests apply to both PNP and NPN transistors. If an ohmmeter is placed between the collector and emitter (C-E), it effectively bridges a two-diode combination in which the diodes are opposing. You should get a high resistance reading with the leads applied both ways. (It's possible to wire the transistor in a circuit which makes the transistor collector-emitter junction act like a single diode. In this case, you could get *DE*. Both results are all right.)

Typical C-E resistance readings for germanium transistors are as follows:

$$\text{Forward biased} \;=\; 80 \text{ ohms}$$
$$\text{Reverse biased} \;=\; 8000 \text{ ohms (8K)}$$

For silicon transistors, you might read:

$$\text{Forward biased} \;=\; 22 \text{ Megohms}$$
$$\text{Reverse biased} \;=\; 190 \text{ Megohms}$$

The high/low ratio is evident.

Place the probes across the collector-to-base junction leads. Reverse the probes. You should observe a low reading in one case and a high reading with the test probe leads reversed (the diode effect). Try the same technique on the base-to-emitter junction leads. Look for the DE. If DE is not present in all the above steps, you can be certain the transistor is bad and needs replacing.

Another way to evaluate a transistor is to measure the bias voltage from the base to the emitter (B-E) on an energized circuit. Confirm the correct supply voltage first; power-supply problems have been known to trick troubleshooters into thinking a certain component has failed.

The B-E forward bias for silicon transistors should be between 0.6 and 0.7 volts dc. If the reading is below 0.5 volt, replace the diode—the diode junction is leaking too much current. If the reading is almost 1 volt, the junction is probably open and, again, the device should be replaced.

B-E Voltage (Forward biased)	Action
0.6–0.7 V	Good, keep
0.5 V	Replace
0.9 V	Replace

Although, in some isolated cases, some other failure could cause the low reading, the most common cause of low bias voltage is failure in the transistor itself.

If the previous tests are inconclusive, there is something else you can try. Measure the voltage across the collector-to-emitter (C-E) junction. If the reading is the same as the source supply (+5 volts for Q1 on the Color/Graphics Adapter card), and you notice on the schematic that there's plenty of resistance in the collector/base circuit, the junction is probably open. Replace the device.

If your reading is close to zero volts, take a small length of wire and short the base to the emitter, removing all the transistor bias. The C-E meter reading should instantly rise. If it doesn't, the transistor is shorting internally and should be replaced. If the C-E voltage does rise, it suggests a failure in the bias circuitry—perhaps a leaky coupling capacitor.

Removing Solder

We used to call them "solder suckers"—those hand-held vacuum pumps with the spring-driven plunger that is used to pull the hot, melted solder off a connector (Fig. 9-12). The process involves heating the old solder until it melts, placing the spring-propelled vacuum pump in the hot solder, then quickly removing the soldering iron while triggering the vacuum pump's spring, sucking the solder up into a storage chamber in the pump.

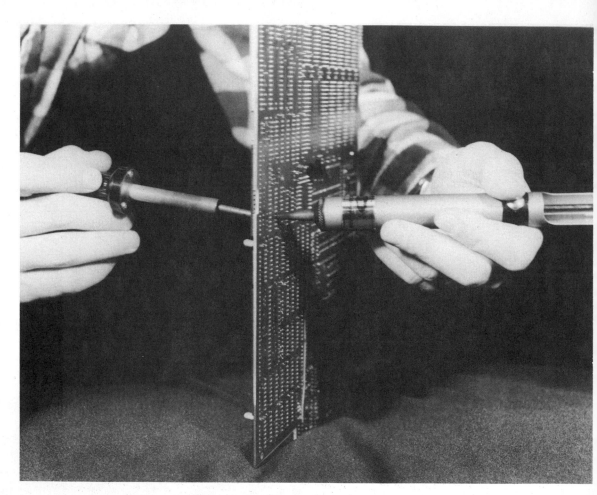

Fig. 9-12. Solder removal tool.

This technique works fine until you try to use it around CMOS chips. Some vacuum pumps produce static electricity, and by now, you should know what that can do to an MOS or CMOS chip.

A safer way to remove solder is to touch the solder with the end of a strip of braided copper. Then, heat the braid just a short distance from the solder, as shown in Fig. 9-13. The copper braid heats quickly, transferring the heat to the solder, which melts and is drawn into the braid by capillary action. Then, cut off the solder-soaked part of the braid and throw it away.

Fig. 9-13. Solder can be quickly removed using a solder wick.

If any solder remains in the circuit-board hole, heat the solder and push a toothpick into the hole as the solder cools. The toothpick will keep the hole open and you can easily insert another wire lead into the hole for soldering.

Another way to remove the residual solder blocking a hole is to drill out the hole with a tiny drill bit. Be sure to remove any debris, filings, or pieces of solder around the hole before energizing the circuit board. Use a magnifying glass to confirm that nothing unwanted remains on the board.

Be careful not to overheat the board during the solder-removal process. Excessive heat can cause part of the circuitry to pull away from the board. It can also damage good components which are mounted nearby.

If you remove the solder from a component and find that a lead is still stuck on some residual solder, take a pair of needle-nose pliers and pinch the lead as you gently wiggle it to break it loose from the solder bond.

Sometimes tightly soldered chips need replacing. The pins of these chips are bonded to the circuit board by a process called *wave soldering*. Wave soldering produces an exceptionally good bond without the added manufacturing expense of a socket. This process helps keep the fabrication costs down, but it makes it more difficult for you to replace the chip.

If the chips are inserted through holes in the board, and then soldered in place, an effective way to remove wave-soldered chips is to cut the chip leads or pins on the component side of the board and then remove the bad chip.

Afterwards, remove the remaining pieces of the pins sticking through the board, using a soldering iron and either solder braid or a vacuum pump.

Some special tools are available to help you remove soldered components. Fig. 9-14 shows a desoldering tip that fits over all the leads of a chip or dual-in-line (DIP) package.

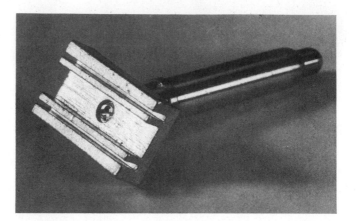

Fig. 9-14.   A desoldering tool.

Fig. 9-15 is a photograph of a spring-loaded dual-in-line extractor tool. By attaching this device to the chip and then applying the desoldering tool shown in Fig. 9-14 to the soldered connections on the opposite side of the board, you can easily desolder the pins of a standard DIP IC, all at one time. Press the load button on the extractor downward and engage the clips, causing the extractor to place an upward spring pressure on the chip. When the solder on the reverse side melts enough, the chip will pop up and off the board.

Fig. 9-15.   A spring-loaded IC extractor tool.

When you replace a chip that was soldered to a printed-circuit board, always solder a socket back in and then plug the replacement chip into this socket. This makes future replacements a lot easier. Be careful to maintain the correct pin 1 alignment.

Soldering Tips

Hand soldering is the most misunderstood and most-often abused function in electronics repair. Not only do many people use poor soldering techniques, but they also use the wrong soldering irons.

Solder isn't simply an adhesive that makes two metals stick together. It actually melts and combines with the metals it is connecting to form a consistent electrical, as well as a mechanical, connection. Time and temperature are critical in this process. The typical hand-type solder job should be accomplished in 15 seconds or less, if the soldering iron and tip are properly selected and then properly maintained.

The nominal solder melting temperature is 361° F. Metal combination between the solder and the metals being joined occurs at temperatures between 500° and 600° F.

Most soldering jobs join the metals, copper and tin, but both of these metals are easily oxidized. Poor or no solder connections are made if the surfaces to be connected are covered by contaminants, such as oils, dirt, etc., so be sure to use solder with a good cleaning flux. The flux prepares the surfaces for best solder metalization. The flux melts first and flows over the metal surfaces removing oxidation and other contaminants. Then the metal heats so that the solder melts and flows, producing a good, shallow bond.

The key to successful soldering is in the soldering iron tip. Most people selecting their first soldering iron jump right into buying a low-wattage iron, but this is a mistake. The soldering-iron tip is used to transfer the heat generated in the iron out to the soldering surface. The iron should heat the tip quickly, and the tip should be as large as possible, yet slightly smaller than any soldering pad on the board. Pick an iron whose tip operating temperature is suited for the circuit board you're to repair. If the tip temperature is too low, the tip sticks to the surface being soldered. If it's too high, it damages the board surface. The ideal working temperature for soldering on your computer's circuit board is between 600° and 700° F.

Soldering-iron tips are made of the same material as some of the contacts you're soldering—copper. Copper quickly conducts heat, but it dissolves in contact with tin. Solder is made of tin and lead. To keep the tin from destroying the copper tip, manufacturers plate a thin layer of iron over the tip. The hot iron (now you know where the term "iron" came from) still melts the solder, but now the tip lasts longer. The iron melts above 820° F, so if the heat produced by the soldering iron stays below 700° F, the solder melts but not the iron plating.

A disadvantage of the iron plating on the tip is that it doesn't conduct heat as well as copper, and it oxidizes rapidly. To counteract this, you can melt a thin coat of solder over the tip. This is called "tinning." This solder layer helps the soldering iron heat quickly and it also prevents oxidation.

The tip of an old soldering iron is usually black or dirty-brown due to oxidation. And it doesn't conduct heat very well. These "burned-out" tips can be cleaned with fine emery cloth and can then be retinned and used.

Wiping the hot tip with a wet sponge just before returning the iron to its holder is a mistake. This removes the protective coating, exposing the tip surface to atmospheric oxidation. It's much better to add some fresh solder to the tip instead. Keep your iron well-tinned.

The proper way to solder a socket or connector lead is to place the tip of the iron on the lead and, after a few seconds, touch the solder to both the soldering tip and the pad at the same time. Be careful not to put too much solder on the tip or it will run out through the bottom of the board through the hole you are soldering.

As the solder pad heats, the tin/lead solder melts and flows evenly over the pin and the pad. Keep the solder shallow and relatively even. When you think your soldering job is complete, carefully inspect your work. Sometimes, if you aren't careful, you can put too much solder on the joint, such that there's not enough solder left on the top or bottom of the connection. It's also possible to get internal voids or hollow places inside the solder joint. Large solder balls or mounds invite "cold solder joints." These are solder joints where contact is only partially made between the component and the board.

Good soldering takes patience, knowledge, and the right tools—a temperature-controlled soldering iron whose tip temperature is maintained in the 500°–600° F range for optimum soldering effect.

Before You Solder It In

A useful thing to do before you solder in a replacement part is to test the device in the circuit. Simply insert the chip or other device into the solder holes and wedge each lead in its hole with a toothpick. Then, energize the circuit and test. After proper function is verified, remove the toothpicks and solder the component into the board.

Circuit-Board Repair

Repairing damaged circuit boards is a lucrative business, and several companies have developed around this activity. For some board failures, you can repair your own circuitry and save some money.

Before soldering in new components, check the board for broken traces and for pads lifting off the board. If a trace is open and is starting to lift away from the board surface, jumper across the broken spot, jumping from one component solder pad to another pad. Use solid #18 or #20 wire, tinned at both ends before soldering.

If a pad or trace lifts free, replace it with an adhesive-backed pad or trace that overlaps the damaged area. Scrape the coating off the pad or from both ends of the trace so the new pad or trace can be soldered firmly to the existing pad or trace. Remove all excess solder and redrill any lead hole that has become covered or plugged with residual solder.

Replacing Surface-Mounted Components

Desoldering and soldering on the IBM PC System Board is not easy—the board construction is such that damage to the board traces and solder points can easily occur if you aren't extremely careful.

CAUTION: Proceed at your own risk.

Be sure you're using a temperature-controlled iron. Locate the component to be replaced. If possible, during chip removal, attach an extractor tool to the component to be replaced. Use a desoldering braided wick to remove the old molten solder, and a temperature-controlled iron to heat the pins until the component comes free. Start at the corners first, and desolder every other pin to avoid overheating one area of the board trace. Clean the solder pads by using the braided wick to remove any excess solder that might be remaining.

To resolder a new surface-mount part onto the circuit board, place the part on the board. Carefully align the part so that all the pins are properly located. Solder one corner at a time, verifying that the part is still lined up right. Once the corners are soldered, move around the part, soldering every other pin until finished.

With surface-mount devices, the components are soldered directly onto the surface of the board. There are no through-holes on the circuit board for device leads. Therefore, when a surface-mount chip is removed, there is no way to install an IC socket in its place on the system board. You must resolder the replacement component directly onto the system board. This is a tough repair. If you don't feel comfortable attempting this job, don't feel bad. Over a hundred thousand repair techs in this country also feel uncomfortable with this repair. They usually opt for board replacement. So can you. But if you want to push ahead, be VERY careful not to overheat the component or the board.

Recommended Troubleshooting and Repair Equipment

If you're planning to tackle failures that usually require Service Center support, you can minimize your investment costs and yet optimize your chances of success by carefully selecting your equipment and tools.

First, get a set of good screwdrivers—both flat blade and Phillips blade. And, get a wide selection of sizes, from the tiny "tweakers" to an 8-inch flat-bladed screwdriver. You might also find a set of jeweler's screwdrivers quite helpful. Then, get several sizes of long-nose or needle-nose pliers. Get several sizes of diagonal cutters, or "dykes," for cutting wire and pins. A good low-wattage soldering iron whose tip temperature is automatically controlled is a must if you intend to replace nonsocketed components. A simple 3½-digit DVM or DMM is useful for test measurements. Another handy tool is the logic probe. If you can afford it, get a 15–25-MHz oscilloscope with dual trace and a time-base range of 200 nanoseconds to 0.5 second. Select a scope with a vertical sensitivity of 10-millivolts per division or better.

Below is an approximate price list for typical troubleshooting and repair equipment.

Tool	Price
Screwdrivers (12 each)	$ 15.00
Pliers (4½-inch short-nose and 5¾-inch long-nose)	15.00
Diagonal cutters (4½-inch flush and 4½-inch midget)	10.00
DMM (3½ digit)	80.00
Logic probe	83.00
Logic pulser	85.00
Current tracer	200.00
Logic clip	80.00
Oscilloscope	1200.00
Logic analyzer	1100.00

You can get by quite nicely for less than $500, using the probe, pulser, tracer, and DMM as your primary equipment. Prices will vary from one manufacturer to another.

Spare Parts

Because of the cost involved, you will probably want to maintain a minimal stock of repair parts, yet you will want to be able to fix your machine quickly when it breaks down. The optimal backup in parts would include one each of every type of chip on your IBM's System Board and Adapter cards. This represents an investment of $100 to $200 in 150 or more chips. Currently, IBM custom chips are available from authorized IBM service centers. The total number of chips in the IBM PC, XT, and AT is higher than the number of chips that you will need as spares because many of the same type of chips are used in different places on the System Boards. In addition, you will only need one of the RAM chips as a spare. Your largest expense in chips will be for the ROMs (unless you are using a $140 8087 coprocessor chip).

Several companies are marketing spare parts packages with schematics, diagnostic tests, and one each of the chips for the IBM System you are using. In Appendix B, you'll find a listing of each chip in your computer, including its designation, name, and location.

Summary

There are four possible ways to optimize the operational life of your computer system.

1. Buy a highly reliable computer with a good performance track record.
2. Buy a good on-site repair contract.
3. Buy a second identical computer to use as a backup during the repair of the first.
4. Become a knowledgeable repair technician yourself.

Armed with the knowledge in this manual, you'll be able to spot the downright poor troubleshooting—the "tech" using a bare cotton swab with low-grade alcohol to "clean" a disk-drive Read head, and the repair person wiping his or her soldering iron on a wet sponge just before putting it back in its holder. These are the mistakes of poorly trained (or poorly motivated) people working on someone else's machine. You'll also be able to recognize the sharp, highly trained technician who uses the right tools and the right procedures to troubleshoot and repair in minimum time.

Then you'll smile to yourself, knowing that you were smart enough to buy this book and do your own repair the right way—the Howard W. Sams way.

Questions for Review and Discussion

1. Describe the differences between a logic probe and a logic pulser.
2. How would you use a logic probe to troubleshoot a suspected circuit and isolate a bad component?

3. You suspect a short-to-ground exists on a 6-inch trace on top of a circuit board. How would you determine where the short is located?

4. What is the best test instrument or equipment to use in finding the elusive glitch?

5. How would you test a suspected bad transistor on the CGA card?

6. At what temperature will solder melt?

7. What is the purpose for flux in the soldering process?

8. How can I test a through-hole replacement part in the circuit before soldering it in permanently?

9. Describe the procedure to follow when soldering a surface-mounted IC onto a circuit board.

10. What's the difference between a logic analyzer and a signature analyzer?

Routine Preventive
Maintenance

In the earlier chapters, you stepped through the detailed troubleshooting and repair of your IBM computer. This chapter will cover a type of maintenance that is not intended to fix a problem but, rather, prevent a problem from ever occurring. *Preventive maintenance* is just as important as corrective maintenance. In this chapter, you'll learn what can damage your computer and cause it to fail, and what you can do to prevent this from happening.

The life-cycle cost of your computer system can be much larger than the initial purchase investment. Often, the price you pay for a microcomputer is actually a small part of the overall system cost. This total cost increases dramatically as the costs for software, books, magazine subscriptions, those extra interface boards, disks, and Service Center repair charges are added in. Service costs can grow over the life of the system to 10 to 50% of your system cost.

Occasionally, a repair expense exceeds the value of the equipment that is broken. It's when we look at high repair costs that "time between failures" and "time to repair" become important. While your IBM PC, PC/XT, or PC AT Personal Computer has an excellent reliability track record, the way you operate your machine and the environment in which you place it become very important to those "time" factors. Your IBM is sturdy and fast, and it performs work easily and accurately. Under most operating conditions, IBM systems are indeed very reliable machines. But, like other machines, they do wear out and fail. Another factor to consider is that you get what you pay for. Those "bargain" interfaces and peripherals that you bought at such a low cost probably have a less than excellent reliability record.

As your computer becomes more and more essential in your home and business, your need for the uninterrupted power of your computer increases. The power of the computer is easiest seen in the impact it has on us when it breaks down. Although many problems can be fixed within a day, you can expect your machine to be gone for one to three weeks if you have to take your computer to a repair shop.

Most large companies take steps to protect their huge computer investments. Accidents and unnecessary failures cost thousands of dollars in lost business. A small business, with a single microcomputer, two disk drives, and a printer, faces just as catastrophic a loss by system failure as does a large company, yet most small businesses don't take steps to prevent such failures. Computers don't burn out. They either wear out or are forced out by human error or adverse operating conditions. If you misuse your computer or don't protect it from the environmental elements, you can be the cause of a failure. Just as you check the oil and water in your car's engine to keep it running right, and then lubricate it, and wash and wax the body to keep it free of dirt and grime to prevent rust, so should you care for and protect your computer. A few moments of care can result in a great many more hours of good, consistent performance. We call this type of care *preventive maintenance*, or just *PM*.

Contributors to System Failure

Proper PM begins with an understanding of what we are fighting. There are primarily six factors that influence the performance of your personal computer (not including the off-the-wall failures like the disk-eating dog or the floppy-bending baby). These factors are heat, cold, dust, noise interference, power-line problems, corrosion, and magnetism. Each is an enemy to smooth system operation. Each acts to cause computer breakdown. This chapter tells how to successfully battle these enemies of reliable performance.

Heat

The IC chips and other devices in your computer are sensitive to high temperatures. During normal operation, the heat that is generated in your IBM is generally tolerable to the circuitry. Usually, leaving your IBM on for long periods of time won't hurt it, because the slots and air vents in the chassis let most of the internal heat dissipate to the outside. The rest of the warm air is drawn into the power supply by its built-in fan and exhausted out the rear of the chassis.

If the components on the system board are not too hot to touch, the amount of heat being produced should not cause any damage. However, heat can become a problem when you begin adding adapter interface boards. The power supply has plenty of voltage margin and is protected against overload, but with the increased power demand, it also produces more heat. The design of the IBM Personal Computer case, with the motherboard lying flat, provides an open space for hot air to rise inside the case, but the air tends to hang over the board rather than move out the vents. Adding adapter boards that connect to the motherboard, or peripheral connectors that plug into the rear of the computer, further restricts any natural air current (or fan suction), and the components get even warmer. The power supply heats up still more as it pumps out even more current to power the piggyback boards and peripherals that derive power from the computer. The piggyback boards, the power supply, and the motherboard all give off heat, and the inside temperatures starts to soar.

Premature aging and failure is caused by excessive heat within a component. The heat produced during operation is not uniform across the component. There are specific locations on the chip that gets most of the heat (generally at the input/output connectors where the leads meet the chip itself). The usual effect of heating and cooling is to break down the contacts or junctions in the device, causing an open-circuit failure. When hot, these devices can produce intermittent "soft errors," with loss of or incorrect data. This effect is known as "thermal wipeout," and is a chronic problem in loaded systems that aren't sufficiently cooled. The continual heating and cooling action present during normal operation also causes the socketed chips to work themselves out of their sockets due to the expanding and contracting of the pins.

Heat can also contribute to disk failure. Disks act just like stereo records when exposed to heat, especially the heat of the sun. If you leave your disks in a hot car, you can be sure some warpage will occur. If the thin disk warps too much, you will lose whatever information you stored on that floppy.

Countering Heat Effects

Heat is seldom a problem for the infrequent PC user. When the use period is increased, generated heat can rise to such a level that degraded performance and reduced component lifetime occurs. The following suggestions should help in preventing heat-related failures:

► Reseat the socketed chips if intermittent failures occur.

► Keep the cooling vents clear.

► Keep your system dust-free, both inside and outside. Do your PMs (preventive maintenance actions) regularly.

► Keep your floppy disks in a cool, dry location.

► Install an external cooling fan if system operation becomes intermittent when heated.

While more and more users struggle with the internal heat problem, a quiet revolution is occurring in fan technology. Brushless DC (direct-current) fans are being designed with thermal-sensor interfaces that can monitor the PC's System Unit temperature, and can cause the fan speed to change relative to the amount of heat sensed. These "smart" fans are also much quieter than the relatively noisy AC (alternating-current) fans you and I have been using for years. As each new computer is born, another potential application for a DC fan appears. These thermal- and speed-sensing fans can provide more efficient, less costly, and longer operating computer systems.

Cold

The effect of cold on computers is an interesting subject. Many top scientists are presently working on getting superconduction devices to work in higher temperatures. Large corporations, who depend on their computers to function at top quality, keep those same computer systems in an air-conditioned room with the temperature normally set at around 65° F. Electronic components operate quite well in cold temperatures, but mechanical components have trouble functioning when the temperature drops. Take disk drives for example. The operating range for a standard floppy disk drive is approximately 40° F to 115° F. At the low end, mechanical sluggishness occurs with an increased possibility of erratic data storage and retrieval. The floppy disk itself can become brittle as it gets cold.

Countering the Effects of Cold

The rule of thumb for extreme cold temperatures is to let the system warm up to room temperature (stabilize) before turning on the power. If the temperature is comfortable for you, chances are it's fine for the system too.

Dust and Other Particles

Just like flies and ants at a picnic site, dust seems to seek out computer equipment. Interestingly, the dust is attracted to the display monitor in much the same manner as it is to a television screen. If the dust is not cleaned from the screen, it will build up, and, eventually, someone will rub it and mar the screen surface. The static electrical charges that build up in the computer and the display monitor attract the dust and dirt. That's why large computer systems are kept in cool, clean computer rooms.

Dust and dirt build-up insulate the circuit devices and prevent the release of the heat that is generated during normal operation. If the devices can't dissipate this heat, the inside temperatures rise higher than normal, causing the chips and other components to wear out even faster. Dust is a major contributor to memory chip failure. Dust seems to be attracted to heat. Have you ever noticed how dust builds up on light bulbs or on the tops of stereos and television sets? The dust particles are charged and are attracted to the magnetic fields around the electrical equipment. Your computer system problems increase in direct proportion to the increase in dust build-up.

Mechanical devices, like printers and disk drives, fall more often than solid-state electronic devices because the mechanical and electromechanical devices have moving parts that get dirty easily, causing overheating and an early failure. Look inside your printer and you'll see dirt and dust collecting. The paper sheds tiny particles as it moves through the printer. These particles become insulators that prevent the heat generated during normal operation from escaping from the equipment and into the surrounding air.

Disk drives have more dust-related problems than printers because they are designed with Read/Write heads that operate on or slightly above the diskette. The space between the head and the disk is extremely small. When the head rides on the disk surface, dust and dirt can cause major problems. Foreign particles, such as dirt, smoke ash, and tiny fibers, can cause catastrophic problems in diskette jackets and in the disk drives, themselves.

The air we breathe is full of air-borne particles, but most of these are too small to even be seen, let alone become a problem. The larger particles in the air cause the computer system problems. Cigarette ash, for example, can settle on a disk surface and move from track to track inside the disk jacket, causing loss of data. Smoking can be catastrophic to drives and computers. Smoke from cigarettes and cigars can coat the internal surfaces of the disk drive with a gummy soot that not only can produce data transfer errors but can also interfere with the mechanical operation, further increasing the wear on the drive. Tobacco is also believed to cause rapid oxidation on pins and connectors, increasing the likelihood of intermittent errors. Most computer centers and computer rooms are off-limits for smoking.

Inside the vinyl jacket surrounding each of your disks is a special lining that traps dirt and dust as the disk spins in the drive. However, this doesn't mean you can get careless about dust and dirt. Dirt on a disk can be swept off by the drive Read/Write head and can gouge out a path on the disk surface, or it can stick on the head and cause other disks to be gouged. The dirt can also cause the head itself to corrode and wear out.

Countering the Effect of Dust

Dust build-up can be controlled. Thoroughly cleaning your computer area every week will do much to contain the dust problem and keep your system in top condition. Dirt and dust can be removed from equipment housings using a damp cloth that is lightly coated with a mild soap.

> **Note:** Turn the power off before you clean your electrical equipment. Be careful you don't wet or moisten the electronic components inside the units.

After washing the surface, rewipe the outside of the equipment with a soft cloth that has been dampened with a mixture of one part liquid fabric softener to three parts water. The chemical makeup of some liquid softeners is almost the same as an antistatic chemical spray. Wiping the case and screen helps to keep static charges from attracting dust to the screen and the tops of the hardware. Most fabric softeners are antimagnetic and prevent the attraction of dust. Often, the chemicals in this inexpensive solution last longer than some antistatic sprays.

Another quite successful technique is the blowing of dust away from the screen with a pressurized can of antistatic dusting spray, as shown in Fig. 10-1. Using this kind of product means you don't have to wipe your equipment off first. Wiping a screen should be done carefully, because you could scratch the screen if some hard dust or dirt particles are on the screen or on your cloth.

Fig. 10-1.   Antistatic spray can be used to clean a screen.

Although the literature from several display manufacturers recommends using window-cleaner spray, be careful. Common household aerosol sprays, solvents, polishes, or cleaning agents may damage your monitor cabinet and screen. The safest cleaning solution is mild soap and water. Associated with their cleaning advice, each manufacturer also includes this important safety precaution:

> **CAUTION:** Make sure the power is off and the plug(s) pulled out of the power socket(s). Use a damp cloth. Don't let any liquid run into or get into your equipment.

For cleaning hard-to-get places, you can use a long plastic nozzle on the end of your vacuum hose to reach inside the hardware. Dust and small particles can be cleaned off the circuit board inside your PC using a soft brush. Fig. 10-2 shows a handy tool for vacuuming out electronic equipment. Be careful you don't damage any of the parts. Brush lightly.

Another control measure is the use of dust covers. You may not have an air-conditioned, air-purified room in which to use your IBM Personal Computer, so dust covers become very important. Plastic covers, made of a static-free material, provide an excellent protection from dust.

Here is a summary of ways to counter dust in your IBM computer system.

► Use dust covers.

► Keep windows closed.

► No smoking near your IBM Personal Computer system.

► No crumb-producing foods near your computer.

► No liquids on any equipment.

► Don't touch the surface of any floppy disk.

► Vacuum the system and the computer area weekly.

► Clean your monitor screen with a static-reducing material.

Noise Interference

Noise can be described as unexpected or undesired random changes in voltage, current, data, or sound. It can be a sudden pulse of energy, a continuous hum in the speaker, or a garbled display of characters. Three types of noise can cause problems: noise that is acoustic and affects you, noise that affects your computer system, and noise that affects other electronic equipment.

Acoustic noise includes the crying of a baby, the blare of an overpowered stereo, and the loud consistent tap-tapping of a computer printer. Also categorized as acoustic noise are high-pitched monitor squeals, and the loud thump

Fig. 10-2. Keyboards can be cleaned with a special vacuum unit.

heard when a disk drive is first accessed. If you listen closely to the motherboard in your system, you will hear a hum that seems to come from the power supply or perhaps from the speaker. Sometimes, hard disks can make all kinds of different noises when being accessed.

Noise that affects the computer and other equipment can be radiated, conducted, or received. It takes the form of *electromagnetic radiation (EMR)*. EMR noise can be further classified as either low- or high-frequency radiation.

If noise occurs in the 1-hertz to 10-kilohertz (1 Hz–10 kHz) range, it is called *electromagnetic interference (EMI)*. If it occurs at a frequency above 10 kHz, it is called *radio-frequency interference (RFI)*. RFI can occur in two forms: conducted RFI, and radiated RFI. *Conducted RFI* occurs when the noise is fed back from a personal computer through the power cord to the high-voltage AC power line. In this case, the power line acts as an antenna, transmitting the noise interference out. When your computer system and its cabling transmits noise, this noise is called *radiated RFI*.

EMI has three primary components. They are transient EMI, internal EMI, and electrostatic discharge (ESD). Power-line transients and electrostatic discharge from the human body are the two most severe forms of externally generated EMI. *Transient EMI* is the undesirable response in electrical equipment when the simple turning on or off of a device causes a large voltage pulse, or "spike," to occur and go smashing through the circuitry.

Internal EMI is the noise generated by the chips and other motherboard devices. With current microelectronic designs, internal noise levels are very low. Thus, other factors, such as connections and the length of leads, have become the main source of noise in printed circuits. Internal noise does become a problem when the components begin to fail or are excessively heated.

The last form of EMI, *electrostatic discharge (ESD)*, has the same effect as what you get from walking across a carpet and then getting shocked upon touching a metal door knob. ESD can cause a "glitch" in electronic circuits and can damage some components.

Noise can even be passed or coupled to nearby equipment on a totally different circuit that is not physically connected to your system. When two conductor wires lie next to each other, one can pick up signals that are coupled across from the other wire. This is known as "crosstalk." Just 10 volts of electricity on one wire will cause a measurable voltage (0.25 volt) on the other wire. Imagine how much crosstalk there could be if the voltage were increased to 100 volts. The induced voltage on the other wire would be 2.5 volts, which is enough to change any information in a stream of data being sent through that second wire.

Computer system noise can originate in many places, including power supplies, fans, and the computer itself. Also, it can come from other equipment, connectors, cables, fluorescent lights, lightning, and electrostatic discharge. The use of high-powered components in switching power supplies has led to widespread problems, with noise being conducted back into the power lines. Switching power supplies have been found to generate EMI in the 10–100 kHz frequency range.

Power-line noise can feed into the computer circuits whenever it exceeds the blocking limits of the power supply. Nearby high-voltage machinery, such as stamping mills, saws, air-conditioning units, and clothes dryers can produce strong magnetic fields in the area around them and, also, in their power cords.

Cables that vibrate and move in a magnetic field can also cause problems. Relays and motors can produce high-voltage transients when they are turned on or off. And television sets and radios can be affected by noise coming from the computer system.

Any digital circuit that uses a clock signal will emit or radiate interference from the cables connected to that circuit. The IBM Personal Computer's CPU operates at a clock speed of over 4 MHz—inside the frequency range of radio and television signals. (Recall that RFI covers all noise that occurs at frequencies above 10 kHz.) If the IBM system were not designed to correct for this type RFI, the CPU transmissions would interfere with the normal operation of nearby radios and television sets. Television sets connected to a cable service would not be affected because the shielded cable allows only the cable-TV program signals to get into the TV antenna input.

Finally, EMI can come from industrial, medical, and scientific equipment, and from electric motors, home appliances, drills, saws, and tool speed controls.

Our computer systems must be able to operate without causing interference to other nearby electronic equipment. They must be able to function without radiating noise, and they must be able to function even in an environment that includes noise being introduced from outside sources. That is why it's important to understand noise and how it can be generated.

Noise Interference Countermeasures

All types of noise interference can produce an undesirable or damaging effect in your IBM system. It can cause garbled screen characters, frozen cursors, and diagonal lines to appear on the screen. Also, programs can be stopped in the middle of an operation, garbage can be read from or written to disks, paper can be jammed in the printer, memory wiped out, and it can even destroy motherboard chips. Noise interference must be prevented by eliminating all noise or by shielding the source. This is not an impossible challenge, but it is a substantial practical and analytical task.

The most effective approach to noise reduction is prevention. But, if you can't prevent noise, you can at least take steps to minimize its impact. The following paragraphs present countermeasures used to prevent various forms of noise interference.

Audible Noise

Most microcomputers don't generate enough audible noise to require acoustic shielding or enclosure. The noisiest part of a computer system is the printer. Most printers don't exceed 70 dB of noise, but the type of noise (tap-tap printing) can become so irritating that many people purchase insulated sound-trapping enclosures, which fit over the printers and cut the noise output in half.

Some computer users place acoustic sound-absorbing foam around their computer system area to achieve a quieter operating place. Acoustic pads placed under disk drives and printers can also significantly reduce noise.

Electromagnetic Interference

While circuit designers try to minimize electromagnetic interference (EMI), it is a natural by-product of aging components, bad solder joints, damaged or corroded connector contacts, and loose connections. EMI is also produced when a burst of electromagnetic or electrostatic energy is conducted or induced through the circuitry. Externally produced EMI enters the computer through the cabling or openings in the case. Sometimes it enters by static discharge, through the case of the disk drive.

Cables are also a source of EMI/RFI. Both internal cables and those cables leading to the external monitor, printer, and any external hard-disk drive can radiate interference. EMI noise can be reduced in the cables by making sure that the cables are not too close to the front of a CRT or are looped together with any power cables. Interface cables are usually insulated, but you can defeat their shielding by placing them in another EMI field.

The case of the IBM Personal Computer is made of metal. It is lightweight, durable, and generally rustproof. While these are good qualities, the most important feature is that metal conducts electricity, so it provides protection against EMI/RFI, and even ESD noise.

The FCC has established specifications that computer equipment must meet regarding the amount of radiated noise that is allowed to exit from the chassis. The FCC places any devices that conduct or radiate EMI frequencies above 10 kHz into one of two categories: Class A devices and Class B devices.

Class A devices are those industrial computing devices sold for use in commercial, business, and industrial environments, and which are not sold to the general public. Class B devices are those consumer computing devices used in commercial, business, and industrial applications, plus personal computers and their associated peripherals.

Both conducted and radiated EMI are regulated. Conducted EMI, in frequencies between 450 kHz and 30 MHz, must be reduced by 48 dB for levels above 1 microvolt. Radiated EMI must be reduced by 46 dB or more when measured 3 meters away from the source.

To meet these requirements, IBM designed a metal shield case for the IBM PC, XT, and AT personal computers. While this brought the EMI within limits, EMI still leaks out of the computer, since it can get out anywhere there is an opening on the chassis—the connector slots on the front of the chassis, the vent holes, around the power-plug jack, and even the keyboard keyholes on top of the detachable keyboard case. Since you won't be changing the circuit board design, you can reduce EMI interference in two ways: (1) prevent it from reaching the motherboard and interface card circuits, and (2) keep it contained within shielded enclosures. To do this, use shielding, grounded cables, filters, and transient absorbers.

Metal enclosures make the best shields. The IBM's switching power supply, a high source of EMI, is enclosed in a metal can. So is the crystal and clock generator circuitry on the PC AT system board. The greater the shield thickness, the better the shield affect. While the metal computer case of your IBM Personal Computer does a decent job of shielding against EMI/RFI, you can improve on the shielding by sealing all openings that aren't being used. Compressible gaskets can be used to close slot holes. At one time, IBM shipped each PC with metal gaskets over each adapter-card access hole. This practice was discontinued, I'm told, because the gaskets kept falling out during shipping. Metal honeycomb ventilation screens can be used over cooling vents.

Use shielded cables. A shield is a conductive coating or envelope placed around a conductor wire, or group of wires, to provide a barrier to electromagnetic interference. Ground the shields. Hook up the ground wires that are attached to some of the peripheral interface cables. A shielded computer that is connected to a poorly shielded peripheral will enable any RFI that is generated inside the computer to be conducted out through the shield weaknesses. Filtering inside the cabling or connectors will also eliminate conducted noise.

Some connectors can be purchased with built-in filter pins to reduce the radiated EMI count around the connnectors. Other EMI-reduction devices include the ferrite "shield beads" which are placed on power-supply leads and connections to ground, or between the stages on the circuit board. These beads are used on the keyboard, clock, and data lines in the PC AT.

Ideally, the shielded connectors should provide a continuous shield from the device, through the connector, and into the shielded cable. Otherwise, the weak shield point becomes a transmission hole for EMI to get out and interfere with other devices or appliances in the area.

One excellent countermeasure to EMI and RFI is the use of fiber-optic cables and connectors. This technology hasn't yet become popular with microcomputer users because the cost is still too high, but the day is coming when fiber-optic data transmission will be the norm rather than the exception.

Electrostatic Discharge (ESD)

It sometimes appears that a wizard with a weird sense of humor secretly loads into every computer a program which intermittently produces random errors, or *glitches*, designed to drive users wild. Chasing and catching such an elusive phantom glitch is a challenge even for experienced repair technicians using expensive and complex troubleshooting equipment. But, you can learn more about this intermittent problem and how to prevent it from affecting your computer operation.

Glitches are electrical disturbances of short duration, but which are often of long enough duration to cause problems in digital circuitry. They are usually the result of an electrostatic discharge (ESD), one of the most severe forms of EMI.

People and objects, such as chairs and desks, can accumulate a substantial electrical charge or potential. The human body can accumulate static charges up to 25,000 volts. It is not unusual to build up and carry charges of 500 to 15,000 volts. Charged objects, or people, can then be discharged (quickly get rid of the voltage) to a grounded surface through another object or person. Remember the times you dragged your feet across a carpet and then shocked someone nearby? This electrical charge is static. It can discharge through your computer, and, when it does, all sorts of undesirable things can occur. If a program is running and a computer user carrying a large potential of electrical charge touches a key on the keyboard, the arc of discharge will find the shortest route to ground, usually through the ICs. The program will bomb to a halt, with data bits "falling away" everywhere. The screen can go wild and display weird characters. Sensitive components can be damaged or destroyed. Even a charge of only 3 volts is enough to create an erroneous bit in most logic circuits.

Electrostatic charges can be of any voltage. The following is a list of some of the sources of ESD glitches:

► People in motion.
► Overheated components.
► Improper grounding.
► Poorly shielded cables.
► Improperly installed shields.
► Missing covers and gaskets.
► Circuit lines too close.
► Poor solder connections.
► Low humidity.

We know that static occurs when two objects are rubbed together. Your movement, walking while wearing wool or polyester slacks, can cause a tremendous charge of electricity to build up on your body. A problem occurs when this charge builds and becomes quite large. Just walking across a carpet can generate over a 1000 volts of charge. If the humidity is low and it is dry in the room, the charge can be substantially higher. (When the relative humidity is 50% or higher, static charges generally don't accumulate.) A built-up static charge will readily arc to any grounded object, such as a disk-drive chassis or the screen of your display.

An ESD release to your disk-drive case won't hurt you, but it can be very damaging to your electronics. The discharge pulse drives through the case to the Read/Write head and then on to the analog-card circuitry, where it can burn out some of the chips. Even if no components are "fried," the damage that is done by this overvoltage spike accumulates and starts to degrade the functioning of some circuit-board components. ESD damage costs has been estimated at millions of dollars annually, but this figure is even higher when components are not totally destroyed, but are degraded. Even so, sooner or later the chip(s) fails completely.

In low humidity, just walking across a synthetic carpet can charge your body to 35,000 volts. Walking over a vinyl floor can charge you with 12,000 volts. A poly bag picked up off a table can develop 20,000 volts. Even sliding off a urethane-foam padded chair can load you with 18,000 volts. Is this a hazard to your PC? Yes. Some electronic devices are very susceptible to low values of ESD voltage.

If your computer occasionally gets the "shock treatment" or pulls the old "disappearing data" trick on you, there are some things you can do. The following list offers some specific solutions to ESD problems.

▶ Use an antistatic spray on your rugs, carpets, and computer equipment. The antistatic spray, when applied with a soft cloth, works both to reduce and control static.

▶ Install a static-free carpet in your computer area.

▶ Place your computer system on antistatic pads.

▶ Install an antistatic floor mat beneath your computer chair. (This is the most popular solution.)

▶ Mop hard floors (noncarpeted) with an antistatic solution. The antistatic floor finish works well, but this is really an expensive solution and is more suited for electronic manufacturing facilities. Most antistatic floor finishes are effective for up to six months.

▶ Install a conductive table top.

▶ Install a humidifier to keep the humidity above 50%.

▶ Keep chips in conductive foam (that black styrofoam-looking material) when not installed.

▶ Touch a grounded metal object (such as the power-supply case) before touching components inside the computer.

You can defeat ESD glitches by paying close attention to static charges in and about the computer system. By making static-charge elimination a part of your preventive maintenance program, you take one more step to extending the longevity of your computer system.

Radio-Frequency Interference

Radio-frequency interference (RFI) is much the same as EMI except that it occurs at frequencies above 10 kHz. RFI is what causes five other garage doors on your street to open when you operate your new automatic garage door opener. You'd really rather it didn't work like that.

Although RFI isn't a health hazard, it's controlled just as EMI is. FCC Rule, Part 15, Subpart J, states that any digital product that generates timing signals or pulses at rates greater than 10 kHz must comply with FCC regulations. In fact, Class B devices like the IBM Personal Computer family are tested over a range of 30 to 1000 MHz to ensure that their emissions fall below the maximum field-strength limits. The computer is also limited in the amount of emission that it can feed back along the power lines (250 microvolts). The same chart that applies to EMI field-strength radiation also applies to RFI. The only sure way to completely block RFI emissions is to completely enclose your computer system in a shield. This is impractical, but there are ways to minimize or reduce the emission of RFI.

There have been reports of interference problems with cordless telephones. The IBM PC has been known to cause low-power telephones to dial or lift off-hook. High-power telephones in the remote area of the computer can cause characters to appear on the screen. Usually the keyboard turns out to be the source of the problem. Here are some ways to minimize RFI around your computer system:

1. Locate your computer at least 6 feet from any television set.
2. Use a directional outdoor TV antenna.
3. Subscribe to cable TV.
4. Connect line filters to your TV.
5. Replace any antenna twin-lead wire to your TV with 75-ohm coaxial cable.

Power-Line Problems

The most important environmental factor for your computer system is good, clean power. If you depend on your local utility to supply this power in steady, reliable consistency, you may be disappointed.

Room-lighting systems can tolerate line-voltage problems that momentarily dim the lights when a large power-hungry machine is switched on; however, computer systems cannot. Computers are more sensitive to power-line disturbances than are other electrical equipment. Undervoltage or overvoltage puts a severe stress on computer components. The effect is to accelerate the conditions under which a device gradually weakens, becomes marginal, and finally wears out.

There are four types of power-line problems that cause concern. These are brownouts (voltage sags), blackouts (voltage loss), transients (voltage spikes), and noise (which was discussed earlier).

Brownouts

Brownouts are those planned (and sometimes unplanned) voltage sags, when less voltage is available to drive the IBM power supply, the display CRT, and the printer motor. (Actually, the plan for less power is for the city's electrical system, not just your little domain.)

Your PC should still work with line voltages that drop and remain at 20 % below the 110-volt rating. But if the supply voltage gets too low, the regulators in your power supply won't be able to pump adequate power into your motherboard, and data can get garbled. During brownouts, computer systems operate intermittently, overheat, or simply shut down and lock up.

Brownouts are far more common than you may realize. And voltage dips are common if you operate your computer near some large electrical equipment such as air conditioners or arc welders. Your line voltage can be drawn down as much as 20% by the heavy momentary drain caused when this nearby equipment is turned on.

By the way, your power supply can also handle a voltage "brown-up," or an increased line voltage, and still provide proper power to your circuit, but the power-supply regulators will generate more heat as they handle the extra incoming voltage.

Blackouts

A power-line blackout, caused by storms and lightning, is a total loss of line voltage. It can be caused by vehicles accidentally knocking down power lines, or even by an improper switching action by a power-station operator. When power is lost, whatever you had in RAM is gone. If you are writing to the disk when power fails, you will have only a partial save—the information that was still in RAM and not yet copied over to your disk is lost. If a scheduled power outage is planned, postpone using your computer. If the weather turns bad and thunder is echoing across the sky, don't turn your computer on. If a blackout occurs or you see lightning, turn your machine off and pull the plug(s) until the storm passes.

When the power goes out, be careful. While the room lights are out and you're muttering under your breath as you feel around for a flashlight, remember what is sure to happen when the power is restored—a tremendous voltage spike will be produced as the lights and motors go back on all over the neighborhood. This could damage your IBM system. Always unplug your computer system when a blackout occurs. Wait until the power has been restored for a few minutes, and then turn your system back on. Don't test your power-supply filters on these kinds of spikes.

Transients

Excluding electrostatic discharge, power-line transients are the most devastating form of noise interference in computer circuits. Transients are large, potentially damaging, spikes of voltage or current that are generated in the power lines feeding electrical power to your community. Spikes can be caused by lightning striking a power line somewhere, by utility company equipment failure, or by the ON/OFF switching action that is common to our using any electrical tool or appliance.

Even though most of these spikes are small and barely noticeable, some voltage spikes as large as 1700 volts have been measured in home wiring. Residential areas experience more large spike transients than do commercial areas.

The line filters in your IBM power supply will protect your system from most high-voltage transients, but sometimes a spike overcomes the power-supply protection and gets to the logic circuitry. The general effect is erased or altered data, but if the spike is too large, sensitive circuit devices in the computer can be destroyed.

The IBM PC, XT, and AT power supplies are normally not affected by the transients generated by ON or OFF switching actions. These actions can produce a short-lived spike that is five times normal line voltage.

Not all spikes are generated outside the computer. Whenever you save a program or file which you've developed, activating the disk drive produces a voltage spike inside your computer. IBM engineers have placed capacitors in strategic locations on the motherboard, and in the disk-drive electronics, to carry spikes harmlessly away to ground, preventing component damage. If any part of the spike reaches the circuit components, the devices are stressed and can become marginal.

Preventing Power-Line Problems

If you live in an area where power outages or brownouts are common, or where electrical storms occur when you aren't ready, or if your computer system occasionally hangs up, you need protection. There are two kinds of approaches to preventing power-line problems. You can condition the power being supplied, or you can provide an auxiliary, or back-up, power source.

Power-line conditioners include an isolator, a regulator, and a filter. Transient suppressors, surge protectors, and isolation devices are examples of *isolators* and will provide protection from voltage and current surges. These devices can keep the line voltage at a proper level even when the line supply is 25% over normal. Some surge protectors can filter out high-frequency spikes, but cannot respond to slow low-frequency transients. One form of surge protector is called a *metal-oxide varistor (MOV)*, a form of diode that will clamp the line voltage at a certain level, preventing overvoltage spikes from getting into your system. These devices are installed across the power-line wires leading into your computer. Isolators cannot provide protection against a brownout or a complete loss of electrical power.

Regulators act to maintain the line voltage within prescribed limits. When the line voltage varies more that 10%, regulators keep the voltage to your IBM system at a near constant and proper level. They are essential if the line voltage varies more than 10% at the computer, but they don't provide protection against voltage spikes and blackouts.

Filters remove noise from the input power line. They short EMI/RFI signals to ground and remove high-frequency signals from the low-frequency 60-Hz power line. Power-line filters work best when they are located immediately next to or at the front end of the power supply. Filters don't stop spikes. Nor are they effective during low- or high-voltage conditions.

When you question whether the power is going to be available on a consistant basis, an auxiliary power source is a necessity. Three choices are available: switching battery backup, uninterruptible power supply (UPS), or a portable generator.

Switching battery backup is becoming very popular in the area of data loss protection. This is primarily because the cost of this backup system is the cheapest (between $150 and $1000) way to supply emergency power. The "battery backup" hooks to the incoming power and supplies power to the system in case a power interruption occurs. When power is interrupted, the "battery backup" switches incoming power from the power supply to the backup battery. The switch from one to the other occurs almost instantaneously (usually within 10 milliseconds), and works well with the PC AT and the PC. The configuration-RAM battery backup in the PC AT is a simplified example of this concept.

If your system is an IBM PC/XT, you may experience problems if you have a "battery backup" installed in the system. One advertised feature of the XT is a beefier power supply that is originally installed in the system. The improved power supply is designed to protect the contents of the system's RAM when there are fluctuations in power. If a XT user has a backup battery installed, the power supply may defeat the backup's purpose. It seems that when a loss of power occurs, and during the 10 milliseconds it takes the "battery backup" to kick in, the power supply resets the system and clears the RAM of all data. If you own a XT, the best bet for power protection is to procure one of the other protection devices discussed next. They may be more expensive (around $2000); however, they are worth it.

The *uninterrupted power supply (UPS)* stores energy when line power is present and then delivers power to the computer when a blackout occurs. These power supplies cost between $1500 and $10,000, depending on what "extras" you want with them, but they are a dependable source of auxiliary power. A UPS is composed of a motor, a generator, and a battery. The motor is driven by power from the utility line while local power is available. The motor turns a generator which produces electricity to charge a battery. When line power is lost, the battery turns the generator to produce AC electricity that can be used by the computer. With a UPS installed, the computer system sees uninterrupted power.

There are four types of UPS equipment that can be used to power your computer system. Each of these are discussed next.

A "continuous-service UPS" changes the AC line voltage to DC to charge a set of batteries. When power is lost, the batteries operate an inverter which changes the DC battery power back to AC to run your computer system.

"Portable and fixed motor generators" are UPSs that are powered by electricity, gasoline, or diesel motors. The generator is turned by the motor and supplies a regulated AC voltage to operate your computer system (and probably many other appliances and lights in your home or business). These devices are often used as emergency backup power for hospitals, police departments, and radio stations. Generators can be expensive, but they can provide backup power throughout the period that line power is not available.

A "forward-transfer UPS" supplies power to your computer system only when line power is lost. It is the classic UPS, in which the line power drives a motor that rotates a generator which charges a battery (or set of batteries). When line power is lost, the batteries take over and provide AC power to the computer through an inverter.

A "reverse-transfer UPS" provides power to the computer from a battery most of the time, and switches to line power only if the UPS fails or is turned off.

Some UPS equipment provides much more than just a power source. One company markets a UPS that provides protection not only against total power loss, but also against power transients, under- and overvoltage fluctuations, brownouts, and dirty (noisy) lines. Most UPS devices can quickly switch to battery power. Once the transfer occurs, the next important consideration is the length of time that the backup will be able to provide power. Some units will keep your computer system running long enough to save what you had in RAM and conduct a normal system shutdown. One popular unit can provide up to an hour of reliable AC power at a systems cost of about $800.

Is extended power during a blackout really important? If you are in an area that has a lot of power problems, consider this: what effect would losing power at the time you were updating your disk directory have on your system? Likely, you'd lose your directory and not be able to retrieve whatever you had on your disk. The problem can be much worse when you connect a hard disk into your system. If a power outage occurs when the hard disk is activated or even simply powered up, there is no way for you to conduct a normal power-down sequence. If your hard disk requires the Read/Write heads to be in a certain position for shutdown, you can't achieve this unless you have a UPS that switches in instantaneously. Failure to properly position the heads can cause drive damage as well as the loss of valuable data.

You have to make some choices. What level of protection do you need? Can you manage adequately without standby power by making backup copies of all your data, and saving to disk often during computer operation? Power-line protection can prevent damage, expensive data loss, and unnecessary downtime.

When selecting a power-line conditioner, consider the speed of response in handling voltage spikes, and its ability to filter out high-frequency noise. Consider the amount of line power it can handle or the range of input voltages it can cover with a clean power output. Another good thing to consider is whether the power-line conditioner has multiple outlets and can handle multiple devices hooked to it.

When selecting a backup power supply, consider the total backup power required to keep your system operating and the length of time you will need that power supplied. The time to switch to standby power is also very important. The availability of built-in line conditioning as well as the availability of under- and overvoltage protection should also be considered.

To determine how much backup power you may require, add the amperage ratings on the label plates of all the computer system equipment (computer, external display monitor, printer, drives, plotters, etc.) and multiply by 120. The result is the approximate wattage, or power, you will require to operate the entire system. Since the larger the amount of power required, the higher your cost, you may want to consider using only the power required to operate the basic system (computer, monitor, and disk drives). You can leave the other peripheral equipment plugged into your standard wall socket and let these fall off (fail) when power is lost. If you do this, don't forget to turn these machines off and unplug the power cords before the power is restored to prevent a big transient from damaging them.

How much power protection to provide is up to you. Many computer users are able to get along quite well with unprotected systems. Others prefer to operate their systems knowing that unseen environmental upheavals won't affect access to their IBM PC, XT, or AT computer system.

Corrosion

All metal connector pins on cables, interface cards, and chip pins are subject to a chemical change in which the metal plating of the pins and sockets is gradually eaten away. This chemical change is called "corrosion." The three types of corrosion that can affect the IBM computer systems are direct oxidation by chemical change, atmospheric corrosion, and galvanic corrosion.

In "direct oxidation," a chemical corrosion occurs. A film of oxide forms on the metal surface, reducing the pin's contact with the socket. During operation, the temperature of these pins increases and, at high temperatures, the oxidation process accelerates. The metal is slowly worn away as the electrical contact surface is converted to an oxide and the oxide crumbles.

"Atmospheric corrosion" occurs when chemicals in the air attack the metals in the computer-system circuitry, causing pitting of the metals and a "rust" build-up. In the early stages of this corrosion, sulfur compounds in the atmosphere are converted to tiny droplets of sulfuric acid that lie on the surface of the connector pins. This acid eats away the metal, causing pits to form. Near the ocean, the presence of salt spray or increased levels of chlorides can cause severe pitting of some metals. When atmospheric corrosion is just beginning to form, the contacts can be wiped clean, restoring the metal brightness. But if the acid is allowed to remain, the long exposure converts it to a sulfate layer that can no longer be wiped away. This reduces the electrical contact between the pins and their sockets.

After an extended period of time, a layer of discolored rust prevents any contact between the pins and their sockets, causing an open circuit. This open circuit can usually be located easily with a meter (or, sometimes, even visually).

It's the in-between stage, when the "almost-open" condition exists, that produces those horrible intermittent failures that can be so hard to find.

In "galvanic corrosion," a tiny crack or hole in the metal plating on a pin or connector lets an electrolyte, such as salt (sodium chloride) in moisture, penetrate between the metal plating and the underlying base metal. A miniature battery forms, with a tiny electric current flowing between the two dissimilar metals. The plating surface becomes scaly and rough as the plating is slowly eaten away. The corrosive action is concentrated on the underlying metal which is exposed at the breaks in the scale, since this is where the "galvanic battery" exists.

The effect is the same as for the other forms of corrosion—the electrical contact between the pin and socket decreases, causing intermittent problems, until the corrosive scale is so complete that the electrical circuit is broken and signals are blocked entirely.

You can actually cause this corrosive action to start if you handle your connectors and PC boards improperly. The oil on your fingers contains enough sodium chloride to begin an oxidation action on those pins. The wrong way to handle printed-circuit boards is demonstrated in Fig. 10-3.

Fig. 10-3.   The wrong way to handle printed-circuit boards.

Corrosion Prevention

A trade-off exists between preventing corrosion and preventing electrostatic discharge, because corrosive action is reduced with a reduction in the relative humidity, but ESD increases.

Electronic manufacturers are aware of the effects of corrosion, and most connectors are made of a combination of metals that resist corrosion but are good conductors of electrical signals. You can choose the type of connectors to use for your cables. You can buy cables and connectors with a tin alloy plating on the pins or with a thin gold plating. You can imagine which type is more expensive. Although you will pay more for the gold-plated connectors, they can be "worth their weight in gold," because they provide superior contact reliability. There are, however, a few inexpensive things you can do yourself to help fight corrosion in your IBM system.

While metal gates and cars can be spray painted to prevent rust (oxidation), this is not an option for preventing corrosion on circuit pins and connectors. The best preventive action is cleaning. By keeping the contacts clean, you can deter oxidation build-up and prevent the occurance of intermittent glitches.

You can clean the pins on some chips by reseating the chips periodically. Chips have a habit of working up out of the sockets after extended use. Turning off all the power, grounding yourself, and carefully pushing these devices back down into their sockets will act to clean the pin surface, restoring (or ensuring) good electrical contact.

> **CAUTION:** Always turn off the power and touch a grounded surface before touching anything in the IBM Personal Computers.

Oxidation on the contacts of connectors can be cleaned with an emery cloth, a soft rubber eraser, a solvent wipe, or a contact cleaner spray. If you use emery cloth, be careful not to grind away the metal plating itself. If you use a rubber eraser, keep the eraser dust away from the computer.

> **CAUTION:** When rubbing to clean contacts, always rub along the pin (lengthwise). Rubbing lengthwise on the pins prevents accidentally pulling a pin contact up off the board.

Solvent wipes are available as part of cleaning kits sold by many computer supply companies. These wipes can clean and then lubricate the contact surface with a film that helps seal out atmospheric corrosion without interfering with the signal flow. Most solvent wipes are individually wrapped in small packages, much like the hand towelettes you get in some restaurants or on some airplane flights.

You can also spray the pins with a contact cleaner spray like those used to clean older television tuner dials. The contact cleaner spray is available at most electronic parts stores and is also an effective corrosion preventive. Contact cleaner wipes and spray are the best methods for removing an oxidation layer.

One final note on the subject of corrosion: high temperatures will increase the corrosive action in the IBM Personal Computer systems. Removing and preventing further corrosion helps keep your computer tuned up and running cool.

Magnetism

The effects of magnetism are especially important in disks and disk drives since these two parts of the computer system are designed to operate on magnetic principles. Each floppy disk is coated with a magnetic oxide, with millions of tiny magnets randomly positioned on its surface. As the drive's Read/Write head passes over the disk surface, a magnetic force is induced in the head by the disk-drive electronics, causing the magnets on the disk surface to line up according to the voltage pulses in the head. These voltage pulses are the computer-generated digital information being converted in the head. This is magnetism that is good for the system.

The voltages used in monitors and television receivers produce strong magnetic fields. Magnetic flux is caused by the presence of a high voltage (115 volts) in computer display monitors and television sets. A color television set produces the strongest magnetic flux, but the high-voltage areas of monitors, printers, telephones, the ballast in fluorescent lights, and even power strips, can be sources of flux. The strength of the flux field depends on the strength of the voltage, which can fluctuate depending on the amount of power being required by the equipment. This is magnetism that is bad for the disks.

If you accidentally place one of your disks in the field, the tiny pole magnets on your disk's tracks can change their alignment. Then, when your disk drive tries to read the disk, the head cannot understand or will misinterpret the information on the disk. You will get garbage, or BDOS read errors.

The moral is: Keep your diskettes, and even your information cables away, from power sources.

Disk Maintenance

Two valuable components in any computer system are the mass storage devices (disks) and the disk drives. The IBM PC, XT, and AT computer systems use 5¼-inch floppy diskettes as the mass storage medium. Since diskettes and disk drives are critical components in all computer systems, it makes sense to do all you can to protect and properly maintain them.

Diskettes are pretty sturdy things, but they are sensitive to magnetic and electrical fields, high temperatures, low temperatures, pressure, bending, and dust. Dust and little airborne fibers are particularly bad for your disks.

The Read/Write head in an IBM floppy disk drive rides on the surface of the most vulnerable part of the mass storage system—the floppy disk. Floppy disks are made of Mylar® or polyethylene terephthalate and are coated with a magnetic iron (ferric) oxide. As the drive head rides on the disk's oxide surface, it causes tiny bits of oxide to rub off the disk. Most of these loose oxide particles are caught and held by the liner, but some of the oxide sticks to the head. Gradually, an oxide layer builds up. This oxide layer has two effects on system operation: (1) It makes the head less sensitive to reading and writing data, and (2) It causes an abrasive action on the disk surface. As the oxide layer builds up, it becomes ragged. This roughness scratches even more oxide off the disk, until the oxide on the disk surface is too thin to support data storage. When oxide is missing from the surface, "drop-outs," or spots where data can no longer be stored, develop. Then the disk fails to read or write properly, and it becomes useless. Keeping the oxide layer from building on the Read/Write head will help extend the life of your disks. The better disks are less likely to spin off oxide particles, so the head stays cleaner longer, and the disks last longer.

With the drive Read/Write head riding on the surface of the disk, any tiny piece of "junk" lying on your disk looks like a huge boulder to the head. A piece of your own hair is about 40 microns (0.0015748 inch) thick. A hair is a huge obstruction to the disk-drive head. Even dust and fingerprints on the disk surface can cause obstacles to the movement of the disk under the head. As shown in Fig. 10-4, to protect the disk medium, and the head, each polyvinyl-chloride disk jacket is lined inside with a dust-catching synthetic fiber. The disk rotates inside the drive at about 300 rpm, and any dust or other particles that may have slipped inside the jacket or settled on the disk are quickly swept off the disk by the liner material. But a build-up of too many particles can overload this protective system.

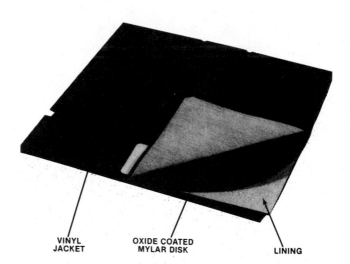

VINYL JACKET OXIDE COATED MYLAR DISK LINING

Fig. 10-4. A typical floppy diskette.

Disks are further protected by the paper storage envelopes, or sleeves, into which the square disk jackets are inserted. Use these envelopes. Don't let your disks lie around outside the envelope inviting dust and dirt trouble.

Disks make different sounds in the disk drive, depending on the type of liner used. Some types of liners provide more wiping action than others. Although the disk may sound like coarse sandpaper when it spins in the drive, that doesn't mean the disk surface or the drive is being harmed. A louder disk may actually be doing a better job than a quieter disk.

Tobacco smoke is also harmful to disks and disk drives. The tars and nicotine that filter up into the air from cigarettes and cigars can settle on your computer system. These sticky chemicals form a gummy ash build-up on any exposed surface, including your diskettes and disk drives. This material literally gums up the drives, eats into the Read/Write head, and scratches the surface of your disks. This is similar to taking a metal file to your favorite record album. Avoid smoking or allowing smoking in your computer area. If you can't do this, then clean your system more often (much more often).

Not all disks are created equal. Some disks are manufactured to better standards and with thicker magnetic oxide coatings. Naturally, these disks are more expensive. Less-expensive disks have thinner oxide coatings and shed their oxide layers easily (not the newer high-capacity disks), further reducing their effective life. Compare disk specifications before you buy. Here is a summary of what you can do to help extend disk life.

1. Buy name-brand disks. Avoid "bargain" disks. The $7.00 disk should last 7 times as long as the $1.50 disk.

2. Never touch the disk surface.

3. Never slam the disk door closed on a disk. You could press the disk-centering hardware into the disk surface instead of the disk hole.

4. Always store disks in their protective jackets.

5. Never write with a pen or pencil on a label that's on a disk (use a felt-tip marker). Ballpoint pens and pencils can cause indentations in the disk surface. Mark the label first, and then put the label on the disk jacket.

6. Store diskettes in a cool, clean, dry place.

7. Don't lay disks in the sun. They warp just as stereo records do.

8. Never allow smoking near your disks or your drive. Smoke lets tars into the air, which can settle on the disk surface (and inside your drive), gumming up the works.

9. Never set disks by monitors or television sets. The magnetic fields can erase data. Also, avoid placing disks near vacuum cleaners or large motors. Even freezers and refrigerators have compressor motors that can alter the data on your disks.

10. Don't bend or fold disks.

11. Store disks vertically. Storing disks horizontally can cause the disk to bind in the jacket, preventing proper speed of rotation, and causing a scratching of the disk surface, resulting in intermittent failure.

12. Don't put disks through airport X-ray machines. Hand them to the security guard for inspection, and have them bypass the X-ray inspection process.

Depending on the quality of your disks, the cleanliness of your computer area, and the condition of your disk drive, the lifetime of your disks could be as short as a week or as long as 17 years (70 million revolutions). Assuming the quality, cleanliness, and condition factors are favorable, disk life is estimated in the number of actual rotations while the disk Read/Write head is in contact with the disk surface, rather than on the total time of existence.

Disk-Drive Maintenance

What kinds of PMs are there for disk drives and hard-disk drives? On hard-disk drives, the head and platters are kept in a vacuum container that should not be opened by anyone but an experienced and authorized technician in a controlled, clean-room environment. It takes sophiticated equipment to perform any kind of adjustments to the tracking and speed, which must (all) be accomplished in this controlled environment. Since hard disks are sealed in dust-tight enclosures, the only PM you can do on these devices is exterior cleaning and proper cable locating to minimize noise interference problems.

Always park the heads before moving a hard-disk drive system, even on those drives that park automatically upon power-down.

According to industry statistics, 64% of all flexible disk-drive failures could be prevented through properly scheduled preventive maintenance. Floppy disk-drive manufacturers' representatives insist that "officially" there isn't any PM for floppy disk drives that the user can do. However, they describe head cleaning as the only routine maintenance that could possibly be done by a novice, although even this is not officially recommended.

Cleaning the Head of a Floppy Drive

Disk-drive heads need regular cleaning to remove the oxides that build up on the leading edge of the head (the side facing the direction of disk rotation). Head cleaning is a PM you can do. Head cleaning diskettes of various kinds are available. The "wet" diskette kind works with a cleaning solvent. Since any cleaning disk works by a rubbing action and by chemical action between the disk fabric and the drive head, there is a potential for abrasion to occur. So you must be careful not to allow the disk to spin in the drive too long. A cleaning disk can spin in a disk drive for about 30 seconds with no apparent damage. With most cleaning disk kits, 45 seconds is too long to keep the cleaning solvent in contact with the drive head. If you buy this type of cleaner, you must use the cleaner just long enough to remove the oxide build-up but not long enough to damage the head.

Nonabrasive head cleaners are now being marketed. These products use fabric-covered disks which are dampened with a cleaning solvent. With the one kit, you sprinkle cleaning solvent on the disk fabric and then insert the disk into your drive for spinning action head cleaning. The disk can be used as many as 13 times. Another kit has cleaning disks that are predampened and individually sealed. You use a cleaning disk once and then throw it away, using another the next time. Both of these products work well.

Drive heads can also be cleaned with alcohol and a cotton swab wrapped in a lint-free material. But, while manually cleaning with alcohol and swab, you could accidentally scrub the pressure pads by mistake, causing more problems than you're preventing. But, if you're careful, manual cleaning can be effective.

Special cleaning materials, such as cellular-foam swabs and chamois leather cloths, are good materials to use for manual head cleaning. Or, you can use a piece of bedsheet wrapped around the cotton swab. Uncovered cotton swabs are dangerous to use because the cotton fibers can catch or pull away, and lie in the drive or on the head, becoming cotton logs on a disk-surface highway, just waiting to get swept into the drive head that rides on the surface of the disk. These fibers can also catch on the ferrite chip in the middle of the ceramic head, loosening it from its mounting and ruining the head.

Surgical isopropyl alcohol or methanol can be used as the cleaning solvent. The solvent used must not leave a residue when it evaporates, so most other alcohol solvents should be avoided. You can also use typewriter cleaner or trichloroethane. In all cases, have plenty of ventilation and make sure the solvent has evaporated before you operate the drive.

How often the head must be cleaned depends on how much the drive is used and what type of diskettes are used. A quality diskette is good for about three million passes, or rotations, against a Read/Write head before enough oxide is worn off so that the head needs cleaning. The "bargain" disks are good for one tenth that rotational life. This means that with bargain disks, instead of 167 hours of access time, you might only get 16 hours or less before the head gets caked with oxide or your disk surface gets too worn to write to or read from. Now you know why your bargain disks don't seem to last very long.

A useful rule of thumb for head cleaning is to clean the Read/Write head every 40 hours of disk operation. This means clean after 40 hours of rotational life if you're using standard disks. You could clean more often or even wait until you start getting Read/Write errors, and then replace or clean the head.

Keeping the drive door closed, unless you are inserting or removing a disk, will help keep dust and dirt out. It also prevents unwelcome visitors (insects and even mice) from climbing into the drive.

To clean the floppy disk drive's head with a drive-cleaning disk, just follow the directions that come with the kit. If no directions were given, the general idea is to dampen the cleaning disk with the solvent supplied and insert the dampened cleaning disk in the drive. Then close the drive door and turn on the computer. With the cleaning disk inside the drive, the disk will simply spin, cleaning as it whirs along. After 20 or 30 seconds, open the drive door, and remove the disk. Turn off the computer and let the drive Read/Write head dry thoroughly before operating the system.

To manually clean the drive head, gather the following tools:

► Flathead screwdriver.

► Phillips-head screwdriver.

► Protective pad.

► Adequate lighting.

► Tray to hold loose screws.

Turn off the computer and disassemble the disk drive, using the procedures found in Appendix B. Disconnect the disk-drive cable from the back of the drive. Remove the two silver flathead screws holding the drive tight to the chassis (Fig. 10-5). On the PC, these are on the side of the unit. On the PC/XT and the PC AT, these screws are in the front of the unit.

Disconnect the power-supply cable from the back of the analog card. Gently remove the drive from the chassis. Carefully remove all cables from the analog card. Carefully remove the two Phillips screws holding the analog card on the drive (Fig. 10-6).

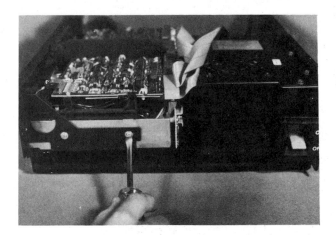

Fig. 10-5.   Remove the two flathead screws holding the disk drive to the chassis.

Remove the analog card. (On the PC and the XT, the analog card slides towards the rear of the drive.) Carefully lift the black head-load arm and look for discoloration (build-up) on the surface of the pad in the PC and XT, or on the Read/Write head (located below). On the AT, there are two heads—one on top and one on the bottom of the head mechanism. Using a special foam or wrapped

Fig. 10-6. Removing the two Phillips screws holding the analog card on the drive mechanism.

cotton swab, dampened with a cleaning solvent, gently rub the head and the pad as shown in Fig. 10-7.

Let the surfaces dry completely before reassembling. When the head and pressure pad are dry, reinstall the drive electronics by carefully placing the analog card on the drive, or by sliding the analog card back into the grooves in the drive mechanism (on the IBM PC and XT). Reinstall the two Phillips screws into the analog card. Reconnect the cable(s), being very careful that no connector pins get broken or shorted. Carefully push the drive mechanism back into the chassis. Connect the power-supply cable to the back-underside of the analog card. On the IBM PC and XT, leave about 2 inches of space when inserting the mechanism into the chassis so that you can get your hands into the back to reconnect the connectors. Then push the drive all the way back into the assembly.

Replace the two silver flathead screws on the sides of the drive in the IBM PC and XT, or in front, if you own an IBM AT. Now power up the computer. Place a COPY of a program disk in the cleaned drive. Have you waited until all the surfaces are dry? Close the drive door. Load and run a program.

If everything runs all right, reassemble the computer. If you have any problems, chances are you have made a mistake in assembling the drive. Go back and check the cables for misalignment or no connection. After the program has run, reassemble the computer and restore the system to full operation. (Note: If you have any problems, refer to the appropriate troubleshooting chapter for your system.)

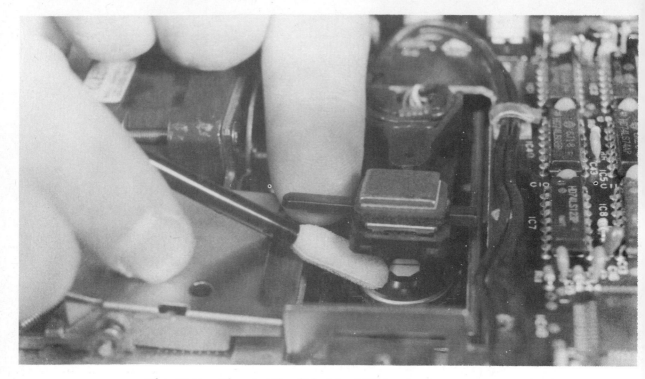

Fig. 10-7.   Cleaning the disk-drive R/W head.

Disk-Drive Head Cleaning Intervals

Cleaning your drive head is like changing the oil in your car. You do it when you feel you've driven enough miles or when the oil looks dirty. Some software manufacturers recommend cleaning the heads every other week. Some repair technicians say clean every six months. Others suggest you don't clean your heads until the disk drive makes mistakes trying to read or write data. Since no hard and fast rule has been offered, I defer to the guidance of the manufacturers (Table 10-1).

Table 10-1.   Disk-Drive Head Cleaning Intervals

System Usage	Cleaning Interval
Over six hours each day	Weekly
Daily	Monthly
Light to moderate	Twice monthly
Occasionally	Every six months

If you live in the smog belt, you may want to clean your heads more often. In any case, it won't hurt for you to clean them at least once a year. If you begin to get Read/Write errors, check and see if PMs are due.

Disk Speed Tests

Although this wasn't mentioned by disk-drive manufacturers as the PMs that you and I could do, a somewhat more detailed, yet handy, PM is the adjusting of the disk-drive speed.

Just as automobile engines need periodic check-ups and engine retuning, disk drives benefit from the same care. You can provide this by correctly adjusting, or tuning, the drive-motor speed. Your IBM PC disk drives rotate at 300 rpm and work with soft-sectored disks. No timing holes are used, as with hard-sectored disks. This makes the speed of rotation critical to the accurate synchronization of the signals stored on the disk. If the speed is off by only 10 rpm, the drive may not be able to correctly read the disk. Variation in speed is caused by normal mechanical drive wear, or by an excessive moving and reconnecting of the drives.

Should the speed be incorrect, data will be written in the wrong location on the disk. The next time you access that area on the track again, the computer will hang up and give you a disk error. While disk speeds between 291 rpm and 309 rpm should be acceptable for Read/Write operation, speeds outside this range cause intermittent or disastrous results. If the speed becomes slower than 270 rpm or faster than 309 rpm, any Write action will erase the synchronization timing marks on the disk, making it useless unless you reinitialize the disk (wiping out the data you had stored).

There are two ways to tune up your drive speed. You can adjust the speed using a disk speed test program, or, if possible, you can adjust the speed using a standard room lamp. Both techniques require your removing the System Unit cover.

Method 1 (IBM PC and PC/XT)

This first disk speed program is for the IBM PC and IBM PC/XT. You start by removing the drive mechanism from the System Unit as discussed earlier. Lay it on its side, as shown in Fig. 10-8. Reconnect the cables to the drive so that it will run properly while on it's side.

CAUTION: Be careful not to touch the electronics inside the drive mechanism while the power is ON.

Turn on power to your computer and insert the disk containing the disk-speed test program into the drive to be adjusted. (Use a backup copy of the program.) Boot the disk in the drive and follow the test procedures outlined in the program's manual.

Most speed test programs display a graduated scale to show the drive's speed. If the speed is out of range, use a jeweler's screwdriver, or a "tweaker" (small screwdriver), and slowly turn the speed-control adjustment potentiometer screw, as shown in Fig. 10-9, until the speed display shows the actual rotation—as close to 300 rpm as possible (within plus or minus 6 milliseconds).

Remove the disk and turn off the power to the system. Disconnect the disk-drive cables and power-supply cable from the drive mechanism and replace the drive in the system, as discussed earlier.

Method 1 (IBM PC AT)

This second version of the use of a disk speed program is for the IBM PC AT. Again, you start by removing the cover to the System Unit, as outlined in Appendix B.

Fig. 10-8. The disk drive, set on its side, with the strobe wheel facing you.

> **CAUTION:** Be careful not to touch the electronics or inside the drive mechanism while the power is ON.

Turn on the computer and insert the disk containing a disk-speed test program into the drive to be adjusted. Boot the disk in the drive and follow the test procedures outlined in the program's manual.

As mentioned in the earlier method for the PC/XT, you should see a graduated scale on your monitor that shows the drive's speed. If the speed is out of range for proper operation, use a jeweler's screwdriver, or a "tweaker" (small screwdriver), and slowly turn the speed-control adjustment potentiometer screw until the speed display (Fig. 10-9) shows the actual rotation—as close to 300 rpm as possible (within plus or minus 6 milliseconds).

Remove the disk and turn off the power to the system. Reassemble the System Unit (refer to the instructions in Appendix B).

Fig. 10-9. Adjusting the speed adjustment potentiometer in a drive on the IBM PC/XT.

Method 2

The use of a tuning lamp enables disk-drive speed adjustments to be made without the need of a speed adust program. Unfortunately, the newer half-height drives, like those on the IBM AT, do not have the tuning-lamp speed-adjustment strobe wheel on the bottom of the drive. Therefore, the only way to adjust the speed on the AT (or one of the newer drives for your PC or XT) is to use Method 1.

However, if you do have the full-height drives, you can adjust the speed by disassembling the drive and setting it on its side, as shown in Fig. 10-8. Then, place an incandescent light lamp near the drive, so the light from the lamp illuminates the speed strobe wheel on the bottom of the drive mechanism (while the drive is running). Locate the timing marks on the strobe disk.

The outer circle of markings is used for the 60-Hz electrical systems common to the United States. The inner circle of strobe markings is used with 50-Hz line power, such as that found in Europe.

This concept of speed adjustment is amazingly simple and quite accurate. By placing the strobe disk in the light of an ordinary room lamp, and causing the disk to spin, you will notice that the strobe disk marks slowly rotate in one direction or another, depending on whether the disk speed is fast or slow. This action is much like the effect seen in a movie film when the stagecoach wheels seem to be rotating in the opposite direction to the movement of the coach. The wheels are rotating at a different speed than that of the film moving through the projector, so you see this weird effect.

The strobe marks on the strobe disk are spaced so they appear stationary when the speed is exactly 300 rpm. With a lighted lamp near the drive, power up the system and insert a blank formatted disk in the drive. Reset the system (CTRL, ALT, DEL), and observe the strobe wheel as the disk spins in the drive.

Using a jeweler's screwdriver or a "tweaker" (small screwdriver), adjust the speed-control potentiometer until the strobe disk seems to be sitting still. Then remove the disk and turn off the power to the computer. Reassemble the drive into the System Unit.

Disk-Drive Alignment

This procedure is not recommended for the novice. The alignment adjustments in the IBM drives set the positioning of the Read/Write head correctly over the tracks on the disk, adjust the disk stop guide, or adjust the collet hub that fits in the hole in your disks. These procedures require special equipment, including a dual-trace oscilloscope, special alignment disks, and various disk alignment tools not usually available to non-IBM repair people.

If a speed adjustment and cleaning doesn't clear up any Read/Write problems you may have, bite the bullet, and take your drive into a Service Center for maintenance.

The most critical alignment adjustment is the Read/Write head alignment, or tracking. Programs require a very accurate alignment of the head over the disk track. If the program loads fine but won't read data, and the disk just spins, you may have a track alignment problem. If you have had to replace the electronics analog card in the drive, you should have the tracking checked. Each card is tuned for the drive, and a new card could affect the head tracking.

Alignment should be checked every year. The easiest way to accomplish this is to format two disks on two different drives, whose speeds have been verified to be correct. Save some programs on each disk, using the same drive on which the formatting was done. Read and write each disk with its drive, to make sure that the individual drives work satisfactorily. Then switch disks and see if each disk works properly in the alternate drive. If one drive reads correctly while the other can't find the data or reads out "garbage," you know you have alignment problems.

Using Heat to Spot Troubles

Thermal Imaging

Imagine having an infrared picture taken of your Personal Computer system board, new and shiny, and operating on a certain program. Comparing this to a second photo taken a year later, when the system has started acting "flaky," shows you that in the middle of the board's RAM, there is a spot that is hotter than it was earlier, indicating that one of the memory chips is about to give out. Replacing this chip returns the system to peak operating potential.

A recent troubleshooting and preventive maintenance technique uses the temperature of the components to determine the condition of the system, much as a doctor takes the temperature of the human body to see if the person is ill. This technique is called "thermal imaging" or "thermography," and is proving to be a remarkably accurate preventive maintenance tool.

Standard photography produces images or pictures from visible light; thermal imaging produces pictures from the invisible heat coming up off the surface of objects. It's a cost-effective maintenance procedure in many large industrial plants.

Several companies sell expensive thermograph machines that will produce heat images in vivid color on high-resolution monitors. These units can measure temperatures all over a printed-circuit board, with a sensitivity of 0.1° C over a temperature range of 0–200° C. If any board has an area on it with a temperature outside specific limits, a computer comparison of the suspected board's temperature image with normal board temperatures will immediately point out the fault. These faults can be shorts, opens, and even marginally defective components. The thermograph units can even diagnose failures in high-density circuit boards—all without touching the board. What's the catch, you ask? Well, unfortunately, the machines cost thousands of dollars. But there's an alternative.

If you own a 35mm camera, you can do your own thermal imaging, using infrared (IR) heat-sensitive film. A good film to get is Kodak HIE-135-36, ASA-25 IR film. If you get color IR film, it is about 50% more expensive. A special filter (Wratten Number 87, 88A, or 89B) makes the picture more effective.

With your Personal Computer open, and running a simple program that continuously repeats, let the computer warm up for about two minutes to let the components reach operating temperatures. Then take a picture of the motherboard. Background light won't matter, because the film is sensitive to heat, not light. Take several shots.

Then, periodically (every 6 months, for example), or when the system starts acting up, take another series of pictures with the same program running in the computer. A comparison of the "before" and "after" pictures will quite likely point out where your system is wearing out, or has failed already.

Heat-Sensitive Liquid Crystals

Another useful technique for finding potential or actual troublespots in your computer is in the use of liquid crystals (LCs). Liquid crystals are organic compounds derived from cholesterol and they react to changes in temperature by changing color. This visual method for testing and evaluating the IBM PC circuit boards is available as a laminate (pressed-layer) film, or as a liquid solution. The liquid solution is recommended for circuit boards. The temperature range for measurement can be specified in increments of 1° C to 50° C, within an operating range of up to 150° C. A testing kit that includes sheets of film, different temperature-range liquid solutions, an aerosol can of black paint, applicator brushes, a sprayer, and solvent for surface and sprayer cleaning, is available from Liquid Crystal Applications, Inc., Clark, New Jersey, for about $250.

Typically, the surface to be tested is first cleaned of all oils and dirt, since these contaminants will give incorrect color readings. Then, it is dried, and the LC solution is brushed or sprayed onto the components and board, leaving a thin, even coat. When the circuit is powered up, the rainbow of colors pinpoint the hot spots on the board or components. If the heat generated at one place on the board doesn't follow the normal circuit heat-up pattern, a failure in that component area can be predicted. On connectors, excessive heat generation indicates a poor connection. Hot spots turn indigo blue, cooling to blue, turquoise, green, and down through yellow and orange to red, and, finally, gray.

The LC solution is useful for testing printed-circuit components for failing chips, solder shorts, and even solder-connection bonds that are breaking apart. The completeness of a bond can be detected by the color changes during normal operation; air in the bond cools more slowly than the surrounding metal. A dark surface shows the color changes best, so the manufacturer adds black dye to the LC solution.

When the test is completed, the solution can be wiped off with a lint-free cloth. The solution won't short out or contaminate the circuit board or the components.

Display Screens and Health Problems

For about 15 years now, this subject has been bandied about. Hobbyists, military and civilian radar operators, and, currently, word-processing operators struggle for answers to the nagging question of whether display screens are harmful to their health. Will long periods of staring at the face of a CRT screen damage the eyes? Is the radiation emitted by the CRT tube dangerous to the user?

The United States government has placed limits on the amount of X-radiation that can be allowed to escape out the face of a CRT tube. This limit is 0.5 milliroentgens per hour, when measured about 2 inches out from the screen. Manufacturers of CRTs added strontium and lead to the glass panels in television sets and monitors to eliminate almost all X-radiation escaping out the front of a display. Many intense tests were conducted by government and civilian organizations to determine how much radiation is emitted by video display terminals. The results were very encouraging. There was no evidence of any damaging radiation coming out of any of the displays tested. Measuring instruments recorded more radiation in the sunlight than in the CRT display light. The overwhelming conclusion by these researchers is that radiation from video displays doesn't threaten our vision.

There are some other issues that need our attention, however. Eyestrain, plus neck and back strains, can all be related to how we use the computer systems. Eyestrain can be caused by what type of display we use. Older screens displayed harsh white letters. Looking at a high-contrast screen of letters and numbers for a long time can cause eye fatigue, headaches, and neck and back strain. Eye fatigue can result from looking at those bright, white letters and numbers on a dark, black, background screen. New CRT phosphors allow the use of green (and now, amber) displays, significantly reducing eyestrain problems. Room light reflections were also linked to eyestrain, so recommendations were made that display terminal users work in a well-lighted room and use nonreflective screens applied to the front of their CRT display screens.

Eye strain can also occur if you set your display monitor to one side of your keyboard, such that you view the screen at a slight angle. The distance between each eye to the screen is slightly different, causing each eye to focus separately. This places a strain on the eye muscles. It's best to look straight on at the display screen.

Neck and back strain, and even some emotional problems have been related to long periods of using a display screen. These issues are being resolved by redesigning the operator work place and work procedures. Poorly designed desks and poor working environments affect computer-operator output. In addition, managers sometimes fail to apply good work practices for people "stuck" on a console for hours on end. Since most managers use computer screens a limited part of each day, it's difficult for them to appreciate the problems that full-time computer operators experience. This may explain why many managers can't relate to display-screen effects on workers and are unsympathetic to their complaints.

Many things can help solve these problems. Display monitors that can tilt and swivel can be used to improve user comfort. Detachable keyboards also help the user to be comfortable. Monitor-height positions that are adjustable, and glare-reducing screens, have become standard for display devices. Also, room lighting can be redesigned for optimum display-screen viewing.

You, as the operator, can act to reduce much of your own eye, neck, or back strain by simply using a hard-back chair instead of a soft, "cushy," slouch-producing recliner. Make sure that you can look straight on at the screen (eyes perpendicular to the screen) and be sure to take frequent, short, rest breaks. When taking a break, stretch for a moment. Develop some simple physical exercises to move unused muscles.

Keep the room well-lighted but not harshly bright. Try using a desk lamp with an incandescent bulb and have it shining on your work and keyboard area from the side. You can also keep an overhead light, both on for background lighting and to cut glare. Set your display unit at a height that feels comfortable for viewing. You'll know if it's correct after a few hours at the keyboard. Adjust the display height as often as necessary. Have your eyes examined at least annually (6 months is better). If you wear glasses, the doctor can prescribe lightly tinted lenses (light blue or light green), which can help to reduce eye strain. You can also increase your intake of foods that are high in Vitamin A (carrots and squash, for example—the "yellow" foods).

There are over 15 million video display units in use today, and twice that many are expected to be in use within two years. As prices come down, perhaps it's time to consider trading in that old, clunky, black-and-white display unit for a new green or amber unit that will serve you better.

Warranties and Service Contracts

Many companies offer service contracts for after-warranty support. If your system is still under warranty, be advised that removing components, and trying to troubleshoot and fix a problem yourself, may void the warranty.

After your warranty runs out, a service contract is advisable if you use your system a lot (like everyday, all day). Getting a contract on an older system may also be wise. Older systems and systems that are used a lot tend to break down more often. A service contract enables you to have the proper maintenance and repair at hand when needed. Service contracts can get expensive, however, depending on how much equipment you want covered and for how long.

If you don't use your system a lot and it isn't old (past 5 years is old), you don't really need a service contract. Also, if you have equipment like oscilliscopes and meters, then you would be better off trying to fix the problem yourself, using books like this one and the *IBM PC Advanced Troubleshooting & Repair* guide (also sold by Howard W Sams & Company).

Summary

This chapter has covered every aspect of routine preventive maintenance necessary to keep the IBM PC, PC/XT, and PC AT systems in peak operating condition. You can find a recommended schedule for routine maintenance at the end of Appendix B. With preventive maintenance, you can keep your system in top shape, always ready when you need it. Remember the six contributors to computer system failures: excessive temperature, dust build-up, noise interference, power-line problems, corrosion, and magnetic fields. For each of these factors, you need to routinely perform some kind of preventive maintenance. Keeping your drives clean and up to par will reduce the chance of you having a large problem occur down the road.

Questions for Review and Discussion

1. How does heat affect long-term system operation?
2. How should a computer system be cleaned?
3. Name four contributors to system failure.
4. What's the difference between EMI and RFI?
5. If I pass a printer cable through a coiled power cable, what form of interference could result?
6. Describe four ways to combat ESD.
7. Describe the four types of uninterrupted power supplies.
8. Name ten ways to extend the life of your disk media.
9. How often should floppy disk drives be cleaned?
10. What are the effects of long-term computer use?

Appendixes

Error Indicators

A number of things can cause a microcomputer to "boot" improperly or not "boot" at all—wrong diskette in the drive, no operating system on the diskette, cables loose, adapter card not fully seated, disk-drive failure, memory chip bad, no clock pulses, or even an unplugged power cord. These system errors will be detected during start-up, and will be indicated by an audible beep, an error-code display, or a completely dead system. In each case, the "boot" process is not completed.

Four types of error indications can occur during the initialization or start-up process—beep indicators from the built-in speaker, system error-code displays, I/O error-code displays, and other error displays. These indicators assist in isolating a failure to a module, subunit, or peripheral.

System error indications are categorized by IBM as shown in Table A-1. Other tables list other error signs.

Table A-1.   System Error Indications

Problem Type	Error Code	Problem Identification
Nothing indicated or an audible beep.	No display.	Undetermined, or as specified by the beep code.
Error code display.	02X	Power.
	1XX	System Board.
	20X	Memory.
	30X	Keyboard.
	4XX	Monochrome display.
	5XX	Color/graphics display.
	6XX	Floppy disk drive.
	9XX	Printer adapter.
	11XX	Asynchronous communications card.

Table A-1. *(cont.)*   System Error Indications

Problem Type	Error Code	Problem Identification
	12XX	Alternate asynchronous communications card.
	13XX	Game control adapter.
	14XX	Printer.
	15XX	SDLC communications adapter.
	17XX	Fixed disk drive.
	18XX	Expansion unit.
	XXXXX ROM	Read-only memory table.

These error indications can be further diagnosed using the following tables. Table A-2 provides a listing of the audible-beep error conditions that can occur during the power-on self test (POST).

Table A-2.   Audible Beep Indicators

Indicator	Problem Area
No beep, nothing happens.	Power, power supply.
Continuous beep.	Power, power supply.
Repeating short beep.	Power, power supply.
1 short beep, blank or incorrect display.	Display circuitry.
1 short beep, Cassette BASIC displayed, no disk boot.	Diskette, drive.
1 long, and 1 short beep.	System Board.
1 long, and 2 short beeps.	Display circuit.
1 long, and 3 short beeps.	EGA card.

Error codes printed on the screen can either be stand-alone codes or can appear in conjunction with amplifying information. Table A-3 describes the error-code displays for various system and I/O malfunctions.

Table A-3.   Error-Code Displays

Code	Problem Area
02X	Power-suppy problem.
100	Option configuration wrong.
101	System Board interrupt circuitry.
102	System Board timer circuitry.
103	System Board timer interrupt.
104	System Board protected mode.
105	System Board last 8042 command.
106	System Board converting logic test.
107	System Board NMI test.
108	System Board timer bus test.
109	DMA test error.

Table A-3. *(cont.)*   Error-Code Displays

Code		Problem Area
121		Unexpected hardware interrupt.
131		Cassette port error.
161		System options (run SETUP). Could be battery failure.
162		System options incorrect (run SETUP).
163		Time and date not set (run SETUP).
164		Memory size setting incorrect (run SETUP).
991		User indicated configuration not correct.
	199 100	Software option configuration wrong. Check switches.
2xx		RAM memory error.
201		Memory test failure.
	xxxx = 201	Memory failure.
	1055 = 201	DIP switches set wrong.
	2055 = 201	DIP switches set wrong.
	xxxx = 201 PARITY CHECK X	RAM chip malfunction.
202		Memory address error.
203		Memory address error.
3xx		Keyboard errors.
301		Keyboard malfunction. (Keyboard cable disconnected, or keyboard did not respond to S/W reset.)
	xx301	Keyboard circuitry malfunction (e.g., stuck key; xx is the hex value representing the scan code of the malfunctioning key).
49 301		Key 73 (49H = 73 decimal) bad.
302		User-indicated error from keyboard test, or AT keyboard is locked.
303		Keyboard or System Unit error.
304		Keyboard or System Unit error; CMOS RAM configuration does not match system.
4xx		Monochrome adapter card error.
401		Monochrome memory, horizontal sync frequency, or video test failed.
408		User-indicated display attribute failure.
416		User-indicated character set failure.
424		User-indicated 80-by-25 mode failure.
432		Parallel port test failure (monochrome adapter card).
5xx		Color/graphics adapter card failure.
501		Color memory test, horizontal sync frequency, or video test failure.
508		User-indicated display attribute failure.
516		User-indicated character set failure.
524		80-by-25 mode failure.
532		40-by-25 mode failure.
540		320-by-200 graphics mode failure.
548		640-by-200 graphics mode failure.
6xx		Diskette drive errors.
601		Diskette power-on diagnostics test failure (interface malfunction).
602		Diskette test failure.
606		Disk verify function failure.

Table A-3. *(cont.)*   Error-Code Displays

Code	Problem Area
607	Diskette is write-protected, disk not inserted properly, write-protect switch is bad, analog card malfunction.
608	Diskette is bad (bad disk status returned).
610	Diskette initialization failure.
611	Drive data cable or disk-drive adapter card is bad (timeout failure).
612	Drive data cable or disk-drive adapter card is bad (bad 765 FDC indicated).
613	Drive data cable or disk-drive adapter card is bad (DMA failure indicated).
621	Drive assembly seek failure.
622	Drive assembly CRC failure.
623	Drive assembly; record not found.
624	Drive assembly; bad address mark.
625	Drive assembly; bad FDC seek.
626	Drive assembly; data compare error.
7xx	Coprocessor error.
9xx	Parallel printer adapter error.
901	Parallel printer adapter test failure. (Could be printer itself bad.)
10xx	Reserved for parallel printer adapter.
11xx	Asynchronous communications adapter error.
1101	Asynchronous communications adapter test failure.
12xx	Alternate asynchronous communications adapter errors.
1201	Alternate asynchronous communications adapter test failure.
13xx	Game control adapter card.
1301	Game control adapter test failure.
1302	Joystick test failure.
14xx	Printer interface errors.
1401	Printer test failure.
1404	Matrix printer failure.
15xx	Synchronous data-link control (SDLC) communications adapter error.
1510	8255 Port B failure.
1511	8255 Port A failure.
1512	8255 Port C failure.
1513	8253 Timer 1 did not reach terminal count.
1514	8253 Timer 1 stuck.
1515	8253 Timer 0 did not reach terminal count.
1516	8253 Timer 0 stuck.
1517	8253 Timer 2 did not reach terminal count.
1518	8253 Timer 2 stuck.
1519	8273 Port B error.
1520	8273 Port A error.
1521	8273 command/read timeout.
1522	Interrupt level-4 failure.
1523	Ring Indicate stuck.
1524	Receive clock stuck.
1525	Transmit clock stuck.

Table A-3. *(cont.)*   Error-Code Displays

Code	Problem Area
1526	Test Indicate stuck.
1527	Ring Indicate not on.
1528	Receive clock not on.
1529	Transmit clock not on.
1530	Test Indicate is not on.
1531	Data Set Ready not on.
1532	Carrier Detect not on.
1533	Clear To Send not on.
1534	Data Set Ready stuck.
1536	Clear To Send stuck.
1537	Level-3 interrupt failure.
1538	Receive interrupt results error.
1539	Wrap data didn't compare.
1540	DMA channel 1 error.
1541	DMA channel 1 error.
1542	8273 error checking or status reporting failure.
1547	Stray interrupt level 4.
1548	Stray interrupt level 3.
1549	Interrupt presentation sequence timeout.
16xx	Display emulation errors (327x, 5520, 525x).
17xx	Fixed disk drive errors.
1701	Fixed disk POST error.
1702	Fixed disk drive adapter error.
1703	Fixed disk drive error.
1704	Fixed disk adapter or drive error.
1780	Fixed disk 0 failure.
1781	Fixed disk 1 failure.
1782	Fixed disk controller failure.
1790	Fixed disk 0 error.
1791	Fixed disk 1 error.
18xx	I/O expansion unit or cable to expansion unit errors.
1801	I/O expansion unit POST error.
1810	Enable/disable failure.
1811	Extender card wrap test failed (disabled).
1812	High-order address lines failure (disabled).
1813	Wait-state failure (disabled).
1814	Enable/disable could not be set.
1815	Wait-state failure (enabled).
1816	Extender card wrap test failed (enabled).
1817	High-order address lines failure (enabled).
1818	Disable not functioning.
1819	Wait request switch not set correctly.
1820	Receiver card wrap test failure; expansion unit cable failure.
1821	Receiver high-order address lines failure.
19xx	3270 PC attachment card errors.
20xx	Binary synchronous communications adapter errors.
2010	8255 Port A failure.
2011	8255 Port B failure.
2012	8255 Port C failure.

Table A-3. *(cont.)*   Error-Code Displays

Code	Problem Area
2013	8253 Timer 1 did not reach terminal count.
2014	8253 Timer 1 stuck on.
2016	8253 Timer 2 did not reach terminal count or Timer 2 stuck on.
2017	Data Set Ready failed to come on.
2018	8251 Clear To Send not sensed.
2019	8251 Data Set Ready stuck on.
2020	8251 Clear To Send stuck on.
2021	8251 hardware Reset failed.
2022	8251 software Reset failed.
2023	8251 software "error reset" failed.
2024	8251 Transmit Ready did not come on.
2025	8251 Receive Ready did not come on.
2026	8251 could not force "overrun" error status.
2027	Interrupt failure—no timer interrupt.
2028	Interrupt failure—transmit, replace card or planar.
2029	Interrupt failure—transmit, replace card.
2030	Interrupt failure—receive, replace card or planar.
2031	Interrupt failure—receive, replace card.
2033	Ring Indicate stuck on.
2034	Receive clock stuck on.
2035	Transmit clock stuck on.
2036	Test Indicate stuck on.
2037	Ring Indicate not on.
2038	Receive clock not on.
2039	Transmit clock not on.
2040	Test Indicate not on.
2041	Data Set Ready not on.
2042	Carrier Detect not on.
2043	Clear To Send not on.
2044	Data Set Ready stuck on.
2045	Carrier Detect stuck on.
2046	Clear To Send stuck on.
2047	Unexpected transmit interrupt.
2048	Unexpected receive interrupt.
2049	Transmit data did not equal receive data.
2050	8251 detected overrun error.
2051	Lost Data Set Ready during data wrap.
2052	Receive timeout during data wrap.
21xx	Alternate binary synchronous communications adapter errors.
2110	8255 Port A failure.
2111	8255 Port B failure.
2112	8255 Port C failure.
2113	8253 Timer 1 did not reach terminal count.
2114	8253 Timer 1 stuck on.
2115	8253 Timer 2 did not reach terminal count or Timer 2 stuck on.
2116	Data Set Ready failed to come on.
2117	8251 Clear To Send not sensed.
2118	8251 Data Set Ready stuck on.

Table A-3. *(cont.)*   Error-Code Displays

Code	Problem Area
2119	8251 Clear To Send stuck on.
2120	8251 hardware Reset failed.
2121	8251 software Reset failed.
2122	8251 software "error reset" failed.
2123	8251 Transmit Ready did not come on.
2124	8251 Receive Ready did not come on.
2125	8251 could not force "overrun" error status.
2126	Interrupt failure—no timer interrupt.
2128	Interrupt failure—transmit, replace card or planar.
2129	Interrupt failure—transmit, replace card.
2130	Interrupt failure—receive, replace card or planar.
2131	Interrupt failure—receive, replace card.
2133	Ring Indicate stuck on.
2134	Receive clock stuck on.
2135	Transmit clock stuck on.
2136	Test Indicate stuck on.
2137	Ring Indicate not on.
2138	Receive clock not on.
2139	Transmit clock not on.
2140	Test Indicate is not on.
2141	Data Set Ready not on.
2142	Carrier Detect not on.
2143	Clear To Send not on.
2144	Data Set Ready stuck on.
2145	Carrier Detect stuck on.
2146	Clear To Send stuck on.
2147	Unexpected transmit interrupt.
2148	Unexpected receive interrupt.
2149	Transmit data did not equal receive data.
2150	8251 detected overrun error.
2151	Lost Data Set Ready during data wrap.
2152	Receive timeout during data wrap.
22xx	Cluster adapter errors.
24xx	Enhanced graphics adapter errors.
29xx	Color matrix printer errors.
30xx	Primary PC network adapter error.
3001	CPU failure.
3002	ROM failure.
3003	ID failure.
3004	RAM failure.
3005	HIC failure.
3006	± 12-V failure.
3007	Digital loopback failure.
3008	Host-detected HIC failure.
3009	Sync failure and No-Go bit.
3010	HIC test OK and No-Go bit.
3011	Go bit and no CMD 41.
3012	Card not present.
3013	Digital failure (fall through).
3015	Analog failure.
3041	Hot carrier (not this card).

Table A-3. *(cont.)*   Error-Code Displays

Code	Problem Area
3042	Hot carrier (THIS CARD!!).
31xx	Secondary network adapter error.
3101	CPU failure.
3102	ROM failure.
3103	ID failure.
3104	RAM failure.
3105	HIC failure.
3106	± 12-V failure.
3107	Digital loopback failure.
3108	Host-detected HIC failure.
3109	Sync failure and No-Go bit.
3110	HIC test OK and No-Go bit.
3111	Go bit and no CMD 41.
3112	Card not present.
3113	Digital failure (fall through).
3115	Analog failure.
3141	Hot carrier (not this card).
3142	Hot carrier (THIS CARD!!).
33xx	Compact printer errors.

A special code is also displayed when a ROM failure occurs. Depending on the computer, ROM failure codes will be displayed as shown in Table A-4.

Table A-4.   ROM Error Codes

Display	Problem ROM
F600 ROM	Cassette BASIC ROM (U29).
F800 ROM	Cassette BASIC ROM (U30).
FA00 ROM	Cassette BASIC ROM (U31).
FC00 ROM	Cassette BASIC ROM (U32).
C8000	Hard-disk adapter ROM.
F0000	System Board failure.
F1000	System Board failure.
F2000	System Board failure.
F3000	System Board failure.
F4000	Empty socket (U28); System Board failure.
F5000	Empty socket (U28); System Board failure.
F6000	Cassette BASIC ROM.
F7000	Cassette BASIC ROM.
F8000	Cassette BASIC ROM.
F9000	Cassette BASIC ROM.
FA000	Cassette BASIC ROM.
FB000	Cassette BASIC ROM.
FC000	Cassette BASIC ROM.

If a RAM failure or parity error is detected, a special error code, followed by the number 201, will appear in the top left corner of the monitor screen. The value 201 identifies a RAM failure; the four-character code preceding the 201 defines the bank and row of memory ICs in which the bad RAM was detected. The first two characters of the four-character code refer to the memory bank, and the last two characters refer to the "bit" position in the RAM bank that failed. For example, if a failure occurs in Bit Position 5 of Bank 1, in a 16K RAM chip system, a 0420 201 error code will appear.

RAM-memory error codes are given in Table A-5. If the third and fourth characters of the error code don't match the code given in the table, swap the entire bank of RAM chips and try again. A cost-saving way to find the bad RAM is to power-down the system and, then, swap each chip, one at a time, with the corresponding bit in an adjacent row. Then, power up and retest. See if the failure has moved to the new bank. The last chip swapped before the failure changed banks is the bad RAM.

Table A-5.   RAM-Memory Failure Error Codes*

System Board Memory Bank (XX)	Failed Chip (XX 201 Parity Check 1)
00 = Bank 0	00 = Parity
04 = Bank 1	01 = D0 chip
08 = Bank 2	02 = D1 chip
0C = Bank 3	04 = D2 chip
	08 = D3 chip
	10 = D4 chip
	20 = D5 chip
	40 = D6 chip
	80 = D7 chip

*For the IBM PC and IBM PC/XT (16K chip). For the 64K RAM memory, refer to Table 7-4, Chapter 7.

B

Miscellaneous Technical Information

The following is an index of the technical information contained in this appendix.

Data Sheet (IBM PC)

Computer: IBM Personal Computer

Manufacturer: IBM Corporation, Armonk, New York

Size: 19.6″ × 16.1″ × 5.5″

Weight: 20.9 pounds without disk drive installed

Power Required: 63.5 watts (maximum)
                        110/220 volts

CPU: 8088 Microprocessor

Data Word Size: 8 bits

CPU Clock Speed: 4.77 MHz

Memory Size: 40K ROM
                     16K–256K bytes on system board
                     1 Mbyte directly addressable memory

Mass Storage Capability: Two disk drives internally
                                 Two disk drives externally
                                 160K bytes—single density
                                 320K bytes—double density

Keyboard Size: 83 keys
                       256 character codes

Display Capability: Monochrome display (MDA)
                            Color graphics display (CGA)
                            Enhanced graphics display (EGA)
                            Professional graphics display (PGA)

Input/Output: Five 62-pin expansion slots
                      Cassette connector
                      2¼-inch speaker
                      Auxiliary power connection
                      Detachable keyboard

Standard Software: PC-DOS Cassette BASIC

Optional Software: MS-DOS
                           Cassette BASIC
                           Advanced BASIC

Data Sheet (IBM PC/XT)

Computer: IBM Personal Computer Enhanced Technology

Manufacturer: IBM Corporation, Armonk, New York

Size: 20″ × 16″ × 5.5″

Weight: 32 pounds

Power Required: 139 watts (maximum)
110/220 volts

CPU: 8088 Microprocessor

Data Word Size: 8 bits

CPU Clock Speed: 4.77 MHz

Memory Size: 40K ROM
256K bytes on system board
1 Mbyte directly addressable memory

Mass Storage Capability: Two disk drives internally
Two disk drives externally
160K bytes—single density
320K bytes—double density
10 Mbytes—hard disk

Keyboard Size: 83 keys, 10 function keys
256 character codes

Display Capability: Monochrome display (MDA)
Color graphics display (CGA)
Enhanced graphics display (EGA)
Professional graphics display (PGA)

Input/Output: Eight 62-pin expansion slots
Detachable keyboard
2¼-inch speaker
Auxiliary power connection

Standard Software: PC-DOS Cassette BASIC (in ROM)

Optional Software: MS-DOS
Disk BASIC
Advanced BASIC

Data Sheet (IBM PC AT)

Computer: IBM Personal Computer Enhanced Technology

Manufacturer: IBM Corporation, Armonk, New York

Size: 21.25″ × 17.28″ × 6.38″

Weight: 37 pounds

Power Required: 192 watts (maximum)
110/220 volts

CPU: 80286 Microprocessor

Data Word Size: 8 and 16 bits

CPU Clock Speed: 6, 8, and 12 MHz

Memory Size: 40K ROM
512K bytes on system board
1 Mbyte directly addressable memory
16 Mbyte of 1.2 gigabyte virtual memory in protected mode

Mass Storage Capability: Three disk drives internally
Two disk drives externally
160K bytes—single density
320K bytes—double density
800K bytes—high density
20–30M bytes—hard disk

Keyboard Size: 84, 101 keys
256 character codes

Display Capability: Monochrome display (MDA)
Color graphics display (CGA)
Enhanced graphics display (EGA)
Professional graphics display (PGA)

Input/Output: Eight 62-pin expansion slots (six have 36-pin enhancement)
Auxiliary power connection
Detachable keyboard
2¼-inch speaker

Standard Software: PC-DOS

Optional Software: MS-DOS
Pascal
FORTRAN
C
COBOL

System-Board Chips (IBM PC)

The following list comprises the devices contained on the IBM PC System Board. Remember to maintain the series code and suffix requirement for the replacement chips.

Label	Integrated Circuit	Description
U1	MC1741	General-purpose operational amplifier
U2	8259	Programmable interrupt controller
U3	8088	Microprocessor
U4	8087	Numeric data processor
U5	74LS30	8-input NAND gate
U6	8288	Bus controller
U7	74LS373	Octal transparent latch
U8	74LS245	TRI-STATE® octal transceiver
U9	74LS373	Octal transparent latch
U10	74LS373	Octal transparent latch
U11	8284	Clock generator
U12	74LS245	TRI-STATE® octal transceiver
U13	74LS245	TRI-STATE® octal transceiver
U14	74LS245	TRI-STATE® octal transceiver
U15	74LS244	TRI-STATE® octal buffer
U16	74LS244	TRI-STATE® octal buffer
U17	74LS244	TRI-STATE® octal buffer
U18	74LS373	Octal transparent latch
U19	74LS670	TRI-STATE® 4 by 4 register file
U20	RN1	4.7K DIP resistor network
U21	SW1	DIP switch
U22	RN2	2K DIP resistor network
U23	74LS244	TRI-STATE® octal buffer
U24	74LS322	8-bit serial/parallel-in register with sign extend
U25	SW2	DIP switch
U26	74LS175	Quad-D flip-flop
U27	74LS02	Quad 2-input NOR gate
U28	Empty	Spare ROM socket
U29	9264 ROM	8K by 8-bit static ROM
U30	9264 ROM	8K by 8-bit static ROM
U31	9264 ROM	8K by 8-bit static ROM
U32	9264 ROM	8K by 8-bit static ROM
U33	9264 ROM	8K by 8-bit static ROM
U34	8253	Programmable interval timer
U35	8237	DMA controller
U36	8255	Programmable peripheral interface
U37–U45	4164 RAM	64K by 1-bit dynamic RAM
U46	74LS138	1/8 decoder/demultiplexer
U47	74LS138	1/8 decoder/demultiplexer
U48	74LS138	1/8 decoder/demultiplexer
U49	74LS08	Quad 2-input AND gate
U50	74LS02	Quad 2-input NOR gate
U51	74LS04	Hex inverter
U52	74LS00	Quad 2-input NAND gate
U53–U61	4164 RAM	64K by 1-bit dynamic RAM
U62	74LS158	Quad 2-input data selector/multiplexer
U63	74LS38	Quad 2-input NAND buffer

Label	Integrated Circuit	Description
U64	74LS20	Dual 4-input NAND gate
U65	74LS138	1/8 decoder/demultiplexer
U66	74LS138	1/8 decoder/demultiplexer
U67	74LS74	Dual-D flip-flop
U68	RN3	4.7K DIP resistor network
U69–U77	4164 RAM	64K by 1-bit dynamic RAM
U78	RN4	30-ohm DIP resistor network
U79	74LS158	Quad 2-input data selector/multiplexer
U80	74LS125	Quad TRI-STATE® buffer
U81	74S00	Quad 2-input NAND gate
U82	74S74	Dual-D flip-flop
U83	74LS04	Hex inverter
U84	74LS10	Triple 3-input NAND gate
U85–U93	4164 RAM	64K by 1-bit dynamic RAM
U94	74LS04	Hex inverter
U95	75477	Relay driver
U96	74LS74	Dual-D flip-flop
U97	74S08	Quad 2-input AND gate
U98	74LS175	Quad-D flip-flop
U99	74LS04	Hex inverter

System-Board Chips (IBM PC/XT)

The following listing comprises the devices contained on the IBM PC/XT System Board. Remember to maintain the series code and suffix requirement for the replacement chips.

Label	Integrated Circuit	Description
U1	8284	Clock generator
U2	74LS245	Octal transceiver
U3	8088	Microprocessor
U4	8087	Numeric processor extension
U5	74LS373	Octal latch
U6	74LS244	TRI-STATE® octal buffer
U7	74LS373	Octal latch
U8	8288	System controller and bus driver
U9	72LS245	Octal transceiver
U10	74LS670	4-by-4 register file
U11	74LS373	Octal latch
U12	74LS244	TRI-STATE® octal buffer
U13	74LS243	Quad transceiver
U14	74LS244	TRI-STATE® octal buffer
U15	74LS245	Octal transceiver
U16	74LS244	TRI-STATE® octal buffer
U17	74LS244	TRI-STATE® octal buffer
U18	MK38036N	ROM
U19	5000027	ROM
U20	74S280	9-bit odd/even parity generator/checker

Label	Integrated Circuit	Description
U21	74LS175	Quad-D flip-flop
U22	74LS04	Hex inverter
U23	74LS27	Triple 3-input NOR gate
U24	74LS00	Quad 2-input NAND gate
U25	8259	Programmable interrupt controller
U26	8253	Programmable interval timer
U27	74LS322	8-bit shift register
U28	8237/9517A	DMA controller
U29	8255	Programmable peripheral interface
U30–U38	4164	64K by 1-bit dynamic RAM
U39	74LS158	Quad 2-input data selector/multiplexer
U40	74LS158	Quad 2-input data selector/multiplexer
U41	74LS244	TRI-STATE® octal buffer
U42	74LS138	1/8 decoder/demultiplexer
U43	74LS138	1/8 decoder/demultiplexer
U44	TBP2410	ROM
U45	74LS138	1/8 decoder/demultiplexer
U46–U54	4164	64K by 1-bit dynamic RAM
U55	74S08	Quad 2-input AND gate
U56	74S138	1/8 decoder/demultiplexer
U57	74LS20	Dual 4-input NAND gate
U58	74LS32	Quad 2-input OR gate
U59–U67	3764	64K by 1-bit dynamic RAM
U68	7407	Hex buffer/driver
U69	74S00	Quad 2-input NAND gate
U70	74S74	Hex inverter
U71	74LS04	Hex inverter
U72	74LS10	Triple 3-input NAND gate
U73	74LS74	Dual-D flip-flop
U74	74LS00	Quad 2-input NAND gate
U75–U83	M3764	64K by 1-bit dynamic RAM
U84	74LS158	Quad 2-input data selector/multiplexer
U85	75477	Dual peripheral NAND driver
U86	74LS74	Dual-D flip-flop
U87	74S08	Qual 2-input AND gate
U88	74LS175	Quad-D flip-flop
U89	74LS04	Hex inverter
U90	74LS32	Quad 2-input OR gate

System-Board Chips (IBM PC AT)

The following listing comprises the devices contained on the IBM PC AT System Board. Remember to maintain the series code and suffix requirement for the replacement chips.

Label	Integrated Circuit	Description
U1–U4	ZA1250NL	RAM
U5	74ALS245	Octal transceiver
U6	74F280	9-bit odd/even parity generator/checker
U7–U10	ZA1250NL	RAM
U11	74ALS245	Octal transceiver
U12	74F280	9-bit odd/even parity generator/checker
U13–U16	ZA1250NL	RAM
U17	MK38097N	32K by 8-bit ROM
U18	8284	Clock generator
U19–U26	ZA1250NL	RAM
U27	MK38097N	32K by 8-bit ROM
U28–U36	ZA1250NL	RAM
U37	74LS590	8-bit binary counter
U38	74ALS245	Octal transceiver
U39–U46	ZA1250NL	RAM
U47	TMM23256P	32K by 8-bit ROM
U48	74ALS245	Octal transceiver
U49	74ALS244	TRI-STATE® octal buffer
U50	74F241	Octal buffer
U51	74F74	Dual-D flip-flop
U52	75477	Dual peripheral NAND driver
U53	74F10	Triple 3-input NAND gate
U54	74F158	Quad 2-input data selector/multiplexer
U55	74F158	Quad 2-input data selector/multiplexer
U56	74ALS573	Octal-D transparent latch
U57	74F10	Triple 3-input NAND gate
U58	74F10	Triple 3-input NAND gate
U59	74F08	Quad 2-input AND gate
U60	74ALS573	Octal-D transparent latch
U61		Time delay
U62	74S51	Dual 2-wide 2-input AND/OR/Invert gate
U63	74F20	Dual 4-input NAND gate
U64	74ALS573	Octal-D transparent latch
U65	74ALS245	Octal transceiver
U66	74ALS245	Octal transceiver
U67	74LS646	Octal bus transceiver/register
U68	74ALS74	Dual-D flip-flop
U69	74LS51	Dual 2-wide 2-input AND/OR/Invert gate
U70	74F11	Triple 3-input AND gate
U71	74F139	Dual 1/4 decoder/demultiplexer
U72	TBP2842	512K by 8-bit PROM
U73	74ALS573	Octal-D transparent latch
U74	80286	Microprocessor
U75	74ALS244	TRI-STATE® octal buffer
U76	80287	Numeric processor extension
U77	74F74	Dual-D flip-flop
U78	74S51	Dual 2-wide 2-input AND/OR/Invert gate

Label	Integrated Circuit	Description
U79	74LS125	Quad 3-state buffer
U80	74ALS32	Quad 2-input OR gate
U81	74ALS04	Hex inverter
U82	82284	Clock generator
U83	82288	Bus controller
U84	74ALS27	Triple 3-input NOR gate
U85	74LS51	Dual 2-wide 2-input AND/OR/Invert gate
U86	74F74	Dual-D flip-flop
U87	1501824	Programmable array logic (PAL)
U88	74LS112	Dual JK flip-flop
U89	74LS245	Octal transceiver
U90	74ALS74	Dual-D flip-flip
U91	74ALS02	Quad 2-input NOR gate
U92	74F08	Quad 2-input AND gate
U93	74F74	Dual-D flip-flop
U94	74ALS00	Quad 2-input NAND gate
U95	74F175	Quad-D flip-flop
U96	74F00	Quad 2-input NAND gate
U97	74F10	Triple 3-input NAND gate
U98	74ALS10	Triple 3-input NAND gate
U99	74ALS02	Quad 2-input NOR gate
U100	74F175	Quad-D flip-flop
U101	74ALS573	Octal-D transparent latch
U102	74ALS245	Octal transceiver
U103	8254	Programmable interval timer
U104	74ALS74	Dual-D flip-flop
U105	74ALS74	Dual-D flip-flop
U106	74ALS74	Dual-D flip-flop
U107	74ALS04	Hex inverter
U108	MC14069/4069	Inverter
U109	74ALS74	Dual-D flip-flop
U110	74ALS08	Quad 2-input AND gate
U111	8237/9517A	DMA controller
U112	74ALS573	Octal-D transparent latch
U113	74ALS245	Octal transceiver
U114	8259	Programmable interrupt controller
U115	63081	PROM
U116	7407	Hex buffer/driver
U117	MC14681/4681	Clock/configuration RAM
U118	74ALS74	Dual-D flip-flop
U119	74F174	Hex-D flip-flop
U120	74ALS00	Quad 2-input NAND gate
U121	74ALS04	Hex inverter
U122	8237/9517	DMA controller
U123	74ALS138	1/8 decoder/demultiplexer
U124	74LS612	Memory mapper
U125	8259	Programmable interrupt controller
U126	8042/P86421505	Keyboard controller
U127	74ALS175	Quad-D flip-flop
U128	74ALS244	TRI-STATE® octal buffer
U129	74F257	Quad 2-line to 1-line data selector/ multiplexer
U130	1503135	Programmable array logic (PAL)

Board-Mounted Frequency Standards

The following list gives the crystals used in the IBM Personal Computers.

Unit	Label	Device	Description
IBM PC	X1	Crystal	14.31818-MHz crystal oscillator
IBM PC/XT	Y1	Crystal	14.31818 MHz
IBM PC AT	Y1	Crystal	14.31818 MHz
IBM PC AT	Y2	Crystal	12 MHz
IBM PC AT	Y3	Crystal	32.768 MHz

Monochrome Monitor/Printer Adapter Chips

The following list comprises the integrated circuits contained on the Monochrome Monitor/Printer Adapter board. Remember to maintain the series code and suffix requirement for the replacement chips.

Label	Integrated Circuit	Description
U1	74LS74	Dual-D edge-triggered flip-flop
U2	74LS04N	Hex inverter
U3	74LS08	Quad 2-input AND gate
U4	74LS74	Dual-D edge-triggered flip-flop
U6	74LS10	Triple 3-input NAND gate
U7	74LS139	1-of-8 decoder/demultiplexer
U8-U15	2114	1K by 4-bit SRAM
U16-U18	74LS157	Quad 2-to-1 multiplexer
U19	74LS244	Three-state octal buffer
U20, U21	74LS374	Three-state octal-D flip-flop
U22	74LS244	Three-state octal buffer
U23	74LS245	Three-state octal bus transceiver
U24	74LS153	Dual 4-to-1 multiplexer
U25	74LS00	Quad 2-input NAND gate
U26	74S11	Triple 3-input AND gate
U27	74LS02	Quad 2-input NOR gate
U28	74LS393	Dual binary ripple counter
U29	74LS175	Quad D-Type flip-flop with Reset
U30	74LS273	Octal D-Type flip-flop with Reset
U31	74LS273	Octal D-Type flip-flop with Reset
U32	74LS166	8-bit Parallel-In/Serial-Out shift register
U33	MK36906	8K character generator ROM
U34	74LS273	Octal D-type flip-flop with Reset
U35	MC6845	CRT controller
U36	74LS125	Quad 3-state buffer
U37	74LS240	Octal 3-state inverter buffer
U38	7405	Open-collector hex inverter
U39	74LS174	Hex-D flip-flop with Reset
U40	74LS244	Octal buffer (3-state)
U41	74LS347	Octal-D flip-flop (3-state)

Label	Integrated Circuit	Description
U42	74LS139	Dual 1-of-4 decoder/demultiplexer
U43	74S32	Quad 2-input OR gate
U44	74LS04	Hex inverter
U45	74LS74	Dual-D edge-triggered flip-flop
U46	74LS08	Quad 2-input AND gate
U47	74LS138	1-of-8 decoder/demultiplexer
U48	74LS138	1-of-8 decoder/demultiplexer
U49	74LS138	1-of-8 decoder/demultiplexer
U50	74LS138	1-of-8 decoder/demultiplexer
U51	74LS138	1-of-8 decoder/demultiplexer
U52	74LS138	1-of-8 decoder/demultiplexer
U53	74LS00	Quad 2-input NAND gate
U54	74S86	Quad 2-input Exclusive-OR gate
U55	74LS174	Hex-D flip-flop with Reset
U56	74LS04	Hex inverter
U57	74LS02	Quad 2-input NOR gate
U58	74LS175	Quad D-type flip-flop with Reset
U59	74LS125	Quad 3-state buffer
U60	74LS244	Octal buffer (3-state)
U61	74LS155	Dual 1-of-4 decoder/demultiplexer
U62	74S20	Dual 4-input NAND gate
U63	74LS157	Quad 2-to-1 multiplexer
U64	74LS244	Three-state octal buffer
U100	74LS32	Quad 2-input OR gate
U101	74LS74	Dual-D edge-triggered flip-flop

Color/Graphics Adapter Chips

The following list comprises the integrated circuits for the Color/Graphics Adapter board. Remember to maintain the series code and suffix requirement for the replacement chips.

Label	Integrated Circuit	Description
U1	74S112	Dual J-K negative edge-triggered flip-flop
U2	74LS74	Dual D-Type edge-triggered flip-flop
U3	74S86	Quad 2-input Exclusive-OR gate
U4, U5	74S174	Hex D-type flip-flop with Reset
U6	74LS04	Hex inverter
U7, U8	74LS166	8-bit Parallel-In/Serial-Out shift register
U9, U10	74153	Dual 4-to-1 multiplexer
U11	74LS74	Dual D-type edge-triggered flip-flop
U12	74LS393	Dual binary ripple counter
U13	74LS08	Quad 2-input AND gate
U14	74LS32	Quad 2-input OR gate
U15	74LS00	Quad 2-input NAND gate
U16	74LS04	Hex inverter
U17, U18, U19	74LS138	1-of-8 decoder/demultiplexer
U20	74LS04	Hex inverter

Label	Integrated Circuit	Description
U21	74LS174	Hex-D flip-flop with Reset
U22	74LS51	Dual AND/OR/Invert gate
U23	74LS32	Quad 2-input OR gate
U24	74LS244	Octal buffer (3-state)
U25	74LS00	Quad 2-input NAND gate
U26	74S04	Hex inverter
U27	74LS51	Dual 2-wide 2-input AOI gate
U28	74LS10	Triple 3-input NAND gate
U29	74S04	Hex inverter
U30	74LS32	Quad 2-input OR gate
U31	74S08	Quad 2-input AND gate
U32	74LS166	8-bit Parallel-In/Serial-Out shift register
U33	8340 (MK36000)	8K character generator ROM
U34, U35	74LS273	Octal D-Type flip-flop with Reset
U36	74LS244	Octal buffer (3-state)
U37	74LS374	Octal-D flip-flop (3-state)
U38	46505 (6845)	CRT controller
U39, U40	74LS174	Hex D-type flip-flop with Reset
U41	74LS08	Quad 2-input AND gate
U42	74LS86	Quad 2-input Exclusive-OR gate
U43	74S74	Dual-D edge-triggered flip-flop
U44	74S74	Dual-D edge-triggered flip-flop
U45	74LS151	8-to-1 multiplexer
U46	74LS00	Quad 2-input NAND gate
U47, U48, U49	74LS51	Dual 2-wide 2-input AOI gate
U50–U57	MK4516N-12 (2118-4)	16K by 1-bit DRAM
U58–U61	74LS374	Three-state octal-D flip-flop
U63	74LS175	Quad-D flip-flop with Reset
U64	74LS164	8-bit Serial-In/Parallel-Out shift register
U65	74LS02	Quad 2-input NOR gate
U66	74LS245	Three-state octal bus transceiver
U67	74LS244	Three-state octal buffer
U68	74LS86	Quad 2-input Exclusive-OR gate
U101	74S174	Hex-D flip-flop with Reset

Enhanced Graphics Adapter Chips

The following list comprises the integrated circuits for the Enhanced Graphics Adapter card. Remember to maintain the series code and suffix requirement for the replacement chips.

Label	Integrated Circuit	Description
U1	4416	16K by 4-bit dynamic RAM
U2	4416	16K by 4-bit dynamic RAM
U3	74LS374	Octal-D flip-flop
U4	74LS258	Quad 2-to-1 multiplexer

Label	Integrated Circuit	Description
U5	74S10	Triple 3-input NAND gate
U6	74S00	Quad 2-input NAND gate
U7		16.257-MHz oscillator
U8	74LS86	Quad 2-input Exclusive-OR gate
U9	74LS125	Quad 3-state buffer
U10	4416	16K by 4-bit dynamic RAM
U11	4414	16K by 4-bit dynamic RAM
U12	74LS374	Octal-D flip-flop
U13	74LS258	Quad 2-to-1 multiplexer
U14	74S04	Hex inverter
U15	74LS153	Dual 4-to-1 multiplexer
U16	74LS27	Triple 3-input NOR gate
U17	74LS32	Quad 2-input OR gate
U18	74LS74	Dual-D flip-flop
U19	74LS374	Octal-D flip-flop
U20	74LS174	Hex-D flip-flop
U21	TC15G022AP-0013	
U22	74LS374	Octal-D flip-flop
U23	74LS157	Quad 2-to-1 multiplexer
U24	TC15G022AP-0014	
U25	74LS138	1-of-8 decoder/demultiplexer
U26	74LS04	Hex inverter
U27	74LS11	Triple 3-input AND gate
U28	74LS138	1-of-8 decoder/demultiplexer
U29	74LS151	8-to-1 multiplexer
U30	74LS32	Quad 2-input OR gate
U31	TC15G022AP-0013	
U32	8622	Prescaler
U33	TC15G008AP-0023	
U34	82137	1K by 4-bit PROM
U35	74LS367	Hex buffer
U36	74LS244	Octal buffer
U37	74LS273	Octal-D flip-flop
U38		4700 by 15 resistor network
U39	74LS245	Octal bus transceiver
U40	4416	16K by 4-bit dynamic RAM
U41	4416	16K by 4-bit dynamic RAM
U42	74LS374	Octal-D flip-flop
U43	74LS258	Quad 2-to-1 multiplexer
U44	8818	Dual modulus prescaler
U45	74LS04	Hex inverter
U46	74LS04	Hex inverter
U47	74LS04	Hex inverter
U48	82137	1K by 4-bit PROM
U49	74LS175	Quad-D flip-flop
U50	4416	16K by 4-bit dynamic RAM
U51	4416	16K by 4-bit dynamic RAM
U52	74LS374	Octal-D flip-flop
U53	74LS258	Quad 2-to-1 multiplexer

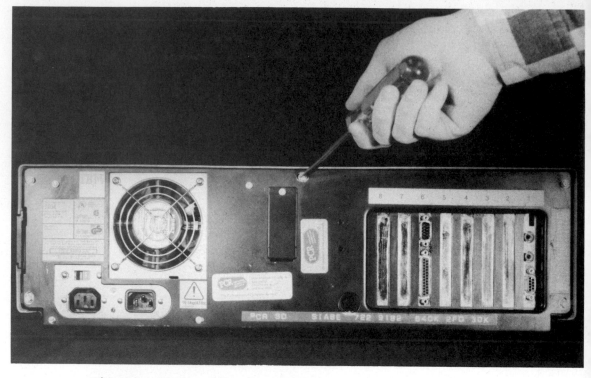

Fig. B-1.   Disassembling the IBM PC AT.

System Unit Disassembly

These procedures apply to those repairs for the IBM PC, PC/XT, and PC AT that require access to the internal subassemblies of the IBM Personal Computer System Unit.

Accessing the System Board

The tools, equipment, and space required are minimal.

- ► #2 flathead screwdriver
- ► Uncluttered workspace
- ► Container to hold screws until reassembly

To access the system board:

1. Turn power off.
2. Unplug the power cord and any peripherals from the rear of the computer.
3. Position the System Unit so the rear of the unit is facing you.

4. Using a flathead screwdriver, remove the five (5) screws from the rear plate (Fig. B-1). **Note:** The IBM AT has a cover on the rear of the unit that is held in place by two plastic fastener strips. Remove this cover, then the five screws on the backplate.

5. Position System Unit so that the front panel is facing you.

6. Place your hands on either side of the cover and slide the cover off of the main unit, pulling towards you as shown in Fig. B-2.

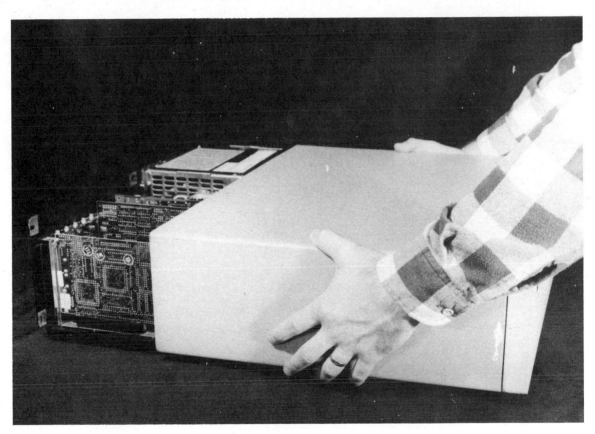

Fig. B-2.   Taking off the cover.

Removing the System Board

1. Refer to the previous section, "Accessing the System Board," and follow Steps 1 through 6.

2. With the cover off, remove all peripheral cards from the System Board.

3. Remove the power connector from the System Board. (This is located in the back, on the right side, when looking from the front.)

4. Remove the speaker cable from the connector on the lower middle section (on the System Board).

5. Remove the System Board mounting screws, as shown in Fig. B-3.

Fig. B-3.   Removing the System Board mounting screws.

6. Slide the System Unit board away from the power supply approximately 2 inches, until the stand-offs can be lifted from their mounting slots.

7. Lift the System Board from the System Unit.

Keyboard Disassembly and Reassembly

Disassembly Procedure

The tools and equipment required are minimal.

▶ Small Phillips-head screwdriver

▶ Uncluttered workspace

▶ Container to hold screws until reassembly

Disassemble the keyboard as follows:

1. Turn the System Unit off.
2. Remove the keyboard from the connector in the back of the System Unit.
3. Turn the keyboard upside down.
4. Remove the four Phillips-head screws from the bottom of the keyboard plate.
5. Lift the top of the plate up and out of the retaining slots in the chassis of the keyboard.
6. Disconnect the cable from the keyboard assembly.
7. Lift the rear of the keyboard out of the chassis.

Reassembly Procedure

This section covers the proper procedures for putting the keyboard back together again.

1. Position the front of keyboard assembly into the front of the keyboard chassis.
2. Lower the back end of the keyboard down into the chassis.
3. Reconnect the cable to the keyboard assembly.
4. Put the tabs on the front of the base into the slots on the front of the keyboard chassis.
5. Slowly lower the back down—don't forget to include the adjustable legs on the bottom of the keyboard.
6. Install the two Phillips-head screws into the mounting holes on the bottom of the keyboard.
7. Reconnect the cable to the System Unit assembly.
8. Power up and test.

Power-Supply Removal and Reassembly

Removing the Power Supply

This section describes the steps required to remove the power supply from the chassis. Minimal tools, space, and equipment are required.

► #2 flathead screwdriver

► Uncluttered workspace

► Container to hold screws until reassembly

Proceed as follows:

1. Turn the power off.
2. Unplug the power cord and any peripherals from the rear of the computer.
3. Position the System Unit so the rear of the unit is facing you.
4. Remove the System Unit cover. (Note: See the procedure for accessing the system board.)
5. Remove the power connector from the System Board. (Note: It is located on the back right-hand side of the unit, when looking at the unit from the front.)
6. If you have drives hooked to the system, disconnect the power cables going to the drive analog cards.
7. Loosen the drives and pull them forward about 2 inches in order to get access to the power supply (see Fig. B-4).
8. Remove the four screws holding the power supply (on the back of the chassis).
9. Push the power supply forward about one half of an inch.
10. To remove the supply, lift up and pull the power supply away from the motherboard.

Reinstalling the Power Supply

This section describes the steps needed to reinstall the power supply in the chassis.

1. Hold the power-supply unit approximately ½ inch from the rear of the chassis, and push the supply toward the motherboard. Then, pull back slightly to align the screw holes in the chassis.
2. Replace the four power-supply mounting screws.

3. Reconnect the disk drives and their power-supply connectors.

4. Reconnect the motherboard power-supply connectors.

5. Reconnect the power cord.

6. Power up and test.

Fig. B-4. Loosen the drives and pull them forward about 2 inches.

System Unit Reassembly

Now that the repair is complete, follow these steps to put the system back together. The simple tools and equipment used to disassemble the unit are all that is necessary for reassembly.

Reinstalling the System Board

1. Position all the stand-offs hooked to the System Board above their mounting holes.

2. Gently push the System Board toward the power supply until you can see that the mounting screw holes are lined up.

3. Reinstall the mounting screws in the System Board.

4. Reconnect the signal wires to the speaker.

5. Install the adapter cards.

6. Reconnect the System Board power-supply connectors.

Reassembling the System Unit Case

1. Gently slide the System Unit case forward over the System Unit.

2. Reinstall the five flathead screws on the back of the chassis. (Note: The older model IBM PC has only two screws on the backplate.)

3. Reconnect all peripherals and the power cord.

Floppy Disk-Drive Disassembly and Reassembly

Drive Disassembly Procedure

The following tools, space, and equipment are required:

- ▶ #2 flat head screwdriver
- ▶ Uncluttered workspace
- ▶ Container to hold screws until reassembly

Proceed as follows:

1. Follow the steps and procedures given for the System Unit disassembly.

2. Remove the signal cable from the analog card on the drive.

3. Some of the peripheral cards will need to be removed to gain access to the drives. Remove them.

4. Remove the two mounting screws on the side of the drive. (The IBM PC AT has the two screws in the front on either side of the drive door.)

5. Slide the drive forward about 1½ inches and remove the power cables from the rear of the drive. Remove any ground wires as well.

6. Remove the drive from the System Unit.

Disk-Drive Reassembly Procedure

To reassemble, follow these simple steps.

1. Slide the drive into the System Unit until about 1½ inches of the drive is left to be inserted. Hook up the power cables to the rear of the drive. Reconnect any ground wires as well.
2. Reinstall the two mounting screws on the side of the drive. (The IBM PC AT has the two screws in the front, on either side of the drive door.)
3. Reconnect the peripheral cards that you removed to get access to the drives.
4. Reconnect the signal cable to the analog card on the drive.
5. Follow the steps given in the earlier procedure for System Unit reassembly.

Fixed Disk-Drive Disassembly and Reassembly

Drive Disassembly Procedure

The following tools, space, and equipment are required.

- ► #2 flathead screwdriver
- ► Uncluttered workspace
- ► Container to hold screws until reassembly

Proceed as follows:

1. Tilt the System Unit up and remove the fixed disk-drive mounting plate screw.
2. Some of the peripheral cards will need to be removed to gain access to the fixed drive.
3. Remove the two mounting screws on the side of the drive.
4. Slide the drive forward about 1½ inches and remove the cables connecting the drive to the adapter card and the power supply. Remove any ground wires as well.
5. Remove the drive from the System Unit.

Drive Reassembly Procedure

To reassemble the fixed drive, proceed as follows:

1. Slide the drive into the System Unit until about 1½ inches is left to be inserted. Hook up the power and data cables to the rear of the drive. Reconnect any ground wires as well.

2. Reinstall the two mounting screws on the side of the drive.

3. Tilt the System Unit up and reinstall the fixed drive mounting plate screw in the bottom of the drive.

4. Reconnect the peripheral cards that had to be removed to gain access to the drive.

5. Follow earlier steps given in the procedure for reassemblying the System Unit.

On/Off Switch Disassembly and Reassembly

Disassembly Instructions

The following tools and equipment are required.

- ► #2 flathead screwdriver
- ► #2 Phillips screwdriver
- ► Uncluttered workspace
- ► Container to hold screws until reassembly

To disassemble the On/Off switch, proceed as follows:

1. First, follow the earlier procedure given for the disassembly of the System Unit.

CAUTION: Be very careful when working with the power supply. Make sure that power has been removed. Remove the plug from the electrical wall outlet.

---

2. Use the flathead screwdriver to press down on the plastic latch on the top of the black On/Off switch cover (see Fig. B-5).

3. The black cover is held on by plastic "catches" on the top and, on the bottom, by long fingers that insert into the power supply.

4. Remove the two Phillips-head screws that hold the switch on the power supply.

5. Slide the switch out and remove the wires going to it. Be very careful to mark exactly which wire went to which terminal.

6. Remove the switch.

Fig. B-5. The IBM Personal Computer On/Off Switch.

Reassembly Instructions

To reassemble the switch, proceed as follows:

1. Attach the wires to the new switch exactly as they were attached before.
2. Slide the switch into its slot on the power supply.
3. Reconnect the two Phillips-head screws that hold the switch on the power supply.
4. Reinstall the black cover over the On/Off switch, by inserting the long fingers on the bottom first and then snapping in the top catches.

ASCII Code Chart

Hexadecimal	ASCII	Hexadecimal	ASCII	Hexadecimal	ASCII
00	^@ (NULL)	2A	*	55	U
01	^A	2B	+	56	V
02	^B	2C	,	57	W
03	^C	2D	–	58	X
04	^D	2E	.	59	Y
05	^E	2F	/	5A	Z
06	^F	30	0	5B	[
07	^G (BELL)	31	1	5C	\
08	^H (BACKSPACE)	32	2	5D	]
09	^I (TAB)	33	3	5E	^
0A	^J (LINEFEED)	34	4	5F	—
0B	^K	35	5	60	`
0C	^L	36	6	61	a
0D	^M	37	7	62	b
0E	^N	38	8	63	c
0F	^O	39	9	64	d
10	^P	3A	:	65	e
11	^Q	3B	;	66	f
12	^R	3C	<	67	g
13	^S	3D	=	68	h
14	^T	3E	>	69	i
15	^U	3F	?	6A	j
16	^V	40	@	6B	k
17	^W	41	A	6C	l
18	^X	42	B	6D	m
19	^Y	43	C	6E	n
1A	^Z	44	D	6F	o
1B	^[(ESCAPE)	45	E	70	p
1C	(CURSOR RIGHT)	46	F	71	q
1D	(CURSOR LEFT)	47	G	72	r
1E	(CURSOR UP)	48	H	73	s
1F	(CURSOR DOWN)	49	I	74	t
20	(SPACE)	4A	J	75	u
21	!	4B	K	76	v
22	"	4C	L	77	w
23	#	4D	M	78	x
24	$	4E	N	79	y
25	%	4F	O	7A	z
26	&	50	P	7B	{
27	'	51	Q	7C		
28	(	52	R	7D	}
29	)	53	S	7E	~
		54	T	7F	DELETE

*Note: The caret symbol ^ represents a control character.

Hexadecimal-to-Decimal Conversion Chart

Hex	Dec	Hex	Dec	Hex	Dec	Hex	Dec	Hex	Dec
$00	00	$34	52	$68	104	$9C	156	$D0	208
$01	01	$35	53	$69	105	$9D	157	$D1	209
$02	02	$36	54	$6A	106	$9E	158	$D2	210
$03	03	$37	55	$6B	107	$9F	159	$D3	211
$04	04	$38	56	$6C	108	$A0	160	$D4	212
$05	05	$39	57	$6D	109	$A1	161	$D5	213
$06	06	$3A	58	$6E	110	$A2	162	$D6	214
$07	07	$3B	59	$6F	111	$A3	163	$D7	215
$08	08	$3C	60	$70	112	$A4	164	$D8	216
$09	09	$3D	61	$71	113	$A5	165	$D9	217
$0A	10	$3E	62	$72	114	$A6	166	$DA	218
$0B	11	$3F	63	$73	115	$A7	167	$DB	219
$0C	12	$40	64	$74	116	$A8	168	$DC	220
$0D	13	$41	65	$75	117	$A9	169	$DD	221
$0E	14	$42	66	$76	118	$AA	170	$DE	222
$0F	15	$43	67	$77	119	$AB	171	$DF	223
$10	16	$44	68	$78	120	$AC	172	$E0	224
$11	17	$45	69	$79	121	$AD	173	$E1	225
$12	18	$46	70	$7A	122	$AE	174	$E2	226
$13	19	$47	71	$7B	123	$AF	175	$E3	227
$14	20	$48	72	$7C	124	$B0	176	$E4	228
$15	21	$49	73	$7D	125	$B1	177	$E5	229
$16	22	$4A	74	$7E	126	$B2	178	$E6	230
$17	23	$4B	75	$7F	127	$B3	179	$E7	231
$18	24	$4C	76	$80	128	$B4	180	$E8	232
$19	25	$4D	77	$81	129	$B5	181	$E9	233
$1A	26	$4E	78	$82	130	$B6	182	$EA	234
$1B	27	$4F	79	$83	131	$B7	183	$EB	235
$1C	28	$50	80	$84	132	$B8	184	$EC	236
$1D	29	$51	81	$85	133	$B9	185	$ED	237
$1E	30	$52	82	$86	134	$BA	186	$EE	238
$1F	31	$53	83	$87	135	$BB	187	$EF	239
$20	32	$54	84	$88	136	$BC	188	$F0	240
$21	33	$55	85	$89	137	$BD	189	$F1	241
$22	34	$56	86	$8A	138	$BE	190	$F2	242
$23	35	$57	87	$8B	139	$BF	191	$F3	243
$24	36	$58	88	$8C	140	$C0	192	$F4	244
$25	37	$59	89	$8D	141	$C1	193	$F5	245
$26	38	$5A	90	$8E	142	$C2	194	$F6	246
$27	39	$5B	91	$8F	143	$C3	195	$F7	247
$28	40	$5C	92	$90	144	$C4	196	$F8	248
$29	41	$5D	93	$91	145	$C5	197	$F9	249
$2A	42	$5E	94	$92	146	$C6	198	$FA	250
$2B	43	$5F	95	$93	147	$C7	199	$FB	251
$2C	44	$60	96	$94	148	$C8	200	$FC	252
$2D	45	$61	97	$95	149	$C9	201	$FD	253
$2E	46	$62	98	$96	150	$CA	202	$FE	254
$2F	47	$63	99	$97	151	$CB	203	$FF	255
$30	48	$64	100	$98	152	$CC	204		
$31	49	$65	101	$99	153	$CD	205		
$32	50	$66	102	$9A	154	$CE	206		
$33	51	$67	103	$9B	155	$CF	207		

Routine Preventive Maintenance Schedule

Preventive maintenance, or PM, is one of the least used techniques for operational cost reduction, yet the savings that can result are substantial. If the equipment doesn't fail, you can't evaluate the bottom-line savings in conducting proper PM. But after the first mind-boggling repair expense, one basic fact will sink in: This failure might have been prevented by doing some easy, routine maintenance.

Many manufacturers are not sure what the optimum PM should be. Some companies prefer you don't do any PMs. (The effect is to cause more equipment repair jobs for you.) Among those who recommend PMs, there is great variation in recommended PM schedules for similar hardware (e.g., disk drives).

The schedule that follows is a consensus of the recommendations of manufacturers, dealers, users, and the author's own personal experience.

You may want to do the PMs even more often if intermittents occur frequently.

Daily

1. Log the operational time. Estimate disk drive "run-light-on" time. Estimate the printer "printing" time. Estimate the computer "power on" time.
2. Monitor the humidity (a measure of static electricity).

Weekly

1. Clean the computer-system work area. Pick up all loose trash, reshelve scattered books, restore magazines to their racks, toss out old printed paper, toss out those "bad" disks you've been saving, wipe down the hardware with an antistatic, dust-absorbing cloth, wipe the desk and bench space with an antistatic cloth, and vacuum the shelves, desk, and floor.
2. Clean the equipment housings and cases. Wipe the chassis with an antistatic cloth, "wash" with a lightly soaped, damp cloth.
3. Clean the display screens. Use an antistatic "dust-off"-type spray or a cloth dampened with an antistatic solution.
4. Clean the floppy disk-drive Read head (after 40 hours of "run-light-on" use).

Monthly

1. Some manufacturers recommend that the floppy disk-drive Read head be demagnetized after 40 hours of "run-light-on" use.

2. Clean inside the computer. Disassemble according to the procedures given in this appendix. Use a soft brush and a long, narrow, vacuum-cleaner hose nozzle, and vacuum the unit. (It helps to spray the nozzle with an antistatic solution first.)

3. Clean inside the printer. Use same technique you used for cleaning inside the computer.

4. Check the ventilation filters in the equipment. Replace, if cleaning is not practical (the filter is worn or badly soiled).

5. Check the connector contacts. Look for signs of corrosion, pitting, or discoloration. Clean contacts if necessary. (Corrosion-removing wipes that also coat the surface with a lubricating coating to protect it from atmospheric corrosion are strongly recommended.)

Every Other Month

1. Reseat all socketed chips on the motherboard and the peripheral cards. Disassemble according to the procedures given in this appendix.

2. Disconnect and then reconnect the cable and connector plugs. This removes corrosion buildup.

3. Apply an antistatic treatment to the computer work area.

4. Clean inside the printer. Using a nonmagnetic, plastic, vacuum-hose nozzle and a soft camel-hair brush, vacuum the printer. (Spray or wipe the nozzle with an antistatic spray or solution first.)

Every Six Months

1. Replace vent filters. This is applicable only if some of the equipment has filters. None are standard in the IBM Personal Computers.

2. Check the floppy disk-drive speed. Speed test programs are advertised in various computer publications. Remember the room light and strobe mark test procedures given in the troubleshooting procedures.

3. Check the floppy disk-drive head alignment. Do this only if you suspect a disk problem.

4. Clean the connector contacts. If you haven't done this during earlier inspection checks, conduct this PM now. Do this PM more often if the computer system is used in a smoggy part of the country or near salt air.

5. Clean the floppy disk-drive Read head. If the system is used daily, the drive heads may need cleaning about now, but this depends very much on the kind and quality of floppy disks that are used.

6. Conduct a printer routine inspection. This is needed every six months, or at about 500,000 lines of print. Check the tightness of the screws and connectors. Conduct a printer self test, as described in the printer owner's manual.

Annually

1. Take a routine maintenance infrared photo (optional). Do this only if you're into this form of PM or troubleshooting.

Glossary

Active High—A positive voltage condition (logic high) necessary to produce an effect.

Active Low—A zero voltage condition necessary to produce an effect.

Adapter Card—An auxiliary device, such as I/O or memory boards, that is used to extend the operation of the PC.

Address—A number that represents a unique bit location in memory.

Address Bus—The collection of wires or traces over which a memory location is sent by the CPU to the memory or I/O device.

Alphanumeric—A character set containing letters, digits, and punctuation marks.

Analog—Electrical information contained in continuously variable physical quantities. The electrical power in your wall socket is an analog voltage.

AND Gate—A computer logic gate whose output is HIGH (or logic 1) if, and only if, all inputs are also HIGH.

ASCII—An acronym for American Standard Code for Information Interchange.

BASIC—An easy-to-learn high-level language. BASIC stands for *B*eginner's *A*ll-purpose *S*ymbolic *I*nstruction *C*ode.

BIOS—The abbreviation for basic input/output system. A software program, usually residing in ROM, which controls the interface communication between I/O devices and the computer circuitry. BIOS defines what occurs when you press a keyboard button, or request the directory of a disk. It is a critical part of the operating system of a computer.

Bit—An abbreviation of *b*inary dig*it*. The smallest unit in a binary notation system.

Blackout—The total loss of electrical power.

Bootstrap—A process by which a short loader program loads itself into memory and then loads a longer program. The program, in effect, pulls itself up by its "bootstrap," bringing itself into a desired state through its own action.

Brownout—A deliberate reduction in the electrical line voltage supplied to you; usually caused by an excessive electrical demand on the electric utility or by an insufficient power-generation capability.

Buffer—A storage area for temporarily holding data.

Bus—A collection of conductors (wires or traces) used for transmitting information, such as data or power signals. For example, the bus can be the 8 wires that transfer the data word in the PC or PC/XT, or the 16 wires that transfer the address word in the PC AT. It can also be a collection of control-signal conductors.

Byte—Eight bits of data operated on as a unit. A byte represents a numerical value between 0 and 255 (decimal). It can also represent a character.

Capacitor—An electrical component that stores an electrical charge.

Cathode-Ray Tube—*See* CRT.

Chip—An integrated circuit. A silicon device mounted in a plastic support package. Often, the complete package is called a *chip*.

Clock—A consistant, periodic signal used to step logic information through a computer circuit.

Cold Start—Initializing the start-up conditions in a computer. The cold-start process assumes no previous activity in the computer; all registers in the machine are set to initial conditions and the power-on self test is conducted in its entirety.

CPU—Abbreviation for central processing unit. The area in which the primary logic decisions are made and the arithmetic manipulations are done. The CPU in the PC and PC/XT is an Intel 8088; in the PC AT, it's an Intel 80286.

CRT—Abbreviation for cathode-ray tube. Basically, the display screen on which you observe the characters and graphics produced by the video adapter card.

Cursor—The display symbol that indicates the position at which the next character will appear.

Data—Computer information, such as numbers, letters, or special symbols. A representation of computer-related information, such as quantity value, instruction code, etc.

Data Bus—The collection of wires or traces over which the data travels in a computer.

DIP—An acronym for dual in-line package. An IC package having two parallel rows of pins.

Disk—The magnetic medium on which you store computer data. The 5¼-inch disk is technically a diskette or minifloppy disk. The 3½-inch disk is a microfloppy disk.

Display—The device on which visual information is presented, using lighted pixels.

Dynamic RAM (DRAM)—A digital memory device, essentially a capacitor, that stores information in a tiny memory cell. DRAMs require periodic access to refresh (restore) any signal charge in the capacitor that may have disappeared (leaked away). The System Board RAM in the PC, PC/XT, and PC AT are examples of DRAM devices.

Enable—To allow circuit or device operation to occur.

Firmware—Programs that are stored in hardware, such as a ROM.

Flip-Flop—An electronic device (chip/IC) that holds a given logic state until acted on by a signal on a certain input pin, at which time the opposite logic state is expressed. Flip-flops are capable of assuming one of two stable binary states, producing an appropriate logic level at their outputs.

Gate—A logic circuit with one or more inputs and a single output, such that the output is determined by the logic level on each of the input lines.

Hardware—The physical components of a computer system. The computer itself, the printer, the monitor display unit, and so on.

Head—A device (mechanical) that is used to read, write, and erase information from a magnetic disk or other medium.

Hexadecimal—Abbreviated hex. The numbering system based on 16 digits, in which the digits above 9 are A, B, C, D, E, and F. Each hexadecimal number can be represented as a 4-bit code.

High Impedance—An electronic state in which the output of a device is isolated from the circuit and appears as nonexistent to the circuit.

IC—The abbreviation for integrated ciruit, a kind of microelectronic device. The IC is the building block of the computer. Also called a "chip," although, technically, the chip is the material on which the IC is mounted.

Initialize—To set the starting values and conditions to predetermined levels.

Input/Output—Abbreviated I/O. The input/output medium (device or channel) through which the computer sends and receives information to and from the outside world (i.e., disk drives, keyboard, display unit, etc.).

Interface—A device or component used to alter or convert signals between circuits, systems, devices, or programs.

Interrupt—The suspension of a process caused by an event external to the process.

K—Symbol for cathode, Kelvin, or kilo. In computer applications, equal to the decimal value 1024. The symbol used to represent the size of memory in a computer. (The term 64K actually means 65,536.) In frequency, kilo refers to 1000. (Thus, 1 kHz is 1000 Hz.)

LED—An acronym for light-emitting diode. A semiconductor that generates visible or infrared light when activated by an applied voltage.

Mega—Abbreviated M and refers to one million. In computer data, this represents a power of 2 that is close to one million (1,048,576). Thus, 12 MHz represents 12 million frequency oscillations per second; 12 Mbytes refers to 12,582,912 bytes of memory.

Modified Frequency Modulation—Abbreviated MFM. A magnetic disk storage technique that varies the amplitude and frequency of the "write" signal to the head.

Monitor—Refers to a CRT display unit.

Motherboard—A name for the System Board that is in generic usage. The large printed-circuit board in the PC on which electronic devices are mounted; the primary or main board in your computer. All other boards receive control signals or information from the motherboard.

Multiplexer—A device capable of interleaving two or more input signals into a serial output sequence.

NAND Gate—A logic gate whose output is HIGH if at least one input is LOW, and LOW if all inputs are HIGH. (An AND gate with an inverter at its output.)

Noise—The interference that results from the presence of an electromagnetic or radio-frequency field in the vicinity of those electrical signals emulating from such equipment as data buses, TVs, or radios.

NOR Gate—A logic gate whose output is LOW if at least one input is HIGH, and HIGH if all inputs are LOW. (An OR gate with an inverter at its output.)

Operating System—A software program in the computer that controls the execution of other programs. It handles I/O control, data management, and resource allocation.

OR Gate—A logic device whose output is HIGH if at least one input is also HIGH.

Parity Bit—A bit that is appended to a data word to make the sum of logic high (1) bits in the word always odd (or even), depending on the design of the system. If a word read out of memory has an improper parity bit appended, the circuitry knows that an error has occurred and that one or more memory chips have failed. Detection of a parity error usually results in a nonmaskable interrupt and a halt in the system operations.

Pin—The small metal connection that protrudes from an IC, or the finger of a circuit trace on the edge of a peripheral adapter card.

Pixel—Short for picture element. A small rectangular unit that is displayed on a video monitor. An example would be the dots on a TV display screen.

Printed-Circuit Board—Also called a printed-circuit card. A (usually) plastic or fiberglass board on which electronic signal and power traces are placed and on which electronic components are mounted. Some boards or cards are layered with ground and power planes sandwiched between data and control-signal path planes. Some boards/cards have components inserted through holes and soldered to the board. Others have nonleaded components soldered to the top of the board (surface mounted).

RAM—Abbreviation for random-access memory. A memory that can be read from or written to by the computer's CPU. Two types exist: static RAM (SRAM) and dynamic RAM (DRAM). The system-board memory in the PC, PC/XT, and PC AT is a DRAM.

Register—A storage device that can contain a bit, a byte, or a computer word.

RF Modulator—A device that converts composite video signals into a TV antenna-level signal.

ROM—Abbreviation for read-only memory. A memory with information permanently stored during manufacture in the device material. The information cannot be changed by the user.

Short Circuit—An extremely low-resistance path for signal or power current. Rather than passing through a component or circuit, a data or control signal can be shorted (usually to ground), causing a loss of process operation and an erroneous output.

Software—The programs that determine and control the actions of the computer.

Spike—A short, high-intensity burst of electrical energy that, if not bypassed (or shorted) to ground, can cause damage to electrical/electronic components.

Static RAM—Abbreviated SRAM. A RAM memory using flip-flops as the memory cells. As long as power is applied, the flip-flops retain the stored information.

Surge—A temporary increase in electrical voltage that lasts long enough to be noticed on a meter.

Synchronization—Adjusting one signal to another to produce a desired relationship of one with the other.

Transient—A brief fluctuation in voltage, shorter than a surge and smaller in magnitude than a spike.

Troubleshoot—To systematically locate a computer hardware or electrical/electronic failure. Software failures are found by systematic debugging.

Volt—The electric potential (pressure) that causes current to flow through an electronic circuit.

Warm Start—The process of restarting the computer without conducting some lengthy initial power-on self-test steps, such as the memory tests. The warm-start process resets the system and reboots DOS just as a cold-start process does.

D

Bibliography

Agrash, Michael and Illowsky, Dan, "Customized Boots," *PC Tech Journal*, February 1985, pp. 150–160.

"All About Mass Storage," Datapro Research Corp., Delran, NJ, July 1988, pp. 101–108.

"All About Microcomputer Displays," Datapro Research Corp., Delran, NJ, April 1988, pp. 101–106.

"Alternatives to the PC AT," *PC Magazine*, November 12, 1985, pp. 109–111.

Anderson, Garry J., "Designer's Guide to the CMOS STD Bus," *Electronic Products*, November 17, 1983, pp. 81–87.

Anderson, Julie, "Irresistible DOS 3.0," *PC Tech Journal*, December 1984, pp. 74–87.

Archer, Rowland, Jr., "The IBM PC XT and DOS 2.00." *Byte Magazine*, November 1983, pp. 294–304.

Archibald, Dale, "The Making of the Magnetic Media for Micros," *Softalk*, February 1982, pp. 160–164.

Arnold, David, "DOS for Beginners," *PC World*, April 1984, pp. 44–51.

Babcoke, Carl, "Practical Information About Testing and Replacing Capacitors," *Electronic Servicing*, July 1970, pp. 28–37.

Babcoke, Carl, "Quick Testing of Transistors," *Electronic Servicing*, November 1970, pp. 26–33.

Babcoke, Carl, "Simple Servicing Tips," *Electronic Servicing & Technology*, July 1983, pp. 44–49.

Baker, Alan, and Mielke, Neal, "Detecting Quality and Reliability Defects in EPROMs," *Electronic Test*, November 1983, pp. 56–62.

Barden, William, Jr., "Getting Your Micro Repaired," *Popular Computing*, May 1983, pp. 54–58.

Bausell, James, "Desoldering Components From High Density PCB's," *Electronics*, February 1984, pp. 97–101.

Bausell, James, "Desoldering Components, Using Continuous Vacuum Solder Extraction," *Electronic Servicing & Technology*, May 1987, pp. 13–18.

Beenker, F.P.M., "Systematic and Structured Methods for Digital Board Testing," *VLSI Systems Design*, January 1987, pp. 50–58.

Belt, Forest, "1-2-3-4 Servicing Simplifies Industrial Electronic Maintenance," *Electronic Servicing*, September 1979, pp. 21–27.

Blumberg, Donald F., "Meeting the IBM Challenge," *Computer/Electronic Service News*, June 1988, pp. 24, 25.

Bohannon, George, "The ABCs of IBM Graphics," *Softalk*, February 1983, pp. 30–36.

Boyd, Alan, "System Notebook," *Softalk*, January 1983, pp. 60–64.

Boyd, Alan, "System Notebook," *Softalk*, February 1983, pp. 82–85.

Boyd, Alan, "System Notebook," *Softalk*, March 1983, pp. 108–110.

Brar, A.S. and Narayan, P.B., "So That's How They Keep the Bits on the Disk!" *Research & Development*, October 1987, pp. 100–104.

Brenner, Robert C., *IBM PC Advanced Troubleshooting & Repair*, Howard W. Sams & Company, Indianapolis, IN, 1988.

Brenner, Robert C., *IBM PC Troubleshooting & Repair Guide*, Howard W. Sams & Company, Indianapolis, IN, 1986.

Bristol, Rod, "Believable Time Measurements With Oscilloscopes," *Electronics Test*, October 1986, pp. 49–47.

Camenker, Brian, "The Making of the IBM PC," *Byte*, November 1983, pp. 254–256.

"Caring for a Personal Computer," *Electronic Servicing & Technology*, June 1985, pp. 42–47.

"Choosing and Using the Proper Soldering Iron," *Electronic Servicing & Technology*, December 1981, pp. 36–39.

Crosby, Mark L., "Singin' the Disk I/O Blues," *Apple Orchard*, Winter 1981/82, pp. 63–68.

Cunningham, John E.,"Troubleshooting Digital Equipment," *Electronic Servicing*, September 1980, pp. 18–21.

Curran, Lawrence J. and Shuford, Richard S., "IBM's Estridge," *Byte*, November 1983, pp. 88–97.

Dale, Alan, "1-2-3-4 Servicing," *Electronic Servicing*, December 1970, pp. 26–30.

Dash, Glen, "Understanding EMI Test Methods Eases Product Acceptance." *EDN*, May 1983, pp. 183–192.

Davidson, Homer L., "Ten Dogs in TV Repair,." *Electronic Servicing & Technology*, September 1984, pp. 12–23.

Davis, Dwight B., "Diagnostics Improve as Computer Systems Proliferate," *Mini-Micro Systems*, August 1982, pp. 115–123.

Desposito, Joe, "Invasion of the Hard Disk Drives," *Creative Computing*, August 1985, pp. 28–35.

Develop Test Technology for VHSIC. RADC-TR-83-148, Rome Air Development Center, Air Force Systems Command, Griffiss AFB, New York, September 1983.

DeVoney, Chris, *IBM's Personal Computer*, Que Corporation, Indianapolis, IN, 1983.

DeVore, John A., "To Solder Easily," *Circuits Manufacturing*, June 1984, pp. 62–70.

Dickinson, John, "Courting Disaster—The IBM PC AT," *PC Magazine*, April 29, 1986, pp. 106–121.

DVorak, John C., "Let's Modernize the Microcomputer," *PC Magazine*, October 28, 1986, p. 77.

Earle, Λ. Scott, "Taking a Closer Look at the RGB Monitor," *PC Magazine*, April 3, 1984, pp. 145–154.

Engel, George M., "Line Cleaner—A Construction Project," *InCider*, August 1983, pp. 108–110.

Eorgoff, M., Satchell, S., and Daneliuk, T., "The IBM PC-XT vs. the Compaq Plus," *PC Products*, June 1984, pp. 31–41.

Fastie, Will, "ATtention to Detail," *PC Tech Journal*, December 1984, p. 5.

Fastie, Will, "Graphics (Again)," *PC Magazine*, July 1985, p. 9.

Fastie, Will, "The IBM Personal Computer," *Creative Computing*, December 1981, pp. 19–40.

Field, Tim, "The IBM PC and the Intel 8087 Coprocessor," *Byte*, August 1983, pp. 331–374.

Field, Tim, "Enhancing Screen Displays for the IBM PC," *Byte*, November 1983, pp. 99–116.

Final Report: The Identification and Assessment of On Chip Self-Test and Repair Concepts, Naval Electronics Systems Command, September 1981.

Freedman, David H., "Designing the Right Enclosure," *Mini-Micro Systems*, August 1983, pp. 229–242.

Freitag, Walter D., "Lubricants for Separable Connectors," *IEEE Transactions on Parts, Hybrids, and Packaging*, March 1977, p. 32.

Glasco, David B., "Using IBM's Marvelous Keyboard," *Byte*, May 1983, pp. 402–415.

Glinert-Cole, Susan, "Upgrading a PC to an 'Xtra T'," *PC Tech Journal*, February 1984, pp. 75–82.

Goldblatt, Robert C., "How Computers Can Test Their Own Memories," *Computer Design*, July 1976, pp. 125–129.

Goodman, Robert, "An Ounce of Prevention," *Electronic Servicing & Technology*, May 1983, pp. 24–39.

Goodman, Robert L., "Techniques for Repairing Intermittents," *Electronic Servicing*, July 1979, pp. 33–39.

Goodstein, Max, "Learning From a Tough Dog TV Repair," *Electronic Servicing & Technology*, April 1987, pp. 25, 57.

Gookin, Dan, "DOS 4.0: The Final Chapter," *ComputorEdge*, September 30, 1988, pp. 14, 16.

Grolle, Carl G., *Electronic Technician's Handbook of Time-Savers and Shortcuts*, Parker Publishing Company, Inc., West Nyack, NY, 1974.

Guidelines: Backup Procedures and Hard Disk Maintenance, DataPro Research Corp., Delran, NJ, June 1987, pp. 251–255.

Hancock, Earle, "A Man of Letters," *InCider*, December 1983, pp. 172–174.

Hancock, Earle, "Do-It-Yourself Disk Drive Repair," *InCider*, November 1983, pp. 32–34.

Harwood, Robert, "Diagnostic and Utility Software," *Personal Computing*, October 1981, pp. 47–54, 166–169.

Hoffmann, Thomas V., "Analyzing the Advanced Technology," *PC Tech Journal*, December 1984, pp. 40–56.

Hoffmann, Thomas V., "Ten By Ten," *PC Tech Journal*, November 1984, pp. 53–70.

Hogan, Thom, "We're Not in Kansas Anymore," *The Portable Companion*, June/July 1982, pp. 11–14.

Howson, Hugh R., "POKEing Around in the IBM PC," *Byte*, November 1983, pp. 121–131.

Hunter, David, "The Roots of DOS," *Softalk*, March 1983, pp. 12–15.

iAPX 286 HARDWARE REFERENCE MANUAL, Intel Corp., Santa Clara, CA, 1983.

IBM PC 5150 COMPUTERFACTS™, Technical Service Data CSCS2, Howard W. Sams & Company, 1984.

IBM PC/AT Model 5170-239 COMPUTERFACTS™, Technical Service Data CSCS17, Howard W. Sams & Company, 1987.

IBM PC-XT Model 5160-086 COMPUTERFACTS™, CSCS10, Howard W. Sams & Company, 1986.

IBM Personal Computer, Datapro Research Corp., Delran, NJ, March 1986, pp. CM11-504MK-101—CM11-504MK-122.

IBM Personal Computer AT, Datapro Research Corp., Delran, NJ, January 1988, pp. 201–210, 801, 802.

IBM Personal Computer Technical Reference, International Business Machines Corp., Boca Raton, FL, 1981.

IBM Personal Computer AT Guide to Operations, International Business Machines Corp., Boca Raton, FL, 1984.

IBM Personal Computer AT Hardware Maintenance and Service, Vols. 1 and 2, International Business Machines Corp., Boca Raton, FL, 1984.

IBM Personal Computer AT Technical Reference, International Business Machines Corp., Boca Raton, FL, 1984.

IBM Personal Computer XT Guide to Operations, International Business Machines Corp., Boca Raton, FL, 1983.

IBM Personal Computer XT Hardware Maintenance and Service, International Business Machines Corp., Boca Raton, FL, 1983.

IBM Personal Computer XT Technical Reference, Vols. 1 and 2, International Business Machines Corp., Boca Raton, FL, 1983.

"IBM Unveils PC AT," *PC Products*, October 1984, pp. 111, 112.

IC MEMORIES DATA BOOK, Hitachi America Ltd., San Jose, CA, 1987.

Illowsky, Dan and Abrash, Michael, "Up, Down, Right, Left & Check," *PC Tech Journal*, February 1984, pp. 93–116.

Introduction to the iAPX 286, Intel Corp., Santa Clara, CA, circa 1984.

Izen, Bud, "Microcomputer Troubleshooting: Components of a Personal Computer." *Electronic Servicing & Technology*, November 1985, pp. 22–27.

Jeffries, Ron, "Mass Storage for the More Perfect PC," *PC Magazine*, October 15, 1985, pp. 99, 100.

Jesson, Joseph E., "Smart Keyboards Help Eliminate Entry Errors," *Computer Design*, October 1982, pp. 137–142.

Kagan, Arvin, "PC/AT Reactions," *PC Tech Journal*, March 1985, p. 14.

Kaminer, David A., "What to Do When Your System Crashes," *Popular Computing*, April 1983, pp. 154–156.

Kear, Fred W., "Board Warp: Causes and Prevention," *Circuits Manufacturing*, December 1983, pp. 95–98.

Lafore, Robert, *Assembly Language Primer for the IBM PC*, Plume/Waite, San Rafael, CA, 1984.

Lancaster, Don, *CMOS Cookbook*, Howard W. Sams & Company, Indianapolis, IN, 1977.

Lehtinen, Rick, "Display Technology Update," *Broadcast Engineering*, July 1988, pp. 64–74.

Lemons, Phil, "The IBM Personal Computer First Impressions," *Byte*, October 1981, pp. 27–34.

Lemons, Wayne, "Streamlined Tests for Transistors." *Electronic Servicing*, August 1977, pp. 34–39.

Lewis, Gordon, "Disks, Drives, and Dirt," *Pro/Files*, September/October 1983, pp. 59–61.

Lieberman, David, "Data Input Alternatives," *Electronic Products*, June 6, 1983, pp. 47–55.

Lieberman, David, "The Clean Connection." *Nibble*, Vol.2/No.8/1981, pp. 159–165.

Little, M. Andre, "System Security." *InCider*, December 1983, pp. 117–121.

Littlefield, Patti, "What to Try Before Taking Your Microcomputer Into the Repair Department," *Educational Computer Magazine*, May–June 1983, p. 73.

Lockwood, Russ, "IBM PC AT," *Creative Computing*, December 1984, pp. 32–40.

LOGIC—TTL DATA MANUAL, Signetics Corp., 1978.

Loop, Roger, "Buying a Digital Scope," *Electronic Products*, May 15, 1987, pp. 38–47.

Machrone, Bill, "How Boca Does It," *PC Magazine*, August 1983, pp. 111–115.

Machrone, Bill, "User-to-User," *PC Magazine*, August 1983, pp. 565–566.

Magid, Lawrence, "Color Discrimination," *PC World*, Vol. 1, No. 2, 1983, pp. 15, 16.

Mann, Timothy J., "Disk Cleaner," *InCider*, October 1983, pp. 166–168.

Margolis, Art, *Troubleshooting & Repairing Personal Computers*, Tab Books, Inc., Blue Ridge Summit, PA, 1983.

May, Larry, "Choosing a Keyboard Technology," *Electronic Products*, September 30, 1983, pp. 91–96.

McCain, John, "Spikes: Pesky Voltage Transients and How to Minimize Their Effects," *Byte*, November 1977, pp. 54–56.

McCann, Scott, "Using a Switch-type Joystick on the IBM PC," *PC Tech Journal*, May 1984, p. 195.

McClain, Larry, "Servicing Your System: Be Prepared," *Personal Computing*, September 1982, pp. 50–55, 148–154.

McLanahan, David, "Here Are Some Sources for Parts and Information," *Electronic Servicing & Technology*, June 1985, pp. 25–28.

McMullen, Barbare E. and John F., "How Blue Can You Get?" *PC Magazine*, April 3, 1984, pp. 112–113.

Miastkowski, Stan, "A Close Look at the IBM Personal Computer," *Popular Computing*, December 1981, pp. 52–57.

Microprocessor and Peripheral Handbook, Intel Corp., Santa Clara, CA, 1984.

Microsystem Components Handbook: Peripherals Volume II, Intel Corp., Santa Clara, CA, 1986.

Miller, Beth, "Microsystem Reliability Testing," *Electronic Test*, November 1983, pp. 48–54.

Milner, Edward J., "Fast Memory Test Checks Individual Bits," *EDN*, October 13, 1983, pp. 222–229.

Morgan, Chris, "IBM's Personal Computer," *Byte*, July 1981, pp. 6–10.

Morgan, Christopher L., *Bluebook of Assembly Routines for the IBM PC*, New American Library, San Rafael, CA, 1984.

Neu, Ed, "Head/Disk Design Not Determined by Design of Any Single Component," *Computer Technology Review*, Summer 1988, pp. 41–44.

Norton, Peter, "Color Me Enhanced," *PC Magazine*, November 12, 1985, pp. 81–85.

Norton, Peter, "Gang of Fourteen: Disk Types for the AT," *PC Magazine*, June 11, 1985, pp. 103–107.

Norton, Peter, "It's Odds and Ends Time," *PC Magazine*, April 16, 1985, pp. 103–105.

Norton, Peter, "Snooping in ROM: The Software Interrupt," *Softalk*, February 1983, pp. 87–89.

Norton, Peter, "Snooping in ROM: The Computer Musician," *Softalk*, March 1983, pp. 79–81.

Norton, Peter, "Snooping in ROM: Which Version Did You Get?" *Softalk*, January 1983, pp. 86–88.

Norton, Peter, "The Good News About DOS 3.x," *PC Magazine*, April 30, 1985, pp. 105–107.

Norton, Peter, "The Trouble with EGA," *PC Magazine*, October 29, 1985, pp. 79–85.

O'Malley, Christopher, "What You Should Know About MS-DOS," *Personal Computing*, August 1985, pp. 43–51.

Perspective: Hard Disk Installation, Datapro Research Corp., Delran, NJ, July 1987, pp. 201–205.

Perspective: Mass Storage, Datapro Research Corp., Delran, NJ, July 1988, pp. 251–257.

Perspective: The ABCs of Video, Datapro Research Corp., Delran, NJ, January 1988, pp. 351–355.

Persson, Conrad, "Oscilloscope: The Eyes of the Technician," *Electronic Servicing & Technology*, April 1987, pp. 10–14.

Petzold, Charles, "The EGA Standard: Monitors That Measure Up," *PC Magazine*, March 25, 1986, pp. 108–120.

Petzold, Charles, "PC Tutor," *PC Magazine*, August 1986, pp. 439, 442.

Pingry, Julie, "The Expanding Real World of the IBM PC," *Digital Design*, February 1984, pp. 80–88.

Poole, Lon, "Under the Hood of the PC," *PC Magazine*, September 1982, pp. 50–58.

RADC Testability Notebook. Final Technical Report: RADC-TR-82-189, Rome Air Development Center, Griffiss AFB, New York, June 1982.

Radding, Alan, "When Your Computer Breaks Down," *Popular Computing*, May 1983, pp. 196–198.

Rampil, Ira, "A Floppy Disk Tutorial," *Byte*, December 1977, pp. 24–45.

Rechsteiner, Emil B., "Keeping Power Clean and Steady," *Mini-Micro Systems*, August 1983, pp. 245–252.

Riccio, Ronald, "How to Avoid Damage When Repairing PC Boards," *Electronic Servicing & Technology*, February 1983, pp. 38–42.

Robinson, J. B., *Modern Digital Troubleshooting*, Data I/O Corporation, Redmond, WA, 1983.

Rollins, Dan, "AT Keyboard Tricks," *PC Magazine*, September 17, 1985, pp. 264–267.

Rosch, Winn L., "300-Megabyte Hard Disks Now in the Works for PCs," *PC Magazine*, April 29, 1986, p. 33.

Rosch, Winn L., "High-Resolution Color Monitors," *PC Magazine*, June 1983, pp. 247–258.

Rosch, Winn L., "IBM AT Hard Disk Difficulties and Alternatives," *PC Magazine*, April 29, 1986, p. 124.

Rosch, Winn L., "Letters to PC Magazine: Hard Disk Heartache," *PC Magazine*, January 14, 1986, pp. 66, 67.

Sandler, Corey, "A Secret Inside the ROM," *PC Magazine*, February 21, 1984, pp. 323, 324.

Sargent, Murry III and Shoemaker, Richard L., *The IBM Personal Computer From the Inside Out*, Addison-Wesley Publishing Co., Reading, MA, 1984.

Satchell, Steve, "IBM's Personal Computer Powerhouse," *PC Products*, January 1985, pp. 21–36.

Schilling, Robert, Jr., "Hardware Diagnostics for the Home," *Popular Computing*, August 1983, pp. 204–210.

Scovern, John L., "No Corrosion with Antistat," *Circuits Manufacturing*, January 1983, pp. 51–53.

Seymour, Jim, "Building in Those Essential 'Options'," *PC Magazine*, March 11, 1986, pp. 87–91.

Seymour, Jim, "The great PC trade-off: Buying up and handing down," *Today's Office*, November 1986, pp. 37–40.

Seymour, Jim, "Two Keys to the PC Graphics Explosion," *PC Magazine*, January 27, 1987, pp. 83–87.

Signetics Logic–TTL Data Manual, Signetics Corp., Sunnyvale, CA, 1978.

Sloop, Joe, "Troubleshooting Logic Systems Logically," *Electronic Servicing & Technology*, July 1983, pp. 26–37.

Socha, John, "The Monochrome/Color Switch," *Softalk*, February 1983, pp. 31–33.

Somerson, Paul, "Goblins, Gremlins & Glitches," *PC Magazine*, October 1983, pp. 111–129.

Somerson, Paul, "User-to-User," *PC Magazine*, June 12, 1984, pp. 434–437.

Somerson, Paul, "User-to-User," *PC Magazine*, October 28, 1986, p. 331.

Stark, Craig, "Monitor Terminology," *PC Magazine*, October 1, 1985, p. 116.

Stolberg, David, "Home Is Where the Office Is," *Computer Dealer*, September 1988, pp. 34–38.

"The AT Arrives," *PC Tech Journal*, November 1984, pp. 208–210.

The Primer of High-Performance In-Circuit Testing, FACTRON, Latham Company, New York, 1985.

The TTL DATA BOOK, Vol. 3, Texas Instruments Incorporated, 1984.

Updegraff, Stephen W., "Better Than Gold—Substrate Coating Surpasses Gold in Hi-Rel Connectors," *Circuits Manufacturing*, December 1983, pp. 54–59.

Victor, Jesse, "Low Noise Topologies, Innovative Designs to Be Spotlighted at Powercon 9," *EDN*, June 9, 1982, pp. 75–84.

Wachtel, Alan, "AT Keyboard's Shortcomings," *PC Magazine*, February 19, 1985, p. 93.

Wattson, Carolyn, "Desoldering Today's Circuit Components," *Electronic Servicing & Technology*, October 1984, pp. 26–28.

Weissman, Ed, "Letters to PC Magazine," *PC Magazine*, August 1986, p. 15.

Whitaker, Lewis A., "Maintenance Alternatives for Personal Computers," *Byte*, June 1982, pp. 452–459.

White, Robert M., "Magnetic disks: storage densities on the rise." *IEEE Spectrum*, August 1983, pp. 32–38.

Williams, Gregg, "A Closer Look at the IBM Personal Computer." *Byte*, January 1982, pp. 36–68.

Williams, Tom, "3½-inch 'floptical' drive packs 25 Mbytes." *Computer Design*, August 15, 1988, p. 9.

"Wohl Talks About Peanuts and Other PCs," *Government Computer News*, December 1983, p. 5.

Zachmann, Mark, "Looking for Compatibility," *PC Magazine*, June 1983, pp. 65–83.

Zachmann, Mark, "PC Tutor," *PC Magazine*, July 1983, pp. 69–74.

Zachmann, Mark, "PC Tutor," *PC Magazine*, October 1983, pp. 577–585.

Zachmann, Mark, "PC Tutor," *PC Magazine*, May 29, 1984, pp. 393–397.

Index